GIVE AND TAKE

**Princeton Studies in Global and Comparative Sociology**
Andreas Wimmer, Series Editor

# Give and Take

## Developmental Foreign Aid and the Pharmaceutical Industry in East Africa

Nitsan Chorev

**PRINCETON UNIVERSITY PRESS**

PRINCETON AND OXFORD

Published by Princeton University Press
41 William Street, Princeton, New Jersey 08540
6 Oxford Street, Woodstock, Oxfordshire OX20 1TR

Requests for permission to reproduce material from this work
should be sent to permissions@press.princeton.edu

press.princeton.edu

LCCN 2019936029
ISBN 9780691187852
ISBN (pbk.) 9780691197845

British Library Cataloging-in-Publication Data is available

Editorial: Meagan Levinson and Jackie Delaney
Production Editorial: Debbie Tegarden
Jacket/Cover Design: Chris Ferrante
Production: Erin Suydam
Publicity: Nathalie Levine and Kathryn Stevens
Copyeditor: Susan Rescigno

Cover credit: Pharmacy in Uganda. Godong / Alamy Stock Photo

This book has been composed in Adobe Text Pro

Printed on acid-free paper. ∞

Printed in the United States of America

10  9  8  7  6  5  4  3  2  1

# CONTENTS

# ACKNOWLEDGMENTS

This is a study on the emergence and upgrading of locally owned drug factories in Kenya, Tanzania, and Uganda. Research on pharmaceutical production in these countries is in some ways geographically contained. In all three countries, most pharmaceutical companies reside in or nearby the industrial area of the main city—Nairobi, Dar es Salaam, and Kampala, respectively—where drug importers, wholesalers and distributors, government authorities, and relevant development agencies also reside. Many of the interviews for this project therefore took place in these three cities. But the study of drug production is also necessarily global. Since the 1990s, most drugs in East Africa (as well as active pharmaceutical ingredients necessary for local drug production) have been imported from India, so I visited New Delhi, Mumbai, Hyderabad, and Ahmedabad—where I conducted interviews with some of India's largest drug producers. I also conducted interviews in China and South Africa, with drug companies that have invested in the East African drug market. To understand the role of foreign aid—from the perspective not only of recipients, but donors as well—I visited the Global Fund to Fight AIDS, Tuberculosis and Malaria and the World Health Organization in Geneva, Switzerland, the United Nations Industrial Development Organization in Vienna, Austria, and met with various German development and humanitarian agencies in Berlin, Bonn, and Tönisvorst. To complement the interviews regarding events in the 1970s and 1980s, I conducted extensive archival research at the World Health Organization.

I would therefore like to first extend my deep gratitude to the very many people—pharmacists, entrepreneurs, activists, government officials, representatives of development agencies, and nongovernmental organizations, and many others—who were willing to spend a few hours with me and educate me about their jobs, experiences, and personal reflections. Almost everything I learned about pharmaceutical production in Kenya, Tanzania, and Uganda—and everything I realized I needed to learn—is thanks to these conversations.

In turn, the many trips that enabled these conversations were made possible by the generous support of my home institution, Brown University. Additionally, in the course of conducting research and then preparing the book manuscript, I was fortunate to spend a year at the Institute for Advanced Study in Princeton, New Jersey, and a few, productive summer months at the

Berlin Social Science center (*Wissenschaftszentrum Berlin für Sozialforschung*) in Germany. Many of the arguments were developed, questioned, redefined, and eventually solidified while presenting my research in academic settings to thoughtful and demanding audiences. I am particularly grateful for the opportunity to present my work at the London School of Economics, University of California—Los Angeles, the Institute for Advanced Study in Princeton, McGill University, Boston University, Princeton University, University of York, Harvard University, University of Notre Dame, CERMES3 in Paris, Boston College, Yale University, Northwestern University, WZB in Berlin, University of Virginia, and Stony Brook University. I wish I could name all those, in these and many other conversations, who offered new directions for me to think about. This book manuscript would have been very different without them. While I fear I would neglect to mention everyone, I want to thank Tatiana Andia, Peter Andreas, Sarah Babb, Emily Barman, Fred Block, Ben Bradlow, Bruce Carruthers, Dalton Conley, Pinar Dogan, Peter Evans, Didier Fassin, Amanda Figgins, Jean-Paul Gaudillière, Oren Gil, Tine Hanrieder, Patrick Heller, Jose Itzigsohn, Margot Jackson, James Jasper, Victoria Johnson, Alexandra Kalev, Greta Krippner, Magali Sarfati Larson, Julia Loktev, Bill Mazza, Ruth Palmon, Irene Pang, Joan Pickard, Dani Rodrik, Andrew Schrank, Gay Seidman, Olga Sezneva, Ken Shadlen, and Barbara Stallings. These supportive colleagues and graduate students, honest readers, undeterred critics, empathetic motivators and/or just dear friends have been constitutive—in direct and some indirect ways—to the making of this book. Finally, a special thanks to everyone at Princeton University Press, especially Andreas Wimmer, Meagan Levinson, and two incredible, albeit anonymous, reviewers.

## ACRONYMS

| | |
|---|---|
| ACT | artemisinin-based combination therapy (antimalarial) |
| AED | Academy for Educational Development |
| AKDN | Aga Khan Development Network |
| AL | artemether-lumefantrine (antimalarial) |
| AMFm | Affordable Medicines Facility—malaria |
| API | active pharmaceutical ingredient |
| ARV | antiretroviral (anti-AIDS) |
| ASU | Administrative Support Unit of the Rural Health Division (Kenya) |
| BHC | Beijing Holley-Cotec |
| BIO | Belgian Investment Company for Developing Countries |
| BMZ | Federal Ministry of Economic Cooperation and Development (Germany) |
| cGMP | current Good Manufacturing Practices |
| CHAI | Clinton Health Access Initiative |
| CMS | Central Medical Stores |
| DANIDA | Danish International Development Agency |
| DAP | Action Programme on Essential Drugs |
| DNDi | Drugs for Neglected Diseases *initiative* |
| DRC | Democratic Republic of Congo |
| EDL | Essential Drugs List |
| EDP | Essential Drugs Programme (Tanzania) |
| EML | Essential Medicines List |
| EU | European Union |
| FDI | foreign direct investment |
| FinnFund | Finnish Fund for Industrial Development |

FINNIDA  Finnish International Development Agency

FKPM  Federation of Kenya Pharmaceutical Manufacturers

GDP  gross domestic product

GMP  Good Manufacturing Practices

GNP  gross national product

GPO  Government Pharmaceutical Organization (Thailand)

GTZ  German Technical Cooperation Agency

HAL  Hindustan Antibiotic Limited (India)

ICDC  Industrial and Commercial Development Corporation (Kenya)

IDPL  Indian Drugs and Pharmaceutical Limited

IMF  International Monetary Fund

INGO  international nongovernmental organization

IPS  Industrial Promotion Services

JMS  Joint Medical Store (Uganda)

KAPI  Kenya Association of Pharmaceutical Industry

KEMSA  Kenya Medical Supplies Authority

KSh  Kenyan shilling

LDC  least developed country

lo-ORS  low-osmolarity Oral Rehydration Salts

MDGs  Millennium Development Goals

MEDS  Mission for Essential Drugs and Supplies (Kenya)

MIT  Ministry of Industries and Trade (Tanzania)

MMV  Medicines for Malaria Venture

MoH  Ministry of Health

MSCU  Medical Supplies Coordinating Unit (Kenya)

MSD  Medical Stores Department (Tanzania)

MSF  Médecins Sans Frontières

NAPCO  National Pharmaceutical Company (Tanzania)

NCI  National Chemical Industries (Tanzania)

NDA  National Drug Authority (Uganda)

NDC  National Development Corporation (Tanzania)

NDQCL  National Drugs Quality Control Laboratory (Uganda)

NEC  National Enterprise Corporation (Uganda)

NGO   nongovernmental organization

NIEO   New International Economic Order

NMS   National Medical Stores (Uganda)

NOC   Non-Objection Certificate

NQCL   National Quality Control Laboratory (Kenya)

NRA   National Resistance Army (Uganda)

NRM   National Resistance Movement (Uganda)

OECD   Organization for Economic Co-operation and Development

ORS   Oral Rehydration Salts

OTC   over-the-counter

PATH   Program for Appropriate Technology in Health (US)

PEPFAR   President's Emergency Plan for AIDS Relief (US)

PHC   Primary Health Care

PIC/S   Pharmaceutical Inspection Convention and Pharmaceutical Inspection Co-operation Scheme

PMI   President's Malaria Initiative (US)

POUZN   Point-of-Use Water Disinfection and Zinc Treatment Project

PPB   Pharmacy and Poisons Board (Kenya)

PQ   prequalification

PSK   Pharmaceutical Society of Kenya

QC   quality control

R&D   research and development

RCT   randomized control trial

RHC   rural health center

RHK   Rural Health Kit

SAP   Structural Adjustment Program

SDGs   Sustainable Development Goals

SIDA   Swedish International Development Cooperation Agency

SOE   state-owned enterprise

SP   sulphadoxine-pyrimethamine (antimalarial)

STC   State Trading Corporation (Tanzania)

TAPI   Tanzanian Association of Pharmaceutical Industry

TFDA   Tanzania Food and Drugs Authority

TPMA Tanzania Pharmaceutical Manufacturers Association

TRIPS Trade-Related Aspects of Intellectual Property Rights

TSh Tanzanian shilling

UDC Uganda Development Corporation

UEDMP Uganda Essential Drugs Management Programme

UEDSP Uganda Essential Drugs Support Programme

UGX Ugandan shilling

UK United Kingdom

UN United Nations

UNAIDS Joint United Nations Programme on HIV/AIDS

UNCTAD United Nations Conference on Trade and Development

UNDP United Nations Development Programme

UNICEF United Nations Children's Fund

UNIDO United Nations Industrial Development Organization

UNIPAC UNICEF Procurement and Assembly Centre

UPL Uganda Pharmaceuticals Ltd.

UPMA Uganda Pharmaceutical Manufacturers Association

UPPA Uganda Pharmaceutical Promoters Association

US United States

USAID United States Agency for International Development

USFDA United States Food and Drugs Administration

WHO World Health Organization

WTO World Trade Organization

GIVE AND TAKE

# 1

# Foreign Aid in Comparative-Historical Perspective

Newspapers in Kenya rarely report on the local pharmaceutical industry, but in November 2011, the *Nairobi Star* heralded some good news: "ARVs to cost 30 % less as WHO clears manufacturer" (Muchangi 2011). The headline referred to a significant turning point for the country's pharmaceutical sector. Earlier that week, the World Health Organization (WHO) certified that a generic antiretroviral (ARV) drug produced by Universal Corporation Ltd., a locally owned pharmaceutical firm, met WHO's stringent quality requirements. Universal could now participate in tenders (bids) for ARVs paid for by the Global Fund to Fight AIDS, Tuberculosis and Malaria, one of the largest funding sources for ARVs in low-income and lower-middle income countries. Although Universal did not end up participating in Global Fund tenders, meeting the WHO quality standards increased the firm's reputation and resulted in sales to other local and international buyers.

That a locally owned firm in a semi-regulated market developed the capabilities to produce complex generic drugs and to follow strict quality standards was a major achievement.[1] Yet, it is impossible to explain Universal's accomplishment without giving donors and international development agencies their due. These donors and development agencies not only established the drug market that Universal was trying to supply and imposed the quality standards that Universal eventually met, but they also, as we will see, provided the technical support that helped Universal meet those standards. This involvement of donors and development agencies has been instrumental to Universal's trajectory and to the trajectories of other pharmaceutical firms in Kenya, as well as Tanzania and Uganda.

———

For decades, scholars have asked whether foreign aid can effectively support countries' development efforts, with diametrically opposed positions but inconclusive evidence (Wright and Winters 2010). One difficulty in reaching credible conclusions is that the literature often measures aid in terms of its volume. The experience of pharmaceutical firms in East Africa suggests, however, that no less important than "how much aid" is "what kind of aid"—What is aid used for? What conditions are attached to it? What type of guidance is offered in meeting those conditions? Sociology has much to offer in answering these questions and my analysis draws heavily on existing sociological insights on development, the state, and entrepreneurship. In turn, I show that foreign aid, which has been largely ignored by sociologists so far, is an important factor in explaining not only development, but also state practices and local entrepreneurship in recipient countries.

In this book, I identify the kind of foreign aid that could advance development in recipient countries by examining, in particular, the case of local industrial production. Based on the experiences of pharmaceutical firms in Kenya, Tanzania, and Uganda since the 1980s, I argue that foreign aid could support the emergence and upgrading of local industry—including the production of more complex products and the pursuit of higher manufacturing standards—when it provides three resources: markets, monitoring, and mentoring. Donor-funded *markets* create demand and therefore new opportunities that shape local entrepreneurs' decision whether and what to produce; effective *monitoring* of the processes used in production can assure performance, quality, or other standards that help with the upgrading of local manufacturing; and *mentoring*, by way of technical support, provides access to know-how, without which local producers would not be able to meet the requested standards and take advantage of the new markets. In the pharmaceutical sectors in East Africa, when foreign aid could be used to procure local drugs, it created markets that gave local entrepreneurs an incentive to produce the kind of drugs for which donors would pay, spurring local production. When donors imposed exacting quality standards on potential recipients of funds as a condition to access those markets, they gave local drug producers an incentive to improve the quality of their products. And when donors provided technology transfer, they gave local producers the know-how necessary to produce more complex drugs and meet the higher quality standards.

These three resources have much in common with resources provided by a "developmental" or "cohesive-capitalist" state—a state with the capacity and coherence to put in place policies conducive to development (Amsden 1989, Wade 1990, Evans 1995, Kohli 2004). It is therefore appropriate to refer to foreign aid that offers markets, monitoring, and mentoring—and thereby helps create pockets of development—as "developmental foreign aid."

The similarity of the resources that are provided by a developmental state, and that I identify as essential for developmental foreign aid, suggest that state policies and foreign aid are complementary rather than competing resources. Demand for commodities could be created by the state, requirements could be imposed by way of industrial policies or regulations, and technical know-how could be acquired by the state (or by local producers utilizing their own means). Developmental foreign aid is therefore particularly welcome when local opportunities are inadequate, regulations are loose, and technical know-how is lacking. Yet, the *impact* of foreign assistance depends on the local conditions in place, including state capacity and local entrepreneurship.[2] Due to this vulnerability to local conditions, as well as foreign aid's own internal contradictions, I will argue in chapter 9 that foreign aid cannot serve as an alternative, only a complement, to a capable state.

Finally, recipient countries have an important role to play in influencing the forms of foreign aid received. It is through political contestations among donors and recipients *within given opportunity structures* that the "how much" and "what kind" of foreign aid is decided. Poor countries are not passive recipients of foreign aid, but they do bargain in the "shadow of power." The focus on local pharmaceutical production in the 1980s and since the early 2000s was in part the result of developing countries constructing local production of drugs as a priority and choosing to use their limited bargaining leverage in support of that priority. At both times, international support of local pharmaceutical production was possible due to certain contingencies, including the taming of multinational drug companies' potential opposition at a time when developed countries looked for concessions they could offer developing countries.

———

Pharmaceutical markets in Kenya, Tanzania and Uganda, were dominated by western pharmaceutical companies from colonial times until the 1990s; since then, they have been dominated by Indian pharmaceutical companies and other importers from the global South (chapter 2 of this book). Nevertheless, local pharmaceutical firms also existed. The experience of local pharmaceutical firms in all three countries included two distinct phases, emergence in the 1980s–1990s and upgrading in the 2000s–2010s. Both phases revealed the role of foreign aid within a particular local context in these firms' trajectories.

In the 1980s, the revelation of abusive marketing practices of multinational pharmaceutical companies in developing countries at a time when these countries were calling for a New International Economic Order (NIEO) forced for the first time an international interest in access to medicine in poor countries. One initiative launched in response was a ration kits program, a foreign-funded program to procure and distribute drugs in rural areas. In Kenya, the program included a local component, which reserved part of the ration kits market for locally produced drugs. This local component was key for the emergence and early resilience of locally owned firms. Foreign aid clearly contributed to local pharmaceutical manufacturing in this case, but only in collaboration with the state, which funded the local part of the program. The presence of capable entrepreneurs in the pharmaceutical field was also important. These entrepreneurs were mostly Kenyans of Indian descent, whose ties with the United Kingdom (UK) and India (a legacy of the British racialized, colonial rule) gave them access to education and technical know-how not available locally; in turn, their networks at home encouraged spread of that knowledge across the entire sector.[3]

In Tanzania and Uganda, the ration kits programs did not have local components; consequently, the local pharmaceutical sectors that emerged were much smaller and more fragile. Local conditions explain why the Tanzanian sector still did somewhat better than the Ugandan one. Whereas Kenya after independence adopted mostly liberal economic policies, Tanzania from the late 1960s until the mid-1980s adopted development projects based on *Ujamaa*, or African socialism. Even in a socialist context, a number of private entrepreneurs were able to draw on local capital or ties abroad to open drug factories. In Uganda, in contrast, a locally owned pharmaceutical sector was late to develop, in part because President Idi Amin expelled Indians in 1972, thereby targeting precisely those local entrepreneurs who could have had access to technical know-how abroad. After Uganda achieved political stability in 1986, a pharmaceutical sector did emerge, but with weaker ties abroad, the sector was small and vulnerable. (We will see that, partly due to these differences during the emergence period, in Kenya mostly older firms took advantage of the new opportunities in the 2000s, whereas in Tanzania and Uganda newly established companies were more likely to do so.)

By 2000, then, Kenya, Tanzania, and Uganda all had local pharmaceutical firms that produced generic versions of off-patent drugs. Because pharmaceutical firms in East Africa had not caught up with novel technologies or with internationally accepted manufacturing standards, these were basic products, such as painkillers, simple antibiotics, simple antimalarial drugs, and vitamins. Within the next decade, though, some top companies began producing complex drugs such as ARVs and antimalarial artemisinin-based combination therapies (ACTs), following quality standards that surpassed those required by national regulations.

As in the 1980s, the health-related foreign assistance provided to Kenya, Tanzania, and Uganda starting in the early 2000s was an outcome of the international political-economic conditions of the time. In the face of the AIDS pandemic, struggles between developing and developed countries over an international agreement to tighten intellectual property protection—with multinational pharmaceutical companies proving their willingness to use that agreement to undermine access to AIDS medicine in countries such as South Africa—led rich countries to fund generous drug donation programs. Consequently, the Global Fund and other global health programs were established. The Global Fund has supported a broad range of programs, but a large component of its funding has been given to governments for the procurement of drugs. It was in order to participate in tenders funded by the Global Fund—or to take advantage of other drug markets created by donors—that pharmaceutical companies in Kenya, including Universal, learned to produce new types of drugs. In turn, it was WHO prequalification (PQ) and other quality requirements, which were put in place to counter multinational pharmaceutical companies' warnings of poor-quality manufacturing in the global South, that encouraged Kenyan companies to invest in quality upgrading. The technical know-how Kenyan manufacturers needed to improve quality standards was made available by foreign assistance.

In Tanzania as well, the promise of markets, the setting of quality-assurance conditions, and the provision of technical assistance enticed the larger manufacturers to invest in producing complex, high-quality drugs. In Uganda, in contrast, most pharmaceutical firms were not exposed to the type of foreign-aid incentives and technical assistance that shaped the Kenyan and Tanzanian sectors, and they did not change their practices much. Yet, one Ugandan company, Quality Chemical Industries Ltd. (QCIL), which was partly owned by one of the largest pharmaceutical companies in India and greatly benefited from unprecedented government support, was able to meet the WHO PQ conditions and sell ARVs and ACTs, including to the Global Fund.

In sum, this book shows that foreign aid effectiveness depends not only on how much aid is given, but also on how it is used. Foreign aid is developmental when it complements local conditions—including state capacity and entrepreneurial competence—by way of markets, monitoring, and mentoring. In the rest of the chapter, I develop my arguments regarding developmental foreign aid and the role of local conditions in the emergence and upgrading of a local industrial sector. Following a section on case selection and research design, I conclude with an outline of the individual chapters.

## Foreign Aid: The Debate on Effectiveness

The first legal statute dealing expressly with official aid, the Colonial Development Act, was passed by the British Parliament in 1929 (Edwards 2014, 39), but it was the Marshall Plan, and US President Harry Truman's 1949 Four Point Speech, that put forward the idea that aid to poor nations was an important component of foreign policy.[4] Although that principle continued to dominate the logic of foreign aid (Eberstadt 1988, Hook 1995), new ideas and changing interests added novel arguments in favor of aid (Lancaster 2007), and, as I discuss below, shaped the many forms that foreign aid has taken since then— including grants and loans, infrastructure (roads, dams, power plants), technology assistance (including for state capacity building), services (e.g., teachers or doctors), commodities (e.g., drugs), and policies.[5]

Given such a broad scope, foreign aid shares some qualities with welfare benefits and, like welfare, it is a contentious terrain, featured in prominent debates in academic journals, popular books, and op-eds in prestigious newspapers. And foreign aid *should* be debated—the stakes are high, first and foremost for the people in recipient countries who are affected by it. In light of these high stakes, the question of aid effectiveness, in particular, leads to the most contentious debates. Critics lament that foreign aid regularly fails to achieve its goals: aid has not been able to reduce poverty, improve human development (i.e., people's freedoms and opportunities), promote democracy, or bring peace. Worse, critics suggest that foreign aid harms—that it breeds corruption, deters democracy and good governance, and ultimately impedes economic growth and increases inequality.[6] At times, the blame falls on the inability of recipients to absorb even well-intended aid programs due to poor state capacity, lack of human capital, and other local conditions (Riddell 2007). More often, critics consider foreign aid programs to be *inherently* ineffective, either because they are designed by paternalistic technocrats, like economists at the World Bank, who are willfully ignorant of countries' specificities (Easterly 2006, 2014), or because they are designed to benefit the donors, not the recipients (Chang 2002). Aid, as a result, "extend[s] the reach" of foreign governments (cf. Ferguson 1990, Li 2007) and reproduces the relations of imposition and dependence between the global North and the global South (Bornschier, Chase-Dunn, and Rubinson 1978, Wood 1986). The promise constructed by the development discourse—a dream of material prosperity and economic progress—has turned into a nightmare (Escobar 1995).

Advocates of foreign aid counter that aid brings positive results through the strengthening of resources, capabilities, and skills.[7] Collier (2007), for example, found that official assistance has helped accelerate gross domestic product (GDP) growth among the poorest nations in the world by approximately one percent per year. These proponents do not normally downplay the challenge of inadequate local resources, but they argue that the right response to that challenge should not be minimal use of foreign assistance, as suggested by many skeptics (Easterly 2008, 25). On the contrary, advocates argue that only aid that is "large enough and [is] maintained long enough" could end countries' "poverty trap" (Sachs et al. 2004, Sachs 2015).

Statistical evidence on aid effectiveness has not been able to resolve the debate, because the complex relations between foreign aid and development outcomes makes any such evidence inconclusive.[8] One challenge for studying the impact of aid on economic growth, for example, is that aid providing emergency relief or given during a humanitarian crisis is likely to be negatively associated with growth, because aid would increase sharply exactly at a time when growth dramatically falls (Radelet 2006). Another challenge is that some types of aid might only affect growth after a long period of time, so the relationship between aid and growth is difficult to detect (Radelet, Clemens, and Bhavnani 2004, Radelet 2006). Wright and Winters (2010, 62) informed their readers that, "this research agenda has in many ways stalled amid criticism related to poor identification, self-inflicted endogeneity, and the general limitations of cross-country growth regressions." In regard to the effect of aid on "governance in the aggregate," Krasner and Weinstein (2014, 133) similarly found "strong reasons to believe that the average effect is not very informative." A consensus seems to have emerged that the debate on aid effectiveness will not be resolved through statistical inquiries.[9]

The qualitative literature, in turn, can be useful for assessing the effectiveness of aid. Although the literature on development in sociology and political science has generally ignored the question of foreign aid (e.g., Evans 1979, 1995, Gereffi 1983, Chibber 2003), what we have learned from relevant studies may support Stiglitz's (2002, 5) assessment that foreign aid, "for all its faults, still has brought benefits to millions, often in ways that have almost gone unnoticed." In sociology, the earlier literature on dependency has been critical—viewing foreign aid as negatively as any other form of foreign intervention (Bornschier 1978, Wood 1986). In contrast, the literature on the developmental state has been cautiously positive when discussing the two countries in which foreign (American) aid could not be ignored, given its magnitude—namely, South Korea and Taiwan.[10] In both cases, scholars concluded that foreign aid had positive, although modest and nondeterminant, impacts on the long-term economic growth of these countries.[11] Among the positive outcomes in South Korea, US aid helped build infrastructure, mines, and factories (Amsden and Chu 2003, Kohli 2004, 81) and improved education (Kohli 2004, 77–78); in Taiwan, "the effects of aid may be said to have been felt in perpetuity . . . in terms of a multiplication of civil engineering projects and know-how and improvements in the administrative capability of the Taiwan technocracy" (Amsden 1985, 91, Wade 1990, 83–84).

The impression of positive but "minor" impact (Amsden 1985, 91) improves, moreover, when scholars consider particular sectors rather than the economy as a whole. One illuminating example is the textiles industry in South Korea, which received the lion's share of the foreign aid given to local industries after the Korean War. Aid by way of subsidized loans initially led to excess capacity, but this was resolved in the 1960s with conditioned government subsidies to exports (Amsden 1989, 64–68). Subsequently, cotton textiles became South Korea's major export item (Amsden 1989, 56). Kohli (2004, 77) lists the revival of the South Korean textiles industry as one of the major accomplishments of American aid.[12] Another example is the construction industry. Amsden (1989, 232) has shown that South Korean construction firms, by serving as civilian sub-contractors to the American forces, obtained surplus equipment, upgraded the quality of their construction work to meet western specifications, and acquired management and quality-control techniques.

Hence, whereas statistical analyses have failed to reach conclusive results regarding the effect of foreign aid on the economy as a whole, historical studies are able to show clear effects when looking at individual sectors. Also in Kenya, Tanzania, and Uganda, foreign aid had a clear impact on local pharmaceutical companies, independently of the effect foreign aid might have had on development as a whole. Next, I discuss the analytical reasons for looking at industrial production—and pharmaceutical manufacturing more specifically—to study aid effectiveness.

## Foreign Aid and the Janus-Faced Pharmaceutical Sector

Most foreign aid, as Radelet (2006, 7) concisely summarizes, is designed to meet one or more of four development objectives: (1) to stimulate economic growth, including through the support of industrial sectors; (2) to strengthen education, health, environmental, or political systems; (3) to provide support, mostly through commodities, during relief operations or humanitarian crises; and (4) to help stabilize an economy following economic shocks. With growing emphasis on individual capabilities and poverty reduction (Sen 2000), western aid has shifted over time away from the objective of economic growth and it is more likely to focus on social issues (i.e., social services, food aid, humanitarian assistance, and poverty alleviation) and political concerns (i.e., democracy, governance, and human rights). Of the eight Millennium Development Goals (MDGs) declared at the United Nations Millennium Summit in 2000, only one refers to the economic realm ("develop a global partnership for development").[13] Funding followed the same logic. For example, in Tanzania, in 1991, "industry" received 24.8 percent of total external assistance disbursements, whereas "health" and "social development" together made up only 11.5 percent of the total.[14] In 2015, in contrast, the $950 million distributed for "social infrastructure" (including health) and "humanitarian assistance" in Tanzania far exceeded the combined sums devoted to "economic infrastructure" ($260 million) and "production" ($150 million).[15]

Prioritization of the social and political over the economic is now changing again, however. Renewed attention to economic issues can be detected, for example, by the greater emphasis on such concerns in the United Nations' (UN) 2015 Sustainable Development Goals (SDGs). The seventeen SDGs make three explicit references to economic issues, including: "Build resilient infrastructure, promote sustainable industrialization, and foster innovation."[16] In addition, new donors from East Asia, especially Japan and South Korea, emphasize economic infrastructure and production facilities in their aid to African countries.[17] Concurrently, in response to the emphasis on individual capabilities, development economists have found it important to reiterate the critical role of *productive* capabilities, which allow for the "transformation in productive structure" and are therefore indispensable for economic development (Andreoni and Chang 2016).

Given this revived interest in utilizing aid in the service of industrial production, it is important to evaluate the conditions under which aid could be effective in that specific realm. (In chapter 9, I will argue that the lessons learned from looking at aid for industrial production could apply to other spheres of aid as well, including the provision of services.) The pharmaceutical sector, in turn, has two qualities that make it particularly suitable to study, given today's challenges of aid in the economic realm.

First, the pharmaceutical sector is a particularly interesting area for looking at both the emergence and upgrading of an industrial sector. As mentioned above, when the US provided aid to South Korea, a major beneficiary was the textiles industry—one of a few consumer-goods industries that developing countries were able to grow through labor-intensive functions of relatively low knowledge intensity. The manufacturing of medicine can in some cases be similarly quite simple but in other cases it can be technologically complex; so studying this sector can shed light on the effect of foreign aid on simple manufacturing, *as well as* on the possibility of climbing up the commodity chain through technical upgrading or even innovation.[18]

Second, the pharmaceutical sector is analytically interesting for reasons that go beyond industrial production *per se*, given that local pharmaceutical production may improve access to affordable medicine and therefore the health situation in the country where it is produced. Aid in support of pharmaceutical production may therefore allow foreign aid aimed at an industrial sector to serve not only economic, but also social objectives, including those declared in the MDGs and SDGs regarding improved access to medicine to fight AIDS, tuberculosis, and malaria. Certainly, supporters of local pharmaceutical production utilized assertions that local production would help improve access to medicine. It is notable, however, that the potential effect of local pharmaceutical production on access to medicine was a double-edged sword because it was at times used to criticize investment in local production, given credible analyses that local production could make drugs costlier than simply importing them from India, for example (Kaplan and Laing 2005). Indeed, justifications for local production in the 2000s focused less on the promise of industrial growth or on the promise of improved access to medicine and more on the need for self-sufficiency. Studying the pharmaceutical industry therefore also gives us an opportunity to analyze the potential tensions between aid for economic development on the one hand and aid for social development on the other—including in regard to the selection of the pharmaceutical sector as a suitable target for aid in the first place, which I discuss in the next section.

## Origins of Developmental Foreign Aid: Bargaining in the Shadow of Power

One assumption often underscored by scholars of foreign aid is that priorities are set by donors rather than recipients (Lancaster 2007). Critics, in particular, are quick to make that claim. For example, the donation of medicine, including ARVs, is often seen as reflecting donors' preference for technological solutions that benefit multinational pharmaceutical companies. Similarly, stringent international quality standards can be seen as a protectionist tool against competition from pharmaceutical companies in developing countries. Scholars recognize, more generally, that foreign aid creates power dynamics that constrain the recipient's action. Given donors' interest in AIDS and malaria treatment, for example, it is difficult for developing countries *not* to prioritize these over other health programs. In regard to the examples above, however, the overwhelming focus on drug donations becomes more difficult to explain once we learn that many of the donated drugs are produced in India, not in the United States (US) or Europe. Support of local pharmaceutical production is similarly puzzling, given the minimal interest in industrial production as a legitimate goal for foreign aid—and the likely opposition of western pharmaceutical companies.

From an analytical perspective, moreover, unreflectively assuming that foreign aid interventions are designed to serve donors' interests runs the risk of overlooking developing countries' active involvement in constructing those interventions.[19] We need instead to investigate the political-economic context in which the preferences of both donors and recipients are constructed. (This is not to imply that countries have unified needs or interests. Rather, clashing political, economic, and other interests are involved. So even when aid priorities are informed by the recipient, it does not mean that these priorities reflect those of the country as a whole.) I argue that aid, not unlike other types of global norms and regulations, emerges through political contestations. In these political contestations, parties are hardly equal—bargaining occurs in the shadow of power.[20] Still, those in the periphery can gain concessions by constructing priorities and choosing battles based on the opportunity structures in place. Hence, even countries with minimal bargaining leverage are not necessarily passive recipients of gifts bestowed on them; rather, they are active manipulators of opportunities when these exist.

Support of local pharmaceutical production in the 1980s and again in the early 2000s was constructed under surprisingly similar political circumstances. At both times, an interest in the production of drugs might not have emerged as a central concern but for the fact that certain events in the course of contentious international negotiations over broader issues created an opportunity for that concern to be addressed. At both times, the opportunity was created by a temporary "taming" of multinational pharmaceutical companies that weakened the impact of their likely opposition.

In the 1980s, at the same time that developing countries were mobilized in support of a NIEO (Chorev 2012b), the revelation of unethical marketing and abusive pricing practices of multinational pharmaceutical companies in poor countries momentarily weakened the political influence of these companies. The scathing exposures were then used to justify reform of pharmaceutical markets, including through the rationalization of procurement and distribution of drugs in developing countries, but also by making local drug production into an industrial priority—using the argument that this was the most effective way to address developing countries' vulnerabilities to the abuse of multinational pharmaceutical companies.

International support of local pharmaceutical production in the early 2000s was similarly an outcome of opportunities in the context of broader developments that weakened the opposition of multinational pharmaceutical companies at a time that developed countries looked for concessions they could offer to developing countries. The trigger was *not* the catastrophic HIV/AIDS pandemic *per se*, but the agreement on Trade-Related Aspects of Intellectual Property Rights (TRIPS), which was negotiated in the course of establishing the World Trade Organization (WTO) and was designed on behalf of multinational companies, including pharmaceutical firms (Sell 2003). TRIPS, which was signed in 1994, required all WTO members to adopt and enforce high minimum standards of intellectual property protection (Sell 2003, Kapczynski 2009, Löfgren and Williams 2013). Countries with loose intellectual property laws, which allowed the development of a thriving generic pharmaceutical sector, as was the case in India (chapter 2), now had to enforce much more stringent patent laws.

The TRIPS agreement contained provisions describing a number of permissible exceptions, or flexibilities, to the protection of intellectual property rights. Concern that TRIPS would limit access to affordable generic drugs, including anti-AIDS drugs, led a number of developing countries, including South Africa, to pass intellectual property laws with explicit references to the controversial exceptions. When multinational pharmaceutical companies tried to challenge the new law in South Africa, the global public outcry against "suing Nelson Mandela" made the multinationals withdraw the case (Chorev 2012a, 842). This "public relations disaster," combined with effective activist mobilization at the global level, put advocates of strict intellectual property rights on the defensive and made developed countries seek ways to pacify poor countries, specifically by demonstrating that TRIPS would not have an effect on access to anti-AIDS and other needed drugs. Hence, in addition to concessions regarding flexibilities, rich countries began to donate unprecedented sums to fight AIDS, as well as tuberculosis and malaria (Chorev 2012a), and they started to actively support local pharmaceutical production.

In short, foreign aid in support of local pharmaceutical production has been the outcome of developing countries constructing priorities and fighting for them given the political opportunities in place. In the next section, I describe the features that made this type of foreign aid "developmental."

## What Makes Foreign Aid "Developmental"?: Markets, Monitoring, and Mentoring

Foreign aid is commonly measured in terms of volume, and aid effectiveness is inferred if more aid is correlated with, for example, greater economic growth. But at least as consequential as how much aid is the question of what *kind* of aid is given and how is it *used*, so when measuring foreign aid only in terms of volume, much of what could make aid effective is lost. More promising than studies that find a positive, negative, or no relationship at all between aid and development are studies that claim a *conditional* relationship between the two. These studies look at the characteristics of recipient countries (e.g., having "good policies"), of donors (e.g., whether aid is bilateral or multilateral), and at the type of activity that the aid supports (e.g., humanitarian aid vs. aid aimed at affecting growth) (Radelet 2006, 10–11). But even that literature falls short of identifying the *kind* of interventions that would allow aid to support development.

When it comes to proposing actual policies, the issue of "what kind" is addressed more explicitly. Skeptics like William Easterly (2008, 25) insist that the only cost-effective interventions are modest ones that directly "make people's lives better." Examples include vaccination, urban water provision, indoor spraying to control malaria, and fertilizer subsidies. An agreeable form of foreign aid, then, involves relatively cheap interventions that have an unmediated and immediate impact on individuals' well-being. These programs should also, to the extent possible, bypass local actors, especially the government. Aid for productive activities is out of the question. Jeffrey Sachs's support of large-scale aid projects is directly opposed to Easterly's, and his list of "bold measures" even leaves room for industrial development. However, Sachs and his collaborators also fail to systematically investigate what kind of aid could be effective and refer, instead, to generic policies such as the provision of export processing zones and industrial parks, tax concessions, and infrastructure. The reference to these policies reflects a relatively hands-off approach to economic growth and pays rudimentary attention to insights from the literature on development (Sachs et al. 2004, Sachs 2014).

The experience of local pharmaceutical producers in East Africa challenges both Easterly's and Sachs's conclusions—and offers a new way of thinking about foreign aid. I argue that similar tools to the ones utilized by a developmental state to promote industrial production as a whole could be provided through foreign aid to advance a specific sector in an otherwise nondevelopmental context. Drawing on insights developed by the economist Alice Amsden (1989), I identify three types of interventions that make foreign aid instrumental in the emergence and upgrading of industrial production: creating markets as incentives to produce; imposing monitorable conditions that improve production practices; and providing access to technical know-how through mentoring.[21]

## MARKETS

According to Amsden (1989, 143), "The first industrial revolution [in Britain] was built on *laissez-faire*, the second [in Germany and the US] on infant industry protection. In late industrialization the foundation is subsidy." Infant industry protection was provided in many industrializing countries based on the understanding that new industries cannot develop without state support—including tariffs, import prohibitions, and investment restrictions—that would limit competition with imports or foreign subsidiaries (Evans 1995, Chang 2002, 3, Rodrik 2008). These protectionist policies were often designed to create a "market reserve" (Evans 1995, 117) for local producers—so they could develop without having to compete too early with established producers.

Foreign aid agencies do not normally have the means available to governments to protect infant industries. Yet, donors can create markets. The provision of commodities by aid agencies often comes in the form of (imported) in-kind donations or in the form of funds earmarked for the purchase of those commodities. In the latter case, donations are often "tied" or for other reasons rely exclusively on imported goods. In such cases, donations are unlikely to benefit local producers. When donations can be used for the procurement of locally produced commodities, however, the availability of these funds offers incentives for local producers to invest in the production of such goods, even if these commodities are more complex or in other ways extend local firms' existing range of products. By creating markets, then, foreign aid can generate conditions that serve a similar function to protectionist measures—namely, providing incentives for local entrepreneurs to produce. Foreign aid may not protect local industries from international competition, but it gives local firms an opportunity to compete in a market that would not have existed otherwise.

In East Africa, foreign aid in the form of markets helped trigger drug production first of simple and then of more complex drugs. In Kenya in the 1980s, in the context of an otherwise very small drug market, the ration kits program, which was designed and funded by development agencies, included government-funded tenders reserved for local producers. This reserved market proved key to the emergence and early resilience of the pharmaceutical sector in the country.[22] No local component was included in the ration kits programs in Tanzania and Uganda, both of which subsequently saw the rise of smaller and more fragile pharmaceutical sectors. When donors made funds available for the procurement of ARVs and ACTs after 2000 without a priori excluding locally made drugs, and even though these donor-funded markets were not normally reserved for local producers, the *possibility* of a market was sufficient to encourage some local pharmaceutical producers to produce these new drugs.

## MONITORING

Infant industry protection risks creating an industry incapable of becoming internationally competitive. Amsden's most innovative insight was that later industrializers were able to prevent such stagnation by the use of *conditioned* subsidies (Amsden 1989, 145). Subsidies were no longer free; rather, "in direct exchange for subsidies, the state exacts certain performance standards from firms," such as meeting export targets (Amsden 1989, 146, Amsden 2001).

Amsden's insight that conditions could alter the behavior of recipients of state subsidies is key to understanding the success of developmental states. I suggest that it should similarly be key to understanding effective foreign aid. Like state support, foreign assistance effectiveness depends on the ability to make recipients meet certain standards. Importantly, the conditions I refer to here are not the same as tied aid or the "conditionalities" that were attached to structural adjustment loans from the World Bank and the International Monetary Fund (Radelet 2006, 13), which involve demands *unrelated* to the effective use of the loans. Rather, here the emphasis is on *performance* and other standards that relate directly to how the funds are used.

In the pharmaceutical sector, standards often focus on quality because the harm from consuming substandard drugs could be significant. In developing countries, the standards required by the government are often lower than the Good Manufacturing Practices (GMP) recommended by the WHO, and enforcement is often lax (Losse, Schneider, and Spennemann 2007). In that context, a monitoring mechanism created by foreign aid had a major impact on the quality of locally produced drugs in Kenya, Tanzania, and Uganda. In the 1980s, the procurement of drugs for the local ration kits did not have conditions attached, and the ration kits program had no impact on the quality standards followed by local pharmaceutical firms. But when donors in the 2000s opened their tenders to local producers, it was under the condition of meeting WHO GMP requirements. As a result, some local producers in East Africa pursued quality standards beyond the level that their respective governments enforced. In short, just as the promise of markets provided an incentive to produce drugs, monitoring provided an incentive to produce *good* (quality-assured) drugs.

This is a case of a weak disciplinary mechanism, however. Rodrik (2008, 28) observes that "sticks" are not only about encouraging investment in productive directions, but also about "weed[ing] out projects and investments that fail." Because international monitoring is voluntary, it has no ability to "weed out" projects. Moreover, because the condition of quality applies to the product, rather than to the performance, improved competitiveness is not an inevitable outcome. The implications are nonetheless significant—a *conditioned* foreign aid, namely, foreign aid that uses requirements to assure quality standards, helped improve production practices of an industry in semi-regulated countries.

## MENTORING

Lall (1992, 112) reminds us that "incentives are not the only part of the story. The ability of firms to respond to incentives depends on their initial base of capabilities and their access to skills within the economy." Amsden (1986, 253) similarly notes that "unlike many natural resources, skills do not grow on trees. Nor, unlike capital, are they easily imported." Rather, they require "a combination of formal education (although not always) and experience," both of which are scarce in developing countries. One of Amsden's (1989) arguments regarding later industrializers, including South Korea and Taiwan, is that, rather than generating new products or processes, they industrialized through *learning*. They developed skills—including technical and market capabilities—by "borrowing" knowledge from elsewhere (Whittaker et al. 2010, 445), through formal learning as well as through licensing and reverse engineering (Amsden 1989).[23] Reliance on borrowed knowledge explains why entrepreneurs in developing countries have often been immigrants who arrived with education or experience (Kohli 2004, 151) or locals who had been working abroad (Saxenian and Hsu 2001; ÓRiain 2004b). Knowledge could also be acquired by hiring foreign consultants (Amsden 1989; Mehri 2015) or, less formally, through commercial channels, such as suppliers of capital goods (Amsden 1989, 233–34; Romer 1993).

I argue that learning can occur—and knowledge can be "borrowed"—with the help of foreign aid. Amsden's analysis of the construction sector in South Korea mentioned above is one example of the success of mentoring. Pharmaceutical production in East Africa is another. Pharmacy schools opened in Kenya and Tanzania only in 1974, and in Uganda in 1988, and these schools did not provide adequate training in industrial pharmacy and were therefore not able to address the severe shortage of qualified technical personnel (Wangwe et al. 2014). Hence, the know-how required for the production of new drugs or for maintaining high quality standards was not available locally. Some local entrepreneurs found private means to access technical know-how that was available only abroad, as I describe below. In addition, technical know-how in the field of pharmaceutical production was provided through foreign aid. In the 1980s, donors provided technology transfer mostly to state-owned companies. After 2000, development agencies offered technical support to privately owned local pharmaceutical companies, with the help of which these companies learned how to produce new types of drugs and follow high quality standards.

In short, commercial opportunities, conditions attached to those opportunities, and guidance provided to help meet those conditions hold the key to foreign aid's impact on industrial production. In East Africa, the promise of new markets generated interest in the production of new drugs, monitoring provided an incentive to produce quality-assured drugs, and mentoring provided the needed know-how.

## Foreign Aid and Local Capabilities

The experience of the pharmaceutical sectors in East Africa led me to conclusions that significantly differ from those usually debated in the literature on foreign aid. Yes, aid can be effective, but its effectiveness depends on what opportunities it creates, what conditions are attached to those opportunities, and with what guidance aid is given. My argument, then, is explicitly sensitive to variations in the type of aid interventions. My analysis is also sensitive to variations in the local context, which, at times, the literature on foreign aid is not. For example, Easterly (2014) certainly considers local conditions, but he implies that local characteristics are equally distorting in all recipient countries. I recognize contradictions and distortions, which I discuss in chapter 9, but show that countries with "good enough governance" (Grindle 2004) and other local capabilities can avoid what Easterly believes is inevitable. Sachs and his collaborators (2004) seem confident that domestic challenges can be successfully addressed. However, we know that local conditions are decisive in shaping the nature and meaning of international interventions, and we know that the local context differs significantly across countries and over time.[24] We should expect, then, that depending on local conditions, the same type of foreign aid would yield different results. (Depending on local conditions, countries may also receive a different kind of foreign aid.) Hence, in addition to asking what makes foreign aid effective, we need to ask what local conditions allow foreign aid to be effectively utilized.

As mentioned earlier, a number of studies do look at how local conditions shape foreign aid effectiveness (Wright and Winters 2010, Matsuzawa 2016). Some suggest, for example, that aid "works better" in countries with "good" institutions and "good" policies (Radelet 2006, 11).[25] Others have argued that the higher the level of human capital or social capital, the more the same amount of aid can "contribute" (Kosack and Tobin 2006, 205; see also, Hout 2002, Baliamoune-Lutz and Mavrotas 2009). Indeed, the experiences of pharmaceutical manufacturing in Kenya, Tanzania, and Uganda show that developmental foreign aid may compensate for inadequate commercial opportunities, loose regulations, *and* lack of technical know-how. At other times, aid can *complement* extant local possibilities, for example, when demand for commodities is created by the state, or when requirements are imposed through industrial policies or regulations, or when technical know-how is acquired by the state or by local entrepreneurs through their own means.

Local conditions, in addition, shape the impact of foreign aid. Here, again, state and private entrepreneurs play important roles. First, foreign aid effectiveness often depends on the capabilities of the relevant state agencies. (This is compatible with what those who are skeptical of the effectiveness of foreign aid would predict. Unlike these skeptics, however, I argue in chapter 9 that donors should invest in state capacity building rather than in looking for ways to bypass the state).[26] Second, foreign aid effectiveness also often depends on the presence of entrepreneurs who can respond to incentives, conditions, and training.

## THE STATE

As Evans (1995, 10) notes, "State involvement [in development] must be taken as one of the sociopolitical determinants of what niche a country ends up occupying in the international division of labor." The literature on the developmental state identified both the institutional features making a state conducive to development, including bureaucratic coherence and administrative capacity, and the tasks such a state may take on, for example, a judicious mix of import substitution and export promotion (Amsden 1989, Wade 1990, Evans 1995, Chibber 2003). Later, scholars identified a different set of tasks, more appropriate for a neo-developmental state in an era of globally fragmented production, including stimulating venture capital investment, creating innovation centers, providing research and development funding, and fostering international networks (ÓRiain 2004a, Breznitz 2007).

Kenya, Tanzania, and Uganda are neither developmental nor neo-developmental states. None of these countries had state capacity or coherence to pursue comprehensive industrial policies. Still, as Evans (1995, 10) reminds us: "State involvement is a given. The appropriate question is not 'how much' but 'what kind.'" State involvement in Kenya, Tanzania, and Uganda included, to a varying degree, an investment in local pharmaceutical production. In the 1980s, all three countries established state-owned pharmaceutical manufacturing facilities, although only Kenya funded a component of the ration kits program that was reserved for local producers and introduced other protectionist policies that contributed to the successful emergence of the sector in the country. In the 2000s, the only pharmaceutical firm in Uganda that took advantage of foreign aid, QCIL, was generously supported by the Ugandan government. All three governments—with foreign insistence and assistance—introduced regulations to monitor quality assurance of drugs in the 1990s, but Tanzania enforced these rules on local manufacturers more strictly than the other two governments, and thereby more effectively discouraged firms with particularly poor quality standards.

## Local Entrepreneurship and Foreign Investment

Industrialization that relies on the private sector requires not only a competent state, but also experienced entrepreneurs (Kohli 2004, 3). The scholarship on the developmental state asserts that entrepreneurship is a condition that the state can help create (Evans 1995, 13). However, all the successfully industrialized countries examined in these studies were countries with an existing availability of competent entrepreneurs, thereby bypassing the question of the "missing entrepreneur"—whether development is likely when a country is not already endowed with experienced private actors (Kohli 2004, 341).[27] What we cannot assume—and what the literature on the developmental state at times implies—is that entrepreneurs emerge organically in response to market opportunities or effective policies (Burt 1992, 34). Rather, becoming an entrepreneur requires available funds or credit, as well as access to technical and managerial know-how, most often through education or experience (Amsden 1986, 253).

Kenya, Tanzania, and Uganda did not have ready-made entrepreneurs, certainly not in the pharmaceutical sector, where specialized know-how is required. Although the situation has improved over time, local capabilities have not caught up with the expanding requirements for capital, technology, and skills. Who, then, were the entrepreneurs who opened pharmaceutical factories and, when available, took advantage of opportunities offered by foreign aid? I suggest that Mark Granovetter's insight regarding inter-local connections applies to transnational connections as well: "The ability to call on *personalized* contacts over a wide geographic area affords considerable advantage in smoothing backward and forward transactions. There are information advantages as well" (Granovetter 1995, 151, emphasis added). Where access to technical know-how is not available locally, entrepreneurs are more likely to come from the ranks of those who have ties abroad.

Indeed, the scholarship on developmental and neo-developmental states offers numerous examples of the developmental role of ties abroad when lack of local skills requires entrepreneurs to borrow knowledge from "elsewhere," as discussed above. And unlike the image of a fully informed, rational global market, in which commercial transactions require no social foundation, entrepreneurs often need to rely on existing informal ties to import needed raw materials or machines, to get jobs abroad where they can gain the necessary experience, or to hire skilled employees from abroad. Even establishing formal commercial relations such as joint ventures often relies on existing informal ties.

During colonialism and after independence, Africans did not generally have ties abroad, but a racialized colonial order and its legacy meant that East Africans of Indian origin did. It is important to distinguish this argument, which focuses on the *structural* characteristics of groups, from arguments that focus on cultural or other essentialist traits (Portes and Zhou 1992).[28] The position of Indians in the racialized social and economic order under colonialism—the one that brought many of them to East Africa in the first place and the one that, in East Africa, provided differentiated educational and economic opportunities to Africans, Indians, and Europeans—enabled them to dominate the region's commercial and industrial sectors after independence (Swainson 1977, Barker et al. 1986). In turn, the development of a flourishing pharmaceutical sector in India—itself a reflection of both domestic and global political-economic processes (chapter 2)—channeled Indians in East Africa into local pharmaceutical production. Specifically, East Africans of Indian origin, especially in Kenya, attended pharmacy schools in the UK or in India when there was not yet a pharmacy school in the region; they got jobs with multinational pharmaceutical companies; and they relied on acquaintances in India to "smooth transactions" for purchasing machines and raw materials. Technical know-how was transferred through informal conversations with suppliers of drugs or raw materials from India; later, East Africans of Indian origin also had an easier time hiring short-term consultants or permanent employees, again from India. In contrast, entrepreneurs without ties abroad (or without political ties at home, as we will see) were often the ones who opened the smaller and less resilient firms.

Over time, pharmaceutical firms in Kenya, Tanzania, and Uganda that were owned by private entrepreneurs and operated as a family business were joined by (or turned into) companies relying on salaried professionals (cf. Amsden 1989, v). In addition, there was a shift from relying on the type of informal, personal ties described above to creating formal, for-profit ties in the form of foreign direct investment (FDI). The literature on development has long debated the traits of foreign-owned companies compared to local firms—but also whether we should expect any differences at all between the two.[29] The pharmaceutical sectors in East Africa remind us of the important advantages foreign companies have over local ones. Although local investors may derive "competitive advantages from local knowledge, experience, and social and political capital in their homelands" (Schrank 2008, 2)—one example is local companies' dominance of the drug market in rural areas (Mujinja et al. 2014)—companies owned by multinational pharmaceutical companies have the advantage of easier access to finance and to technical know-how. Significantly, this changed in important ways the companies' relationship to opportunities and incentives, including those offered by foreign aid. Companies owned by multinational pharmaceutical companies were less likely than local companies to be responsive to foreign assistance, as I also discuss in chapter 9.

In addition to ties abroad, entrepreneurs benefit from the diffusion of information through *local* networks across the industry.[30] Among pharmaceutical manufacturers in East Africa, the strength of local networks depended on the presence of common business interests (manufacturers who did not engage in importation of drugs had different interests than manufacturers who did); common concerns (likely among manufacturers with similarly sized enterprises or similar levels of technical sophistication); educational and professional background (when entrepreneurs were also pharmacists); geographical proximity (given the poor infrastructure and challenging business environment in East Africa, physical proximity made it easier to meet); and, importantly, social (nonmarket-based) ties.

The scholarship on middleman minorities, which looks at the social structure of ethnic communities to explain their success in certain occupations, is useful for understanding how social ties matter, and why they are likely to be found among ethnic minorities, including Indians in East Africa (Bonacich 1973).[31] Most importantly, ethnic minorities have the advantage of "bounded solidarity" and "enforceable trust" (Portes and Zhou 1992), which act against the violation of group norms, such as malfeasance among entrepreneurs, and in favor of mutual support. Notably, bounded solidarity emerges not out of spontaneous feelings due to, say, common ethnicity. Rather, it is a reaction by "a class of people faced with common adversities" (Portes and Sensenbrenner 1993, 1325) and a product of the enforcement capacity of the ethnic community, including "ostracism of violators [and] cutting them off from sources of credit and opportunity" (Portes and Zhou 1992, 514), in a context in which members do not have employment options outside of kin (Granovetter 1995).[32] Others have shown that friendships among competitors enhance collaboration and mitigate harmful competition (Ingram and Roberts 2000) and that relations among minority group members improve availability of information

TABLE 1.1. Foreign aid and local factors that shaped local pharmaceutical production in Kenya, Tanzania, and Uganda, 1980s–90s & 2000s–2010s

|  |  | Market | Monitoring | Mentoring | Outcome |
|---|---|---|---|---|---|
| Emergence 1980s–90s | Kenya | Foreign aid; State |  | Local entrepreneurs | (+) Emergence, resilient |
|  | Tanzania |  |  | Local entrepreneurs | (~) Emergence, fragile |
|  | Uganda |  |  |  | (–) Late emergence, fragile |
| Upgrading 2000s–2010s | Kenya | Foreign aid | Foreign aid | Foreign aid | (+) Upgrading |
|  | Tanzania | Foreign aid | Foreign aid; State | Foreign aid | (+) Upgrading |
|  | Uganda | Foreign aid |  |  | (–) No upgrading |
|  | Uganda* | Foreign aid; State | Foreign aid; FDI | FDI | (+) Upgrading of one company |

* Indicates a case of one firm with an exceptional trajectory. FDI = foreign direct investment.

(Ody-Brasier and Fernandez-Mateo 2017). Similarly, the social ties of Kenyans of Indian origin were an important factor in the diffusion of information across manufacturers over the years, including in regard to opportunities provided by foreign aid.

Social ties, and local networks more generally, may strengthen a sector's trade association and therefore its political influence (Samford 2017; see also Evans 1995, Sen and Te Velde 2009). In East Africa, however, trade associations of pharmaceutical manufacturers did not have the "institutionalized channels for the continual negotiation and renegotiation of goals and policies" that Evans (1995, 12) describes in his analysis of embedded autonomy. An interest in local drug production by either the state or aid agencies triggered, rather than was in response to, an association's activities. The exception was Kenya in the 1980s, where the trade association—created by manufacturers with extant social ties— did gain some early concessions.

In sum, developing countries rely on foreign aid for markets, monitoring, and mentoring because they have only small markets, because regulations are loose and difficult to enforce, and because local skills are lacking. This is not to say that states and other local actors cannot provide a foundation for developmental foreign aid, however. Table 1.1 offers a summary of the complementarity of foreign aid and domestic capabilities in Kenya, Tanzania, and Uganda that led to the emergence and upgrading of the local pharmaceutical sector in these countries (see also book outline below).

## Toward a Comparative-Historical Analysis of Foreign Aid

This book offers a comparative-historical analysis of the effects of foreign aid on local pharmaceutical production in Kenya, Tanzania, and Uganda. I examine the political-economic history of each country starting with the colonial era, but I focus on the periods most significant to the stated research question: the 1980s–1990s, where I study the effects of foreign aid on the *emergence* of pharmaceutical firms, and the 2000s–2010s, where I study the effects of foreign aid on the *upgrading* of pharmaceutical firms in each country.

Earlier in this chapter I explained why local pharmaceutical production is a politically important and analytically interesting field for studying the effects of foreign aid. Kenya, Tanzania, and Uganda, in turn, offer rich sites for such a study. In all three countries, pharmaceutical production has been affected by numerous types of foreign aid over a long period of time, including aid given to the state and aid given directly to the sector; aid aimed at industrialization, aid granted for the procurement of drugs, and aid for state capacity building; and aid given bilaterally as well as multilaterally. This provides a rich arena to look at whether and which types of aid work. At the same time, the effects are sufficiently contained to permit analysis of almost every pharmaceutical firm in the history of each country.

The pharmaceutical sectors in Kenya, Tanzania, and Uganda are also particularly suitable for a comparative analysis across countries and over time. First, the pharmaceutical sectors in all three countries were exposed to extensive foreign aid interventions, unlike pharmaceutical sectors in other countries, such as India and China. Second, both in the 1980s–1990s and in the 2000s–2010s, the kind of foreign aid interventions, as well as the local context that these interventions met, were sufficiently similar to convincingly isolate the factors that led to differences in outcomes. The similarities in the local context include a relatively common colonial history and similar economic and political reforms following liberalization. As mentioned previously, there are important differences as well. After independence in the early 1960s, the three countries followed different political-economic regimes: liberalism in Kenya, African socialism in Tanzania, and military dictatorship followed by civil unrest in Uganda. And, already under British rule, Kenya was industrially and financially more developed than Tanzania and Uganda, and its economy continued to perform better later on.[33] The cases are also interdependent, to some extent. Kenyan drug producers, for example, export their drugs to Tanzania and Uganda. Accordingly, the analysis incorporates points of intersection and mutual influence between the cases.

My study of the pharmaceutical sector in each country is constructed largely through the experience of individual companies. To establish the emergence and upgrading stories of each firm (including those that have closed), I relied on interviews, along with archival materials and public documents. Altogether, I conducted approximately 240 interviews. In Kenya (95 interviews), Tanzania (37), and Uganda (43), I interviewed founders of local pharmaceutical firms, current managing directors, and industrial pharmacists working in those firms. I also interviewed importers and distributors of drugs, civil servants in the relevant government agencies, and representatives of professional and trade associations, international organizations and bilateral development agencies, and local and foreign nongovernmental organizations (NGOs). In Kenya, I participated in a conference organized by the Pharmaceutical Society of Kenya and attended one meeting of the Federation of Kenya Pharmaceutical Manufacturers. To situate local production in the larger global pharmaceutical market, I also conducted interviews in India (25), China (15), and South Africa (2). In India, I interviewed owners and representatives of pharmaceutical companies that export to African countries, as well as representatives of professional and trade associations, and of local and foreign NGOs. I also participated in a conference organized by the Indian Drug Manufacturers' Association. In China, I interviewed representatives of pharmaceutical companies that export to African countries and consulted with others involved in the pharmaceutical and biotech sectors. To obtain the perspective of foreign aid providers, I interviewed officials at the WHO and the Global Fund in Geneva, Switzerland, at UNIDO in Vienna, Austria, and, in Germany, I interviewed representatives of the German Technical Cooperation Agency (GIZ), the Federal Ministry of Economic Cooperation and Development (BMZ), and the medical aid nongovernmental organization action medeor. I also interviewed representatives of the pharmaceutical company Roche in Basel, Switzerland. In addition, I conducted extensive archival research at the WHO library and archives.[34]

## Pharmaceutical Production in East Africa and an Outline of the Book

The pharmaceutical sectors that emerged in Kenya, Tanzania, and Uganda in the 1980s and 1990s were all small, but the available measures indicate that the Kenyan pharmaceutical sector fared better than the Tanzanian and Ugandan ones. The Ugandan sector's performance was particularly poor. In 1990, the estimated market shares of total drug sales of local drug manufacturers were 20 percent in Kenya, less than 10 percent in Tanzania, and negligible in Uganda.[35] In addition to one or two state-owned enterprises (SOEs), which all three countries established, Kenya had twelve privately owned companies, while Tanzania had four, and Uganda only one. Other indicators show similarly pronounced differences. By 1990, Kenya had the total capacity to manufacture 8 billion tablets and 800 million coated tablets per year, whereas Tanzania only had the capacity to produce 3 billion tablets per year.[36] The Kenyan

TABLE 1.2. Local pharmaceutical production in Kenya, Tanzania, and Uganda, 1990

|  | Kenya | Tanzania | Uganda |
|---|---|---|---|
| Local market share | Est. 20% | Est. less than 10% | Negligible |
| No. of firms | 1 SOE + 12 private | 2 SOEs + 4 private | 1 SOE + 1 private |
| Value | $15 million (1987) | $4.9 million | Negligible |
| No. of employees | Over 1,000 | Est. 340 | N/A |
| Total manufacturing capacity | 8 billion tablets | 3 billion tablets | N/A |
|  | 800 million coated tablets | 69 million capsules |  |
|  | 1 billion capsules | 430,000 liters |  |
|  | 10.8 million liters | 1 million bottles |  |
|  | 20 million bottles | 40,000 kg |  |
|  | 800,000 kg creams | 10.5 million vials |  |
|  | 50 million vials | 0.5 million liters of semi-solids |  |
|  | 26.5 million ampoules | 0.5 million aerosol |  |

*Source:* Compiled by the author; see chapters 3, 4, 5. SOE = state-owned enterprise.

pharmaceutical sector employed three times the number of workers that the Tanzanian sector employed, and the value of the Kenyan pharmaceutical sector was estimated to be three times larger.[37] Although we have no credible data on Uganda, we can safely assume that the production capacity, employment, and value of the pharmaceutical sector in Uganda at the time were all minor. Table 1.2 summarizes the above indicators.

By 2000, Kenya, Tanzania, and Uganda all had local pharmaceutical firms that produced generic versions of simple drugs. But then, in all three countries, some companies increased their production capabilities, producing more complex drugs and following higher quality standards. In all three countries the contributions of the pharmaceutical sectors to GDP remained small, but there were also significant differences.[38] The Kenyan sector remained the largest of the three; indeed, measured by value, Kenya was one of the three largest local producers of medicine in the region (not counting South Africa), behind Nigeria but on par with Ghana (IFC 2007, figure A3.2, UNIDO 2011b, Simonetti, Clark, and Wamae 2016). In the most recent data available, estimated market share of the local pharmaceutical sector in Kenya was 28 percent, compared to an estimated market share of 10–15 percent in both Uganda and Tanzania (UNIDO 2010a, Wangwe et al. 2014a). By 2010, Kenya had twenty firms producing drugs, compared to nine in Tanzania and eleven in Uganda; and the estimated value of the pharmaceutical sector in Kenya in 2008 was $103 million, compared to $46 million in Tanzania, and $27.6 million in Uganda

TABLE 1.3. Local pharmaceutical production in Kenya, Tanzania, and Uganda, 2010

|  | Kenya | Tanzania | Uganda |
|---|---|---|---|
| Local market share | 28% (2008) | Est. 10–15% | Est. 10–15% |
| No. of firms | 20 | 9 | 11 |
| Value | $103 million (2008) | $46 million (2008) | $27.6 million (2008) |
| No. of employees | 3,389 | N/A | 1,216 |
| New drugs | ARVs; | ARVs; | ARVs;* |
|  | ACTs | ACTs; | ACTs* |
|  |  | Zinc/lo-ORS |  |
| Quality standards | WHO PQ; | WHO PQ; | WHO PQ* |
|  | PIC/S; | PIC/S; |  |
|  | Roche audit | Roche audit |  |

*Source:* Compiled by the author; see chapters 6, 7, 8.

* Indicates a firm with an exceptional trajectory. ARV = antiretroviral, ACT = artemisinin-based combination therapy, lo-ORS = low-osmolality oral rehydration salts, WHO PQ = World Health Organization prequalification, PIC/S = Pharmaceutical Inspection Convention and Pharmaceutical Inspection Cooperation Scheme.

(UNIDO 2010a, 2010b, UNDP 2016). In Kenya, 3,389 persons were employed in the sector, whereas in Uganda 1,216 were employed (UNIDO 2010a, 2010b). Although we have no equivalent estimates for employment in the pharmaceutical sector in Tanzania (Losse et al. 2007), we can assume it was much smaller than in Kenya because in 2010, 4,687 persons in total were employed in the country's 37 chemical firms, only a handful of which produced pharmaceutical products (UNIDO 2010c).

In terms of the range of drugs manufactured and of quality standards, however, both Kenya and Tanzania fared better than Uganda. Not only did the top companies in Kenya and Tanzania register a larger number of drugs than top Ugandan companies (chapter 2), but the top pharmaceutical companies in Kenya and Tanzania learned to produce new types of drugs, including ARVs, ACTs and, for treating diarrhea in children, zinc and low-osmolarity oral rehydration salts (lo-ORS), following high quality standards, whereas the larger companies in Uganda, with the exception of one company with a unique trajectory, did not. In Kenya, two companies pursued WHO PQ (one successfully), six companies pursued a European certificate (PIC/S), and three passed an audit conducted by Roche. In Tanzania, although pharmaceutical firms did not seek WHO PQ for ARVs or ACTs, two companies pursued WHO PQ for zinc, one company pursued PIC/S, and two passed the Roche audit. Table 1.3 summarizes some of the indicators mentioned above.

In the rest of the book, I offer a detailed empirical investigation of the emergence and the upgrading experiences of pharmaceutical companies in Kenya, Tanzania, and Uganda, as indicated in the measures above. Because locally produced drugs capture only a small share of the drug market in East Africa, however, the analysis would not be complete without situating local firms in that larger context. Chapter 2 documents the shift in the pharmaceutical markets in Kenya, Tanzania, and Uganda from markets dominated by originator (brand-name) drugs produced by western companies to markets dominated by generic drugs produced in the global South, most prominently, in India. The chapter also describes the ongoing efforts by multinational pharmaceutical companies to slow down that shift—especially by strengthening intellectual property rights. The chapter contributes to the scholarship on industrial production in developing countries by identifying the role African markets played in the growth of the Indian pharmaceutical sector. As for the concern that TRIPS has pushed Indian drug manufacturers out of poor countries, I show that the data do not indicate such a "flight," but that it reveals changes with a direct effect on access to affordable medicine—including increased reliance on drug donations to attract large drug companies into these markets. Finally, the chapter examines why reports on the prevalence of Chinese drugs in East Africa are greatly exaggerated.

The following three chapters describe the *emergence* of the pharmaceutical sectors in Kenya, Tanzania, and Uganda respectively. Chapter 3 begins with the international political-economic context, in which developing countries were able to make local pharmaceutical manufacturing part of "development" in the 1970s–1980s, thereby encouraging foreign assistance in that field and enhancing interest in local pharmaceutical production in many countries. The chapter then describes the interplay between foreign aid and state policies in Kenya that together contributed to the emergence of a small yet robust locally owned pharmaceutical sector. Most important was a "ration kits" program that helped rationalize the procurement and distribution of drugs in rural areas. As part of that program, a government-funded component was used to specifically purchase locally produced drugs. This proved critical for the emergence and growth of the Kenyan pharmaceutical sector. Other policies in support of the state-owned pharmaceutical firm also indirectly pushed for and later assisted privately owned pharmaceutical firms. With the support of foreign aid, then, the Kenyan government was able to create a market for local producers. Foreign assistance did not come with technology transfer (mentoring), and access to technical know-how was predominantly available to Kenyans of Indian origin, whose social position during colonialism and after independence granted them educational, commercial, and cultural ties abroad. There was little attention to quality standards (monitoring).

Chapter 4 examines the limited growth of the local pharmaceutical sector in Tanzania, compared to Kenya. Tanzania, too, relied on a ration kits program funded by donors, but development agencies rejected suggestions for a local component for ration kits, and donors offered only limited support—in the form of raw materials—to state-owned pharmaceutical enterprises. Without a domestic component, the ration kits turned from a potential facilitator of local pharmaceutical production, as was the case in Kenya, into a factor undermining it. Limiting domestic opportunities in the context of a socialist economy further inhibited the emergence of privately owned pharmaceutical factories. Nevertheless, a number of private companies did open, and their trajectories again illustrate the role education and ties abroad could play in the creation of a private sector in a context in which technical skills were not available locally.

Concluding this section, chapter 5 explains why a local pharmaceutical sector did not emerge in Uganda in the 1980s, and why it was fragile when it ultimately did emerge in the 1990s. Uganda's political-economic situation during Idi Amin's military dictatorship between 1971 and 1979, and until the end of the civil war in 1986, was inhospitable for both state-owned and private pharmaceutical manufacturing. Moreover, when Amin expelled Indians in 1972, Ugandan entrepreneurs' ties abroad were severed, delaying the emergence of a private pharmaceutical sector in the country. A ration kits program was launched in Uganda only in 1986, and it did not have a local component. A pharmaceutical sector cautiously emerged only in the 1990s. The vacuum created during the Amin regime now enabled broader access to the pharmaceutical field, including indigenous Africans on the one hand and non-Ugandans on the other. However, without ties abroad, in addition to lack of state support or foreign assistance, many pharmaceutical firms that opened at the time were quite fragile.

The following three chapters describe the upgrading of the pharmaceutical sectors in Kenya, Tanzania, and Uganda in the 2000s and 2010s—a period shaped by the liberalization of the East African markets back in the 1990s, negotiations over TRIPS, and the international response to AIDS. Chapter 6 describes the conditions that led pharmaceutical manufacturers in Kenya to invest in the production of a broader range of drugs, and to improve quality standards beyond what was required by local regulations. The chapter begins with the contentious negotiations over TRIPS—including in regard to developing countries' concern that producers of generic drugs would no longer be able to make the types of generic drugs needed in poor countries. I describe how these negotiations resulted in donors providing to some developing countries not only markets, as they did in the 1980s, but also monitoring and mentoring. In Kenya, a new market of interest to local manufacturers, for anti-AIDS and antimalarial drugs, was created when the Global Fund to Fight AIDS, Tuberculosis and Malaria, among other donors, did not a priori exclude local manufacturers from tenders. To participate in these tenders, however, drugs manufacturers had to receive WHO PQ confirming that their drugs were produced following international, rather than only local, quality standards. This monitoring gave local producers an incentive to improve their manufacturing practices. In turn, development agencies offered training and other forms of mentoring—giving local producers the means to learn *how* to produce drugs following these higher quality standards.

Chapter 7 describes the transition of the pharmaceutical sector in Tanzania from a small, vulnerable sector to a still small but more sophisticated one. The chapter shows that, as in Kenya, upgrading was thanks to developmental foreign aid that offered markets, monitoring, and mentoring. Fewer pharmaceutical companies in Tanzania were able to respond to the incentives created by the Global Fund market, but they responded positively to tailored offers made by development agencies, which involved help with creating domestic demand. Another difference between Tanzania and Kenya was the complementary regulatory roles played in Tanzania by the state and, potentially, foreign investors.

Chapter 8 identifies the conditions that led even the largest Ugandan pharmaceutical companies to forgo production of complex drugs or quality upgrading, with the exception of one firm with a unique trajectory. In Uganda, the Global Fund did not operate through the drug procurement state agency, which made the Global Fund market less approachable for most local producers. Additionally, Ugandan producers were not offered the mentoring made available to Kenyan and Tanzanian drug companies. Without potential markets and adequate mentoring, local producers did not have the incentives or capabilities to change their strategies, and local pharmaceutical firms in Uganda continued to produce simple drugs. The exception was a joint venture between a Ugandan firm and one of the largest pharmaceutical companies in India. With unprecedented support from the state, it was able to successfully achieve a WHO certificate and take advantage of the Global Fund and other markets.

Finally, chapter 9 summarizes the book's main arguments regarding developmental foreign aid in the pharmaceutical field and suggests that similar conclusions apply to other industrial sectors, as well as to other (nonindustrial) sectors of interest to foreign aid, including the provision of services and the distribution of essential commodities. The chapter then identifies a number of contradictions and tensions inherent to developmental foreign aid, including in regard to its effects on the state. First, given that the cases examined in the book confirm the importance of state capacity for foreign aid effectiveness, the chapter takes on the highly contested question of whether foreign aid could contribute to state capacity-building. I suggest that although there are obvious challenges, there are also convincing indications that both pharmaceutical regulation and enforcement by state agencies have significantly increased thanks to foreign aid support. Second, given the difficulties in increasing state capacity, maybe aid programs could simply bypass the state? The chapter explains why even developmental foreign aid should not—but also cannot—replace the state.

Foreign aid can be effective and therefore requires our support. But the type of foreign aid that is likely to be effective is not parachuting aid that evades local institutions and actors but, rather, foreign aid that relies on the institutions and actors in place. Finally, the last section of chapter 9 considers the recent wave of FDI in the pharmaceutical sector in East Africa. It suggests that this development, too, makes the state more rather than less essential.

# 2

# Global Pharmaceuticals and East Africa

The pharmaceutical industry traces its origin to the merging of two types of firms: apothecaries that moved into wholesale production of drugs such as morphine, quinine, and strychnine in the middle of the nineteenth century, and dye and chemical companies that established research labs and discovered medical applications for their products starting in the 1880s. In the early 1930s, the medicines that were developed in the US and Europe were still mostly compounded locally by pharmacists, however. The discovery and the beginning of commercial production of sulfa drugs and penicillin in the 1930s and 1940s generated a revolution in drug therapy and, with it, the making of the modern pharmaceutical company. Following World War II, in particular, pharmaceutical firms in the US, Europe and Japan became vertically integrated, with extensive investments in inhouse research and development (R&D), and marketing. Products were promoted by brand names and protected by patents (UNCTC 1979, Chandler 2005, Chemical & Engineering News 2005).

When an invention is granted a patent, for a period of time, others cannot use this invention without the patent owner's consent. The granting of patents in the pharmaceutical field created a tiered industry that produces two types of drugs, "originator" (also "innovator," or "brand-name") drugs and "generic" drugs. An originator drug is manufactured by the firm that owns the patent on the discovery of that drug. A generic drug is an identical copy of the originator drug in dosage form, safety, strength, route of administration, quality, and performance characteristics. A generic drug can only be sold if the drug is off-patent or, if the drug is under patent, with the permission of the patent holder. Originator drugs are always branded (e.g., Advil), which is why they are also called brand-name drugs. Generic drugs are often sold under the generic name of the drug (e.g., Ibuprofen), that is, the scientific name based on the active ingredients used ("nonbranded generics" or "generic generics"), but generic drugs could also be sold under their own brand name ("branded generics"). Generic drugs (both nonbranded and branded) are considerably cheaper than originator drugs (UNCTAD 2011b).

The patent system and aggressive marketing allowed manufacturers of originator drugs to control the market worldwide. By the 1990s, however, the global pharmaceutical market had gone through two transformations. First, the market has become, in terms of volume of sales, largely dominated by generic drugs (Kaplan and Mathers 2011). Because originator drugs are so much more expensive than generics, the trend is less visible when it comes to value of sales. Yet even in terms of value, the generic market has been growing, making up about 30 percent of total global sales as of 2000. In low-income countries, generics represented almost two-thirds of the value of total sales that year.[1]

Second, countries in the global South were manufacturing these generic drugs. Following the R&D stage, the actual production of drugs—of both originator drugs and their generic equivalents—involves three stages: bulk drug production (the production of active pharmaceutical ingredients or APIs); formulation (the processing of bulk drugs, together with other inactive components, including excipients, into finished dosage forms—such as tablets, capsules, ointments, liquids, powders, injectables and the like); and packaging (the packaging of finished products in final container and labeling, or repackaging of bulk finished products).[2] The technologies of bulk drug production are sophisticated, whereas formulation and packaging, especially of simple drugs, require no more than "relatively simple equipment and the following of well spelled-out directions" (Wortzel 1971, 3). In contrast, because APIs are produced in an enclosed system so that the production environment does not affect quality, whereas final formulations are exposed to the environment and therefore require a laboratory-type setting, quality standards are more difficult to meet in formulation than in bulk production (Sensenbrenner 1987).

Bulk drug production was the first to move to the global South—partly due to the introduction of pollution controls in Europe, which made it much less expensive to produce APIs in countries without such rules.[3] Final formulation of generics has followed. In the 1970s, developed market economies and centrally planned economies contributed nearly 90 percent of total production of pharmaceutical products in value (UNCTC 1984, 2). In 2000, high-income countries still accounted for more than 90 percent of world pharmaceutical production in value (WHO 2004, figure 1.1). In volume, however, changes have been dramatic, including the rise of India as the "pharmacy for the developing countries" (UNCTAD 2011b, 15). That year, the Indian pharmaceutical sector was the fourth largest in the world in terms of volume, accounting for 8 percent of the world's production (it was thirteenth largest in terms of value, accounting for 1 percent of the world's production) (WHO 2004, 4). In short, a global pharmaceutical market that was earlier monopolized by research-based companies in the global North has come to be shared with generic drug producers in the global South. As a consequence, the price of drugs in many parts of the world has become more affordable.

The growth of the generic drug market, and the production of these drugs in the global South, has been nothing short of radical. But the shift has not been inevitable—and legal and political changes in intellectual property protection and quality standards since the 1990s have been pointing at a possible reversal. Indeed, brand-name pharmaceutical companies ("Big Pharma") have been fighting hard to keep their markets, by seeking patent protection across the globe and by questioning the quality of generic drugs produced in the global South (Chorev 2015).

Patent laws are national laws, and many countries, including India in 1970, chose not to have stringent intellectual property protection on pharmaceutical products, exactly in order to strengthen local drug production. In 1994, however, all member states of the World Trade Organization (WTO) signed the Agreement on Trade-Related Aspects of Intellectual Property Rights (TRIPS), which required them to adopt and enforce high minimum standards of intellectual property protection, including for pharmaceuticals (Sell 2003, Kapczynski 2009, Löfgren and Williams 2013). To comply with TRIPS, India revised its intellectual property law in 2005. Under the revised law, Indian drug manufacturers had to wait much longer before they could copy new drugs (Chaudhuri 2005). Critics of TRIPS argued that strengthened intellectual property protection would delay access to affordable drugs to people who need them. An added concern was that, even though TRIPS—following bitter political struggles—allows low-income countries under certain conditions to export drugs under patent, these markets would be too small to make it attractive for Indian manufacturers (Shadlen 2007).

In addition to patent protection, brand-name pharmaceutical companies used concerns regarding poor manufacturing standards in industrializing countries as a way to deter governments, doctors, and patients from using generics. Indeed, whereas the formulation of drugs is simple, one characteristic that sets the pharmaceutical sector apart from other industries is quality concerns because, if not manufactured correctly, drugs "could potentially have dire health consequences for the user" (UNCTAD 2011b, 9). To avoid cross-contamination, production out of specifications, mislabeling, and so on, detailed standards have been developed, known as Good Manufacturing Practices (GMP).[4] Based on GMP guidelines developed by the World Health Organization (WHO), many industrializing countries developed their own national GMP regulations (WHO 1995a, 2007, 9). The stringency of the standards and the level of enforcement differ across countries, however, and loose standards and poor enforcement have been used by brand-name pharmaceutical companies to discredit generic manufacturers (Chorev 2015).[5] While high quality standards are unequivocally supported also by public health officials and health activists, there are concerns that quality standards are used as a protectionist tool. There are also concerns that measures designed to assure the quality of drugs produced in the global South—including the WHO prequalification (PQ) scheme—would lead manufacturers to abandon semi-regulated markets in favor of the more profitable regulated countries that they can now access.

In this chapter, I document the shifts from brand-names to generics and from the global North to the global South in East Africa. Looking at the global pharmaceutical market through the experiences of Kenya, Tanzania, and Uganda offers new arguments regarding both the original transformation and the extent to which it has been possibly reversed after TRIPS.

In regard to the original transformation, I show that the rise of Indian exports was not simply a consequence of conditions in India, as it is often suggested. In East Africa, it was also a consequence of market liberalization imposed through Structural Adjustment Programs (SAPs) on the three countries in the 1980s and 1990s. Specifically, the removal of foreign exchange restrictions—combined with inadequate regulation of the pharmaceutical market—allowed an unmonitored entry of drugs into the private market. The result initially was the flooding of the market with drugs of various quality (Peterson 2014). However, more stringent regulation was eventually introduced. Over time, although concerns remained regarding the presence of counterfeit and substandard drugs—often sold in unlicensed chemist stores known as "quack shops"—the situation has markedly improved (Chorev 2015). In turn, thanks to the imports of drugs especially from India, East Africans gained access to affordable, quality drugs that they would not have had otherwise.

The drug markets in Kenya, Tanzania, and Uganda also reveal some of the effects that TRIPS had on countries that rely on Indian drug imports—in regard to whether and which Indian companies have maintained their interest in the East African markets. I show that, between 2001 and 2010, the number of drugs from India that was introduced to the East African markets continued to increase every year. I also show that, although there was quite a high turnover of Indian companies (new drugs were often introduced by new companies)—the number of *reputed* Indian companies, namely, those that follow high quality standards, remained considerable. At the same time, the interest of these established companies in the East African market may be dependent on their sales to donors—so that if donors left these markets, so would these manufacturers. Additionally, the drugs these companies introduce to the markets that are not for the donors may be targeting only a small strata of the middle-class.

Finally, given the reputation of China as the "factory of the world," and its enormous domestic pharmaceutical market, there is an expectation that China, like India, would be present in the global pharmaceutical market. Indeed, there are frequent references in official reports to imports of drugs from India and China to East Africa as if they were of similar significance (UNIDO 2010a, 53, 2010b, 51). In fact, Chinese drug manufacturers have so far had only minimal presence in East Africa. Based in part on my interviews in East Africa, India, and China, in the last section of this chapter, I identify a number of factors that explain the prevalence in East Africa of Indian but not of Chinese drugs. First, the Indian domestic drug market was less attractive than the Chinese domestic market, which pushed Indian manufacturers to seek export markets earlier on. Second, conditions in East Africa were more welcoming to Indian than to Chinese manufacturers: as latecomers, Chinese drug manufacturers faced more stringent regulatory requirements; and because these requirements involved much documentation and paperwork in English, the language barrier created an additional challenge. Third, Chinese manufacturers were disadvantaged by the fact that many of the importers and distributors of drugs in East Africa were of Indian descent, and they preferred to work with Indian manufacturers.

## Originator Drugs in East Africa under Colonialism and after Independence

Western medicine was introduced in Kenya, Tanganyika (comprising the mainland part of present-day Tanzania), and Uganda at the time of colonial rule.[6] Most pharmaceuticals were imported, often from national companies, for use by colonial officials and settlers. A few pharmaceutical companies also established subsidiaries in Kenya, where they produced a small number of mostly consumer products, such as cough sweets and baby foods (UNCTC 1984). Government imports were purchased through the Crown Agents for Overseas Administration; other drugs were brought by import-export houses, such as Howse and McGeorge.[7] Merchandising companies that were operating through Kenya were also importing medicine and other commodities to Uganda and Tanganyika (Rweyemamu 1973, 33, Barker and Wield 1978, 317). The importation of drugs via Kenya—as well as the fact that the foreign subsidiaries of western pharmaceutical companies were all in Kenya—was part of a larger pattern that institutionalized Kenya's commercial and industrial advantages in the region.[8]

After independence, medicine in Kenya, Tanzania, and Uganda continued to mostly come from brand-name companies from the global North, and the few firms manufacturing pharmaceuticals in Kenya in the early 1970s were still all subsidiaries of multinational corporations.[9] In the early 1970s, the largest exporters of drugs to East Africa were the UK, the US, West Germany, France, Switzerland, Italy, and Belgium.[10] Drugs continued to be distributed by some of the same companies that had done so during colonialism. In Uganda in the 1970s, for example, drugs for the Government were imported through

Crown Agents.[11] Similarly, the private foreign retail and wholesale establishments active in East Africa were often reincarnations of the older import-export houses, including Howse and McGeorge from the UK, and Hoechst East Africa and Jos. Hansen & Soehne from Germany.[12]

Although "multinational [drug companies] played a fairly big part" in the 1970s, "there were generic manufacturers even then."[13] In Kenya, retail shop owners imported generic drugs from Hungary, Poland, and Russia, as well as "the most basic [medicine] from India," and "only a few medicines" from China.[14] Still, "the volume of business they transacted was fairly small."[15] In Uganda and Tanzania as well, some drugs came from Eastern Europe, Egypt, and India.[16] Tanzania also purchased drugs from China at "extremely favorable prices."[17] As for the quality of these drugs, one report asserted that although many of the pharmaceutical manufacturers selling in East Africa at the time were "of world reputation," others were "companies probably operating outside the quality control system of any government."[18]

## Manufacturing Generics in the Global South: The Rise of India

This grip of western multinationals on the drug market in East Africa substantially loosened in the 1980s and 1990s. Brand-name drugs no longer dominated the market and most foreign subsidiaries had left Kenya.[19] Instead, drugs have been imported also from countries in the global South. This was part of a larger global trend, as we have seen, and developing countries, both as producers and as *buyers*, were active participants in making it happen.

In high-income countries, the trend in favor of originator drugs was reversed with a wave of patent expirations for widely prescribed drugs, combined with a declining rate of innovation. Equally important was increased cost-consciousness on the part of many governments, leading to policies encouraging the use of generics (UNCTC 1979, WHO 1988, 29, Carpenter 2010). In the US, for example, the Drug Price Competition and Patent Restoration Act (Waxman-Hatch Act) in 1984 famously took steps to open up the generic market in the country (WHO 1988, 29). In 1965, only about 10 percent of the total number of prescriptions written in the US were for generic drugs (Wortzel 1971); by 2006, the number went up to 56 percent (Greene 2007, 23). In 2015, generic drugs accounted for around 70 percent of the US drug market by volume; in Europe, they accounted for around 50 percent (Sun Pharmaceutical Industries 2016).

For countries in the global South, relations with multinational pharmaceutical companies were one aspect of broader relations of dependence on the global North. In 1984, 98.4 percent of the drugs imported into Africa still came from Europe and North America (WHO 1988). In international forums, developing countries denounced the exploitation of Big Pharma and called for various remedies, such as a code of conduct for the marketing of pharmaceutical products. Many of these efforts failed, but a few initiatives, including the formulation of national lists of essential drugs, were instrumental in reserving governments' limited health budgets for the purchase of generic drugs (chapter 3, Chorev 2012b).[20]

As industrializing countries saw it at the time, the issue of *which* drugs were purchased was tightly connected with *where* the drugs were produced. As the Prime Minister of India Indira Ghandi said in her address to the WHO's Assembly in 1981, "Medicines which may be of the utmost value to poorer countries can be bought by us only at exorbitant prices, *since we are unable to have adequate independent bases of research and production*" (cited in Patel 1983, 165, emphasis added). Another remedy, then, was local pharmaceutical production—and India was at the forefront of that effort.

Indeed, industrial policies provided by the government greatly helped the spectacular growth of the Indian pharmaceutical sector, as I briefly describe below (Aggarwal 2004, 5, Chaudhuri 2005, 10, Kapczynski 2009). In addition, and in line with an argument I make in chapter 1, India had entrepreneurs who were able to take advantage of those policies. As Chaudhuri (2005) convincingly described, the seeds of the sector were in the Indian government's earlier investment in public research institutions from where future entrepreneurs originated, including two public-sector drug companies, Hindustan Antibiotic Limited (HAL) and Indian Drugs and Pharmaceutical Limited (IDPL). In line with another argument I make in chapter 1, these institutions benefited by learning from foreign technology. HAL was established by the government in 1954, with technical assistance provided by the WHO and imported equipment supplied by the United Nations Children's Fund (UNICEF); the IDPL was established in 1961, with technical assistance from the Soviet Union (Aggarwal 2004, Chaudhuri 2005). Industrialization through learning (Amsden 1989) was intertwined with indigenous knowledge both times. The technical data and blueprint provided by the WHO to HAL were prepared by two Indian nationals, who had been previously at the Haffkine Institute, one of the oldest biomedical research institutes in India. "Thus, indigenous technology was routed through an international body" (Chaudhuri 2005, 31). In the case of IDPL, "various modifications [of the technology provided by the Soviet Union] were necessary owing to technological imperfections and also to match the Indian conditions" (Chaudhuri 2005, 32). HAL and IDPL were instrumental in creating domestic capabilities and fostering nascent entrepreneurs, especially because universities in India at the time did not provide the type of specialized training required by pharmaceutical companies (Chaudhuri 2005, 34). As an expert on the Indian pharmaceutical sector told me in an interview, "All Indian pharma entrepreneurs came out of IDPL."[21]

These nascent Indian entrepreneurs benefited from supportive state policies.[22] Most known is the *Patent Act 1970* that, by maintaining patent protection on the process but not the product, enabled indigenous firms to copy new drugs as long as they could use a process not mentioned in the patent of the innovator company (Chaudhuri 2005). The Act is considered to be "perhaps the single most significant policy initiative . . . that laid the foundation of the modern pharmaceutical industry" in India (Aggarwal 2004, 5). By the late 1970s, Indian firms mastered the technology of 97.5 percent of the formulations (and more than 75 percent of the bulk drugs) available in the Indian market (Horner 2013, 14). Within a decade, they captured a substantial proportion of the domestic market (UNCTC 1984, 53), and by 1991, the "Indianization of the pharmaceutical industry" in the country was "virtually complete" (SCRIP 1991a, 12).

## LIBERALIZATION AND EXPORTING INDIAN
## DRUGS TO EAST AFRICA, 1980–2000

Pharmaceutical production in India was initially almost entirely focused on the domestic market, however, and exports constituted only 1 to 5 percent of total production. Yet from the mid-1980s, exports began to steadily increase. In the 1990s, more than a quarter of production was directed to the export markets, and by the end of that decade, the rate of exports was one third of total production (Aggarwal 2004, 26, Chaudhuri 2005, 41–46). Exports were partly driven by incentives adopted by the Indian government in the mid-1980s, which included exemptions for exports from some restrictive provisions of the 1986 New Drug Policy and the Foreign Exchange Regulation Act (Joseph 2009, 15). The small market of exports that existed already in the early 1980s was directed at the Soviet Union, the Middle East, and Africa (UNCTC 1984, 53), and even as exports became more central to the industry, they continued to be directed at under-regulated markets—ultimately leading to the crowning of India as the pharmacy of the developing world. African markets, specifically, were seldom the primary markets for Indian drug companies—as early as 1994–95, Africa was only around 10 percent of total Indian exports of pharmaceutical products (Chaudhuri, Park, and Gopakumar 2010, 37)—but they were often the first export markets for small manufacturers. For many African countries, moreover, a small share of Indian exports constituted a very large part of their drug markets.

One reason for the successful introduction of Indian drugs in African markets was that Africans could more easily afford these drugs.[23] Not only were these generics, price controls in India combined with domestic competition also meant that prices of drugs fell substantially, becoming among the lowest in the world (Horner 2013). As a pharmacist who worked for a brand-name company in Kenya put it, "So the price aspect is really one of their [Indian firms] key . . .

advantages, which has given them entry to the markets."[24] Interestingly, price controls and domestic competition drove many Indian drug manufacturers to seek out export markets in the first place.[25]

In turn, the entry of Indian drugs—or what critics see as the "flood of imported pharmaceuticals" (UNIDO 2010a, 50)—also depended on conditions in the receiving countries. As Peterson (2012) rightly emphasizes, the "flood" was enabled by market liberalization in many developing countries, imposed through SAPs in the 1980s and 1990s. SAPs started with the World Bank's launching of a Structural Adjustment Facility that offered loans not for projects—as was the norm with the Bank until then—but for balance-of-payments support, and in exchange for policy reforms. These policy reforms, in turn, were aimed at changing the underlying structure of national economies to promote exports and economic growth. In 1986, the International Monetary Fund (IMF) inaugurated a structural adjustment facility of its own and began systematically to require market-liberalizing policy reforms in addition to the macroeconomic reforms it had required in the past. Under SAPs, developing countries' governments privatized state-owned industries, liberalized domestic capital markets, removed price controls and trade barriers, and generally moved towards decreased reliance on state intervention in their economies (Babb 2013).

In Africa, Kenya was one of the first countries to receive a World Bank Structural Adjustment Loan and an IMF standby agreement, both in 1980. Tanzania, under President Nyerere, first resisted settling with the IMF, but it eventually signed an agreement with the IMF in 1986. Uganda, too, entered an agreement in 1986, soon after President Museveni took power. With the market liberalization that followed, one Kenyan industrial pharmacist commented, "everybody could sell anything here."[26] Another pharmacist explained, "SAP from the World Bank and IMF forced liberalization of the local market, including pharmaceuticals."[27] "When the economy opened . . . , Indian drugs came in," said another pharmacist.[28]

An open market was a radical departure from the way drugs had been procured and distributed in all three countries. In Kenya, the drug market was generally open even before liberalization, but the market was still constrained by foreign exchange restrictions—importers in Kenya had to obtain a foreign exchange allocation license. A Kenyan importer explained that, "For the import license, [the government] had a category of products to whom to give priority. And pharmaceuticals . . . came in that category. [But it was still] dependent on the foreign exchange available in the country." So, drug importers could be denied a license when "there was no foreign exchange in the country."[29] In both Tanzania and Uganda, until the late 1990s, a state agency had been distributing drugs for the private sector—the National Pharmaceutical Company (NAPCO) in Tanzania, and the Uganda Pharmaceuticals Ltd. (UPL) in Uganda. Medicine supply through private channels started in Tanzania already in the early 1990s (Häfele-Abah 2010, 40), and small private importers and distributors opened stores in Uganda following the end of Idi Amin's regime (IFC 2007), but it was liberalization that truly changed the nature of the drug market.

In all three countries, the removal of foreign exchange restrictions impacted drug imports after liberalization the most.[30]A Kenyan pharmacist explained, "Liberalization was a turning point, because . . . the government stopped the active regulation of foreign exchange . . . . And this is what really changed the dynamics. Because then there was no restriction" on obtaining foreign currency for procuring drugs abroad.[31] In addition, trading in general in East Africa became more widespread thanks to easier credit from commercial banks, and, later on, thanks to technological developments that made it easier to establish connections abroad. Referring to the Internet, a Tanzanian drug importer explained, "In the past, only Indians could know about Indian [drugs]. Now everyone can."[32] In some cases, "once the market opened, people from [East Africa] started going to India and buy[ing] drugs there."[33] In other cases, manufacturers from India came to East Africa looking for "credible partners."[34] Here, the fact that many importers, distributors and wholesalers in East Africa were of Indian descent, smoothed the interaction (chapter 1). The outcome, then, was the wide opening of the drug import trade—including informal trade—with "wholesalers everywhere."[35]

"When you open importation liberally, then the headache of *regulating* it becomes a huge task," a Kenyan pharmacist complained.[36] Because before liberalization drugs had been mostly imported by the government and came from brand-name drug manufacturers located in regulated economies, regulation of drugs in Kenya, Tanzania, and Uganda had been a relatively minor affair. The private sector, which was small, was also effectively monitored. With some nostalgic undertone, one Kenyan drug importer described, "[In the 1970s] the number of retail outlets was very limited. It was a very disciplined business in the sense that each and every outlet . . . was . . . properly registered with the Ministry of Health. [Every outlet] had a . . . qualified pharmacist, and there was a fair amount of checks and balances in place."[37] In contrast, with the mushrooming of private traders bringing drugs from semi-regulated countries, the regulatory tasks were much more exacting. With liberalization, according to a Kenyan pharmacist, drugs were "brought in briefcases. It was not the law. But people took advantage [of inadequate enforcement, and] bypassed the legal authorities."[38] An official in the inspectorate department in Kenya's drug regulatory agency similarly described, "We opened the borders for everybody. [They] came in with very small consignments. You can walk in. After two days, you dispose. [You leave]. You come again."[39] Importers confirmed that, "A lot of them were substandard."[40] The market also saw an explosion in the number of unlicensed drug shops, where substandard and counterfeit drugs were often sold.[41]

Over time, however, in an attempt to protect consumers from the consequences of a "free" market, all three countries strengthened their drug regulations. Consequently, as I describe in the respective chapters, registration of drugs, inspection of factories, and post-marketing surveillance improved. The requirements were looser than the ones in regulated markets and the enforcement weaker, enabling the operation of illegal drug outlets (UNIDO 2010a) and the entry of substandard drugs to continue.[42] Still, the quality of drugs improved over time. In Kenya, partly thanks to government action, including the employment of more inspectors, more raids, and the closing of unauthorized retailers, the failure rates of drugs went down.[43] By 2010, studies found a particularly low prevalence of substandard antimalarial drugs in the country (WHO 2010, 2011).[44] Also in Uganda, importers were less likely to purchase drugs on the grey or black markets and more willing to source only from factories approved by the Ugandan government (Klissas et al. 2010).

In short, generic drugs made it to East Africa when drug manufacturers in India were looking for export markets at the same time that distributors in Kenya, Tanzania, and Uganda took advantage of liberalization to import drugs. Initially, a free market of drugs led to the importation of poor-quality drugs, through both legal and illegal channels. However, liberalization ultimately triggered additional regulation and enforcement, and India became "a source of low-cost but high-quality drugs" (Chaudhuri 2005). In what follows, I offer empirical evidence of the growing reliance in Kenya, Tanzania, and Uganda on Indian drugs.

———

I asked an Indian importer in Kenya when Indians first started importing drugs to the country, and he jokingly answered, "When did the first Indian arrive?" That first Indian supposedly brought with him a suitcase filled with medicine.[45] In reality, Indian drugs made it to the Kenyan market in a systematic fashion only in the late 1980s, and increasingly so since the mid-1990s. By value, Big Pharma continued to have the largest market share. Estimates suggest that in the early 1990s, around 47 percent of drug imports came from Europe, the UK, and the US (WHO 1995a, 142); by 2008, the market share of brand-names was even larger, with around 55 percent of drug imports coming from the global North (UNIDO 2010a, 42).[46] Still, even in terms of value, Indian presence was impressive, with estimates suggesting that between 2001 and 2009, imports to Kenya from India were on average 24.5 percent of total imports every year (Anand Rathi Research 2010, UNIDO 2010a, 41). In terms of volume, Indian drugs dominated.[47] There is no accurate data on the volume of imported drugs; but, to be legally sold, every drug in Kenya (since 1982), Tanzania (since 2000),

TABLE 2.1. Number and rate of imported drugs registered in Kenya, 1982–2010

| | 1982–90 | | 1991–2000 | | 2001–2010 | |
|---|---|---|---|---|---|---|
| | Drugs | % imports | Drugs | %imports | Drugs | % imports |
| Global North | 1,135 | 90 | 1,216 | 45 | 961 | 21 |
| Global South | 122 | 10 | 1,504 | 55 | 3,577 | 79 |

*Note*: The "global North" includes the US, all European countries, Canada, Japan, and Australia. The "global South" includes all countries that are not in the global North, not counting Kenya.

and Uganda (since 1997) had to be registered by the respective government agency, and registration data offer an alternative way of assessing the composition of the drug market. Because in Kenya registration started relatively early, the data also allow for comparison over time.[48]

Table 2.1 shows the number and rate of imported drugs (not counting locally produced drugs) registered in Kenya from the global North and the global South. In the 1980s (1982–1990), 90 percent of the registered drugs (1,135 drugs) came from the global North and 10 percent (122) from the global South. Measured by the rate of drugs registered, then, pharmaceutical companies from the global North clearly dominated the market. But they were losing their dominance in the 1990s (1991–2000): during that decade, only 45 percent of the registered drugs (1,216) came from the global North whereas 55 percent (1,504) came from the global South. Notably, the *number* of drugs registered by companies from the global North in the 1980s and the 1990s stayed almost the same, whereas the number of drugs registered by producers from the global South multiplied more than tenfold. This trend intensified in the 2000s (2001–2010), with only 21 percent (961) of registered drugs coming from the global North, and 79 percent (3,577) coming from the global South.

In regard to which countries imported drugs to Kenya, two developments are important. First, over time, more countries were registering drugs in Kenya—from 34 countries in the 1980s to 58 in the 2000s. Second, in the 2000s, even the main importing counties had a lower share of the market than the main importing countries had had in the 1980s, with one prominent exception. Table 2.2 lists the top six registering countries in each decade and their relative share of the total. In the 1980s, not counting Kenya, the UK and the US had the largest number of registered drugs (16 percent each) followed by Germany (11 percent) and Switzerland (6 percent). In the 1990s, the relative share of the UK and the US went down (8 and 7 percent, respectively), followed by Germany (6 percent) and Switzerland (3 percent). By the 2000s, Pakistan had the second highest share, with 5 percent, and Bangladesh had 4 percent; the UK and the US each had 3 percent. The very notable exception for the

TABLE 2.2. Top six registering countries in Kenya, 1982–2010

| 1982–90 | | | 1991–2000 | | | 2001–2010 | | |
|---|---|---|---|---|---|---|---|---|
| Country | Drugs | % drugs | Country | Drugs | % drugs | Country | Drugs | % drugs |
| Kenya | 387 | 24 | India | 1027 | 30 | India | 2,505 | 48 |
| UK | 262 | 16 | Kenya | 819 | 24 | Kenya | 751 | 14 |
| US | 248 | 16 | UK | 283 | 8 | Pakistan | 246 | 5 |
| Germany | 170 | 11 | US | 248 | 7 | Bangladesh | 216 | 4 |
| Switzerland | 103 | 6 | Germany | 193 | 6 | UK | 179 | 3 |
| India | 72 | 5 | Switzerland | 118 | 3 | US | 177 | 3 |

tendency of smaller market shares was India. India had only 5 percent of the registered drugs in the 1980s; but the rate went up to 30 percent in the 1990s and to 48 percent in the 2000s.

In Tanzania as well, back in the early 1990s, imported pharmaceuticals came from the global North, including the UK, Germany, Italy, Denmark, Switzerland, the Netherlands, and Belgium. Tanzania also imported from Kenya.[49] Similar to Kenya, the turning point was the mid-1990s, with drugs arriving from Egypt, India, and other countries in the global South. By 2000, when registration began in Tanzania, the market was already largely controlled by drugs from the global South, especially India. In terms of value, according to one estimate, between 2001 and 2009, 27.5 percent of drug imports to Tanzania came from India (Anand Rathi Research 2010, 17); based on the UN COMTRADE database, a UNDP report (2016, table 2) calculated that in 2012 the figure was 36.8 percent.[50] India's dominance is also evident in the registration data.[51] As of 2012, 76 percent of the imported drugs registered were from the global South (see table 2.3). India was dominant with 46 percent of the registered drugs. Kenya, which was second, had 7 percent of registered drugs, followed by (after Tanzania) Germany, UK, Egypt, Cyprus, Pakistan, South Africa, China, and Switzerland (see table 2.4).

Uganda, too, saw growing imports of generic drugs from the global South, starting in the 1990s. Major suppliers, in descending order, were India, Kenya, the UK, France, and Germany (UNCTAD 2001, 37). In terms of value, according to one estimate, between 2001 and 2009, 25.3 percent of drug imports to Uganda came from India (Anand Rathi Research 2010, 17). In terms of volume, estimates suggest that by 2009 India supplied around 60 percent of the country's pharmaceutical imports.[52] Registration data, which started in 1997, tell a similar story.[53] As of 2012, 83 percent of all imported drugs registered in Uganda came from the global South (see table 2.5). India was dominant with 56 percent of the registered imports. Kenya, which was second, had only

TABLE 2.3. Number and rate of imported drugs registered
in Tanzania, as of 2012

|  | Drugs | % imports |
| --- | --- | --- |
| Global North | 716 | 24 |
| Global South | 2,283 | 76 |

*Note*: The "global North" includes the US, all European countries,
Canada, Japan and Australia. The "global South" includes all countries that are not in the global North, not counting Tanzania.

TABLE 2.4. Top eleven registering countries in Tanzania,
as of 2012

| Country | Drugs | % drugs |
| --- | --- | --- |
| India | 1,615 | 46 |
| Kenya | 247 | 7 |
| Tanzania | 214 | 6 |
| Germany | 116 | 3 |
| UK | 106 | 3 |
| Egypt | 102 | 3 |
| Cyprus | 91 | 3 |
| Pakistan | 91 | 3 |
| South Africa | 80 | 2 |
| China | 67 | 2 |
| Switzerland | 67 | 2 |

8 percent of registered drugs, followed by (after Uganda) China, Pakistan, Germany, UK, Egypt, Cyprus, Malaysia, and South Africa (see table 2.6).

Big Pharma maintained its market share by selling to the government,
donors, as well as to a fraction of the population in each country that could
pay out of pocket for brand-name drugs or had insurance that covered them.
In Kenya, a frequently cited estimate was that, "the top 5 percent of the private market is 100 percent multinationals," that is, the richest 5 percent of
Kenyans only bought brand-name drugs from multinational pharmaceutical
companies.[54] This also explained the greater presence of brand-name drugs
in Kenya, where purchasing power was higher and health insurance schemes
more developed, than in Tanzania and Uganda. The less affluent bought branded
generics. Everyone else bought nonbranded generics.[55] Local purchasing
power also explains why Indian drugs, which were cheap even compared to

TABLE 2.5. Number and rate of imported drugs registered in Uganda, as of 2012

|  | Drugs | % imports |
| --- | --- | --- |
| Global North | 535 | 17 |
| Global South | 2,702 | 83 |

*Note*: The "global North" includes the US, all European countries, Canada, Japan, and Australia. The "global South" includes all countries that are in not the global North, not counting Uganda.

TABLE 2.6. Top eleven registering countries in Uganda, as of 2012

| Country | Drugs | % |
| --- | --- | --- |
| India | 1,876 | 56 |
| Kenya | 259 | 8 |
| Uganda | 143 | 4 |
| China | 133 | 4 |
| Pakistan | 97 | 3 |
| Germany | 89 | 3 |
| UK | 88 | 3 |
| Egypt | 80 | 2 |
| Cyprus | 73 | 2 |
| Malaysia | 66 | 2 |
| South Africa | 63 | 2 |

other generics, were so dominant. In addition to price, also the type of drugs produced in India—including drugs that had demand mostly in low-income countries—made Indian drugs attractive and made experts warn that as Indian drug manufacturers started complying with TRIPS, they would abandon the African markets.

## TRIPS AND EXPORTING INDIAN DRUGS TO EAST AFRICA SINCE 2000

East Africans' acceptance of drugs made in India was not certain, as importers met resistance from distributors, medical practitioners, and others, who were used to European-made originator drugs. This attitude eventually changed—in part thanks to the successful production of antiretrovirals (ARVs) in India.

Because of TRIPS, it was unclear initially whether generic versions of patented ARVs could be legally produced. To defend their market, brand-name pharmaceutical companies claimed that the importation or local production of generic ARVs violated the international obligations of WTO member states. It was only thanks to bitter (and ongoing) political struggles that "flexibilities" in the TRIPS agreement were confirmed to allow countries under certain conditions to import (or locally produce) generics of patented drugs, and the legality of generic production and sales of ARVs was accepted (Chorev 2012a). It was then that major Indian drug companies, including Cipla and Ranbaxy (which already had other drugs registered in Kenya), but also Hetero Drugs, Aurobindo Pharma, and Cadila Healthcare (which did not), started exporting ARVs *and other drugs* to Kenya, Tanzania, and Uganda (SCRIP 2001).[56] The initial volumes of ARVs were small, but after additional struggles, the two largest donors of anti-AIDS and antimalarial drugs—the Global Fund to Fight AIDS, Tuberculosis and Malaria, and the US President's Emergency Plan for AIDS Relief (PEPFAR)—began to procure generic drugs, which greatly increased the demand for Indian drugs (Venkatesh, Mayer, and Carpenter 2012).

But these successes did not settle all concerns regarding the impact TRIPS would have on poor countries' access to generics of relatively new drugs. Although many of the political struggles were over the right of generic manufacturers to produce on-patent drugs, another concern has been whether drug producers would be interested in utilizing that hard-won right. With the reintroduction of drug product patent protection in India in 2005, India's drug companies were permitted to manufacture new drugs only by relying on the TRIPS flexibilities (Chaudhuri 2013).[57] TRIPS flexibilities involved, however, many bureaucratic hurdles. Another concern has been that leading generic manufacturers might not invest in producing copies of new drugs needed in poor countries—and risk legal confrontations with the innovator company—for such limited markets (Shadlen 2007, Sampat, Shadlen, and Amin 2012).

An additional factor that could make leading Indian manufacturers less likely to challenge patents was a wave of foreign direct investment (FDI) in the pharmaceutical sector in India, starting around 2008. Responding to the loosening of restrictions on FDI in India—and encouraged by the relaxation of price controls and a growing domestic branded market—multinational brand-name pharmaceutical companies bought a few of the largest generic pharmaceutical companies in India (WHO 2011e). The most notable examples were Ranbaxy, which was acquired in 2008 by a Japanese company, Daiichi-Sankyo (Chaudhuri 2008), and Piramal Healthcare, which was acquired in 2010 by an American company, Abbott Laboratories (Tewathia 2014). Other prominent Indian manufacturers entered contract manufacturing agreements with Big Pharma (Greene 2007, table 7, Chaudhuri 2013, table 6.1). Both scholars and health activists worried that generic companies that are owned or otherwise dependent on multinational companies (MNCs) would become less combative in challenging patents, or even in introducing generics to the market as soon as patents expired.[58] As one health activist ruefully said, "While [activists] were fighting for the laws that would allow Indian generic manufacturers to sell patents, the MNCs bypassed the entire system by buying those generics."[59]

Another concern was that once the leading Indian manufacturers "acquired the maturity to venture into the more difficult developed country markets" (Chaudhuri 2008, 12), they would lose interest in the African market. In some ways, a move from markets in the global South to markets in the global North is an expected trajectory of a successful industrial sector (Amsden 1986). In this case, this "acquired maturity" was accelerated by TRIPS, which made the Indian pharmaceutical companies' copying strategies illegal, forcing them to find alternative ones. Paradoxically, "maturity" was also accelerated by the quality assurance required by the Global Fund and PEPFAR—WHO PQ and US Food and Drug Administration (USFDA) approval, respectively—which encouraged many of the larger Indian pharmaceutical companies to certify the quality of their drugs and factories and in that way gave them a path to regulated markets. In the US, the FDA launched an expedited, cheaper procedure for PEPFAR drugs. This procedure did not give the approved drugs access to the American market, but Indian manufacturers found that once they had one drug approved, it was subsequently easier for them to get regular approval for other drugs made in the same factory.[60] In 1990, only ten manufacturing facilities in India were approved by the USFDA for the production of both bulk drugs and formulations, but by 2013, 238 bulk drug and 142 formulation sites had been approved by the USFDA.[61] By then, between 30 to 40 percent of the generic medicines taken in the US were made by Indian companies (Kazmin 2015).[62]

In short, major changes in opportunities, interests, and capabilities led to increased entry of the leading Indian pharmaceutical companies to regulated markets, but we are yet to know what effect this had on their practices in semi-regulated markets. I show that one can begin to decipher that question by looking at registration data in Kenya, Tanzania, and Uganda.

First, as I described above, registration data show that Indian drug manufacturers continued to export drugs to East Africa, and in growing numbers. As we have seen, 48 percent of the registered drugs in Kenya between 2001 and 2010 came from India; as of 2012, 46 percent of the registered drugs in Tanzania, and 56 percent in Uganda came from India. Other studies show that Africa as a whole came to constitute an expanding market for India's pharmaceutical exports: up from 10.6 percent of total Indian exports of drugs and pharmaceuticals in 1994–95 to 14.7 percent in 2007–2009 (Chaudhuri et al. 2010). The question, then, is not *whether* Indian drug companies kept exporting to East Africa, but *which* Indian companies.

Second, there was a relatively high turnover of Indian companies in East Africa. In Kenya, many companies that had registered drugs in the past no longer did so; at the same time many other companies registered drugs in Kenya for the first time only after 2005.[63] Some of the companies that stopped registering new drugs were among the same leading Indian companies that entered regulated markets. For example, Dr. Reddy's Laboratories, one of the largest pharmaceutical companies in India, closed its operations in Africa in 2009, when it decided to focus only on the large and more profitable regulated markets. Top companies also left because, given the additional costs of maintaining high quality standards, they could no longer compete in price-sensitive markets (Chaudhuri et al. 2010, 36). Additionally, the East African markets depended on old drugs, which some of the top Indian companies no longer produced.

Third, even as some reputed Indian companies left East Africa, many stayed. To estimate the reputation of Indian companies who stayed in East Africa, I compared the list of the Indian companies that have registered drugs in Uganda as of 2012 with four different sources: the top 179 companies compiled by the Centre for Monitoring Indian Economy (Chaudhuri et al. 2010), the top 200 Indian pharmaceutical companies in 2007–2008 based on their revenue (Cygnus 2008), Indian companies with USFDA approval (Pharmexcil 2013), and Indian companies with WHO PQ. Of the 111 Indian companies that registered drugs in Uganda in 2012, 58 appeared in at least one of the four sources, which means that 52 percent of the Indian companies that registered drugs in Uganda that year were reputed companies. As for the relative *number* of registered drugs made by reputed companies, 1,072 of the 1,829 Indian drugs that were registered in Uganda—or 59 percent—were made by reputed companies.[64] Given the ratio of all Indian drug companies (around 6,000) to top companies (200–300), this is impressive.[65]

The Indian pharmaceutical companies that stayed in East Africa, then, included not only small companies, but, in contrast to the concerns described above, also leading companies. This was partly because once a firm produced a drug, the cost to enter the African market was relatively minimal; and once they put operations in place (as many leading companies did), some companies did not move out no matter how low the profits might have been.[66] But it also seems to be the case that reputed companies entered and/or stayed in East Africa mostly because of the markets created by the Global Fund and PEPFAR. This is made clear by the fact that many of the drugs registered by these companies in East Africa, as of 2010, were ARVs, antimalarials and anti-tuberculosis drugs; and it is possible that only because these companies were *already* present in the markets through the Global Fund and PEPFAR that they were *also* registering other drugs. One example is the Indian pharmaceutical company Cipla. Until the 2000s, Cipla's focus was on the Indian market. In 1992, for example, exports were only around 10.6 percent of its sales. But in 2001, Cipla transformed the global ARV market when it offered its "all-in-one" ARV pill at $600 per patient per year to all African governments, and at $350 to the humanitarian organization Médecins Sans Frontières (Chorev 2012a). Cipla had been selling in African countries before, but the "main thrust for Cipla in Africa came after 2000."[67] Together with ARVs, Cipla introduced other medicine, including asthma, malaria, anti-cancer, cardiac, and antibiotics.[68] Other Indian companies had similar experiences. For example, Hetero, given its focus on generics of the latest molecules, considered the African market "unsuitable," but after it started selling ARVs, it also introduced other branded generics to the African market that "at least some of the people can afford."[69] Yet only 15 percent of Hetero's sales in Africa were non-ARVs, confirming their main interest in the donors markets.[70] Indeed, for most major Indian companies Africa was a trivial market, but it was a more significant market for those who sold for the Global Fund or PEPFAR. Africa accounted for 14.1 percent of Cipla's sales in 2006–2007, 6.9 percent of Ranbaxy's formulations sales in 2006, and 7.7 percent of IPCA's total income (Chaudhuri, Mackintosh, and Mujinja 2010, 5).

As confirmed by Hetero's experience, when selling in the private market, these larger firms did not necessarily compete with the smaller suppliers, as they often marketed drugs that were branded for the urban, middle-class niche market.[71] This targeting, however, "hardly satisfies the cause of most of the poor people who need essential drugs" (Chaudhuri et al. 2010, 37).

In short, what we may be witnessing is not a moving out of the leading Indian pharmaceutical firms from the East African markets altogether, but a focus on the donors market and, as for the local market, a focus on the private sector and on medicine that could only be afforded by the middle class.

Fourth, even if leading Indian manufacturers stayed, many Indian drugs in East Africa were produced by "second-tier" firms. They were sold in unregulated markets exactly because they did not follow the requirements of the regulated markets. A drug trader in Uganda mentioned, "In India there are good manufacturers, but they do business in Europe and the US, not Africa. It's the 'others' who are ready to make something for you."[72] A managing director of an Indian company confirmed in a newspaper interview, "For small and mid-sized companies who do not have adequate infrastructure to meet the EU or USFDA [standards] . . . countries in Africa offer [a] good business opportunity. The regulatory authorities are liberal" (Das 2011). What was the quality of these "second-tier" drugs? These drugs were produced by small companies that relied on price advantage, their factories were not always adequately inspected, and they were therefore more likely to get away with "using shortcuts."[73] Yet the quality of drugs made by less reputable Indian companies in 2010 was still higher than the quality of drugs made by Indian companies earlier on. This was in part thanks to changed regulations in India. Schedule

M of the *Drugs and Cosmetics Act, 1940*, which governs the quality of drugs in the country, became stricter over time, even if the new regulations were not always effectively implemented.[74] Interestingly, one incentive for the more stringent domestic regulation in India was increased quality expectations by under-regulated export markets. A news service for the global pharmaceutical industry reported, "The move [introducing quality control standards in India] is designed to reduce the export of substandard pharmaceuticals to developing countries, many of which are beginning to insist on proper certification for the medicinal products they import" (SCRIP 1999). So regulation in other semi-regulated countries, including Kenya, Tanzania, and Uganda, contributed to the increased quality of imported "second-tier" Indian drugs.

To summarize, the maturing of major pharmaceutical companies in India did not mean that they left the African markets. It is possible that the presence of those that did stay in East Africa depended on sales to donor programs, however. At the same time, the quality standards of the smaller drug companies from India that continued to sell in East Africa depended on the enforcement mechanisms in both India and the respective East African country, both of which somewhat improved over time.

## Manufacturing—but Not Yet Exporting— Generic Drugs in China

Reports on the drug markets in East Africa often refer to drugs from China as if they were as common in the region as drugs from India (UNIDO 2010a, 53, 2010b, 51). Given the reputation of China as the "factory of the world," and its enormous domestic pharmaceutical market, there would be nothing surprising if China was as present as India in the global pharmaceutical market. However, this is not the case. Chinese firms, as of 2010, only had a fraction of the market share in Kenya, Tanzania, or Uganda.

Some Chinese drugs did arrive to the region, including earlier on. For example, Tanzania bought discounted drugs from China starting in the early 1980s.[75] In general, however, the volume was minimal and remained small, even if the number of Chinese companies and the number of drugs from China did increase over time. In Kenya, only three drugs and two companies from China were registered from 1982 to 1990, whereas 40 drugs made by 16 companies were registered from 1991 to 2000, and 122 drugs and additional 42 companies registered from 2001 to 2010. Altogether, only 60 companies from China had drugs registered in Kenya (compared to 334 companies from India), and they made only 2 percent of the drugs registered. In Tanzania, as of 2012, China only had 2 percent of the registered drugs, imported by only 19 companies. According to the United Nations Development Programme (UNDP 2016), in terms of value, China had only 3.9 percent of imports to Tanzania—around one-tenth of the value of Indian companies. In Uganda, as of 2012, China had 4 percent of the registered drugs, imported by only 18 companies. Haakonsson (2009a) estimates that drug imports from China were negligible in 1995 and captured only 2.6 percent of the market in 2005.

Given China's manufacturing capabilities, the greater success of Indian pharmaceutical companies compared to the Chinese is a puzzling reversal. I argue that this can be explained in part by the fact that the Chinese pharmaceutical sector developed later and faced no pressures to move from the local market to exports. By the time Chinese pharmaceutical companies entered the East African markets, moreover, these were regulated to a greater extent than when the Indian companies had first entered. In addition, Chinese pharmaceutical companies, more than their Indian counterparts, found it challenging to follow the required documentation and paperwork.

The chemical pharmaceutical industry in China started, as it did in India, in the 1950s, shortly after the Communist Party took over power. Similarly to India at this time, the industry received technology transfer from the Soviet Union, which supported the founding of some of China's top domestic drug producers (Van Den Bulcke, Zhang, and Li 1999, 359). The ten-year Cultural Revolution (1966–1976), however, almost destroyed the Chinese research base and obstructed the development of manufacturing technology (Wang 1999)— and it took time for the pharmaceutical industry to revive. Following the economic reforms under Deng Xiaoping in the late 1970s, China by 1985 was producing chemical drugs in 839 plants, but production facilities were small-scale, duplicative, and greatly uneven in quality; many relied on the outdated foreign technology acquired before the 1960s (Sensenbrenner 1987, Wang 1999, Tang et al. 2007). By 2005, following liberalization that "provided opportunities for newcomers with cash" (Wang 1999, 462), the number of pharmaceutical manufacturers producing both western and traditional medicines rose to over 4,600 (Bumpas and Betsch 2009, Watanabe and Shi 2011). The majority of new domestic producers were still single-factory companies, however, "producing oversupplied old bulk actives on a small scale with obsolete technology and outdated management" (Wang 1999, 462–63).

These companies were also mostly producing poor-quality drugs. The first GMP standards were issued in China in 1988 (Pefile et al. 2005, 46). These standards have become more stringent over the years—today they resemble WHO and European standards—but enforcement has been challenging.[76] In 1998, the Chinese State Drug Administration gave pharmaceutical companies until 2004 to meet GMP standards. Later the director of the agency was found guilty for accepting bribes in exchange for speedy approvals and other special favors (Liu 2012); other challenges included lack of compliance procedures, light punishments, poor quality of inspectors, and the cracking down on quality to pressure firms on unrelated issues, such as prices. Instances of undeserved accreditation and other challenges notwithstanding, by the deadline, nearly 2,000 manufacturers lost their production licenses (Liu 2012); a total of 3,731 bulk and final formulator manufacturers got GMP approval (Pefile et al. 2005).

Poor manufacturing practices—including *poorly documented* manufacturing practices—made it more difficult to export drugs from China, compared to other commodities, even to semi-regulated markets. The regulatory requirements regarding pharmaceutical products tend to exceed what is normally asked of other imported commodities. Notably, the requirements include not just post-hoc documentation, but documentation done as an integral part of the process of production. According to many interviewers, the use of English, in particular, was a major barrier for Chinese drug manufacturers, especially for the older generation.[77]

In East Africa, Chinese importers also suffered a slight bias against them, as many of the importers and distributors were of Indian descent and had developed close ties with Indian drug manufacturers and exporters. One distributor in Kenya explained that he did not bring many drugs from China because he did not like to travel there—China was too vast, and there were language issues. Like others, this distributor questioned the quality standards in China. Contributing to the challenge of establishing trust in the quality of Chinese drugs was lack of information—whereas in India, manufacturers are ranked (ORG rating), in China, they are not.[78]

In turn, different domestic conditions explain why exports of final formulations would be less attractive to Chinese manufacturers than to Indians. One difference was China's particularly large domestic market, in spite of the very low prices for generic medicine there (WHO 2004). According to one estimate, in 2015, the Chinese spending on medicine was $115 billion—second only to the American market ($430 billion). That year, India reportedly spent only one-tenth of what China spent, $12 billion (Sun Pharmaceutical Industries 2016).

In spite of these numerous barriers, the expectation is that just the way Chinese producers have caught up with Indian API production, they will do the same with final formulations. An expert on pharmaceuticals in China claimed, "They say it took India 30 years to become international—and we just started!"[79] One indication is a growing number of instances in which manufacturers, both in India and in East Africa, rely on contract manufacturing in China where it is cheaper to produce.[80] Another is that a growing number of Chinese pharmaceutical companies have made it to regulated markets, as indicated by their ability to achieve USFDA approval. In 1988, there were no formulation plants from China that had FDA approval (World Bank 1988). In 2007, there were still "only a few" Chinese drug companies that had been approved by the USFDA (Tremblay 2007). By 2013, 43 sites owned by 36 companies had received USFDA approval (compared to 142 sites owned by 79 companies from India).[81] Chinese pharmaceutical companies also began seeking WHO PQ for final formulations. In 2017, 23 drugs from China from 11 companies were prequalified by the WHO.[82]

Of the 23 WHO prequalified drugs from China, 13 were antimalarial drugs, and 11 of those were produced by one company, Guilin. (The other two antimalarial drugs were produced under the license of Novartis, a Swiss company). Guilin was one of three antimalarial Chinese producers that had a presence in East Africa in 2012. The other two companies were Kunming and Beijing Holley-Cotec, and the trajectories of these companies illustrate three different ways by which Chinese drugs did make it to East Africa.

The reason for the relative prominence of antimalarial drugs in China's drug exports to East Africa was that China played an important role in developing the drug that since 2001 has been considered the most effective medicine for malaria treatment. In 1972, Chinese scientists successfully isolated the active ingredients from the sweet wormwood plant (Artemisia annua), and produced a new drug—artemisinin (Pefile et al. 2005). China had poor drug development capabilities at the time, and the first drug brought to the market, Coartem, was owned not by a Chinese company, but by the Swiss company Novartis (Tremblay 2007). The drug received international licensing approval in 1999, and two years later the WHO recommended the use of artemisinin-based combination therapies (ACTs) for malaria treatment (Pefile et al. 2005). WHO also called against the use of artemisinin *mono*therapies, which was considered a major contributing factor to the development of resistance to artemisinin derivatives.

In Kenya, in addition to Coartem, which was registered in 1999, another registered antimalarial was an artemisinin monotherapy produced by Guilin. Originally state-owned, in 2004 Guilin became a subsidiary of Fosun Pharma, one of the top 20 pharmaceutical companies in China.[83] When the WHO banned artemisinin monotherapies, Guilin was able to register a combination therapy in Kenya in 2005. Guilin received WHO PQ in 2006—the first WHO-prequalified ACT from the global South. The drug was also certified by the USFDA.[84]

The second company, Kunming, was the Chinese partner of Novartis when Coartem was first developed, and it owned the Coartem license in China.[85] Kunming had an ACT registered in Kenya, Tanzania, and Uganda, branded as Arco, but it was not WHO-prequalified. Consequently, the drug was only sold in the private market.[86] Kunming's ACT also made it to East Africa as donations from the Chinese government.[87] A small crisis erupted when Wikileaks published US cables that revealed that, "In January 2010, the Chinese Ambassador to Uganda . . . delivered 240,000 doses of two Chinese antimalaria drugs to Uganda at a public event that was featured in large paid advertisements in local papers." This included 144,000 doses of Arco, produced by Kunming. "It was later revealed that one of the drugs, Arco, had not been [pre]qualified by the WHO, and that part of the funding for the malaria clinic in Mulago Hospital was earmarked for testing of these drugs" (Gyezaho 2011).

The other ACT offered as donation in that same event were 100,000 doses of Duo-Cotexin, produced by Beijing Holley-Cotec (BHC). These, too, were not WHO prequalified, although BHC has been trying to achieve the certification since 2005.[88] Kunming and BHC were part of the same larger company—Holley Group. Indicating the minimal interest of Chinese companies in export markets, antimalarials were the only drugs exported by the Holley Group; all the company's other pharmaceutical products were for the domestic market.

In short, as of 2010, drug manufacturers from China had only a limited presence in Kenya, Tanzania, and Uganda. The experience of Guilin, Kunming, and BHC suggest that the larger drug companies in China focused either on the domestic market or regulated markets, and much less so on semi-regulated export markets. In turn, small Chinese companies still met real challenges in entering even semi-regulated markets.

## Discussion

Under colonialism and long after independence, Kenya, Tanzania, and Uganda relied on multinational pharmaceutical companies for the supply of drugs. Starting in the 1990s, however, these markets have been taken over in terms of volume by generic drugs, mostly from India. In this chapter, I provided evidence that demonstrates just how remarkable that shift has been. I also argued that the entry of Indian drugs to the East African markets was the result not only of domestic conditions and policies in India, but also of changing conditions in Kenya, Tanzania, and Uganda—specifically, the move in all three countries from an unregulated but closed market to an open market. Before the 1990s, regulation of pharmaceuticals hardly existed in Kenya, Tanzania, and Uganda. Presumably, governments could trust the quality of the drugs they were buying, given that these were manufactured in highly regulated markets. In fact, this was not the case. Some multinational pharmaceutical companies not only overcharged for their drugs, but also were willing to sell mislabeled, expired, and other types of substandard drugs to governments in the global South, as I describe in chapter 3. Still, liberalization made developing countries more vulnerable to the entrance of substandard drugs. The removal of foreign currency restrictions, among other policies, initially allowed for entirely unsupervised drug markets with traders opening unlicensed quack shops where they could sell smuggled drugs, many of which were unregistered. Over time, however, regulation was able to limit to some extent the unruliness of the private market. Access to good, affordable medicine is still limited in Kenya, Tanzania, and Uganda—but it has greatly improved thanks to manufacturers of generics in the global South.

The analysis of this chapter has additional theoretical implications. In the debate over the consequences of "south-south trade," Amsden (1986, 255) argued that manufacturing for exports to other developing countries tends to be relatively skill-intensive and that "it is arguable that historically, the production of commodities destined to Southern markets has facilitated North-bound trade." This has proven to be the trajectory of some Indian drug manufacturers and is likely to become the trajectory of Chinese drug manufacturers as well. As important, however, is the impact "south-south trade" has on the receiving party. Here it seems relevant to consider trade in pharmaceuticals in the context of current debates over China's—and, to a lesser extent, India's—investment in Africa.[89] Whether companies and governments from the global South exercise a new form of neo-colonialism, or whether they can trade (and provide aid) without exploitation, is usually addressed by looking at the extraction of natural resources or the conditions imposed on recipients for the provision of aid.[90] Yet, even the relatively mundane case of trading in pharmaceuticals could be illuminating—and it suggests that there is nothing in the "nationality" of companies that would make them more or less likely to exploit. The same question that Peter Evans (1976, 129) asked in regard to multinational versus local companies could be rephrased to apply to the case here: Is it reasonable to expect that the decisions made autonomously by an Indian or a Chinese entrepreneur would be any different than those made by a European one, assuming that both were facing the same economic situation? It is not. Rather, it is regulations—both at home and in the receiving market—that change a company's behavior. East Africans received drugs that manufacturers in India and China could not sell in markets in the global North. This, to repeat, has also been the case at times with drugs manufactured by pharmaceutical companies from the global North. It is inherently exploitative to sell substandard products to vulnerable populations. In contrast, regulation that puts an adequate threshold allows for a market that is differentiated, legitimately, not by quality, but by cost—from which both producers and consumers in the global South could benefit.

The rise of a pharmaceutical industry in India in the 1970s–1980s was partly triggered by international discussions over ways by which poor countries could reduce their dependence on multinational drug companies. India was not alone, as many other industrializing countries experimented with local pharmaceutical production at the same time. The following three chapters describe the emergence of pharmaceutical sectors in Kenya, Tanzania, and Uganda.

# 3

# Kenya in the 1980s

## INTERNATIONAL ORIGINS OF LOCAL PRODUCTION

When western medicine was introduced in East Africa, at the time of colonial rule, most pharmaceuticals available in Kenya were produced in factories in Europe, although a few pharmaceutical companies established subsidiaries in Kenya. Both practices continued undisrupted after independence, but by 1990, as I show in chapter 2, generic drugs from India came to dominate the Kenyan market, and, with the exception of Glaxo (later, GlaxoSmithKline or GSK), foreign subsidiaries had left.

In Kenya, in addition to the increase in generic imports from other countries in the global South, a number of locally owned (as opposed to foreign subsidiaries) pharmaceutical firms had also opened. So, although the market continued to be predominantly served by imports, a Kenyan pharmaceutical sector was established and had grown over time. From 1977 to 1987, the value of drug imports grew four-fold, from 200 million Kenyan shillings (KSh) to almost 800 million KSh, at the same time that local production increased six-fold, from 40 million KSh to more than 240 million KSh.[1] Locally owned pharmaceutical firms included one state-owned company, Dawa Pharmaceuticals Ltd., and a dozen private companies.[2] One private firm, Beta Healthcare, was a take-over of the foreign subsidiary of Boots (UK). The other privately owned firms were newly established. A few of them had started producing "informally" already in the 1970s, but they opened large-scale pharmaceutical plants only later on.[3] With the exception of Beta Healthcare, which was owned by prominent African Kenyans, all plants were owned by Kenyans of Indian descent.[4] Already in 1990, local pharmaceutical companies had an estimated 20 percent market share. The pharmaceutical sector at the time employed more than 1,000 workers, and it was valued at around $15 million.[5] Many of the firms have not only survived into the 2010s, but they have also remained the largest drug companies manufacturing in Kenya.

In this chapter, I identify the domestic circumstances that enabled the emergence of a pharmaceutical sector in Kenya. A number of political-economic conditions led traders of pharmaceuticals into manufacturing, including state policies that, through various protectionist measures, were able to create a "market reserve" for local drug producers. In addition, racialized colonial legacies created a class of Kenyan entrepreneurs of Indian origin that, thanks to ties abroad, had access to education, jobs, and technical know-how. Indian Kenyans' community ties at home, in turn, provided for the effective diffusion of the acquired know-how.

In this chapter, I also show that foreign aid was instrumental in the emergence and growth of locally owned pharmaceutical firms in Kenya. As part of the call for a New International Economic Order (NIEO), and as the abusive marketing practices of multinational pharmaceutical companies were exposed, developing countries' demand for a more even distribution of pharmaceutical production between industrialized and industrializing countries made pharmaceutical manufacturing a legitimate aspect of investment in "development." This triggered principled and practical support of local pharmaceutical production from a number of international organizations, which shaped the Kenyan government's initial interest in establishing a state-owned pharmaceutical factory and later support of a private pharmaceutical sector as well. With World Health Organization (WHO) guidance the Kenyan government introduced an Essential Drugs List (EDL), which not only rationalized the procurement of drugs in the country, but did so in a way that prioritized locally produced drugs. As part of a ration kits program for the procurement and distribution of essential drugs in rural areas, which was designed and funded by the Swedish and Danish development agencies, the Kenyan government was able to create a market reserved only for local producers that proved to be key for the sector's continued resilience.

In what follows, I first describe the international struggles over improved access to affordable medicine, including by means of local production. In the following sections, I show how the Kenyan government's adoption and *adaptation* of international models—including the establishment of a state-owned factory, a national list of essential drugs, and a ration kits program—contributed to the emergence and success of a locally owned pharmaceutical sector. I then describe how colonial legacies and ties to India gave Kenyans of Indian origin access to technical know-how not available locally, which then got diffused through community ties at home. I conclude with a description of the outcome: the Kenyan pharmaceutical sector by the beginning of the 1990s.

## How Pharmaceuticals Became "Development": Bargaining in the Shadow of Power

The end of colonialism brought to newly independent countries sovereignty and membership *as sovereigns* in international organizations. By the 1970s, developing countries became a majority in the UN, and they attempted to use their numbers to make operative demands. One significant achievement was the "Declaration on the Establishment of a New International Economic Order," which passed unanimously at the Sixth Special Session of the UN General Assembly in 1974.[6] Developing countries' main demand in their call for a NIEO was that of economic development, but that goal intersected with other development concerns, including health (Chorev 2012b).

Health disparities in the world were a particular cause of concern. One study presented to the WHO, for example, estimated a 21-year difference in life expectancy between industrialized and low-income countries and reported that child and infant mortality were 13.5 and 8 times higher, respectively, in low-income countries than industrialized countries (Chorev 2012b, 55). Under the leadership of director-general Halfdan T. Mahler, the WHO responded to developing countries' demands by committing the organization to addressing these disparities, ambitiously declaring that, "the main social target of governments and WHO . . . should be the attainment by all citizens of the world by the year 2000 of a level of health that will permit them to lead a socially and economically productive life" (WHO 1978).[7] The objective of "Health for All by the Year 2000" (HFA/2000) was to be achieved through Primary Health Care (PHC).[8] In turn, one key component of PHC, and a "special strategy for achieving the goal of HFA/2000," was the provision of *essential* medicines.

This emphasis on better access to affordable medicines was informed in part by developing countries' fierce critique against the marketing practices of multinational pharmaceutical companies in their countries. A 1975 WHO report confirmed many of the documented allegations others had made:

> Drugs not authorized for sale in the country of origin—or withdrawn from the market for reasons of safety or lack of efficacy—are sometimes exported and marketed in developing countries; other drugs are promoted and advertised in those countries for indications that are not approved by regulatory agencies of the countries of origin. Products not meeting the quality requirements of the exporting country, including products beyond their expiry date, may be exported to developing countries that are not in a position to carry out quality control measures.[9]

In addition, price manipulations and aggressive marketing meant that drugs represented the bulk of national health budgets in poor countries (Mamdani

1992, 2). Due to a colonial legacy of biased health-care infrastructure, many needed drugs were only available to the urban population (Melrose 1983, 182).

The revelations of such abusive practices momentarily tamed the influence of multinational pharmaceutical companies and—at a time that international organizations were already under pressure to address developing countries' grievances—forced the WHO and other international organizations into action (Chorev 2012b). Although developing countries and health activists failed to convince WHO members to support an international code of conduct to regulate the marketing of pharmaceutical products (Chorev 2012b, Andia and Chorev 2017), they were able to take advantage of the political vulnerability of multinational pharmaceutical companies to advance other initiatives. Specifically, the WHO joined other international organizations and bilateral development agencies in support of three policies: local production of drugs "wherever feasible," a selection of essential drugs "to meet [developing countries'] real needs," and a ration kits program.[10] These strategies drew on extant policies in several developing countries, but the WHO helped institutionalize and diffuse them to other countries, including Kenya. I discuss the model list of essential drugs and the ration kits program later in the chapter. Here I focus on local production of drugs.

## LOCAL PRODUCTION OF ESSENTIAL DRUGS

For developing countries, the solution for "the main difficulty . . . [of ensuring] the supply of drugs at reasonable prices" was disassociation from multinational pharmaceutical companies, to the extent possible.[11] Local pharmaceutical production was therefore considered the most direct way to resolve developing countries' vulnerabilities to the abuse of multinational pharmaceutical companies. Linking public health concerns with the goal of economic growth, developing countries argued that the "crux of the problem" was the unequal distribution of industrial capacity, where 90 percent of the drugs were produced in developed countries; 5 percent in three developing countries, India, Brazil and Mexico; and the remaining 5 percent in all other developing countries.[12] "The long-term solution," therefore, "clearly rested with local production of essential drugs."[13] Local pharmaceutical production, a WHO document promised, would "facilitate regular and sufficient availability of essential drugs of internationally acceptable quality, which is essential to maintenance of health care at reasonable cost." It would also "enable flexibility of drug supply corresponding to local needs, including sudden catastrophic epidemics and other emergency conditions."[14] By reducing the need for hard currency used for the procurement of imported drugs, local production also promised to relieve poor countries from "one of the heaviest burdens on import payments."[15] And it would "create local employment opportunities and strengthen manpower development," as well as a multiplier effect on supporting industries.[16]

Most developing countries, however, lacked the know-how to establish a pharmaceutical sector on their own. Already in 1966, therefore, a document submitted to an African Symposium asked "that the [Economic Commission for Africa], in association with WHO, prepare a comprehensive report . . . on . . . the assistance that Africa may and can obtain for [the development of a pharmaceutical industry] and the possible safe and reliable sources of technology, experience, and otherwise."[17] Similarly, the Fifth Conference of Non-Aligned Countries at Colombo, Sri Lanka, in August 1976, endorsed "the establishment by each developing country of its own pharmaceutical industry as appropriate," and invited "the relevant international organizations . . . to assist in the achievement" of this objective.[18]

In response, the United Nations Industrial Development Organization (UNIDO), the United Nations Conference on Trade and Development (UNCTAD), the United Nations Development Programme (UNDP), and the WHO, among others, declared their support of initiatives for the creation of indigenous production capabilities.[19] The Lima Declaration and Plan of Action, which UNIDO famously adopted in 1975, set ambitious targets for promoting industrialization, including that by the year 2000, 25 percent of the world's pharmaceuticals should be produced in developing countries (UNIDO 1975). At the WHO, in 1978, Resolution WHA31.32 declared that local production of essential drugs and vaccines was a "legitimate aspiration" of developing countries.

Alongside symbolic support, UN agencies launched programs aimed at "the establishment of . . . production facilities for pharmaceuticals." The primary responsibility fell on UNIDO, as this was "an essential part of its effort to foster . . . industrialization" (UNCTC 1984, 77). From 1976 onward, UNIDO conducted feasibility studies and offered technical assistance to a few countries trying to start up local production of finished essential drugs (UNCTC 1979, Guimier, Lee, and Grupper 2004, 12). Attempts to elicit the support of developed countries included conferences on the "Transfer and Development of Technology to Developing Countries Under More Favorable Conditions in the Pharmaceutical Industry."[20] In turn, commitment to the principle of *appropriate* technology (Chorev 2012b, chapter 4) meant a preference for *low-cost* pharmaceutical plants. The goal was to design a Model Plant, consisting of buildings, equipment, instruments and infrastructure, "which . . . fulfil technical criteria including health and safety standards, GMP guidelines and ecological considerations for waste disposal *at the least possible investment cost* and greater reliability to enable the manufacture and control of manufacture of essential drugs in developing countries."[21]

Given its pharmacological expertise, the WHO's assistance focused on providing guidance on what drugs to produce based on the therapeutic needs of countries, assessment of the efficacy and safety of the drugs produced, and assistance with pharmaceutical quality.[22] From early on, then, the WHO offered *guidelines* and *standards*. Already in 1969, for example, Resolution WHA22.50

endorsed requirements for Good Practices in the Manufacture and Quality Control of Drugs (later known as Good Manufacturing Practices, or GMP). In subsequent years, many developing countries incorporated into their national legislation versions of these requirements adapted to local conditions. In this case, as with the Model List of Essential Drugs, the role of the WHO in diffusing norms and practices has been remarkable.[23]

Through the 1970s, international organizations expressed confidence that the goal of local production of drugs was attainable. One WHO official assured member states, for example, that local drug production "could be started out almost anywhere using very simple methods."[24] Another promised that, "production technology for essential drugs was not as complicated as might be feared."[25] A note from the WHO regional office for the Western Pacific stated that, "development of local formulation of limited items of drugs . . . required relatively large numbers of unskilled personnel and a relatively low level of investment."[26]

Others warned of potential challenges, however. A study prepared in cooperation with UNIDO (Lall 1978, 1) stated:

> The difficulties that developing countries encounter in the development of pharmaceuticals [range] from the strictly technological problem common to most industries of obtaining know-how . . . to the *economic* difficulties of reducing the costs of buying technology and products in highly imperfect and oligopolistic markets, the medical difficulties of ensuring rational and effective therapeutic practice, the *social* difficulties of providing for the basic health needs of large numbers of poor people, the *legal* difficulties of defining property right contracts and obligations . . . and the *political* difficulties of countering abuses in the present system . . . . Consequently, the task of pharmaceutical development is formidable.

Indeed, by the 1980s, support for local production was fading, in part due to "substantial economic, infrastructural and technical problems."[27] Support was fading also due to intensified opposition from rich countries, as discussions evolved into issues such as a code of conduct for the marketing of pharmaceutical products (Chorev 2012b, 111–21). The WHO, in particular, faced criticisms from the US government that it was "not so well equipped" to provide support in the field of "drug supply infrastructure."[28] To avoid conflict, the WHO chose to deflate early promises, and director-general Mahler announced that local production of drugs was going beyond what the organization could in fact deliver (Chorev 2012b, 120).[29] UNIDO also shifted its focus. In 1980, UNIDO still asserted that, "Each developing country should accept a commitment to establish a strong local pharmaceutical industry" (UNIDO 1980, 12). By the end of the decade, UNIDO's publications were more concerned with effective procurement and quality control of imported drugs, development of medicine from indigenous medicinal plants, and support for ancillary industries, especially packaging materials (Foster 1999).

A diminished interest in pharmaceutical production was also justified by a new argument that local production of drugs was not (or was no longer) economically rational for *most* developing countries. The success of some developing countries and the subsequent rise of a global market for generics led to a significant price decrease of many drugs, which worked against local manufacturers in other countries who were not able to produce drugs at competitive prices (Foster 1986, 5–6, Guimier et al. 2004). In 1984, one report argued: "Few, if any, drugs can be produced locally if pure economic justification is the only justification."[30] By then, there was also a growing sense that, "the establishment of local pharmaceutical production has been modest and fallen far short of expectations." The reasons cited contradicted many of the views expressed back in the early 1970s: "Drug formulation has a limited value-added component; it is complicated technology; quality is often difficult to assess; and processes require importation of know-how, raw materials and machinery."[31]

Although international political support for local production turned out to be short-lived (Häfele-Abah 2010), the initiatives, programs, and policy models that were put in place had deeply affected local pharmaceutical production in many developing countries. In Kenya, the government established a state-own pharmaceutical plant, and it was involved in two programs supported by foreign aid: the creation of a national list of essential drugs and what came to be known as the ration kits program.

## Making Medicines in Kenya: A State-Owned Factory

As an interest in local pharmaceutical production was pushed into the international agenda by developing countries in the 1970s and early 1980s and effectively disseminated through debates, international programs, and policy models, many governments added pharmaceutical production to their industrialization agenda, often by establishing state-owned pharmaceutical plants. In Kenya, a state-controlled pharmaceutical company was established in 1977. The company, Dawa Pharmaceuticals Ltd.—*dawa* means drug in Swahili—was 34 percent owned by the Kenyan Industrial and Commercial Development Corporation (ICDC), 8 percent by its subsidiary ICDC Investment Co. (ICDCi), 34 percent by a private Yugoslav company, Krka Pharmaceuticals, and the rest (24 percent) by three "private Kenyan investors."[32]

The ICDC was the Kenyan government financing institution responsible for the promotion of industry and for reversing the three-tiered, racialized system under British rule that had inhibited African-owned industry. Under colonial rule, Kenya's primary economic activities initially focused on primary production, providing raw materials for industries in Britain, and serving as a "captive market for [Britain's] manufactured goods" (Amutabi 2006, 84). Until 1945, industry consisted mostly of processing agricultural goods, although factories producing basic consumer goods for the domestic and regional markets (such as cement, soda, beer, cigarettes, soap, and canned fruits and vegetables) were also opened (Brett 1973, 277, Swainson 1979, Mwega and Ndung'u 2008, 354). Africans were not allowed to participate in production of trade goods and only "controlled petty trade, subsistence farming and subsistence pastoral agriculture." Asians, unlike Africans, were allowed light, small-scale manufacturing, and they "controlled smaller import-export firms, most of the retail shops in cities and towns . . . and small-scale manufacturing." Europeans controlled "the larger import-export firms, shipping, mining . . . plantations, large farms, large scale food processing firms . . . and the larger commercial firms in urban areas" (quoted in Gachino 2009, 142–43). Although industrial policies shifted after World War II, the racialized system did not. So even as the British colonial policy in Kenya began to encourage local participation in industry, subsidiaries of multinational corporations and settler enterprises were "clearly and explicitly favored" (Swainson 1977, 1987, 140–41). As a result, subsidiaries of multinationals set up many of the biggest companies; the smaller and medium enterprises were owned by European settlers and local Indians (utilizing capital they were able to accumulate before and during the war), and indigenous Africans were not significantly involved (Swainson 1980). In an effort to reverse that unequal system, after independence the ICDC and the ICDCi, which was a parastatal body (government corporation) created by ICDC, were tasked with the goal of enabling *African* development (Gregory 1993, 299).

The ICDC decision to invest in Dawa, which was a state-controlled company, rather than encouraging private African investment, was typical for the time. Earlier on, the Kenyan government pursued an export-oriented growth strategy based on incentives for private industrial investment, not state participation. A scarcity of privately owned financial capital, however, forced the state to assume a more active role already in the late 1960s (Fahnbulleh 2006). Dawa was established at a time that state participation in the productive sectors increased even further, in response to the economic turmoil of the 1970s—including a balance of payments crisis in the early 1970s, a severe drought in 1973, the rise in petroleum prices in 1974, the closing of the Ugandan and Tanzanian markets to Kenyan exports in 1977, and over-commitments following a short-lived rise in export prices for coffee and tea in 1976–77 (Swainson 1980, 208, Fahnbulleh 2006). In 1983, there were 200 parastatals (World Bank 1983, 41), representing a doubling of state involvement compared to only four years earlier (Fahnbulleh 2006).

The decision to join forces with foreign investors was also typical (Swainson 1980, 208). Soon after independence, in order to halt capital flight, the government passed the *1964 Foreign Investment Protection Act*, which guaranteed foreign firms the repatriation of earnings and capital without restrictions, among other concessions and incentives. And the Kenyan government made explicit (in such documents as the "Sessional Paper 10 on African Socialism and Its Application to Planning in Kenya," published in 1965) its ambition to develop a free-market economy, where foreign investors were welcome (Fahnbulleh 2006, Mwega and Ndung'u 2008, 354). Similarly, although the ICDC was responsible mainly for stimulating small industrial and commercial enterprises under African ownership and management, it was also mandated to participate in joint ventures with foreign investors (Swainson 1987, Fahnbulleh 2006). Foreign investment was welcomed in state enterprises in part as a way to access technical know-how, which was the role of Krka Pharmaceuticals in the case of Dawa.[33]

Finally, also common was the participation of prominent private Kenyan investors (Swainson 1987, 152). Industrial policies in Kenya often followed a neo-patrimonial logic, and under President Jomo Kenyatta, who held that position from independence until 1978, much of the country's prosperity was concentrated in the hands of the president's family and his ethnic group, the Kikuyu (Sandbrook 1993, 68). Neo-patrimonialism, this time benefiting the Kalenjin people and other ethnic groups in the Rift Valley, was arguably worse under the second President of Kenya, Daniel arap Moi (Barkan 2004, Sundet and Moen 2009). Measures taken over the years to Africanize the commercial sector were therefore selective (Swainson 1977). In the case of Dawa, the three private investors were all "prominent" entrepreneurs, who "belong[ed] to [President Kenyatta's] district" and were "with political backing."[34]

Dawa had a good reputation, and it did well for a while (it later experienced difficulties)—as did other state-owned companies in Kenya at the time.[35] One assessment described Dawa as "a very well managed . . . unit," that "follows the GMP as recommended by WHO."[36] In the early years, Dawa enjoyed minimal local competition—in the late 1970s, the local pharmaceutical sector was still made of foreign subsidiaries, which were less likely to produce the essential medicines that Dawa did.[37] A few local pharmacists had started producing some medicine, but it was still on an informal, noncommercial basis, and no match to Dawa's investment of 3 million KSh in a new plant (Swainson 1977).

As for competition with imported drugs, here government support was crucial. In Kenya, the policy of import-substitution industrialization often took the form of sector-specific policies, such as high tariffs, import quotas (expressed as specified quantities or foreign exchange allocations), and restrictive licenses (Hopcraft 1979, World Bank 1994). Given public health concerns that advised against protectionist measures and Kenya's dependence on imported drugs, some of these policies were hard to utilize in the pharmaceutical sector. The Kenyan government, for example, generally did not use foreign exchange allocation to regulate the entry of drugs. Instead, the Kenyan government aimed to block imports only of drugs that could be produced by Dawa.[38] For that purpose, the government used the Non-Objection Certificate (NOC) system, where local firms (in this case, Dawa) had to approve the import license applications submitted by importers of drugs before an application could be officially considered by the government.[39] According to one Kenyan manufacturer, the NOC created a "virtual monopoly" for Dawa. Although likely an overstatement, it clearly benefitted the company.

NOC was an atypical policy instrument, but two other policies that the Kenyan government used to support Dawa were adapted from international initiatives: the national list of essential drugs and the ration kits program.

### THE NATIONAL LIST OF ESSENTIAL DRUGS IN KENYA

Aggressive marketing practices of multinational pharmaceutical companies meant that many developing countries spent scarce resources on drugs they did not need and could not afford. In 1977, a WHO expert panel prepared a "Model List" of a little more than 200 essential drugs and vaccines, with the idea that such a list—if properly adapted for the needs of each country—could rationalize the procurement decisions of developing countries and help them counter both misinformation and pressure from multinational pharmaceutical companies. The drugs included in the EDL, later renamed Essential Medicines List or EML, had to be of acceptable quality, safety and efficacy; had to be affordable; and had to be indispensable for the health needs of the local population (Chorev 2012b, 93–100). Countries received guidelines for how to prepare their own national lists, suitable for their morbidity patterns, available financial resources, and local preferences. The guidelines indicated a preference for generic names. Reflecting support for local production, the guidelines indicated preference to drugs for which local, reliable manufacturing facilities existed (Chorev 2012b, 96).

When the model list of essential drugs was introduced to WHO members, it was considered—more than local pharmaceutical production—a real and immediate threat to the interests of brand-name pharmaceutical companies. After all, the stated goal of the list was exactly to help governments procure a limited number of drugs, with preference for generic names (Reich 1987, 49–50, Mamdani 1992, 19). Multinational companies' opposition was partly neutralized by their damaged reputation at the time, given the evidence that they took advantage of governments and sold them expensive and unnecessary drugs. But the opposition was sufficiently effective to force the WHO to make some compromises—most importantly, the WHO promised that such lists would be utilized only in developing (not developed) countries, and only in regard to public (not private) procurement (Chorev 2012b, 93–100). Although limited to public procurement in poor countries, the list of essential drugs nonetheless proved a remarkably consequential and long-lasting program. In spite of multinational companies' continued opposition (Reich 1987, 49–50, Mamdani 1992, 19), already in 1984, the WHO could proudly state that, "more than 80, perhaps as many as 100, countries have already developed a list of essential drugs based on the WHO model list."[40]

To disseminate the EDL, the WHO established the Action Programme on Essential Drugs (APED, later called DAP).[41] DAP offered "a spirited marketing of the [EDL] concept," including in the African region, which was a "priority of DAP involvement."[42] In Kenya, with technical support from the Danish International Development Agency (DANIDA), the first National List of Essential Drugs was published in 1981 (Quick and Ndemo 1991).[43] Kenya's list, which contained nearly 300 active ingredients, included some outdated products and dosage forms, did not include specified process or criteria for revisions, and hospitals were able to use drugs not listed. Nonetheless, the list "has provided a sound basis for public sector drug supply" from then on (Quick and Ndemo 1991, 3). Remarkably, a much later survey, from 2009, found that around 93 percent of medicine prescribed in Kenya adhered to the national EML (MMS and MPHS 2009, 2). In addition, the rationalization of procurement through adherence to a national list of essential drugs also contributed to the goal of local pharmaceutical production, as the government commitment to the purchasing of essential drugs made it more likely to procure the kind of drugs Dawa was able to produce. In that way, the national list of essential drugs preserved part of the public market for Dawa.

## THE RATION KITS PROGRAM

In 1981, Kenya's Administrative Support Unit of the Rural Health Division (ASU) set up the "New Management System of Drug Supplies to Rural Health Facilities," which later became known as the "ration kits" program.[44] In contrast to the list of essential drugs that favored Dawa's drugs only indirectly, the ration kits program as adapted by the Kenyan government did so directly. However, like the EDL, the ration kits program was designed by and diffused with the support of international organizations and bilateral development agencies, including the WHO, DANIDA, and the Swedish International Development Cooperation Agency (SIDA).[45]

The challenge motivating the ration kits program was the lack of access to essential drugs in rural areas. In Kenya, the rural population in the early 1980s was approximately 80 percent of the total population of 16 million people; but the bulk of the health budget was allocated to secondary and tertiary hospital services located mostly in cities, and rural health centers were neglected (Moore 1982, Swamy 1994). The first goal of the program was to rationalize procurement. For that purpose, a Drug Selection Committee, with specialists from Kenya's Ministry of Health, the WHO, and DANIDA, created one list of thirty-nine essential drugs specifically for rural health centers and another list of thirty-one items specifically for rural dispensaries.[46] The second goal of the ration kits system was to rationalize the distribution of these drugs. In Kenya, delivery of drugs faced "problems of loss, pilferage and damage in transit and storage." To overcome these obstacles, a WHO report explained, "*sealed* boxes with standardized content (items and quantities) were chosen." The content for each sealed box was calculated to be sufficient for the average health facility for one month.[47] The sealed boxes—or "ration kits"—were centrally packaged and then delivered from the Medical Supplies Coordinating Unit (MSCU) in Nairobi to the rural health units.[48] The system, which started in 1981 with a pilot project in three districts, turned into a national program in 1985.[49] By 1988, it was serving 381 health centers and 982 dispensaries, with a total of 46,300 kits per year.[50]

There were some obvious disadvantages to sealed kits. For example, all kits included the same essential drugs in spite of geographical variation in therapeutic needs, leading to surpluses of drugs in some places and shortages in other. One critical evaluation reported that, "severe shortages of drugs for rural facilities and hospitals still occur regularly." The same evaluation described delays in processing contracts, delays in payment, debts for past drug deliveries, and large emergency procurements—presumably resulting in higher prices (Quick and Ndemo 1991, 38). One Ministry of Health official even complained of "major pilfering."[51] Nevertheless, the program was considered a success, and "an innovative step in reducing the problems encountered in distribution."[52] In 1987, Gerald Moore summarized, "It is not the perfect system . . . But at least it gives the health units the basic drugs, month after month, which with a little careful training of health workers can enable them to treat 70–80% of the cases seen in such units."[53] The program subsequently became the subject of several international workshops and a model for aid agencies in other countries in the region, including Tanzania and Uganda (Quick and Ndemo 1991).

Like the EDL, moreover, the ration kits program contained an industrial objective. One evaluation of the ration kits program stated: "In achieving the objective of making available essential drugs to the whole population, one of the intentions is to *encourage local manufacturing with the aim of self-sufficiency*."[54] Although never achieving self-sufficiency, thanks to the Kenyan government, the ration kits program did contribute to the emergence and resilience of local pharmaceutical production in Kenya, and it did play a decisive role in the success of Dawa.

The ration kits program was originally designed to rely on imported drugs, but the Kenyan government, with the support of the development agencies involved, decided, "as far as possible . . . to take advantage of local production/

repackaging facilities."[55] To facilitate local production, every ration kit was divided into two. Ration Kit I was provided from overseas suppliers under a tender from abroad; but Ration Kit II was supplied by local manufacturers under a tender open only to them.[56] DANIDA and SIDA paid for Ration Kit I, and the Kenyan government paid for Ration Kit II.[57]

The decision to have a local component was justified as a way to "facilitate control and supervision of production/repackaging operations."[58] More pressing, however, were the industrial ambitions involved. Kenya's ASU wrote: "[This] will be in accordance with the Kenya Government's policy of developing local industry."[59] Writing on behalf of the WHO, Dr. Moore stated that, "a healthy local pharmaceutical industry in Kenya is necessary . . . so that the country can eventually achieve self-sufficiency in a very important sector."[60] ASU also expressed the hope that, "where necessary, local management skills and capacities will be upgraded."[61] There was no assumption that local drugs would be cheaper than imported drugs (Haak and Hogerzeil 1991), although kits were heavy, which meant saving on transportation costs.[62]

Initially, few local producers from which to buy drugs existed. Dr. Moore in 1979 concluded that, "practically the only local manufacturer who has the necessary product range, quality control repackaging know-how and production capacity to work with the ASU is Dawa."[63] Elsewhere, Dr. Moore again referred to Dawa as "key to the whole project."[64] Only Dawa, then, was initially in a position to reap the benefits of the government's procurement of local ration kits, and these benefits were substantial. In 1983, for example, about 65 percent of the drug needs for the ration kits program by volume were supplied locally.[65] In 1987, the Kenyan Government paid $4 million on the procurement of ration kits sourced locally, whereas DANIDA and SIDA paid $3 million for drugs provided by overseas producers.[66]

Dawa's reliance on the public sector is made clear by the fact that, in 1985, 70 percent of its sales were to the government. Dawa had presence in the private market as well. One indication of Dawa's investment in the private market is its marketing. In 1981, Dawa was the only local company among the top ten advertisers in Kenya—the other nine (of which five were distributors of pharmaceutical products) were either multinationals or foreign subsidiaries (Jouet 1984).[67] In addition, Dawa was exporting 10–20 percent of its products to neighboring African countries. Dawa had its own label, as well as contract manufacturing agreements with multinational pharmaceutical companies, including Beecham and Glaxo. According to one estimate, as of 1983, Dawa had a similar market share to the foreign subsidiaries of Wellcome, and was ahead of Sterling and Glaxo (Owino 1991). UNCTC (1984) reported that in 1984 Dawa was responsible for more than 25 percent of the local production. At that time, Dawa had 200 workers, with estimated annual sales of $8 million. Moreover, evaluations were positive. A WHO report concluded that "Dawa functions satisfactorily with reference to facilities, staffing, GMP, reliability, and productivity."[68]

In short, government support was fundamental for Dawa's emergence and growth. The government provided Dawa initial financial investment, prevented international competition through NOC, and created procurement schemes that gave priority to its products—indirectly through the government's adoption of an EDL, and directly through the government's funding of local drugs for ration kits. In turn, the Kenyan government's decision to establish a state-owned pharmaceutical company and a few of its supportive policies were clearly informed by the international discussions and initiatives at the WHO and UNIDO that stemmed from developing countries' call for a NIEO. Foreign aid, then, was critical. State policies and foreign aid have been instrumental also in the making of a private pharmaceutical sector, as I describe in the next section.

## Making Medicines in Kenya: A Private Sector

The World Bank (1983) warned that, "industrial expansion by financial participation by the Government" could lead to selective distribution, if the Government "participate[d] in one firm in an industry while leaving other firms to fend for themselves." In Kenya, however, Dawa's growth came together with the rise of a locally owned private pharmaceutical sector. Indeed, although the Kenyan government did not develop a comprehensive industrial policy to promote that sector, state and international programs—including those that supported Dawa—were partly responsible for the move of some drug distributors and traders into manufacturing.

In general, the policies pursued by the Kenyan government "have not been particularly conducive to an integrated development of the pharmaceutical industry in Kenya" (UNCTC 1984, 106). This was in part due to the government's "need to ensure the provision of adequate amounts of quality drugs," which ruled out policies such as preferential pricing in government contracts (UNCTC 1984, 106), but it was also consistent with a World Bank's (1983, 10) assessment that Kenya's industrial policies were often "ad hoc responses to the needs of particular industries" and firms. Other policies not only failed to protect local drug manufacturers, but also introduced additional burdens on them. For example, there were no import duties on final formulations, but duties ranging from 20 to 33 percent were imposed on raw materials, packing equipment, and machines and spares used for the manufacturing of medicines.[69] Other barriers included, "the lengthy procedures for the procurement and importation of raw materials . . . for processing of Foreign Exchange Allocation License, shipping time, inspection time, and delays at ports for clearance."[70]

Still, the state's support of Dawa created conditions favorable to the emergence of a private industry.[71] Policies that protected Dawa pushed some local drug traders and distributors to look into other opportunities, including manufacturing, at the same time that a spillover effect of the same policies allowed manufacturers other than Dawa to also benefit.

Particularly threatening for drug importers was the Non-Objection Certificate system, which required them to get approval from Dawa before they could receive an import license. A critical report alleged that, "Dawa used its political connections and the NOC to bar most pharmaceutical imports into the country while selling its products well above their real market value" (Nyong'o 1988, 25). Although this statement is likely an exaggeration, interviews confirm that Dawa used the NOC to block a large number of drugs, impacting local importers and distributors, who now found their supply of drugs cut short. Importers also resented the need to disclose their business plans to a competitor (various interviews).

A number of local importers reacted by "put[ting] up their own local industries."[72] As the chairman of Lab & Allied described, "So once this [NOC] rule was established and people who were importing were affected, [they] started to think about getting into manufacturing."[73] Such a response by importers to protectionist policies is not uncommon. The economist Albert Hirschman (1968, 9–10) argued: "As [local] industry is started primarily to substitute imports, *those engaged in the foreign trade sector are likely to play a substantial role in the process.* This is the reason for the industrial prominence of . . . former importers [in Latin America]" (emphasis added). Indeed, locally owned drug manufacturing firms that opened in Kenya in the early 1980s were retail or wholesale enterprises first. Lab & Allied, for example, was first incorporated in 1970 as a trading company dealing mainly in general healthcare sundries, toiletries, and laboratory chemicals. It diversified into pharmaceutical wholesaling in 1971 and moved to pharmaceutical production only in 1979 (Ciuri 2015). Cosmos Pharmaceutical, P.M.C., Mac's, and Pac's Laboratories started in a similar way.[74] The two brothers who opened Universal in 1996 also started by first buying a trading company.[75]

Pressures to *leave* the trading business were complemented by incentives to *enter* local production. The banning of imports of some drugs due to the NOC, for example, "created impetus to fulfill market demand by owning productive facilities."[76] Later on, pressure from those who turned to manufacturing led the government to pass *The Customs and Excise (Remission)(Medicaments) Order, 1982* (CAP 472), which cancelled the import duties on raw materials used by local pharmaceutical manufacturers.[77]

Still, local manufacturers reported that the most consequential factor contributing to their success was, as was the case with Dawa, the ration kits system.[78] As we have seen, Dawa was initially the only local manufacturer considered for the ration kits program. This was not only because of its manufacturing capabilities. A newspaper article reported that, "Dr. Maneno [head of ASU] argues that to bring in more firms would bring back all the delays and disappearance or nonappearance of some drugs inherent in the present distribution system."[79] Yet local firms were understandably "unhappy that they are not being given a fair slice of the rural drug cake,"[80] and the ASU eventually yielded. Especially given Kenya's small private market and the government's limited health budget, the ration kits orders made a big difference for locally owned firms, leading to "sustained growth."[81] Lab & Allied recounted in the Africa Business Directory how, as the firm became a "leading supplier to the . . . Essential Drugs Kits system," "the modest manufacturing facility . . . was soon outstripped in through-put capacity."[82] A WHO report stated that procuring from local producers created "a stable market for local manufacturers and [helped] them grow."[83]

With growth came improvements, including "increase[d] manufacturing capacity and capability."[84] Dr. Moore enthusiastically reported: "Under the impetus of the new system, the local pharmaceutical producers, which until then had languished under import discriminations, doubtful manufacturing practices and questionable quality control procedures, began to get their act together."[85] He explained the reason for the changes: "Suddenly here was a golden opportunity—a ready-made, high volume market with a good possibility of actually getting paid!"[86] Thanks to the ration kits, local firms also focused on manufacturing essential medicines rather than consumer products like toiletries; they adopted generic labeling and developed better packaging; and they lowered their prices and improved their quality standards.[87]

The increased "capacity and capability" allowed for the production of a broader range of products, and it made other market opportunities available.[88] For example, in the late 1980s, the Mission for Essential Drugs and Supplies (MEDS)—the joint Catholic and Protestant health services in Kenya—bought more than 75 percent of essential drugs items from local manufacturers (even as it was complaining of "the high cost of some local drugs").[89] At the time, MEDS provided up to 35 percent of health care in Kenya's rural areas and interviews confirm the reliance of local manufacturers, including Cosmos, Elys, and Biodeal, on MEDS.[90] Notably, MEDS, like the Kenyan government, was heavily dependent on donor funding, including from the Dutch, Swedish, and German governments.[91] Kenyan manufacturers also supplied drugs to international nongovernmental organizations (INGOs) that worked in "war-torn countries" in the region, when these INGOs needed an immediate supply of drugs.[92]

Finally, local drug manufacturers also developed an "export business," mostly to Tanzania and Uganda, including through both formal channels and smuggling.[93] In general, Kenya's trade relations with Tanzania and Uganda had been already institutionalized to Kenya's advantages before independence, and they were affected by the fact that Kenya was a settler colony. Under colonialism, imports reached the East African region *via* Kenya. In addition, the British allowed for some industrial development in Kenya earlier on, and foreign subsidiaries often produced there and then exported to the other territories (Honey 1974, 64–66). At independence, Kenya, Tanzania, and Uganda had a common market, a common external tariff, a common currency, and common services managed from Nairobi—the Railways and Harbors, Posts and Telecommunications, Customs and Excise, and the East African Airways. These continued links served to maintain Kenya's dominance at the expense of Uganda and Tanzania (Rweyemamu 1973, 45–46, Coulson 2013, 356). To address this imbalance, the countries signed in 1964 the Kampala Agreement, which urged inter-regional allocation of major new industries. The agreement failed to resolve the imbalance, however, as multinationals continued investing in Kenya, undercutting the factories that opened in Uganda and Tanzania (Coulson 2013, 356, Lofchie 2014, 68). In 1977, the East African Community, the most recent regional integration arrangement, collapsed, and the ensuing closure of borders barred Kenya's industrial production from next-door markets until the mid-1980s. Yet dire political and economic conditions in Uganda and Tanzania in the early 1980s meant that both countries had to rely heavily on imports to satisfy basic needs, without having sufficient foreign currency to pay, and one of the only places to obtain the needed commodities was Kenya. In Uganda, moreover, a British economic embargo meant that traders instead "went shopping [in Kenya]" (Mamdani 1983, 96–97). A Kenyan told me: "People were just coming, buying [drugs] in baskets with boxes and so forth, and going [back] across the borders."[94] Another stated: "Kenya had the benefit of being surrounded by countries with a lot of violence and wars. So [these countries] require drugs, without having their own. So [they] got the medicines from Kenya."[95] In spite of the closure of borders, then, between 1977 and 1987, formal exports of drugs from Kenya went up from 26 million KSh to 86 million KSh.[96] Although the growth trajectory is clear, the small value reflects both the limited capability of Kenyan manufacturers and the small size of the Tanzanian and Ugandan markets, though Kenyan drugs were also found in Ethiopia, Congo, Zambia, and Malawi.

In short, a locally owned private pharmaceutical sector was established in Kenya due to supportive government policies. As one experienced Kenyan pharmacist succinctly summarized, "the Essential Drugs List inspired the government to start the kit program, and it was the kit program that inspired the growth [of the locally-owned pharmaceutical sector]."[97] The presence of international assistance in both these programs—the EDL and the ration kits—is easily detectable and historically crucial, as I showed above. However, state and international programs could not have led to local manufacturing without the presence of entrepreneurs who were in a position to exploit the new market opportunities. In the next section, I describe the conditions leading to the presence of nascent entrepreneurs in Kenya.

## Making Entrepreneurs in Colonial and Post-Colonial Kenya

By prioritizing essential drugs, and by committing public funds for purchasing these drugs, the Kenyan government provided novel opportunities to nascent entrepreneurs. However, opportunities do not make entrepreneurs. Rather, entrepreneurs endowed with capital can exploit opportunities presented to them. In the case of pharmaceutical manufacturing, capital includes technical know-how—what machines are required and how to use them, where to buy raw materials, how to maintain quality standards, and more. This technical know-how was not generally available in Kenya.

In the 1980s, indigenous Africans' entry into pharmaceutical manufacturing was through arm's-length financial investment of politically connected individuals. Both in the case of Dawa and in the case of the only private company that was owned by Africans at the time, Beta Healthcare, investors had no pharmaceutical background and hired professionals to manage the company.[98] Kenyans of Indian descent usually did not have political connections. Yet, as I described above, the racial structure of British colonialism in Kenya gave them access to commerce and industry, and Indian Kenyans maintained advantageous position in the economy, including in the retail market, after independence. In addition to financial capital, their position under colonialism and their unique relations with India gave Indian Kenyans access to education, job experience, and technical know-how, which enabled them, in turn, to take advantage of the opportunities granted by the government and foreign assistance in the pharmaceutical sector.

### BEING INDIAN IN KENYA: FROM TRADING TO MANUFACTURING

Most Indians in East Africa arrived during colonial time, either to work on the Uganda railroad (which was constructed starting in the 1890s to link the interiors of Uganda and Kenya with the Indian Ocean port of Mombasa in Kenya) or in small shops, often catering to the railway workers (Bharati 1972). Under British rule, certain opportunities—due to land-holding restrictions, for example—were closed to Indians in Kenya, but commerce was open to them (and closed to indigenous Africans). During colonialism, then, the main occupation of Indians in Kenya was commerce; public employment was the second most important occupation (Delf 1963, Ghai and Ghai 1971, Mwega and Ndung'u 2008, 353–4). Following Kenya's independence, the government's goal of reversing the racialized system by way of "Kenyanization" meant that employment depended on one's citizenship status, which not all Indians could get, and not all Indians wanted (Ghai and Ghai 1971, Bharati 1972, Aiyar 2015).[99] Kenyanization also meant that public sector jobs were not likely to be open to Indians, even as citizens; and commerce—consisting of importing manufactured products, wholesaling, retailing, purchase of produce, and exporting— remained their primary vocation (Gregory 1993, 43).

Kenyanization and other government measures also meant to improve Africans' standing in commerce. Laws such as *The Trade Licensing Act of 1967,* which limited the areas of the country in which noncitizens could engage in trade, were specifically designed to help indigenous Africans penetrate the retail and wholesale sectors (Swainson 1987). Swainson (1977) estimates that "about 80% of the loans [from ICDC] up to 1971 had been advanced to indigenous traders in order to assist them in acquiring businesses from noncitizen Asians." Indian citizens were also affected. For instance, in early 1975, the government cancelled the trade licenses of sixty-nine large wholesale/retail stores in Nairobi owned by Indians with Kenyan citizenship, on the grounds that they were importing goods illegally (Swainson 1977, 43).

In the pharmaceutical sector, the Indian traders who became manufacturers had Kenyan citizenship, with the exception of Prakash Patel, the founder of Cosmos, who was born in India and kept his Indian citizenship. According to Patel, as a noncitizen, he was required to sell some shares of the retail store that he owned, E. T. Monks & Co, to a Kenyan; and disagreements with the new partner were part of what led him to leave the shop and launch a manufacturing firm.[100] Indian drug traders with Kenyan citizenship were not directly affected by Kenyanization. Still, retail in the pharmaceutical sector in the 1960s and 1970s was "dominated by . . . non-Black Kenyans," and Kenyanization helped increase the number of African-owned pharmacies in the 1980s.[101] With newcomers entering the field, some Indian Kenyans felt pushed out, which contributed to their shift to manufacturing. As one pharmacist told me:

> With so many Africans . . . setting up small little pharmacies in the outbacks of town, they started eating into the retail market [until then controlled by Indians]. [As a result], it was [no longer] as lucrative. So [Indians] started now to go into manufacturing. Because they have been selling pharmaceuticals, they knew what are high volume products, yeah? . . . That's when you have Mac's Pharmaceuticals, you have Cosmos . . . Pac's Laboratories . . . All of them now came off from retail. This is now in the '80s.[102]

A World Bank (1994, 5) report confirmed that, "ironically, entry restrictions on Asians regarding retail and wholesale trade led many of them into the light manufacturing industry."

Indians in Kenya had invested in manufacturing already under colonial rule, when a more interventionist economic strategy following World War II advanced industrialization in Kenya. As mentioned above, this mostly benefited British and other foreign firms, but it also benefited local Indians, who emerged from the war with sizable savings from trade and artistry, which they then invested in factories (Swainson 1980, World Bank 1994). Gregory (1993, 292) finds that in 1948 "a census report revealed a surprising 7,351 Asians in manufacturing as compared to 10,265 in commerce." In 1962, 13.6 percent of "economically active Asians" were in manufacturing, compared with 44.5 percent in commerce and banking and 31.3 percent in public services (Gregory 1993, 23).

As with commerce, the government after independence attempted to redress colonial legacies and reverse Europeans' and Indians' domination also in manufacturing. Policies targeted both the public sector—top posts in parastatals were generally reserved for indigenous Africans (World Bank 1994)—and the private sector, with the support of the ICDC (Swainson 1987, 150). These measures were not able to prevent the preservation of an ethnically tiered industrial sector, however, by both specialization and size. Indigenous African companies concentrated in the production (processing), as well as distribution of agricultural goods, whereas companies owned by Indian Kenyans were distributed more equally among a number of different sectors (Swainson 1977, table 2). As for size, the World Bank identified "a clear pattern: the large industries are dominated by parastatals and multinationals, the small to medium-sized firms by Asians, and the micro and informal sector ones by Africans" (World Bank 1994, 7).[103]

Also in the pharmaceutical sector, all firms, with the exception of Dawa (a parastatal) and Beta Healthcare, were owned by Indian Kenyans. Thanks to systematic advantages under colonialism, Indians in Kenya also had access to financial capital after independence, and—through ties abroad—they had access to education, job experience, and the technical know-how needed for adequate pharmaceutical manufacturing. Community ties at home, in turn, enabled local support, diffusion of knowledge, and some political influence.

## LEGACIES OF RACIAL COLONIALISM: EDUCATION ABROAD AND ON-THE-JOB EXPERIENCE

Drug production requires knowledge that is generally gained in a school of pharmacy. Entrepreneurs could employ pharmacists (as Dawa and Beta Healthcare did), but in Kenya most pharmaceutical firms were small, family-owned enterprises, so it was more likely for the entrepreneurs themselves to have attained pharmaceutical knowledge.[104] Before the mid-1970s, Indians in Kenya had easier access to pharmacy education than indigenous Africans. This was a reflection of a general gap in access to education between Africans and Indians in East Africa during, but also after, colonialism.

The colonial era featured minimal investment in education in general, and a grossly unequal distribution of resources in the racially segregated educational systems, with Indians having much better access to primary and secondary education than Africans (Delf 1963, Ghai and Ghai 1971). Indians also had clear advantage when it came to getting a university degree abroad, which was much more desirable than a local or regional degree. For example, in 1955, 887 of the 997 students from Kenya who were studying abroad were Indian or European (Goldthorpe 1965, 17). In contrast, Kenyan Africans who attended college mostly went to Makerere College, in Uganda.[105] Studying abroad was the *only* way to become a pharmacist, because pharmacy degrees were not offered in East Africa until 1974. Because studying abroad was attainable mostly to Indians, they "were among the first . . . pharmacists in East Africa" (Gregory 1993, 217). In 1962, according to the *Kenya Population Census*, there were no African pharmacists in Kenya. Of 119 pharmacists , 74 were Indian and 45 were European. In 1972, of 144 pharmacists, 102 were Indian, 28 were European, and only 14 were African (Gregory 1993, 225–26).

Some of these pharmacists later became wholesalers, and then entered manufacturing. Indeed, founders of local pharmaceutical companies in Kenya normally had a pharmacy degree that they had obtained either in the UK or India.[106] As most pharmaceutical firms in Kenya continued as family businesses, relatives joined the company after receiving advanced degrees, again mostly from abroad—often in pharmacy, but other times in accounting, law, business administration, or related disciplines (various interviews).

In short, access to pharmacy schools abroad at a time in which there was no way to pursue a degree locally provided Indian Kenyans with the foundational skills that later on allowed them to move to manufacturing. As the founder of Elys put it, the local pharmaceutical industry came up because of "[Kenyans of] Asian origin becoming pharmacists in England."[107]

By the time the founders' sons and daughters decided whether and where to pursue a pharmacy degree, one could be attained in Kenya. A School of Pharmacy opened in 1974, at the University of Nairobi, and since then, twenty to thirty pharmacy students have graduated annually.[108] Upon graduation, African Kenyans were more likely than Indian Kenyans to get government jobs due to preferential hiring practices. Others, as suggested above, opened small chemist shops, often in rural areas. They did not have the financial capital, however, to become wholesalers or to turn to manufacturing (this happened later; see chapter 6). Another reason Africans did not go into manufacturing was that the School of Pharmacy in Kenya did not focus on industrial pharmacy, so graduates did not have the appropriate training.[109] Finally, Africans did not go into manufacturing in the 1980s and 1990s because they lacked practical experience, which Indian Kenyans again had thanks to ties abroad.

Indeed, having a pharmacy degree does not mean that one knows how to produce drugs—but attending a pharmacy school can get one a job, which is where one learns. Access to education abroad before the opening of a pharmacy school in Nairobi got Indian Kenyans jobs in multinational companies, both in Kenya and the UK—in retail, wholesale, and importing, as well as in drug manufacturing.[110] This gave them both experience and confidence to later open their own businesses. As the chairman of Elys summarized: "[They] started in retail shops or worked for MNCs [multinational corporations]. This experience allowed them to have their own, initially very small, productive facilities."[111] For example, the founder of Regal Pharmaceuticals worked for Burroughs Wellcome and was involved in setting up a factory before he opened his own facility.[112] Others gained experience by relying on less formal connections. For example, after his studies in India, the founder of Lab & Allied, Vithal Patel, worked in Kenya as a medical sales representative for a German pharmaceutical company. As one newspaper article described, "the marketing job gave [Patel] experience with drugs, [and] valuable exposure that would later set him on the path to open [his own] business" (Ciuri 2015). As part of his job, Patel used to visit many manufacturing facilities abroad and through interactions with drug manufacturers in India, he learned how to produce medicine.[113]

## TIES ABROAD: INFORMAL AND FORMAL ACCESS TO TECHNICAL KNOW-HOW

Although multinational companies in Kenya played a positive role in providing their skilled employees experience that they could later use to establish their own business, there were no other channels of information spillover. As one report regarding "the transfer of . . . dosage form fabrication technology" concisely summarized, "when production activities are conducted in [least developed countries] by the multinational firms, little of the technology reaches local firms, except perhaps through former employees" (Wortzel 1971). Indeed, one Kenyan drug manufacturer suggested that foreign subsidiaries did not help local manufacturers. "No. They were secretive. You could not enter their block."[114] A different way of gaining access to technical know-how—open to those with pharmacy education and means to open an importing business—was through interpersonal ties with pharmaceutical manufacturers.

For Indian Kenyans, this was particularly true in regard to pharmaceutical manufacturers in India.[115] For example, when Prakash Patel, the founder of Cosmos, decided to try out manufacturing, he didn't know much about drug production other than "experimenting" with mixing drugs in the back of his old shop. However, after his son had received a pharmacy degree in the UK, Patel (who was originally from India and moved to Kenya after he had completed his studies in India and worked in the UK) arranged for him an apprenticeship in two reputable pharmaceutical manufacturing firms in India. Patel was able to arrange these apprenticeships thanks to old connections from his school days and new ones he had developed when he owned a retail store.[116] The founders of Lab & Allied and Elys also learned from pharmacists in India. This was possible thanks to commercial, but also cultural, ties to India (Gregory 1993). The founder of Elys told me that he "knew stuff from his experience with imports" because of his "connections with pharmacists." He knew pharmacists from Italy, Spain, the Netherlands, and Germany, but they "wouldn't give information." In contrast, "in India, friends that I made through business connections" gladly helped.[117] He elaborated:

> And then we learned slowly [from] friends from India . . . how to manufacture, what process to be taken, and so on . . . We knew lot[s] of manufacturing companies from when we used to import. [So] we had lot[s] of connection[s] with lot[s] of . . . pharmacists. And of course, they would advise if there was a problem in the product, how to go about it. . . . [Others] did not give such information.[118]

In addition to technical know-how, ties with Indian drug manufacturers provided Indian Kenyans easy access to second-hand machines and raw materials, as India became a major exporter of active pharmaceutical ingredients. Additionally, Indian Kenyans hired experienced pharmacists from India as consultants, again to compensate for lack of local skills.[119]

Finally, not only technical knowledge, but also confidence in the pharmaceutical business traveled from India to Kenya. In reflecting on his decision, the founder of Cosmos told me that his "itch" to move to manufacturing was "inspired" by observing his classmates from pharmacy school back in India founding some of the most successful Indian pharmaceutical companies.[120]

## COMMUNITY AND SOCIAL TIES AT HOME

For Indian Kenyans, colonial legacies created unique connections abroad. At home, the racial colonial project positioned them as a "middleman" minority (Bonacich 1973). Cable (1969, 222) describes the utility for the British of putting Indians between them and the indigenous population: "Indians could perform the vital retail and clerical functions, not only eliminating the need for training Africans but attracting the natural unpopularity of petty traders and bureaucrats, siphoning off hostility from the [colonial] administration." One result of this social position, as I discuss in chapter 1, was that Indians in Kenya—like the Chinese in Southeast Asia, the Syrians in West Africa, and the Parsis in India—developed "bounded solidarity" and "enforceable trust"

(Portes and Zhou 1992, Ferrand 1999), which established mutual support and prevented members from violating group norms.

This was also the case in the pharmaceutical sector. Indian Kenyans entered pharmaceutical manufacturing as a group and relied on each other for support. I was told that the sector came into being when the founders of Elys, Cosmos, Regal, and Lab & Allied "got together and decided to open manufacturing facilities."[121] These men knew each other, could trust each other, and helped each other when possible. According to one of the founders' sons: "[It was a] small community. They were all friends. If one of them didn't manage to produce something, [he] would call someone else and ask for advice."[122] Moreover, lack of opportunities elsewhere kept the next generation in the family business (see Granovetter 1995). This diffusion of knowledge also contributed to the fact that the Kenyan sector at the time was relatively level—with companies following a similar business model and having a similar degree of sophistication. This solidarity based on the ethnic composition of the sector was further cemented by geographical proximity—all of the factories were located in Nairobi—and it was strengthened by common concerns. Because local manufacturers in Kenya did not engage in importation of drugs, they could all support policies that would prioritize locally produced drugs over imports.

In turn, solidarity combined with mutual interests helped local manufacturers' political activities. The founders of the local pharmaceutical firms early on established the Federation of Kenya Pharmaceutical Manufacturers (FKPM) that is still active today. Echoing the informal origins of many of the firms, as well as the fact that the manufacturers all knew each other socially, FKPM in some form "dates back to the 1970s," although it was formally established only in 1981. All the locally incorporated private companies were members, and Dawa and the foreign subsidiary Howse and McGeorge also joined. FKPM was often concerned with practical matters, such as improving the timely payment for tenders, but the association was also at times instrumental in changing more consequential policy issues, including the discriminatory duties structure, mentioned above.[123] The influence of FKPM should not be overstated, however. It had fewer resources and less access to the government than the Kenya Association of Pharmaceutical Industry (KAPI), which represented the interests of multinational pharmaceutical companies doing business in Kenya. Rather, when FKPM's policy suggestions were addressed, it was often when similar recommendations were also made by international organizations or aid agencies (see chapter 6).

To summarize, the know-how required for pharmaceutical manufacturing was not available in Kenya in the 1970s and 1980s. This was why Dawa required foreign participation. Private enterprises did not have the capital or the state support to launch purely commercial relations with foreign investors. However, Kenyans of Indian descent—advantaged by colonial rules that made them dominant in the commercial and industry sectors—were able to acquire the necessary know-how by obtaining pharmacy degrees in the UK or India, getting jobs with foreign companies, and using social relations to "borrow" (Whittaker et al. 2010) technical knowledge from manufacturers in India, where pharmaceutical production was already advanced, in addition to purchasing second-hand machines and raw materials. Acquired skills and practices spread through community ties at home. Thanks to such learning, these entrepreneurs were able to take advantage of the market created by the state and foreign aid. In the next section, I describe the sector that has emerged as a result.

## The Kenyan Pharmaceutical Sector in the 1990s

One of the drug manufacturers in Kenya told me that to learn how to make aspirin back in the late 1960s, he bought a hand-filling machine that he put at the back of his shop. At the end of each day, he worked on the machine; later he bought more machines and hired low-skilled women to work for him. Only then did he move to an actual manufacturing facility. Others started in a similar way. Even as they grew in size, local firms in Kenya limited their activities to final formulation and packaging (they imported their raw materials, including active pharmaceutical ingredients and excipients), and they produced simple generics, mostly (but not only) nonbranded.[124] Still, the sector by 1990 was formalized, relatively large, sufficiently resilient, and with mostly acceptable quality standards.

Not all the drug companies that opened in Kenya in the 1980s survived, but many did—and the number of locally owned firms grew over time. In 1990, there were 13 firms, which together employed more than 1,000 employees.[125] By then, most companies moved to larger premises, which allowed for greater capacity and a broader range of drugs. For example, when Regal was first founded, the firm manufactured oral syrups in rented premises with a staff of eight; five years later, it moved into a custom-built factory.[126] Lab & Allied moved in 1990 to new premises that were five times larger than the previous facility.[127] By 1990, Kenya's drug factories were able to manufacture 8 billion tablets, 800 million coated tablets, one billion capsules, 10.8 million liters of liquids, 20 million bottles of dry syrups, 800,000 kg of ointments, 50 million vials of injection vials, and 26.5 million ampoules a year.[128]

There is no credible data on sales to assess manufacturers' growth over time. However, local producers often refer to the number of drugs they produce as an indication of their overall success, and we do have information on that, through Kenya's registration data (see chapter 2).[129] Although the list of registered drugs cannot say much about either the volume or value of the drugs in the Kenyan market, it indicates which drugs were introduced to the Kenyan market each year, and as such, is useful for measuring the *activity* of individual companies over time—and local companies' activities have certainly increased. When drugs first had to be registered in Kenya in 1982, seven locally owned firms registered a total of 72 drugs. By 1990, locally owned firms registered a total of 255 drugs. In 1990, Lab & Allied had the largest number of registered drugs (60), followed by Dawa and Cosmos, respectively (50 each). Regal, which later became one of the largest firms, only had 11 drugs registered at the time. This gap notwithstanding, companies had similar levels of manufacturing sophistication and knowledge, as a result of which they produced similar types of drugs.

As for market share, one credible report estimates that local producers in the 1980s captured an impressive 20 percent of the total market.[130] Registration data also confirm the active presence of locally owned pharmaceutical companies in relative terms. Between 1982 and 1990, locally owned firms registered almost 16 percent of the total drugs listed.[131]

As for quality standards, one pharmacist told me that when local pharmaceutical manufacturing just began, "regulations were not there," and quality standards were "awful." Manufacturers, for example, allegedly made syrups with equipment intended for filling juices, or they calculated the expiration date based on the day they put the product in the store rather than the day the product was manufactured.[132] In 1981, *The Pharmacy and Poisons (Registration of Drugs) Rules* required registration for the importation or manufacturing of drugs in the country.[133] The main motivation was to avoid the dumping of obsolete imported pharmaceutical products on the Kenyan market, but another aim was to monitor local manufacturing (Jouet 1984). Registration at the time, however, was not effective in assuring quality, as lack of physical, financial, and human resources seriously constrained the Ministry of Health's regulatory quality-control programs (Owino 1991).[134] A local importer commented that "it took a while for [the government] to establish facilities, manpower, capacity to evaluate their products and do licensing." Registration at the time required only a three-page form, and especially in the first few years, companies filed applications for a lot of products to take advantage of the fact that the system of evaluation and registration was not very complicated.[135] As a result, the process of registration could not prevent the presence of poorly manufactured drugs, even among the legally registered ones (WHO 1995a). Indeed, given the poor enforcement, not all local manufacturers in the 1980s followed GMP.[136] According to one report, due to lack of enforcement, GMP were respected only in Dawa among the locally owned firms and only in four of the seven foreign subsidiaries (UNCTC 1984). A report from 1989 similarly asserted that "many manufacturers . . . do not meet GMP standards."[137] More forgiving reports offered a more positive view, however. An assessment from 1990 mentioned that "most local manufacturing units have reasonable quality control laboratories, manned by qualified personnel."[138] In evaluating the ration kits program, Haak and Hogerzeil (1991) concluded: "In general, quality has not been a problem and most manufacturers have been able to deliver good quality goods."

In short, a locally owned pharmaceutical sector emerged in Kenya in the 1980s, and it grew over time. Firms remained relatively small; they produced simple, cheap drugs; and they kept, at best, "reasonable" quality standards. Still, the number of firms grew over time, individual firms expanded, and many of the firms that opened up in the early 1980s are still functioning successfully today.

## Discussion

Pharmaceutical production is not an obvious choice for industrial development. The drug industry does not have easy backward linkages, it requires some financial capital as well as technical knowledge, and public health concerns should make governments reluctant to protect local manufacturers from international competition, as it would likely increase the price of drugs. Still, a locally owned pharmaceutical sector emerged in Kenya in the 1980s and has become relatively successful.

We cannot fully comprehend the investment in local pharmaceutical production in Kenya and across the industrializing world in the late 1970s without noting the fierce international debates over access to affordable medicine. Revelations of abusive marketing practices of multinational pharmaceutical companies in developing countries triggered an interest in self-sufficiency in the provision of medicine and, as part of their response to the NIEO, led international organizations and their members to support local pharmaceutical production, endorse the concept of essential drugs, and fund the distribution of drugs in rural areas. Kenya's policies in the pharmaceutical sector were a reflection of these international developments, and they were often guided and funded by international development agencies—including the WHO, DANIDA, and SIDA.

However, Kenya's experience was also uniquely Kenyan—as the government's decision to finance part of the ration kits program in order to allow national tenders clearly demonstrates. The Kenyan government had the administrative and financial capabilities to create a market for local manufacturers, and it was that market that supported both the state-owned company and privately owned firms. (I later show that a ration kits scheme based on international tenders only would have been at best inconsequential and potentially harmful for local production.) Kenya also had nascent entrepreneurs that could take advantage of the market opportunities the government created. As a result of racialized colonial legacies, Kenyans of Indian descent had capital and, through ties abroad, access to education, jobs, and technical know-how that did not exist in Kenya at the time.

Hence, foreign aid in Kenya in the 1980s was instrumental but, on its own, limited in its nature and effects. Foreign aid offered potential producers incentives by introducing a program that, with the help of the government, created a market for them. Without it, a successful pharmaceutical sector would not have emerged. Still, there was no effective monitoring of quality standards and no guided mentoring. Therefore, it was only the synergy between foreign aid and domestic conditions that led to the emergence of a local pharmaceutical sector in Kenya. In the next two chapters, I show how a different interplay between local conditions and foreign aid, delayed and in other ways restricted the growth of a local pharmaceutical sector in Tanzania and Uganda.

# 4

# Tanzania in the 1980s

## THE LIMITS OF LIMITED AID

In the midst of a severe economic crisis, Tanzania's access to hard currency in the late 1970s was so limited that it caused widespread shortages of imports, including essential goods. Lofchie (2014, 29) describes the effect this had on health care services and medicines,

> As the foreign exchange shortage deepened, the country's public services deteriorated as well. Tanzania was unable to afford . . . the medications and equipment necessary for its public hospitals and rural clinics. . . . Hospitals were so short of anesthetics, antibiotic medication, antidiarrheal drugs, saline kits, and even ordinary bandages that patients were frequently required to bring their own.

The health care sector's need for hard currency was due to its almost exclusive reliance on imported medicines, because drug production in Tanzania at the time was at its infancy (although hard currency would have been required for raw materials for local production as well, as I describe below). Under British mandate, practically all pharmaceuticals were imported to Tanganyika from Europe. In addition, a few drugs were imported from "international companies in Kenya," indicating the tendency of multinational companies to invest in Kenya rather than either Tanganyika or Uganda.[1] In the early 1970s, therefore, Tanzania had "no pharmaceutical product manufacturing" (Wortzel 1971), with the exception of three extremely small factories that together employed no more than twenty workers (Rweyemamu 1973, 206). Yet, around the same time the Kenyan government opened Dawa, Tanzania established two state-owned pharmaceutical companies as well: Keko Pharmaceutical Industries opened in 1975–76 in Dar es Salaam; and Tanzania Pharmaceutical Industries (TPI) opened in 1980 in Arusha.[2] A small number of privately owned companies also opened. In addition to Mansoor Daya Chemicals Ltd. in Dar es Salaam, which had opened n 1964, another company, Khanbhai Pharmaceuticals, opened in Tanga in the 1970s. By 1979, reports indicate that Tanzania had "started to repack formulated drugs and process bulk drugs into dosage forms" (UNCTC 1979, 48). Subsequently, Shelys Pharmaceuticals opened in Dar es Salaam in 1981, and Interchem Pharmaceuticals opened in Moshi in 1987.

Yet, the private pharmaceutical companies in Tanzania were few in number, opened years apart from each other, and were based in different cities (Dar es Salaam, Tanga, and Moshi). This suggests that, unlike Kenya, there was no one set of conditions at a particular moment that triggered their formation. The pharmaceutical sector in Tanzania was small with limited capacity and low capacity utilization. In 1990, compared to Kenya where local companies had 20 percent of the market share (chapter 3), local pharmaceutical companies in Tanzania had the capacity to produce no more than 10 percent of the country's drug requirements (World Bank 1990), and because the companies did not produce in full capacity, actual market share was even smaller.

The growth of a local pharmaceutical sector was inhibited by the fact that Tanzania did not have the same kind of policies to support the local pharmaceutical sector that Kenya had. Tanzania did have some supportive policies, especially for the two state-owned companies—including policies that were informed by a Task Force that was established in 1980 in response to the shortages in medicine, described above. The Task Force, which was dominated by representatives of international development agencies, called for a national list of essential drugs, a ration kits program, and the strengthening of local pharmaceutical production. The ration kits program in Tanzania, however, did not include a local component. Without a local component, local manufacturers could not benefit from the ration kits market. Moreover, without a local component, the ration kits program turned into a factor undermining local production instead of becoming a facilitator of it.

Still, a few entrepreneurs did open small factories, as we have seen—and their trajectories again illustrate the role that ties abroad could play in the creation of a private sector in a context in which technical skills were not available locally. In Tanzania, colonial legacies and political-economic opportunities after independence led to different types of ties abroad than in Kenya, however, and to different types of social ties at home—both contributing to the fragility of the sector.

The chapter begins with a brief review of the health care system in Tanzania during the socialist period and up until the economic crisis, which led to the creation of the internationally dominated Task Force and the launching in Tanzania of an ambitious Essential Drugs Programme (EDP). The chapter then describes the effect of EDP policies on local pharmaceutical production in the larger context of Tanzania's political economy. The Tanzanian government established two state-owned pharmaceutical factories, and the drug procurement agencies in the country purchased drugs from these factories; but I show that limited opportunities through foreign aid made it difficult even for these companies to function. I then describe how colonial legacies and conditions after independence shaped local entrepreneurship and entrepreneurs' ties abroad and at home, allowing for the emergence of a few drug companies, but all small and quite fragile. The chapter concludes with a mapping of the pharmaceutical field in Tanzania in 1990, which, I argue, was the outcome of limited international support and limiting domestic opportunities, as described in the course of the analysis.

## Health Care Systems after Independence: From Arusha to Essential Drugs Programme

The colonial medical service offered minimal services for anyone other than expatriates and senior civil servants, and when Tanzania gained independence in 1961, it inherited a biased and inadequate health care system that included 100 small hospitals, 22 health centers, and 835 dispensaries—for a population of 10 million. Most of these were run by voluntary agencies rather than the government. Life expectancy at the time was 35 years.[3] Although health services was a low priority in the first years after independence (Iliffe 1998, 201), this changed by the end of the decade, when the Tanzanian government placed social welfare, including health, at the very center of its development vision (Jennings 2015). Under the political leadership of Tanzania's first President, Julius Kambarage Nyerere, the state promoted a version of African socialism, *Ujamaa*, which included as a core tenet equitable access to health services.[4] The Arusha Declaration in 1967 promised to mobilize "all the resources of this country towards the elimination of poverty, ignorance, and disease."[5] That promise resulted in solid improvements in literacy, access to primary education, and health care. By 1983, primary school enrollment increased from 15 percent in 1961 to 96 percent, and clean and potable drinking water was provided to about half of the villages in the country (Jonsson 1986, 746). In the health domain, the focus was on delivery of basic health care services in rural areas (WHO 1975, 57–62). Between 1971 and 1984, the number of rural health centers (RHCs) increased from 87 to 239, and the number of rural dispensaries grew from 1,436 to 2,644 (Orubuloye and Oyeneye 1982, 685, Kanji, Munishi, and Sterky 1989, 7, Iliffe 1998, 203). By the late 1980s, 93 percent of the population lived within 10 km of a health facility (Kanji et al. 1989, 3).[6]

President Nyerere had a "towering influence" at home (Lofchie 2014, 5) as well as at the international level, and Tanzania was one of the leaders of the

Non-Aligned Movement—an organization of states that refused to align themselves with either the US or the Soviet Union (Chorev 2012a, 46). In the realm
of health, Tanzania's focus on basic health needs helped shape the international
agenda at the time—including the Word Health Organization's adoption of
the Primary Health Care (PHC) approach in the Alma Ata Declaration in 1978
(chapter 3).[7] Indeed, "The Alma Ata declaration . . . was welcomed by Tanzania as embodying the same principles that it was trying to implement" (Kanji,
Munishi, and Sterky 1989, 7). This recursivity—from Tanzania to the WHO and
back to Tanzania, as we will see—is an important reminder that international
models adopted by member states are not exogenous forces, but are embedded
in existing national practices and experiences, including in the global South
(Chorev 2012a).

In Tanzania, just like at the international level, an important component of
PHC was access to medicine.[8] However, Tanzania's dependence on imported
drugs made it vulnerable to abuse. UNICEF reported that expenditure on
drugs in Tanzania rose at 33 percent per year, until by 1975–76 drugs consumed
20 percent of the total recurrent expenditure on health.[9] This was due in part
to widespread prescribing of expensive drugs, linked to excessive promotional
activity by international drug companies.[10]

Such expenditures were wasteful in regular times, but they became intoler-
able when an economic crisis hit Tanzania, at a particularly vulnerable moment.
Because of Britain's under-development of the territory, at independence Tanganyika had been one of the world's poorest countries, with an economic base
composed solely of subsistence agriculture and a few estate crops (Kanji et al.
1989, 6). Socialist policies did not "affect the fundamental productive basis of
the economy" (Campbell and Stein 1992, 5), and both the low productivity
in the agricultural sector (exacerbated by the *Ujamaa* policy of forced villagi-
zation) and the low level of industrialization continued. With deteriorating
returns for cash crops, moreover, Tanzania—like other African countries—
suffered a severe balance of payments crisis (Campbell and Stein 1992, 5).
The country's trade balance was also deeply affected by the quadrupling of oil
prices following the oil shocks of 1973 and 1979; a severe drought in 1974 that
greatly damaged agricultural production and led to unprecedented imports
of food; and Tanzania's effort to do away with the Amin Regime in Uganda and
the break-up of the East African Community in 1977. In the late 1970s, the Tanzanian economy practically collapsed (Mans 2002, 353, Coulson 2013, 354–60).

The health care system almost collapsed as well. From the mid-1970s to the
late 1980s, only donor support prevented the per capita expenditure on health
care from severely declining.[11] Access to medicine was especially affected. As
mentioned earlier, one of the major manifestations of the economic crisis was
growing trade imbalance, leading to a particularly severe shortage of foreign
currency. Because drugs in Tanzania were almost all imported, "the national

health service [had] come under severe strain due to shortages of drugs" in the late 1970s.[12] A few years later, "even the most essential medicaments could not be found in the health units."[13] The shortage was particularly felt in rural areas; only 15 percent of the drugs that were still available in the country reached rural health facilities, which handled 60 percent of total outpatient visits.[14]

In trying to develop a long-term solution to the acute shortage of drugs in Tanzania in 1980 the Ministry of Health (MoH) appointed a Task Force to carry out an analysis of the problems and make recommendations for their resolution. The Task Force was funded by the Danish International Development Agency (DANIDA) and included representatives from the WHO, UNICEF, and the MoH, with technical assistance from DANIDA. Hence, whereas Tanzania had pioneered some of the ideas that were adopted and disseminated by international organizations, the composition of the Task Force shows that these international organizations subsequently had great influence on the country's programs.[15] The Task Force concluded that three major factors were at play: increasing demand by a growing population, a severe shortage of foreign currency, and "wastage due to inefficiencies in planning, procurement, storage, distribution and usage" of drugs.[16] The EDP, which was established to implement the Task Force's recommendations, was in a position to address only the third factor. Still, the EDP was an ambitious exercise, with four major components aimed at ensuring the availability of essential drugs in the rural health services. In line with existing international programs at the time, these were: an essential drugs list (EDL), a ration kits system, support of local production of essential drugs, and quality assurance.[17] The next section describes the origins of state-owned pharmaceutical companies in Tanzania and the various ways by which government and foreign programs—including the EDP—either facilitated or neglected their growth.

## Making Medicines in Tanzania: Two State-Owned Factories

The Task Force's call for local production and the EDP's plan "to enhance self-reliance in the production of essential drugs" (MOH Tanzania1990, section 1.3.8) reflected a long-standing commitment by international agencies in support of local pharmaceutical production in Tanzania. In 1969, a UNIDO study already reported approvingly that, "Tanzania wished to establish immediately a national pharmaceutical industry," and a WHO mission two years later stated that such a national project "deserves encouragement and support."[18] Later on, the shortages of foreign currency gave the plan particular urgency, based on the expectation that "formulating pharmaceuticals locally" would "reduce [the country's] drug bill—getting more pharmaceuticals for the same sum or getting the same amount of drugs for less money."[19] Pointing out that, "present local production of pharmaceuticals is more expensive than imports of drugs," a UNICEF report nevertheless supported investment in local production, due to the promised savings of *foreign* funds. "The foreign reserves to be used for raw materials etc. for a local production must be considerably below the foreign reserves needed for the purchase of . . . similar drugs from abroad."[20]

In line with these sentiments, by the time the Task Force made its recommendations, there were already two state-owned pharmaceutical industries in mainland Tanzania: Keko Pharmaceutical Industries and TPI. The two companies were part of the government's investment in state-led industrialization and were as vulnerable as other industries in the wake of the economic crisis.

## STATE-LED INDUSTRIALIZATION AND THE ORIGINS OF STATE-OWNED PHARMACEUTICAL FACTORIES

Investment in local pharmaceutical production as a means to address the drug needs of the country was consistent with the Arusha Declaration and with the broader state-led industrialization efforts at the time. Tanzania's starting point was especially wanting, however, given German and British neglect, which left it with a particularly small industrial base (Honey 1974, Coulson 2013). Under German rule, a very small-scale industry concentrated on first-stage processing of primary products for export and on provision of only a few consumer goods for the settlers (Barker and Wield 1978, 317). During World War I, scarcity of materials led to the production of some manufactured goods normally imported from Europe, including a few medical supplies: the German-run Amani Agricultural Research Institute made quinine and twelve varieties of medicines and medicaments (Rweyemamu 1973, 116). But even this minimal effort was blunted by the British takeover. British policy in Tanganyika was based on the understanding that colonial production was not to compete with manufacturers back in Britain, and when economic development of the colonies was later on advanced, the British preferred to invest in Kenya, which was a settler colony, than in Tanganyika. Therefore, with the exception of agricultural processing industries that could not otherwise be exported, and small-scale or craft industries requiring minimal capital investment and little specialization, the British made the decision not to industrialize (Barker and Wield 1978, Coulson 2013). After World War II, the colonial government began to encourage some consumer-based secondary industries (Honey 1974, 65). However, Tanganyika continued to stay in the shadow of Kenya and was able to only attract a small share of capital invested in the region (Barker et al. 1986, 44–46). Between 1946 and 1958, 3,380 private companies opened in Kenya, valued at £120 million, compared with 2,650 companies valued at £81 million in Tanganyika and Uganda combined (Honey 1974, 66). Kenyan companies could also more easily compete with local ones in the Tanzanian market because of regional arrangements that eliminated all inter-territorial trade barriers (Honey 1974). In the pharmaceutical sector, foreign subsidiaries manufacturing in or importing to Kenya sold their products in Tanzania. A pharmacist who worked at Glaxo in Kenya, told me, "So a lot of the multinationals were using Kenya as a base to get into the other countries. I mean, for instance, when we [Glaxo] joined, we used to supply east and south and southern African countries."[21]

Under President Nyerere, the Arusha Declaration offered a development strategy that involved the government taking industrialization in its own hands, rather than relying on private capital. Subsequent policies resulted in major nationalization of private businesses that opened during the colonial era or after independence—including of commercial banks, firms involved in sisal and grain milling, import-export houses, insurance firms, subsidiaries of multinational corporations, cooperative unions, and some privately owned buildings. Most of these properties were owned by foreign companies or by Tanzanians of Indian origin (Coulson 2013). The government also acquired a controlling share in major industrial firms (Edwards 2014, 74), although the policy was to retain those previously employed and to leave management responsibility to the private partners (World Bank 1971, 14–15, Gregory 1993, 296–97). In addition, the government established a number of large-scale, state-owned industries, many through joint ventures with foreign capital.[22] As state-owned companies, therefore, the two pharmaceutical factories, Keko and TPI, were consistent with what was typical for Tanzania at the time— although rather than joint ventures, technical transfer came in the form of foreign aid.

Keko was set up in 1975–76 as a unit under the MoH, and later transferred to the Ministry of Industries and Trade (MIT), where it was 100 percent owned by the National Chemical Industries (NCI).[23] TPI was from its inception in 1980 under MIT, with 82 percent of its shares owned by NCI and 18 percent by the National Pharmaceutical Company (NAPCO), a government agency that procured and distributed drugs for the private sector from 1973 to 1997 (World Bank 1990).

Technology transfer for Keko, including both expertise and machinery, came from the People's Republic of China.[24] China's support reflected the special relations between the two countries at the time. Starting with the construction of the Tanzania-Zambia Railway in the early 1970s, Tanzania was one of the first African countries where China developed a major economic presence (Lofchie 2014, 222), partly enabled by the diplomatic crises between Tanzania and its traditionally important foreign donors: West Germany (over Tanzania's recognition of East Germany), the US (over rumors that the US was plotting to overthrow President Nyerere), and the UK (over the Rhodesian Unilateral Declaration of Independence) (Rweyemamu 1973, 43–44, Coulson 2013, 219).

By 1981, however, Keko was already exclusively staffed by local Tanzanians. This, combined with a report on "an anticipated unavailability of spare parts for the Chinese manufacturing machines," suggests that China's support of the factory was short-lived.[25]

TPI, too, relied on foreign assistance. The Government of Finland paid for technical consultancy services provided by a private Finnish pharmaceutical company, Orion-yhtymä Oy (Orion). Orion helped to set up the pharmaceutical plant and provided support for the management and operation of the plant.[26] The United Nations Conference on Trade and Development (UNCTAD) noted in a congratulatory report that the National Development Corporation (NDC), Tanzania's development agency, in negotiations with Finland promoted local technological capacities by securing training of locals both by expatriates on the TPI staff in Tanzania and with Orion back in Finland.[27] TPI continued to use technical assistance provided by one technical manager and one production superintendent from Orion also after the plant was fully under the local management of NCI.[28]

Keko, which was established to "produce fluids for intravenous infusions and common drugs in tablet form," was small—with only 1,350 square meters (14,500 square feet) of production premises.[29] In comparison, "the investment in Arusha [TPI] was much larger."[30] Indeed, TPI was opened because NCI wanted to increase production so as to meet "approx. one third of the country's estimated requirements."[31] With 3,150 square meters (34,000 square feet) of production premises, TPI was "one of the largest pharmaceutical plants in East Africa" at the time.[32] Whereas Keko "geared to lower technology," TPI was designed to be "modern," offer more products, and follow better quality standards.[33]

These differences mattered little as both Keko and TPI struggled to establish themselves in the midst of a severe economic crisis that led to the near collapse of the manufacturing sector in Tanzania by the early 1980s.[34] Many industrial enterprises closed, and those that remained open operated far below production capacity. The main obstacle was "lack of essential imported inputs" due to insufficient foreign currency.[35] Combined with transport problems, shortages of credit, machine breakdowns, and water and power shortages, capacity utilization of industries fell from 75 percent in 1975 to 25 percent by 1985 (Stewart, Lall, and Wangwe 1992, 16, Lofchie 2014, 91). Keko and TPI met a similar fate. When TPI for the first time placed a request for foreign reserves for the purchase of raw materials with the Central Bank of Tanzania, it was granted less than one-tenth of the amount it had asked for.[36] In 1981, a review for DANIDA estimated that Keko's production "was not more than 25% of [its] capacity," whereas TPI "has been working around 10% capacity or less."[37] Through the 1980s, "the production trends at the TPI well correlate[d] with the scarcity of foreign exchange facing the country."[38]

This low capacity utilization was particularly frustrating given the desperate drug situation prevailing in the country. Indeed, this was an unfortunate paradox: the lack of foreign currency that caused shortages in imported drugs—thereby providing an opportunity for local manufacturers—also paralyzed local production. The need to resolve this paradox led the Task Force to call for the strengthening of local production as part of EDP. A joint report by the Government of Tanzania and UNICEF commented: "Local production of pharmaceuticals is considered high priority for the Government and the Party. This has become increasingly more important in light of the effect that the foreign exchange shortage has had on . . . the procurement of drugs."[39]

However, the government had only limited resources, and foreign assistance proved lacking. Although they helped with the upgrading of facilities and offered some hard currency for the purchase of raw materials, development agencies were more likely to provide imported drugs than to fund the procurement of local ones. This applied also to the ration kits program.

## FOREIGN AND GOVERNMENT SUPPORT

The minimal production that was taking place in Keko and TPI was possible mostly thanks to foreign support. First, foreign donors helped with the upgrading of Keko, the older of the two state-owned companies. In 1982, Keko "received a DANIDA grant . . . for physical plant rehabilitation," which was used for rebuilding the section for infusions (World Bank 1990, 105). DANIDA's support also included training, and from 1985 to 1988, an engineer and a pharmacist from Denmark were placed to assist the company.[40] Second, foreign donors provided both factories some desperately needed hard currency. The Swedish International Development Cooperation Agency (SIDA) granted Keko a "raw material allocation" of 3.7 million TSh (approx. $450,000), while TPI in 1981/1982 received 4.7 million TSh (approx. $575,000), in addition to 1 million TSh ($122,000) from the Tanzanian Government.[41] In 1990, it was reported that, "most raw materials are being donated by Finland or Norway" (World Bank 1990, 106).

These donations were hardly sufficient to fully utilize the factories' production capacity, but there was only limited demand for their drugs.[42] At the time, drugs in Tanzania were provided almost exclusively through either the Central Medical Stores (CMS), an agency under the MoH that procured and distributed drugs for the public health sector, or NAPCO, for the private sector. TPI and Keko, therefore, could only sell their products to the government; and although CMS and NAPCO purchased drugs from TPI and Keko, they could do so only to a limited extent (World Bank 1990, 105).

The CMS's procurement logic followed the international model diffused by the WHO. The WHO, as we have seen in chapter 3, had a "keen interest in a determined propagation of the concept of essential drugs," and one of the Task Force's recommendations in Tanzania, and the first component of the EDP, was formulating a national EDL.[43] The goal was to cope with the acute shortage of drugs, but also to rationalize a disorderly system of quantification and distribution in which drugs had been procured on a permanent ad hoc basis.[44] Once a list of essential drugs was drawn in Tanzania in 1981, CMS was expected to procure drugs based on that list.[45] CMS's commitment to only procure essential medicines could have potentially created a market for local producers, and CMS did purchase around 10 percent of its pharmaceutical needs locally, mostly from TPI and Keko. That CMS purchased only one-tenth of its needs from local sources in part reflected the capabilities of these local companies at the time, as it was difficult for the two companies to respond to orders on time. More importantly, CMS purchased "almost the entire amount" of pharmaceutical products with the help of donations, which had "compensatory clauses" that required the funds to be used largely in the markets of the donating countries.[46] Hence, CMS had to buy drugs from companies in donor countries, which left CMS with discretion only in regard to a small budget.

NAPCO was created as a *for-profit* government enterprise in the wake of the nationalization wave, and it functioned differently than CMS. For one, NAPCO did not have to adhere to the EDL (World Bank 1990, 104); and to the dismay of those advocating for the EDL concept—NAPCO preferred to sell more profitable brand-names over generics.[47] Moreover, NAPCO sold its brand-name products with a 30–40 percent mark-up, which made the price of its drugs exceptionally high (World Bank 1990, 104). Profitability, too, was high. In 1983, NAPCO was considered "one of the most successful undertakings in Tanzania."[48] The focus on expensive brand-names meant that NAPCO imported most of its drugs. In addition, NAPCO, like CMS, relied on donations that came with the obligation to purchase imported drugs.[49] Yet NAPCO owned 18 percent of TPI, and TPI and Keko were both based in the Ministry of Industries and Trade and were also motivated by profit. That meant that TPI and Keko, too, emphasized "brand name [generic]s that give higher profits than [nonbranded] generics," even if that inclination was opposed to the MoH drugs policy.[50] Hence, in spite of reservations regarding the ability of TPI and Keko "to deliver products of good quality on time," NAPCO did purchase drugs from these two companies, and to a greater extent than CMS.[51] Estimates suggest that 20 percent of NAPCO's needs were "met through [Keko] and TPI."[52]

In short, foreign aid provided the state-owned pharmaceutical companies in Tanzania technical support and some funds for raw materials. In addition, both CMS and NAPCO purchased drugs from these two companies. However, given CMS's and NAPCO's limited budgets and tied donations, these purchases were quite modest. A much larger public market existed through the ration kits program—in 1990–91, the kits provided 27.2 percent of the country's drug supply, compared to CMS that provided only 11.4 percent of the supply.[53] However, as I describe below, funds donated for the ration kits program were not used for the procurement of local drugs. Nor were they used for the procurement of raw materials for local production.

## RATION KITS

In addition to deficiencies in drug selection, which the list of essential drugs meant to improve, Tanzania had issues with inadequate storing and drug management, which meant that, "on the shelves of the CMS [were] drugs so obviously expired or damaged as to be useless or harmful."[54] Distribution, too, was inadequate. An urban bias meant that, "Rural Health Facilities handle[d] 60% of total out-patient visits, yet receive[d] only 15% of total drug budgetary allocations." Additionally, "Pilferage and loss *en route* [took] away a part of this already meager allocation."[55] A solution was found in Kenya. An external evaluation of the WHO's program reported:

> The implementation of the ration kit programme for rural health facilities in Kenya provided WHO with a "model case" which could be publicized and serve as an encouraging example for other countries. Thus, as part of its advocacy campaign, WHO organized an inter-regional Workshop on Essential Drugs in Nairobi in 1982. Participants to the workshop were taken on field trips to see the functioning of the programme. Documents from this workshop were widely disseminated. A similar workshop was again organized in 1983. . . . It is difficult to assess the effect of these workshops but in 1983, neighboring Tanzania embarked upon an essential drugs programme conceptually similar to the Kenyan programme.[56]

In 1983, then, Tanzania adopted a ration kits scheme, "based on . . . the Kenyan model."[57] DANIDA provided $30 million for the program, WHO provided technical assistance, and UNICEF was the executing agency in partnership with the Tanzanian MoH. The first kits arrived in Tanzania in January 1984 and all regions were covered by August of that year.[58] By 1987, the ration kits program was serving 300 RHCs and 2,690 dispensaries, with a total of 35,880 kits per year.[59]

Evaluations of the ration kits program in Tanzania were largely positive—notwithstanding the inevitable irresponsiveness to local variations across regions and other challenges.[60] A survey from 1984 showed 90 percent availability of essential drugs in dispensaries and health centers in the program areas, compared to availability of 53 percent in dispensaries and 47 percent in health centers in the pre-program areas (Jonsson 1986). A later report confirmed: "Drugs are now readily available in remote health units of Tanzania. . . . There has also been an increase in the population that attends the health units and this can partially be associated with the availability of drugs."[61] The historian John Iliffe (1998, 206) referred to it as "one of tropical Africa's better supply systems."

The success of the program had no impact on local production, however. In contrast to the Kenyan experience, here all funds *and* all the drugs sealed in the ration kits came from overseas (Haak and Hogerzeil 1995). There was no local component that was preserved for local producers.[62] The absence of a local component was not due to lack of interest. Over the years, there was much talk about local production as part of the program, supported both by the Tanzanian government and donors—including some at DANIDA and UNICEF. Interest in local pharmaceutical production seemed particularly legitimate when, in the context of severe drug shortages, local products were wasted. A UNICEF report lamented, "In 1981, certain drugs were in stock in Arusha [TPI] at the time when foreign donors were called upon to supply emergency drugs."[63]

Importantly, there was confidence in the ability of the state-owned companies to supply at least few of the drugs.[64] Learning how to produce the drugs for the kits was considered easy. In 1981, a DANIDA consultant stated: "The drugs are supplied with an information sheet indicating in English composition, indications, and appropriate use, as well as shelf life and storage requirements. It would be a simple matter to review and translate these information sheets so as to serve as a basic manual." He estimated that, "12 of the drugs on the Tanzania list of essential drugs can without difficulty be produced in [TPI]," and whereas Keko was smaller, "a range of essential drugs on the national list can be produced there."[65] In the late 1980s, experts from the University of Dar es Salaam reported: "The situation indicates that there is a lot of installed capacity that could be exploited to enhance the objectives of the EDP. . . . TPI is said to be able to contribute 28 items in the EDP present drug list. . . . [Keko] can contribute about 12 items."[66] Another DANIDA consultant similarly "recommended that up to 10 drugs of the essential drug kits should be manufactured locally."[67]

The obstacle for incorporating locally-produced drugs into the ration kits program was not lack of manufacturing capabilities then.[68] Rather, the challenge for at least some development agencies was the state. To begin with, the government was in no position to fund local ration kits, which meant that, unlike in Kenya, donors would have to pay for the locally produced drugs. Even if funded by development agencies, a local component would have required heavy reliance on the state—and, in spite of the great achievements in the health regime described earlier, donors did not believe that the Tanzanian government was up to the task. To begin with, there were institutional deficiencies that made coordination of local production difficult. The same DANIDA consultant who evaluated local companies positively, was less encouraging when it came to other state agencies. The consultant reported:

> A series of structural obstacles to the exploitation of the national potential for the production of essential drugs was identified: The Treasury, The Central Bank of Tanzania, The Ministry of Industries, and the Ministry of Health operate according to rules which do not allow a coordinated effort to secure a local production of essential pharmaceuticals with the purpose to procure urgently needed medicine.[69]

Similarly, an evaluation prepared for the WHO reported that, "in Tanzania, the government's request to donors for local production support has been considerably weakened by the lack of consensus and coordination between the ministries."[70]

Other concerns focused on CMS. The ration kits program in Tanzania was initially designed so that it bypassed CMS—kits were delivered directly to the regions—which made it more complicated to integrate locally produced drugs into the existing distribution system. The system was designed in such a way due to distrust in CMS capacity. "A fact-finding mission . . . had found [that] the operations of CMS and customs bureaucracies were a great impediment to an efficient and effective procurement. Thus, for the EDP to realize its goals it was judged necessary to make the EDP procurement centralized and vertical programme-wise."[71] Hence, UNICEF established a commodity chain that bypassed CMS entirely. "[The Tanzanian MoH] . . . communicates with UNICEF's country office. The local UNICEF office sends demands to UNIPAC [the Copenhagen-based UNICEF Procurement and Assembly Centre]. UNIPAC searches and contacts drug manufacturers and suppliers. UNIPAC then packages the kits, [and] allots the kits into containers."[72] After arriving to Tanzania, the kits were sent "directly to the zonal stores." A local component would have forced a CMS involvement, which donors sought to avoid.[73]

Moreover, local production required CMS involvement beyond distribution. Kits of imported drugs were assembled and sealed in Copenhagen.[74] For local producers to participate in the ration kits, however, packing had to be done locally, because it made little sense to invest in locally produced drugs only to have them shipped to Copenhagen.[75] But such packing facilities were expected to be established at the CMS, and the challenges seemed for some too difficult to overcome. First, CMS had to be "fully rehabilitated to give room for a packaging area."[76] In addition, there was "the problem of locally produced packaging material." A DANIDA Mission Team explained: "To import packing material just in order to do the packaging locally does not seem cost effective. Establishment of a packing line is stipulated for 1987–88. It is likely that such a line will be delayed."[77] Indeed, a local packing line was still not in place in 1990.[78]

Concern with local challenges notwithstanding, also relevant is the fact that the decision to import all ration kits drugs benefited UNICEF, as well as pharmaceutical companies in donor countries. At the time, the WHO and UNICEF had just abandoned their attempt to establish a group bulk purchasing scheme; and in seeking alternative channels, "the obvious answer was to increase the capacity of . . . UNIPAC . . . which was already buying large quantities of essential drugs on the world market, had long experience of shipping supplies to developing countries, and [had] a new warehouse which allowed the possibility of handling a greatly increased volume." Tanzania's ration kits program allowed for such increased volumes. "With the establishment of the Tanzanian programme . . . UNIPAC's supply operation increased considerably. The volume of drugs handled moved from US$17 million in 1982 to . . . $60 million in 1986."[79]

Not everyone was happy with the decision not to integrate local production into the ration kits program. One report summarized the frustrations: "As far as we can see, not many recommendations were implemented by the Government towards integration of local production and EDP."[80] Other critics, in turn, highlighted the related paradox of accepting drug donations at the same time that local producers were unable to produce drugs due to lack of raw materials, and they suggested that funds should be used if not for purchasing of local drugs than at least for providing the raw materials local producers needed. A DANIDA consultant remarked that "the temporary respite in the drug situation has . . . been met mostly through the importation of finished drugs, while the local production facilities have been more or less idle." "Early in 1981 an emergency order for mainly essential drugs was placed abroad. . . . Part of the drugs . . . might urgently have been produced in the country, if only the donor countries had been aware of that possibility and consequently shipped the raw materials to Tanzania instead of manufactured pharmaceuticals."[81] Almost a decade later, a Tanzanian report still expressed similar frustrations: "Perhaps EDP could have done something in making drug industries acquire raw materials more easily than . . . is the present case."[82] The report suggested: "The EDP could make a great impact if it assisted in procuring some essential raw materials to manufacture drugs that could enter the kits in the eventuality that [they are] locally packed."[83] However, no ration kits funds were channeled for that purpose, due to donors' lack of interest in the matter and the government's lack of influence on donors' decisions. The DANIDA consultant reported that, "the Ministry of Health was not in the position to . . . request donor countries to supply urgent raw materials for the local production rather than shipments of manufactured drugs."[84] The Tanzanian report concluded: "Unfortunately . . . under the present internationalized and verticalized EDP drug procurement system an 'EDP-sponsored import support money' for the purchase of raw materials for the local manufacturers is not possible."[85]

In sum, in spite of a motivated government and a stated commitment to local pharmaceutical production, foreign support for it proved to be minimal. Donor countries helped with the upgrading of Keko and TPI and provided some funds for the purchasing of raw materials, but they did not devote any of the ration kits funds to locally produced drugs or to the purchasing of imported raw materials that would enable local production. Without contribution to the ration kits program, state-owned companies had only a small local market available to them. Nevertheless, state-owned pharmaceutical companies still did better than their counterparts in the private sector, as I describe below.

## Obstacles to Entrepreneurship in the Private Sector

In Tanzania, the two state-owned pharmaceutical firms did not help with the emergence of a private sector, as Dawa did in Kenya. Only four private pharmaceutical factories functioned by 1990, Mansoor Daya, Shelys, Interchem, and Khanbhai. The last two were so small that they were rarely featured in evaluations and reports.

The private pharmaceutical sector in Tanzania was small because there were no state or foreign aid programs conducive to private pharmaceutical production, and it was small because there were very few pharmacists-entrepreneurs who could take advantage of the opportunities that did exist. Entrepreneurship in the pharmaceutical field was rare due to limited educational opportunities, which meant that there were only a few pharmacists in Tanzania; and it was rare due to limited commercial opportunities, which meant that there were very few private pharmaceutical wholesalers or importers, from the ranks of which pharmaceutical manufacturers usually emerged. The entrepreneurs in Tanzania who did open pharmaceutical factories followed a slightly different pattern than the one we saw in Kenya (chapter 3)—one company owned by indigenous Africans was based on financial capital accumulated locally, whereas the other companies were owned by East Africans of Indian descent who had ties abroad. In Tanzania, however, colonial legacies meant that the ties abroad were somewhat different than the ones utilized by Kenyan pharmacists-entrepreneurs; there was no reliance on community or on social ties at home.

### NO GOVERNMENT OR FOREIGN SUPPORT, NO MARKET OPPORTUNITIES

The Tanzanian government did not actively support private pharmaceutical enterprises, and in some cases it undermined their competitiveness through, for example, discriminatory duties (which the Kenyan government eliminated in 1982). To make drugs available "to the greatest possible number of people," there were no taxes or customs duties on most imported drugs, yet there was a 15 percent customs duty on imported raw materials for pharmaceuticals.[86] Although CMS and NAPCO bought from the two-state owned drug factories, as we have seen, the Tanzanian government only minimally utilized public procurement of drugs to support private local production. CMS still bought some drugs from Mansoor Daya and Shelys in the early 1980s, but it no longer did so by the end of the decade, and NAPCO only purchased marginal volumes from the two factories (World Bank 1990, 106–107). Foreign aid also did not help create a local market, because, as we have seen, the ration kits program did not include a local component and did not devote funds for the purchasing of raw materials for local producers. Private pharmaceutical firms also found it difficult to sell to the third sector, and the church mission health services purchased drugs from private manufacturing companies in Tanzania only "to a very small extent." Exports were also minimal, although there are indications that Mansoor Daya products were sold in Kenya, Rwanda, and Burundi.[87]

## NO PHARMACY EDUCATION, NO PHARMACISTS

In addition to lack of supportive policies, Tanzania acutely suffered from the problem of the missing entrepreneur (Kohli 2004). In the pharmaceutical field, entrepreneurship in Tanzania was constrained most directly by the difficulty of gaining a pharmacy degree, either in Tanzania or abroad.

Under British rule, investment in education in Tanganyika was minimal (Brett 1973, 77, Coulson 2013, 115), and as elsewhere in the region, three parallel education systems were developed, with a markedly differentiated financial support and rate of attendance. For example, in 1946, the colonial government's net expenditure per student was £38 on Europeans, compared to £4.4 on Indians, and £1.9 on Africans (Mbilinyi 1979, 237–38). Approximately 30 percent of Indians but only 2 percent of Africans attended primary school (Mbilinyi 1979, table 7.2). In addition, Africans were not generally given opportunities to go beyond secondary school (Barker et al. 1986, 47). In 1962, less than fifteen Tanganyikan Africans—a shockingly low number— graduated from Makerere College in Uganda, the only college in the region (Coulson 2013, 122, Edwards 2014, 66). Children of Indians in Tanzania, in contrast, had easier access to university degrees and professional qualifications outside the region, including in Britain, India, and Pakistan (Honey 1974, 67, Barker et al. 1986, 47).[88]

Because there was no pharmacy school in Tanzania, access to higher education abroad was necessary to gain a pharmacy degree.[89] After independence only a few Tanzanians had such opportunities—mostly in the Soviet Union, other Eastern Bloc countries, or India.[90] As a result, there were only few pharmacists practicing in Tanzania. In 1971, there were at most 50 pharmacists in the country, 12 of which were African Tanzanians and 38 of which were non-Africans.[91] This "deplorable" shortage of pharmacists led in 1974 to the setting up of a Department of Pharmacy in the University of Dar es Salaam, with support from the British Council and the University of Aston, in the UK.[92] In the 1980s, the annual output of pharmacists was around fifteen, and the pharmaceutical sector continued to experience shortages of suitable personnel.[93]

## NO PRIVATE TRADING, NO CLEAR PATH TO PRIVATE MANUFACTURING

Pharmaceutical manufacturing in developing countries was often taken up by entrepreneurs with a pharmacy degree already working in the sector as wholesalers or traders, as was the case in Kenya (chapter 3). However, this channel was less available in Tanzania. Although the shortage of pharmacists was one reason for the small number of drug wholesalers and importers, another was the absence of commercial ties abroad—part of a general lack of investment in commercial and industrial activities in Tanganyika under colonial rule. Kenyan retailers and wholesalers had direct links to European and other suppliers, but traders in Tanganyika often traded through Kenya, as we have seen. A subsequent constraint was that under Tanzania's *Ujamaa*—especially with the establishment of NAPCO—there were fewer opportunities to engage in commercial activities in the private sector.

Under colonial rule, commercial activities in Tanganyika, to the extent they existed, were dominated by Indians. These were initially Indian merchants who had controlled the internal market trade in Zanzibar from the beginnings of the nineteenth century and had moved onto the mainland once East Africa had been partitioned among European powers in the 1890s. They were later joined by contract railway construction workers and shopkeepers, also from India (Honey 1974, Barker et al. 1986, 41–43, Gregory 1993, 10).[94] As in Kenya, this Indian concentration in retail and wholesale—and later on, also in industry— was enabled by explicit discriminatory policies, as Africans were not initially allowed trading licenses (Tripp 1997, 94), and the fact that commerce was almost the only business opportunity for Indians (Coulson 2013, 109). After independence, half of all shopkeepers were Indian, and the largest shopkeepers were either of Indian or Arab descent (Tripp 1997, 35). The violence of the Zanzibar Revolution in 1964, the attempted coup in Tanganyika the same year, and fears regarding the consequences of Africanization, had many of the 92,000 Indians in Tanzania at the time leave the country, mostly to the UK and Canada.[95] Still, among Indians who stayed, "an overwhelming preoccupation with retail and wholesale trade" remained (Gregory 1993, 22–23).[96]

For those in retail and wholesale, including Tanzanians of Indian origin, the Arusha Declaration was a severe blow, as it was seen as an attempt to exert state control over their businesses, especially as the government formed the State

Trading Corporation (STC).[97] Initially, however, the STC was responsible for only a fraction of total imports, and many small Indian Tanzanian importers remained (Coulson 2013, 339–40), including in the pharmaceutical field. In 1971, there were still thirty-two drug-selling establishments, most of which engaged in both retail and wholesale activities, and they were all importers.[98] Then, in 1973, "one branch of the STC . . . became NAPCO." This was "a parastatal agency with a right to import and trade drugs and related ware . . . for the governmental as well as for the private health sector in Tanzania."[99] Once established, NAPCO took over most pharmacies in Tanzania, and although starting in the mid-1980s, some new pharmacies did open, in 1988, there were still only twenty-six privately owned pharmacies in the country; there were 35 licensed private importers by 1995 (WHO 1995a, 161).[100] NAPCO dismantled in 1997.

This does not mean that NAPCO failed to contribute to local pharmaceutical production. As we have seen, NAPCO owned one of the state-owned pharmaceutical companies and bought drugs from both Keko and TPI. But NAPCO did ignore the private pharmaceutical companies that existed and, by centralizing the procurement of drugs, it indirectly narrowed opportunities for gaining experience and skills in the pharmaceutical field.

In short, for both Indian and African Tanzanians, it was difficult to attain a pharmacy degree, and there were minimal openings for private pharmaceutical trades. As a result, there were few opportunities for job experience or exposure to manufacturing facilities through trading. Without an access to technical know-how, only few entrepreneurs could go into pharmaceutical manufacturing. Some of those in Tanzania who did open pharmaceutical manufacturing facilities had obtained a pharmacy degree (or related educational background) from abroad, and/or they owned a retail pharmacy first, as was the case in Kenya. Other Tanzanians, however, differed from Indian Kenyans regarding the kind of ties abroad upon which they relied.

## TIES ABROAD AND TIES AT HOME IN TANZANIA

Four privately owned pharmaceutical companies opened in Tanzania and survived into the 1990s. (No new pharmaceutical factory opened in Tanzania in the 1990s). Each company opened at a different time and in a different political-economic context. The first private pharmaceutical factory, Mansoor Daya Chemicals (named after the founder), opened during the short period of "investment boom" in Tanzania, between 1955 and 1965 (Coulson 2013, 210–11).[101] This was prior to the Arusha Declaration and Tanzania's development plans still focused on the private sector, with specific attempts to attract foreign capital (Barker et al. 1986, 49–50). Many of the largest companies were owned by multinational companies (Rweyemamu 1973, 113). Other investors, mostly

in light manufacturing, included locals of Indian origin. There were also investors from neighboring Kenya and Uganda, who were also often of Indian origin
(Coulson 2013, 201–11, Honey 1974, 68).[102] Indeed, this was the background of
Mansoor Daya, who was born in Kenya to Indian parents. With the exception
of his move to Tanzania, Daya's trajectory was similar to that of other pharmaceutical manufacturers in Kenya. He went to a pharmacy school in Edinburgh,
Scotland, in 1956. Upon graduation, he returned to Kenya, where for two years
he worked in a chemist shop in Nairobi. He then moved to Dar es Salaam in
Tanzania, where his brother was a doctor. There, Mansoor Daya opened a retail
pharmacy and, shortly after independence, in 1964, he established a small pharmaceutical factory.[103]

In the wake of the Arusha Declaration, fear of nationalizations, as well as
limited access to commercial loans and insurance, led private enterprises to cut
down their investments and operations. Still, although the state had become
the largest owner of capital, private capital accumulation continued, especially
with the loosening of restrictions in the late 1970s (Barker and Wield 1978,
table 2, Chachage 1987, Coulson 2013, 369). It was during this period that
Khanbhai Pharmaceuticals was established in Tanga. Khanbhai Pharmaceuticals was part of a diversified company, owned by the Khanbhai family, originally from Gujarat, India. In 1946, Taher Khanbhai was sent from Tanzania to
England to train as a pharmacist; and, upon his return, he established the Khanbhai Pharmacy, which became, according to his brother, Bashir Khanbhai, "the
seed of our family pharmacy business for 50 years!"[104] Bashir Khanbhai also
received a pharmacy degree from the University of London in 1966. He then
joined the family business, where he helped establish various businesses, including the pharmaceutical plant.[105] Over the years, Khanbhai reportedly became
"a household name," with presence both in wholesale and retail pharmacies, as
well as pharmaceutical formulations (Srinivasan 1999). Although the Khanbhai
pharmaceutical factory resembled the trajectory of other Kenyan and Tanzanian pharmaceutical enterprises, Khanbhai was a diversified family business,
and the pharmaceutical factory was hardly at the center of their operations—it
was small to begin with (smaller than Mansoor Daya), remained small, and the
Khanbhai name survived even after the pharmaceutical factory closed in 2000
(Center for Pharmaceutical Management 2003, 20).

Shelys Pharmaceuticals was established in 1981 in Dar es Salaam by an Indian
Tanzanian medical practitioner, Dr. R. S. Patel. We do not know what made
Dr. Patel shift from medical practice to pharmaceutical manufacturing, but it
might have mattered that he was relative of Ashok Patel, the founder of Elys in
Kenya. Dr. Patel was able to get a loan from a Tanzanian investment bank, which
he used to buy a range of machinery, mainly from India, and to build a large
factory hall. This factory was established next to another factory, also owned by
Patel, for "small, lowest-technology production of 'beauty preparations' from

exclusively local raw materials."[106] In 1984, Shelys was bought by the Sumaria Group. The Sumaria Group was founded in Kenya back in the 1940s by K. P. Shah, who was originally from India, and his six brothers, following the pattern among Indian entrepreneurs of intra-family partnerships—which we have also seen with Khanbhai.[107] The firm, which began as a small general trading business, extended its operations into Tanganyika in 1957, where it started to manufacture plastic goods that it had formerly imported. In the 1970s, the company turned into a diversified multinational firm, with a large number of companies in plastics, food processing, edible oils, soaps, cement, textiles, real estate, and soft drinks (Sutton and Olomi 2012). Like Khanbhai, then, Shelys was one enterprise of a larger business conglomerate, although with a much better trajectory later on (chapter 7).[108]

Interchem Pharmaceuticals, too, was a small factory that was part of a larger business conglomerate. It was founded in 1987 in Moshi and soon thereafter was sold to Benjamin Mengi, who became the managing director of the firm, and to his older and more successful brother, Reginald Abraham Mengi (East African 2008). An African Tanzanian, Reginald Mengi obtained an education in the UK and then worked in Tanzania for the multinational accounting firm of Coopers & Lybrand (which later became PriceWaterHouseCooper), where he eventually became the firm's chairman and managing partner. In the late 1980s, Reginald Mengi went on to start his own companies. Mengi's IPP Group, which became one of the largest industrial groups in East Africa, included IPP Media, one of the most successful media conglomerates in Africa, and IPP Resources, which mined coal, copper, chrome, gold, and uranium (Frontani 2015, Mackintosh et al. 2016). Compared to this, Interchem was a particularly small endeavor. It closed in 2008.

In Tanzania as in Kenya, then, education and ties abroad were an important aspect of nascent pharmaceutical entrepreneurship: Mansoor Daya and two members of the Khanbhai family received pharmacy degrees abroad, and the founder of Shelys had ties with pharmaceutical manufacturers both in India and Kenya. However, none of the entrepreneurs had experience working with multinational pharmaceutical companies, or—possibly with the exception of Khanbhai—had import businesses that could have given them exposure to drug manufacturing. Investment in pharmaceutical production in Tanzania, instead, at times relied on links with Kenya—through migration, family relations, as well as commercial investment. Indeed, Tanzania illustrates another possible path for local pharmaceutical production, which was less common in the Kenyan pharmaceutical field—investment by an industrial group, at times without any previous interest in the pharmaceutical field. We will see that after 2000 this path became at least as common as the pharmacist-entrepreneur trajectory.

In turn, there is no indication that social or other ties at home played any role in Tanzania, in contrast to Kenya, where domestic solidarity allowed for diffusion of information that strengthened the sector as a whole. In Tanzania, geography, national origins, religion, and other differences might have prevented the creation of a trusting community. The factories were not all owned by pharmacists, and they were geographically dispersed, with two in Dar es Salaam, one in Tanga, and one in Moshi. Of the four companies, one was owned by indigenous Africans, and the other three were established by Indians, one of them was from Kenya and the three belonged to different communities.

In short, limited educational and commercial opportunities both at home and abroad restricted in Tanzania the access to technical know-how needed in the pharmaceutical field and hence the number of pharmacists-entrepreneurs interested in drug manufacturing. Although a private pharmaceutical sector still emerged, it was smaller and much less resilient than the one that emerged at around the same time in Kenya, as I describe below.

## The Tanzanian Pharmaceutical Sector in the 1990s

The Tanzanian pharmaceutical sector started with a disadvantage of having no industrial infrastructure or technical know-how—and for many years after independence, it was difficult for both state-owned companies and private entrepreneurs to catch up. Without the support of foreign aid, the Tanzanian government could only create a limited market, while barriers to education and job experience—as well as broader restrictions on private entrepreneurship—prevented growth of the industrial sector even as the market was opening up. As a result, the Tanzanian pharmaceutical sector that emerged was small and quite fragile. The two state-owned pharmaceutical companies, Keko and TPI, did much better than the private firms, but still produced a limited range of products, and they continuously struggled with limited utilization of their (relatively large) capacity. In turn, there were only four privately owned pharmaceutical companies that operated in the 1990s. Both Mansoor Daya and Shelys were small, but they were still larger than the two "minor production plants," Khanbhai and Interchem, which already in the 1980s "had not . . . significantly contributed to the drug supplies of Tanzania."[109] Later on, Shelys became one of the more successful pharmaceutical manufacturers in Tanzania, but Mansoor Daya remained small and both Khanbhai and Interchem eventually closed (chapter 7).

Installed production capacity shows the (unfulfilled) potential of the state-owned factories and the very basic starting point of even the two larger privately owned firms. In total (calculating only these four companies), the installed annual production capacity of local pharmaceutical companies by 1990 included: 3 billion tablets, 69 million capsules, 430,000 liters of liquids,

40 thousand kg powders and creams, 1 million liters of infusion solution, 10.5 million injection vials, 500,000 liters of liquid semi-solids, and 500,000 aerosol units (World Bank 1990). This was substantially smaller than Kenya's total manufacturing capacity at the time (chapter 3). As for individual companies, TPI and Keko were significantly larger than Mansoor Daya and Shelys. For example, Keko and TPI had capacity for 2.7 billion out of the country's total capacity of 3 billion tablets, and TPI had capacity for 50 million out of the total capacity of 69 million capsules. In comparison, Mansoor Daya had the capacity to produce 300 million tablets, and Shelys had the capacity to only produce 35 million tablets (World Bank 1990).

Yet, as we have seen, these pharmaceutical companies had major difficulties utilizing the capacity they had. During the economic crisis in the 1980s, this was largely due to insufficient foreign exchange allocations.[110] Later on, capacity utilization improved somewhat but still remained low, and stayed lower than Kenya's.[111] An expert report estimated that, "Most of the time the [pharmaceutical] industry [in Tanzania] utilizes 30% to 50% of its installed capacity."[112] Employment data similarly reflect the small size of the sector and its minimal production activity. In 1990, at a time that Kenya's sector employed around 1,000 workers, Tanzanian firms employed only about 340 workers—TPI had 130 employees, Keko had 120, Mansoor Daya had 50, and Shelys had 39.[113]

Aside from having limited capacity utilization, Tanzanian pharmaceutical companies also only produced a small number and a limited range of drugs.[114] Whereas Dawa in Kenya produced 100 drugs in the early 1980s, Keko in 1990 had the capacity to produce 14 products, and in practice it only produced 4 tablets (aspirin, paracetamol, chloroquine, and tetracycline); TPI had the capacity to produce 36 products but produced only 24.[115] Mansoor Daya "produced only a few basic items."[116]

Not surprisingly, then, the market share of local producers was minimal. In 1990, local firms' combined capacity amounted to about 10 percent of the country's "drug requirements" (World Bank 1990, 105); given their underutilized capacity, these firms' actual market share was much lower.

Even within these constraints, however, the companies were seemingly profitable. As a 1990 World Bank report explained: "Pharmaceutical products are simple and cheap to manufacture. . . . It is therefore not surprising that all the companies now make profits despite severe underutilization of capacity and the other constraints." Still, the World Bank also noted that Keko's recent profits "may only be paper profits reflecting inventory valuation gains due to devaluation," and another report warned that TPI's turnover was not as significant as Keko's, though its level of long-term debt was five times higher.[117] The privately owned companies were even less profitable (World Bank 1990, 106).

Finally, in terms of quality standards, lack of regulation and later monitoring enabled inadequate adherence to quality standards, although one of the state-owned factories was doing relatively well. As for the regulations in place, in 1978 the *Pharmaceuticals and Poisons Act No. 9* became the legal instrument for the regulation of drugs in Tanzania.[118] The act established the Pharmacy Board, which was responsible for the issuance of licenses to manufacturers, wholesalers, and retail outlets and for evaluating and registering drugs. At the time that the MoH Task Force was established in 1980, however, regulations for the act had not yet passed.[119] As quality assurance mechanisms were considered fundamental to an adequate essential drugs program, they became part of the Task Force agenda; and a fourth EDP component, quality assurance, was to be achieved by "rehabilitating" the recently established Pharmacy Board, which was "very thin in manpower and equipment, and mostly ineffective."[120]

Initially there were only minimal improvements, and neither imported nor locally manufactured facilities were inspected by the Board: "The Board's inspectors are supposed to visit [Keko], TPI and other [local] manufacturers but practically no visits have been made."[121] Without inspectors or adequate quality testing facilities, "[it] is left to the suppliers that they adhere to GMP [Good Manufacturing Practices]."[122] Consequently, suppliers, including local pharmaceutical companies, did not generally follow strict quality standards. An industrial pharmacist, who was sent by the United Nations Industrial Development Organization (UNIDO) to Tanzania in 1980, had this to say on Keko, Mansoor Daya, and Khanbhai:

> All the plants were designed improperly, the performance of production equipment was far below expected levels, and good manufacturing practices were almost nonexistent. The managerial and technical staff was handicapped by the absence of proper guidance and training and consequently the operation of the plant is founded on principles learned through self-experience with the result that it is devoid of acknowledged systems and procedures for assuring the quality, integrity and safety of the products on the one hand and efficiency, productivity and economy on the other.[123]

The consultant promised that "all these shortcomings were surmountable;" however, a decade later Mansoor Daya did not improve.[124] Keko was doing somewhat better, enough for one report to remark that, "quality and control facilities exist to some satisfactory levels,"[125] although another report noted, "quality control is poor."[126] The reports on Shelys were only slightly more forgiving. "Physical plant and production facilities are good, but still need improvement. Quality control of the manufactured product is adequate, but none of the currently marketed formulations have been properly tested" (World Bank 1990, 106). TPI was evaluated more positively.[127] One report maintained that, "the plant was built in accordance with GMP and the layout and flow of material is suitable." Also, "the plant is . . . in possession of the know-how and the technical skills to produce . . . products in a satisfactory quality."[128] In 1990, another positive review stated that "the physical plant is well designed and maintained. . . . Quality control is good, and there is an excellent laboratory for all necessary tests" (World Bank 1990). In regard to both TPI and Keko, the understanding was that "their in-house process operations do not correspond *strictly* to GMP recommendations but the quality of their products is *acceptable*."[129] This suggests a flexibility in regard to quality standards—a flexibility that the WHO later abandoned, as I describe in later chapters.

## Discussion

Like Kenya, Tanzania adopted a national list of essential drugs and relied on a ration kits program funded by donors to improve the distribution of drugs to rural areas. In Tanzania, however, the government was in no position to fund a local component for ration kits, and donors, too, refused to support such a local component. Without a domestic component, the ration kits program could not facilitate local pharmaceutical production. In a poor country in the midst of a severe economic crisis, this left pharmaceutical firms with no credible market to exploit. The frustration of those supporting local pharmaceutical production stemmed exactly from the fact that a local component of the ration kits program could have had (as it had in Kenya) a significant impact on the local industry, given the substantial size of the funds for ration kits relative to Tanzania's overall public health budget. Indeed, the Tanzanian pharmaceutical sector that emerged was small and notably fragile—even the state-owned pharmaceutical companies, which had been doing better than the privately owned ones, were weaker than their Kenyan counterparts. The Tanzanian case also shows how foreign aid that is not designed to facilitate domestic interests may easily become a factor undermining them. Donors may have been right in focusing on the urgent need of providing essential medicines rather than supporting local production, but the result was that local manufacturers had to compete with imported drugs that were essentially provided to the government for free.

The Tanzanian case sheds light on another aspect of foreign aid, that of aid allocation. I showed that the decision by donors not to have a local component of the ration kits program (or in other ways to meaningfully support local pharmaceutical production) was a response to perceived local conditions. Concerned with the public health situation in Tanzania, donors committed funds to help resolve the acute issue of severe drug shortages. In principle, they considered local pharmaceutical production an integral part of the solution. In practice, a perceived lack of state capacity—specifically, in regard to CMS—helped donors rule against supporting local procurement of local drugs. This suggests that lack of state capacity at times be doubly consequential: it does not only rule out effective state action, but may also block access to foreign assistance that is not "internationalized and verticalized."

Lack of market opportunities was one factor contributing to the fragility of the pharmaceutical sector in Tanzania in the 1980s and 1990s. Another was lack of access to technical skills. Few in Tanzania had access to a pharmacy degree abroad, and in a socialist economy there was limited private trade in pharmaceutical products, which in Kenya was a channel of getting access to technical know-how. In turn, the few private companies that did open in Tanzania confirm the role of pharmacy education, job experience, and ties abroad in facilitating pharmaceutical manufacturing. In Tanzania, however, these manufacturers belonged to different nationalities and communities, and not all of them were pharmacists. Combined with the fact that factories were set up years apart and in different locations, this diminished social relations among them, and the potential for diffusion or political influence.

# 5

# Uganda in the 1980s and 1990s

## THE MISSING ENTREPRENEURS

In 1989, a World Health Organization (WHO) evaluation of the ration kits program in Uganda expressed cautious optimism about integration of locally produced drugs into the sealed kits and about pharmaceutical production in the country more generally:

> Though still in its infancy, the local Ugandan pharmaceutical industry is said to be developing plans for a sizeable entry into the market. This is not likely to be a major force within the next one–two years. However, bulk procurement of individual items [plus] local kit packing will enable selected products of local production to be considered and thereby help to strengthen the local industry leading to more self-reliance.

Tellingly, the same report mentioned that, "probably at least half the present drug kit contents could be purchased at internationally competitive prices from Kenya, using Uganda shillings."[1] By that year, as we have seen, Kenya's first generation of locally owned pharmaceutical firms was already established (chapter 3), and even Tanzania's more fragile sector was in place (chapter 4). In Uganda, even this cautious report proved overly optimistic, and it took another decade before a small and quite vulnerable sector emerged.

Like Tanzania, Uganda imported its drugs from multinational pharmaceutical companies, both under colonialism and long after independence (Wortzel 1971).[2] However, in 1979, at a time that Tanzania and Kenya were already described as "countries which have started to repack formulated drugs and process bulk drugs into dosage forms," Uganda was still listed under "countries which have no manufacturing facilities" (UNCTC 1984, 48). One state-owned company, Uganda Pharmaceuticals Ltd. (UPL), opened in 1973 and had two drug factories, but they offered only minimal contribution to the pharmaceutical market in Uganda. Another state-owned pharmaceutical company, NEC Pharmaceuticals, opened two decades later in 1991, and this factory did not thrive either. The private sector initially performed just as poorly. There were a few establishments producing drugs in the 1960s, but they were all extremely small extensions of retail shops or wholesalers, and they all disappeared in the 1970s.[3] Only two privately owned companies opened in the 1980s—Medipharm Industries (EA), in 1982, and Inlex, in 1986. A slightly more stable private pharmaceutical sector developed in Uganda in the 1990s, with the opening of Kampala Pharmaceutical Industries (KPI), Mavid Pharmaceuticals, Bychem Laboratories, Rene Industries, and Kisakye Industries, and with the privatization of UPL in 1996. However, half of these companies eventually closed down. The more successful ones had financial backing and/or access to technical know-how, including through ties abroad, as was the case in Tanzania and Kenya.

Foreign aid played no role in the emergence of the Ugandan pharmaceutical sector. Indeed, I argue in this chapter that lack of foreign support—including lack of a local component of the ration kits program—contributed to the sector's slow and tenuous development, especially in comparison to Kenya. Developing agencies' decision against a local component was based on the assessment that, unlike in Kenya or even Tanzania, there were no local manufacturing capabilities upon which to draw.

In this chapter, I describe the local conditions that prevented the emergence of a pharmaceutical sector in the 1980s, and that shaped the characteristics of the sector when it finally did emerge in the 1990s. I describe how both the public and the private industrial sectors in Uganda were devastated under Idi Amin's rule from 1971 to 1979—nationalization overwhelmed the public sector, and the expulsion of Indians in 1972 greatly exacerbated the country's scarcity of nascent entrepreneurs, including in the pharmaceutical field. Unrest continued after Amin's fall in 1979 and up until 1986, when the National Resistance Army (NRA) led by Yoweri Museveni took over. Only then did Ugandan (and non-Ugandan) entrepreneurs, including indigenous Africans, begin to experiment with drug production. I show that some entrepreneurs had similar backgrounds to the pharmacists-entrepreneurs in Kenya and Tanzania; namely, they were traders with a pharmaceutical background and/or ties abroad. Others opened drug manufacturing facilities without much capital or background in pharmacy. Without either state or foreign assistance, these firms remained vulnerable, and many eventually closed down. One that survived, Medipharm, was an early recipient of foreign assistance—the only instance of foreign aid to the pharmaceutical industry in Uganda at the time.

The chapter begins with a brief review of the health care system and access to medicine during the Amin regime and the years of civil war. It then describes the ration kits program in Uganda, which started in 1986 but did not have a local component. The chapter then identifies local conditions, from colonial legacies to the situation during and following the Amin regime, that hindered the emergence of a resilient local pharmaceutical sector. It then describes the pharmaceutical sector that finally emerged in the 1990s and the sources of its vulnerability.

## Health Care Systems and Access to Medicine: Idi Amin and the Civil War Years

In Uganda under colonialism, "health services funded by the state were overwhelmingly geared to the needs of the European and Asian community" (Jørgensen 1981, 62) and were focused on curative care in the cities (Hutchinson 2001, 409). After independence in 1962, government efforts concentrated on improving primary care, and Ugandans experienced steadily improving health indicators. Indeed, until the 1970s, Uganda's health sector was considered to be one of the best in Africa (Hutchinson 2001, 407–409). This was enabled by the fact that Uganda had one of the more prosperous economies in Africa at the time, with an annual growth rate of 6 percent between 1962 and 1971 (Mbabazi and Mokhawa 2005, 134). All progress, however, was summarily destroyed following Idi Amin's *coup d'état* in 1971. Amin's regime was overthrown in 1979, but it was followed by a five-year war. Given the broader context of the early 1980s global economic crisis, these events "have all combined to produce a situation in the health sector *that is critical*."[4]

"During the era of Idi Amin," one report described, "practically all social services were run down and neglected."[5] According to another report: "Many hospitals were without access to power supply and water, and many rural health units were destroyed or were lacking basic facilities and adequate staff."[6] "What was left intact was eventually plundered to near-total destruction during and immediately following the [1978–79] war of liberation."[7] By 1979, "The overall breakdown of services in the country was so great . . . that health services ceased to exist in many areas" (Dodge 1986, 755). The government could only service about 20 percent of the medical needs of the country.[8] By the 1980s, the health care system collapsed.[9] Uganda, which was previously at the top among African countries in terms of health status, was by then fortieth (Macrae, Zwi, and Gilson 1996, 1096).[10]

A severe shortage of drugs ensued, "due in part to the difficulty of obtaining foreign exchange" (WHO 1995b, 13). In 1980, "[the shortage] meant that the individual units in the rural districts had to manage with their normal supply for 3 weeks for a 2-months' period."[11] A report prepared by the Ugandan Ministry of Health (MoH), the United Nations International Children's Fund (UNICEF) and the Danish Red Cross described:

The health sector has been faced a decreasing budgetary allocation for several years now. The national foreign exchange constraints have hit the health sector (especially the drugs supply) very hard. Uganda . . . imports all her drug requirements. The very limited foreign exchange allocations are irregular thus leading to an insufficient and irregular supply of drugs to the health units.[12]

The drugs that were available came mostly with the help of donations; after Museveni took power, ration kits were also introduced into the country.[13]

## Essential Drugs and Ration Kits

The implementation of the Primary Health Care (PHC) strategy in Uganda could only take place with foreign support (WHO 1995a). In 1979, the Ugandan Ministry of Planning requested UNICEF assistance in the provision of essential drugs to selected health centers. The Ugandan MoH, WHO, and UNICEF then agreed on a package of 45 essential drugs intended to fulfill most of these health centers' needs. Following some delays, between 1982 and 1985, UNICEF helped rehabilitate about 100 health centers in a program that also included the provision of pre-packed kits containing essential drugs.[14]

Although modest, the program was considered a promising endeavor. "There are tremendous advantages to be gained from the coordination of the procurement of basic drugs, both in terms of lower prices and in terms of economizing on quality control, clearance charges, transportation from Mombasa [in Kenya] to Entebbe [in Uganda] and distribution within Uganda."[15] A more critical account, however, suggested that, "UNICEF essential drug list contains many items which are not strictly essential, some of the most essential items are mostly inadequate to cover the patient load, and a few items exceed the requirement for the RHCs [rural health centers]."[16] The report suggested that the frequent shortages of drugs in the UNICEF-supported health centers were due to higher attendance rate than was originally anticipated, but also leakages; as one report diplomatically stated: "It is believed that the frequent lack of some drugs in RHCs is not unconnected with their easy availability in the private sector."[17]

In 1986, this program was replaced by a Danish International Development Agency (DANIDA)-funded Uganda Essential Drugs Management Programme (UEDMP), which later changed its name to Uganda Essential Drugs Support Programme (UEDSP) (WHO 1995a, 56). The UEDMP was explicitly inspired by the ration kits programs in Kenya and Tanzania. As one report stated: "DANIDA had previous experiences in Kenya and Tanzania in drug supplies and desired to transfer its expertise to Uganda" (WHO 1995a, 13). In Uganda, development agencies were concerned with servicing the private sector as well, so in addition to working with the government, DANIDA also worked with the faith-based Joint Medical Store (JMS), which received one-third of the total donations.[18] From 1985 to 1987, Phase I of UEDMP focused on emergency drug supply to rural units and to hospital out-patient clinics (WHO 1995a). In evaluating that phase, a WHO report asserted: "The civil unrest seen in the area around the capital which coincided with the launch of the programme was an obvious disruption" (WHO 1995a, 13). Still, the program was positively evaluated:

> The drug kits . . . answered a pressing need when they were first introduced in 1986/87. There was a national emergency shortage of drugs in the country and pre-packed kits containing the most needed items were an effective means of getting these drugs quickly and safely to the end users, the rural health facilities.[19]

Phase II of UEDMP, which was implemented from 1988 to 1990 (WHO 1995a, 14), focused on the importation of kits of essential drugs, which included at the time fifteen "core medicines."[20] The contribution of the drug kits to Uganda's overall procurement of medicine was substantial. In 1989, the value of the essential drugs kits was $4 million. In comparison, the Ugandan government spent $3 million on additional essential drugs "through the tender system as individual, bulk items."[21] By the end of Phase III in 1996, UEDSP's contribution was even higher: the program provided 85 percent of the drugs for the public sector.[22]

Although the drug kits program was considered a positive experience, as elsewhere, concerns surfaced regarding its inflexibility. "The drug kit system [cannot] respond quickly to different needs in the country. . . . Unless such differences are ironed out by regular redistribution, shortages and suffering may result in some areas, wastage in others."[23] Another concern was that rather than helping with state capacity, the program weakened it.

> The drug kit system effectively takes away responsibility for the purchasing, quality control and management of drugs from the national staff. At each stage of the drug supply chain, the national personnel have little to do. . . . Thus, the drug kit system does not give much opportunity to develop the drug management skills, including procurement, of national staff, and this may be a serious lack when donor support phases out or when the need for a drug kit system is over and the drugs are once again procured in bulk for individual packing and distribution.[24]

A similar concern with local capabilities could have been raised—as it was in Kenya and Tanzania—in regard to manufacturing. In Uganda, however, there was never a call for, nor a serious consideration of, a local component of the ration kits program as a way to secure part of this market for local producers.

There was a call for local packaging, but unlike in Tanzania, this was not motivated by the possibility of local production but, rather, because packing the kits locally was seen as "a more efficient method."[25] This lack of interest in local manufacturing was a reflection of the fact that there was no manufacturing facility at the time in Uganda that could produce the needed drugs. In the following sections, I first describe the particularly weak state-owned pharmaceutical sector under both Idi Amin and President Museveni. I then describe the paralysis of the private pharmaceutical sector under Amin and the emergence of a pharmaceutical sector in the 1990s, though still small and fragile.

## Making Medicine (1): Unmaking the Public Sector

In 1984, reports discussing Uganda's dependence on imported drugs mentioned that, "Uganda has no pharmaceutical industries."[26] Uganda, which did not inherit an industrial base from the British, did have one state-owned and a few small privately owned pharmaceutical factories that opened in the 1970s, but these did not survive the industrial collapse under the Amin regime.

Like Tanzania, Uganda experienced deliberate underdevelopment under colonialism through a policy of nonindustrialization and reliance on a primary-products exporting economy (Stoutjesdijk 1967, Mamdani 1976). Only in the early 1950s, the colonial administration adopted an official commitment to industrialization and founded the Uganda Development Corporation (UDC), which carried out its task of promoting industrialization through partnerships with foreign (British) capital (Mamdani 1976, 250–56, Okuku 2006). Enormous rises in the prices for Uganda's traditional exports, in turn, made it possible to finance basic infrastructure, including the construction of the Owen Falls Dam in Jinja, roads, railways, and telecommunication lines. Even then, the main investment was in the processing of agricultural products. A substantial part of other manufacturing activities, such as sugar and tobacco manufacturing, was also directly related to the agricultural sector, whereas other manufacturing enterprises focused mostly on goods with high transport costs (Stoutjesdijk 1967). Hence, "industrial deepening has not yet taken place by the early 1960s." The economy was agrarian, dominated by "African farm enterprise," and industry was an insignificant sector in the economy (Obwona et al. 2014, 3). There were only 264 manufacturing establishments reported in 1963 (Okuku 2006, 124).

Uganda remained predominantly an agricultural country after independence. As for industrial strategy, the government initially followed a market-based, state-led import-substitution industrialization, with the state maintaining a central position in the sector. Of the 3,600-registered commercial and industrial enterprises in 1968, only 10 percent were publicly owned (77 percent were privately owned, and 13 percent were foreign owned); however, the enterprises owned by the state were the larger ones, including the 44 largest manufacturing establishments, with a share of 74 percent of total turnover (Stoutjesdijk 1967, 28, Mamdani 1976, 258–59).

This mixed structure of private, public, local, and foreign participation in the manufacturing sector was to be transformed by President Milton Obote's "Move to the Left" strategy. In 1969, inspired by the Arusha Declaration in Tanzania, President Obote launched the Common Man's Charter, which stated: "We affirm that the guiding economic principle will be that the means of production and distribution must be in the hands of the people as a whole" (cited in Okuku 2006, 135). That goal was to be achieved through nationalization. In all, about 100 large firms were to be impacted, although in the end, some companies did not lose majority control, and only 78 enterprises were nationalized (Gregory 1993, 84, Kibikyo 2008).

In 1971, Idi Amin took power in a military *coup*. Under Amin, drastic nationalization led to an unprecedented transfer of private property to the state. Amin promised to place the economy in the hands of African traders, and toward that end he ordered the expulsion of Ugandans of Indian origin in 1972, giving them ninety days to leave the country and seizing their assets. Although later Amin ordered that only noncitizens would be expelled, the effect was the same. Approximately 49,000 Indians, both citizens and noncitizens, left Uganda, and only about 4,000 stayed in the country. This left the Ugandan government with an "abandoned" property of 5,655 firms, factories, ranches, and agricultural estates (Jørgensen 1981, 285–88).[27]

Much of that expropriated property went to government departments and ministries, parastatals, and the UDC, leading to a vastly expanded role of the public sector in the economy. The UDC, for example, more than doubled the number of companies it ran (Okuku 2006, Kibikyo 2008). As I discuss below, this larger role proved to weaken, rather than strengthen, the state's economic performance—and this was clearly the case with the state-owned pharmaceutical company, Uganda Pharmaceutical Ltd., which was opened in 1973.

A year earlier, in 1972, the WHO sent a consultant to Uganda with the task of "considering the advisability of presenting a request to UNIDO to establish a pharmaceutical industry in Uganda."[28] After a thorough examination, the consultant, Prof. G. Osuide, Head of Department of Pharmacy and Pharmacology at Ahmadu Bello University in Nigeria, concluded:

> The Government should implement its plan to increase manufacture of drugs at Entebbe [Central] Medical Stores for use in government hospitals as this measure would greatly reduce government expenditure on drugs in terms of costs and foreign exchange, make commonly used drugs readily available, enhance the government's position in enforcing . . . drug registration and price control, provide experience and more professionally satisfying

jobs for pharmacists, and provide the necessary experience to start a national drug industry at a later stage, in the private sector.[29]

In other words, the consultant supported local production but advised to first focus on basic production in existing facilities.[30] This recommendation was similar to an earlier assessment of UNIDO.[31] The consultant also encouraged the government to ask UNIDO for assistance "in developing the existing Medical Stores at Entebbe."[32] The type of technical support UNIDO was expected to provide indicates the low level of know-how available in Uganda at the time.

> A four-year period of assistance is proposed. . . . The assistance should include the following: (1) A principal expert in pharmaceutical manufacture who would organize conversion of the facilities of the existing medical stores, take charge of the production of drugs at the outset and train local staff. (2) A technician skilled in the installation and maintenance of pharmaceutical equipment who would be in charge of the equipment during installation and operation of the project and would train local technicians. (3) Seven fellowships (i) One of six months for the Chief Pharmacist to enable him to visit drug manufacturing establishments and study drug registration and inspection procedures in developed countries, and observe quality control laboratories. . . . (iv) Two of one year for two pharmacists, to enable them [to] study drug manufacture in industrial firms overseas. . . . (4) Equipment.[33]

There is no evidence to suggest that any of these recommendations were implemented. Instead, the government opened two drug manufacturing facilities. In 1973, the government established UPL as the government pharmacy, under the Ministry of Commerce.[34] Like the National Pharmaceutical Company (NAPCO) in Tanzania (chapter 4), UPL acted as an importer and distributor of pharmaceutical products for the private system of pharmacies.[35] UPL, again like NAPCO, seemed to have a high mark-up of drug prices. Comparing the price of drugs sold by UPL in the private sector to the price of drugs sold by Central Medical Stores (CMS) in the public sector, one report found that "[UPL] sells in Uganda at ten times the price of the CMS."[36] Against the advice of the WHO consultant, UPL had a manufacturing arm that included two drug factories. This again resembled NAPCO, which owned 18 percent of one of the state-owned pharmaceutical firms in Tanzania. One of UPL's factories, in Jinja, produced "a wide range of products" "under the name of Opa Ltd. and Aerosols Ltd."[37] Another factory, in Kampala, "manufactured a small range of antibiotics, aspirin tablets, and also toothpaste."[38]

There is little available information on the sources of capital and know-how, or on the experience of these factories until 1979.[39] We do know that most industries were devastated during the Amin regime. As Amin forced out hundreds of Indian managers, engineers, accountants, and other professional personnel (Okuku 2006, 140), enterprises, many owned by the state, lost technical background and experience, international market connections, and access to capital (Livingstone 1998, 46).[40] Industries also suffered from shortages of foreign currency, which they needed for importing raw materials, components parts and spares (Mamdani 1983, 48), and from political interference (Ddumba-Ssentamu and Mugume 2001, 10). When the Amin regime was finally overthrown in 1979, there was additional widespread destruction of infrastructure and of industrial plants, many of which were looted (Livingstone 1998, 38). By 1980, then, the manufacturing sector had all but collapsed. Out of 930 manufacturing enterprises registered in 1971, only 300 remained in operation. Factories that survived operated on very low capacity utilization of just 5 percent on average (Livingstone 1998, 38). In 1986, industrial output was estimated to be little more than one-third of peak levels that had been achieved in 1970–72 (Brett 1996, 332). The two pharmaceutical factories faced a similar fate. Both were vandalized in 1979, and no activity was undertaken in the factories for the following few years.[41]

Recovery attempts for the pharmaceutical factories were planned but did not materialize. At the end of 1981, for example, in response to UPL's request, the Swiss pharmaceutical company Ciba-Geigy prepared proposals for rehabilitation and upgrading of both the Jinja and Kampala plants. A later report, from 1986, seemed to similarly support the possibility of upgrading: "While the facilities will need drastic improvements to meet the standards of Good Manufacturing Practices . . . the equipment of very high standard is available."[42] According to a WHO report from 1987, however, "Since [1981] the situation has remained the same."[43] Another report stated that, "due to internal problems the factories in Jinja and Kampala are barely carrying out what can be termed production."[44] Indeed, this was not an opportune time for industrial production. Between 1979 and 1986, Uganda went through economic turmoil, including structural adjustment programs (SAPs) and severe political conflicts, including a guerrilla war by the NRA waged between 1981 and 1986 (Livingstone 1998, 38). In the late 1985, the economy again collapsed (Mbabazi and Mokhawa 2005, 134). By the time the National Resistance Movement (NRM) formed a new government in 1986, with Museveni as President, the manufacturing sector was reduced to a mere 3.5 percent of GDP. Infrastructure was destroyed, there was no utility sector, and factories suffered from obsolete capacity with no access to proper maintenance or replacement due to scarcity of foreign exchange (Siggel and Ssemogerere 2004, Mbabazi and Mokhawa 2005, 135, Kibikyo 2008).[45]

With the emergence of political and economic stability, an evaluation from 1986 reported that, "the Government in Uganda is keen to start [pharmaceutical] production" and "is willing to rehabilitate the production unit in Kampala."[46]

Although the new government invested in UPL, including moving the factory to new premises, the company incurred heavy loses and was eventually privatized in 1996, during a wave of privatization of parastatals undertaken as part of Uganda's SAP.[47]

Five years earlier, in 1991, the National Enterprise Corporation (NEC), the commercial arm of Uganda's Defense Forces, opened its own pharmaceutical company, NEC Pharmaceuticals.[48] DANIDA skeptically reported that NEC's "potential production capacity is estimated to cover approximately 70% of Uganda's need for some 5–10 simple items within [Uganda's EDL]. This does not seem realistic within the time-frame of 1–2 years set up by NEC Pharmaceuticals, especially in view of the limited access to trained professional staff."[49]

Indeed, there is little information about any production taking place in the factory in the following few years. The factory's subsequent attempts to establish itself, mostly through joint ventures, also did not work very well. In 1999–2000, NEC Pharmaceuticals negotiated a joint venture agreement with a German group, Heinz Haupt Pharmaceutical. In the course of the negotiations, it was disclosed that although $10 million were allegedly spent on procuring equipment for the factory, such equipment had never been installed, and the assets of the company were valued at only around $6 million (Pharma Letter 2000). The agreement with Heinz Haupt was also dogged by allegations that in return to financial inducements given by the German group to top NEC officials, the NEC Board undervalued the subsidiary considerably, allowing the group to acquire a majority shareholding at a low cost (Tangri and Mwenda 2013, 142). By 2005, NEC entered a different joint venture, with Healthworld Group, and the company changed its name to NEC Health World Pharmaceuticals (Losse et al. 2007). According to local pharmacists, however, the company never produced anything. NEC Pharmaceuticals eventually closed down (Parliament of Ugnada 2015, 11).

In short, the Ugandan government only minimally invested in state-owned pharmaceutical production. Without either state or foreign support, the pharmaceutical factories in the public sector existed mostly on paper. Until the 1990s, there was also no private pharmaceutical sector to speak of, and the factories that eventually opened were initially small and fragile, as I describe below.

## Making Medicine (2): Unmaking, Then Remaking Entrepreneurs

Although there was no private pharmaceutical industry in Uganda in the 1970s, the nineteen retail and wholesale pharmacies that operated in the country then also engaged in some form of small-scale basic production. They mostly produced skin preparations, solutions and suspensions intended for oral administration, composite powders, eye lotions, and dietetic preparations.[50] Production in these facilities did not follow basic quality standards. A report mentioned that these producers made no records of the manufacture or distribution of the drugs, and the labels did not give a batch number or the date of manufacture; there were spelling errors and misleading claims on some labels.[51] Only three establishments manufactured "sufficient quantities" to be mentioned by name in official reports. These were Opa Laboratories, Nakivubo Chemists, and Universal Pharmacy.[52] We know little of these factories other than that Nakivubo and Universal Pharmacy "operate on such a small scale that they may not be able to afford all quality control facilities."[53] Opa Laboratories, which opened in the late 1950s in Jinja, was more established. It had large premises, made tablets, and exported drugs to neighboring countries.[54] A WHO consultant in 1973 referred to it as "the only important drug manufacturer" in Uganda and assessed the following:

> This factory could make a real contribution to the drug manufacture in Uganda, but great improvements are needed. The drugs are manufactured under very unhygienic conditions, without supervision by qualified personnel, identification of raw materials or any other form of quality control at any stage of manufacture. There are four tablet machines, two granulators and one drying oven in the small tableting room. This could easily result in mixing of powders and leaves, and other errors. There is no order at all in the raw materials store. . . . The writer understands that some of the samples taken from the factory by the inspector did not meet the standard specifications, as could be expected in view of the operating conditions.[55]

Minimal production capacity was partly due to weak industrial policies; for example, the consultant noted that Uganda "imposes customs duties on some raw materials while finished products made with the same raw materials are exempt from duty."[56] Lack of manufacturing standards, too, was the result of insufficient government action.

> The problem is that the Government, even if it wanted to, could not enforce quality control of its own products or those of other establishments . . . as it has insufficient facilities and personnel to control all the products manufactured in Uganda today. . . . Moreover, the Government has insufficient staff for inspection of the drug factories. Even if it did assign some of the government pharmacists as drug inspectors, none at present has sufficient experience of drug manufacture and quality control to adequately advice manufacturers on various technical aspects of drug manufacture and control. [57]

Whatever potential these establishments had to become formal pharmaceutical factories—the local manufacturers that opened in Kenya in the 1980s had also started as small facilities (chapter 3)—the political transformations in

Uganda drastically reversed their trajectory. The report from 1973 mentioned that "Nakivubo expanded its plant and acquired new equipment, but the writer is reliably informed that they have recently decided to abandon the project," and that "Universal Pharmacy has reduced its production, and the management intends to sell the business."[58]

Not only did existing establishments close down, but also no new establishments opened up. When Museveni took power in 1986, drug production in Uganda was reported to be "negligible."[59] Haakonsson (2009b) quotes an officer at the Ugandan National Drugs Authority (NDA) saying: "All the factories stopped. Some facilities were closed down and some were not cared for." There were no raw materials, basic packing materials, water supply, or electricity. Equipment was broken down. There was no technical know-how."[60] Lack of know-how was exacerbated by the fact that by expelling Indians, Amin expelled the commercial, industrial, and professional elite of the country. In what follows, I describe the conditions in the private sector and the means by which entrepreneurship was first unmade, and then somewhat revived.

## NO PHARMACY EDUCATION, NO PHARMACISTS

As in Kenya and Tanganyika, the British government neglected the education of the population in Uganda. At the end of World War I, mission schools, aided by state subsidies, had only about 90,000 African students enrolled out of population of more than 3 million (Jørgensen 1981, 62); and only in the 1920s did the British government take direct control of education in the territory (Mamdani 1976, 160–61). As in Kenya and Tanganyika, a racialized colonial order meant that Indians in Uganda fared better than Africans.[61] As for higher education, Uganda had the distinction of having the first college in the region, Makerere College, which opened in 1922; and enrollment at the College favored Ugandans over students from Kenya or Tanganyika (Mamdani 1976, 163). A decade later, the courses offered included medicine, engineering, agriculture, and veterinary science. They did not include pharmacy (Goldthorpe 1965, 9–10). University status was granted in 1949 through special relations with the University of London, and the College's name changed to Makerere College, the University College of East Africa (Goldthorpe 1965, 12). With independence, the special relations with the University of London were terminated, and the newly renamed Makerere University College became part of a regional conglomerate called the University of East Africa, with the Royal College of Nairobi in Kenya and the University College of Dar es Salaam in Tanzania. This cooperation disbanded in 1970, and Makerere became an independent national university. After independence the university experienced a "period of vitality," but Amin's rise to power marked "the beginning of the university's spiral of deterioration" (Byaruhanga 2013, 21). Amin imposed cutbacks in resources, and, combined with an outflow of professors to countries abroad, the University's academic prestige was destroyed. As a result, Uganda was falling behind its neighbors in professional education (Byaruhanga 2013, 21). Whereas Kenya and Tanzania opened a pharmacy school in 1974, Uganda opened one—at Makerere University—only in 1988. In the early 1990s, the intake was about ten students per year (WHO 1994a, 5).[62]

Uganda also faced difficulties sending students to pharmacy schools abroad, though Indians again had easier access abroad than indigenous Africans. According to a WHO report, only 25 African and 31 Indian students from Uganda were pursuing pharmacy degrees abroad in 1973.[63] Of the 25 African students, moreover, 17 studied at institutions that were not recognized by the Pharmaceutical Society of Uganda and would not be able to work as pharmacists upon their return. (However, at least one student who had graduated from such an institution later worked as a senior dispenser at Mulago hospital.) The remaining African students included 3 studying in the UK and 1 in Canada; a student in the UK "abandoned pharmacy," and there was "no trace" of 2 students in the US. Of the Indian Ugandan students, 30 studied in the UK and 1 in the US, all in schools with qualifications recognized in Uganda.[64]

A slightly condescending WHO report listed the disadvantages of foreign training compared to domestic one.

> The present intention of the [Ugandan] Government . . . is to train its pharmacists abroad. The pharmacy courses are very competitive in the countries whose qualifications are acceptable to the Pharmaceutical Society of Uganda. This poses a big problem as it is highly unlikely that the Government will be able to place its students in the institutions of the countries in question, by normal admission arrangements. If, however, the Government makes special arrangements to place a large number of students, it will probably have to pay the full cost . . . of training instead of the normal fees only. . . . [The cost] may well prove more expensive in cash and kind than starting a school of pharmacy in Makerere. Also, training students overseas involves greater wastage owing to problems of climate and adjustment in the foreign environment. Also, it may be assumed that students have knowledge which was not in fact taught during their pre-university education in their own countries. . . . Finally, training in overseas institutions is geared to meet the needs of those countries which are technologically advanced and have highly trained personnel. [65]

As a result of these limited educational opportunities, both at home and abroad, there were very few pharmacists in Uganda, and—reflecting the unequal access since colonialism—the majority of them were of Indian origin. In 1971, there were at most 75 pharmacists in Uganda, "only about 10 of which are Ugandan nationals." Amin's expulsion of Indian Ugandans that year therefore devastated the profession.[66] By 1979, the number of pharmacists declined to 15 (Dodge 1986, 755). It wasn't until the opening of the pharmacy school in Makerere University in 1988 that those numbers started to go back up significantly—by the mid-1990s there were about 100 registered pharmacists in the country (WHO 1994a, 5).

## EXPELLING, AND THEN REVIVING, THE COMMERCIAL CLASS

A shortage of pharmacists limited the number of retail pharmacies and wholesalers.[67] In 1971, there were only eighteen registered retailers in the entire country (most also engaged in wholesale activities).[68] Even these modest commercial seeds were effectively suppressed during the Amin era. The parastatal UPL monopolized trade in pharmaceutical products in the private market; and, in a move that proved to be crucial to pharmaceutical trading, Amin expelled the Indians, who were at the heart of commerce in Uganda. The dominance of Ugandans of Indian origin in the commercial sector in the country was, like their higher level of education, a colonial legacy—helped by discriminatory policies put in place by the British. Even in the 1950s, after the colonial government instituted policies favoring African small entrepreneurship, the approximately 12,000 African traders constituted more than 70 percent of all traders in numbers, but they controlled only one-third of the retail trade; the rest of the retail industry was either in the hands of Indians or of British export-import houses. After independence, in spite of the government's attempts to expand the base of African retail trade, the Indian community continued to dominate the wholesale and retail trade (Mamdani 1976). Even under Obote's Move to the Left, "the measures to effect Africanization of commerce were enforced . . . slowly . . . and loosely" (Jørgensen 1981, 248). Certainly in the pharmaceutical field, expelling the Indian community meant expelling those who had "formed the backbone of the trading community which linked the pharmaceutical industry in distribution of medical supplies throughout the country" (Dodge 1986, 755). A decade later, in 1980, there were still only sixteen private pharmacies in Uganda.[69]

Commerce expanded with political stability, and by the 1990s there were around 120 pharmacies in Uganda (WHO 1994a, 4). Many small drug importing businesses also opened. The revived commercial pharmaceutical sector included indigenous Africans—thanks to the opening of the pharmacy school, but also to the vacuum created by the expulsion of the commercial elite. Still, a large share of the commercial sector in pharmaceutical goods was taken over by entrepreneurs who were not indigenous Africans. These included some Indian Ugandan "returnees," as after the overthrow of the Amin regime, subsequent governments asked them to return with the promise of returned property.[70] However, returnees did not generally show an interest in pharmaceuticals and were instead more likely to invest in real estate or the hospitality sector.[71] Other entrepreneurs in the pharmaceutical field included Kenyans and Tanzanians of Indian origin, and Indian nationals coming from India. This was the case with the Ugandan economy more generally, which saw many of the investors coming from abroad (Bigsten and Kayizzi-Mugerwa 2001). Indian nationals were particularly active in the pharmaceutical commercial sector: because there was no "trading infrastructure" in that field and minimal local competition, non-Ugandans found it easy to "take the first part of the market."[72] Indeed, starting in the 1990s, Indian nationals reportedly dominated the "pharmacy village" on William Street in Kampala, where dozens of pharmaceutical importers have been selling their goods.[73]

## PHARMACEUTICAL MANUFACTURING AFTER AMIN

In pharmaceutical manufacturing, as in commerce, there was hardly any infrastructure to draw on—so while a pharmaceutical sector did emerge in the 1990s, it was small and fragile. Similarly to Kenya and Tanzania, some of the first entrepreneurs were locals of Indian origin who relied on access to education and ties abroad to establish their businesses. However, Uganda also saw, as part of its first wave of post-Amin entrepreneurship, a new type of investors—locals without much capital or ties abroad.

Indian Ugandan entrepreneurship in the pharmaceutical field echoed a general dominance in the industrial sector that, as was the case in the commercial sector, started under colonialism and was greatly shaped by the British racialized colonial order. Indians' move to industry in this case was in part in response to the fact that starting in the 1940s, the colonial state was acquiring ginneries from Indians and transferring them to African cooperatives. According to Mamdani (1976): "Expelled from the processing sector of the economy, Indian capital looked for other profitable investment opportunities," which they found in the manufacturing sector that the British state created after World War II. After independence, as mentioned above, industry was mainly state-controlled, but Indian Ugandans were able to expand their manufacturing investments through partnerships with the parastatal UDC. In fact, they played such a dominant role that "by 1966, more significant than the state's investments in manufacturing were those of Uganda Indian capitalists" (Mamdani 1976, 258). Other investors included large Indian groups from Kenya and Tanzania (Stoutjesdijk 1967, 11, Mamdani 1976, 259–60).

The expulsion of Indian businessmen left a serious gap in terms of investment in manufacturing, as it did in commerce, especially in such fields as pharmaceuticals, which required technical background, experience, and international connections (Livingstone 1998, 46). When industrial production again increased after 1986, a number of returnees were among the first to establish pharmaceutical production facilities. These returnees had similar trajectories as the entrepreneurs in Kenya and in Tanzania, with an overseas pharmacy education, experience in pharmaceutical trading, and reliance on ties with India. These companies grew over time and proved relatively resilient.

Kampala Pharmaceutical Industries (KPI) was opened in 1992. The founder, Aziz Damani, was born in Kampala. He had UK citizenship and attended pharmacy school in the UK, graduating in 1966. After graduation, he worked in the pharmaceutical sectors in the UK, Tanzania, and Zambia. In the late 1980s, he was back in the UK, where he owned two pharmacies. With the encouragement of his brother, Karim Hirji, who had stayed in Uganda during the Amin regime and had become one of the most successful businessmen in the country, in 1991 Damani returned to Uganda and set up a pharmaceutical factory. Damani reportedly invested $3.2 million in the factory, and he was proud of the fact that in 1994 President Museveni officially presided over the opening of the plant. Damani hired twelve experts from India to run the factory—including in production, quality control, and engineering. In 1996, Damani sold the company to the Industrial Promotion Services (IPS), a for-profit company under the Aga Khan Fund for Economic Development (chapter 8).[74]

The origins of Rene Industries are similar, albeit more modest. The company was founded by a married couple, Rishi and Meera Vadodaria. Rishi Vadodaria, a Ugandan of Indian origin, received a degree in chemistry in Pune, India. (He later also pursued an MBA). Meera Vadodaria also received a chemistry degree in Pune, and after returning to Uganda, she pursued a pharmacy degree from Makerere University. When they returned in 1984, they initially opened a small business that had nothing to do with pharmaceuticals; a few years later they opened an import drug company, Rene Pharmacy, on William Street. In 1998, they opened the manufacturing company, Rene Industries. This firm, too, hired Indian nationals with experience in pharmaceutical manufacturing.[75]

The Dawda Group, which acquired UPL when it was privatized in 1996, followed a different path—similar to the experience of Khanbhai and Shelys in Tanzania. The Group was founded by a Kenyan of Indian origin, Hasmukh Dawda, and began investing in a variety of businesses in Uganda starting in 1990. In addition to large industrial enterprises, Dawda also owned pharmacies and, at the time, was a wholesale agent for a number of Indian pharmaceutical companies. In the early 2000s, Dawda sold 70 percent of its UPL shares to Libyan investors, however, who closed UPL in 2010 (chapter 8).

Importantly, Uganda in the 1990s also saw the emergence of African Ugandan entrepreneurs in the pharmaceutical commercial and industrial sectors, who were generally absent in Kenya's or Tanzania's first generation of pharmaceutical manufacturers. According to Livingstone (1998), this was thanks to the fact that, "the vacuum created [by the expulsion of the Asians] has stimulated the growth of an African business class, while it is evident that the economy has now been effectively Ugandanized in terms of managers, technicians and skilled workers, whatever problems exist in respect of acquired skills and experience at all levels." In the pharmaceutical sector, these entrepreneurs at times faced serious difficulties—often because they were not pharmacists, lacked ties at home or abroad, and had little business experience.

Inlex, which opened in 1986, was unique in being a partnership between an Indian Ugandan and two African Ugandans. The company had "modern laboratories and factory equipment for the production of various drugs," but, according to reports, it was from the beginning "marred by ownership wrangles, poor management and sheer greed for money at the expense of international pharmacology standards." The managing director of Uganda Development Bank allegedly authorized a large loan of $2.7 million to Inlex in return for 25 percent of the shares in the company, which he then gave to his son who was still a student at the time. This came up in a dispute, in the course of which, "The Board Chairman and founder of the company, Mr. Dilip Adatia [was] locked out of the company by his fellow directors." The company's reputation suffered independently of this specific dispute. For example, a newspaper article in *Weekly Topic*, with the headline "Beware: firm produces 2mn expired tablets" claimed that Inlex manufactured chloroquine phosphate tablets out of materials that had expired.[76]

In addition to Inlex, four other pharmaceutical firms were owned by African Ugandans.[77] Bychem Laboratories, which Livingtone Kintu Ssalongo opened in 1997, was closed within a decade, but not before getting into an ugly battle with another pharmaceutical company, Mavid Pharmaceuticals, which was opened by Sulaiman Bukenya in 1995 but which also ultimately closed (UNIDO 1997, Kaaya 2014). The other two companies fared better. Kisakye Industries was opened by Kitumba Benjamin Benson in 1999. Although the founder was not a pharmacist, he had a "diploma in medicine" and worked in government hospitals for three years before first owning a drug shop and then two pharmacies/wholesales.[78] He later started manufacturing, albeit initially without machines and with only one product, cough syrup. He eventually had machines fabricated locally and was then able to import machines from India as well, although production remained on a very small scale.[79]

Finally, of the small factories, the "most interesting" and likely the most successful one was Medipharm Industries (EA), which was opened in 1982 by an African Ugandan couple, Rogers Collins Seguya and Rebecca Seguya.[80] Before turning to manufacturing, they had opened a company for the importation and retailing of drugs and medical devices in 1971, called Overseas Trading Company. In 1978, they started a small mixing and compounding unit, still in their small retail outlet on William Street. Eventually they moved to a manufacturing unit and started production in 1984. Foreign aid was instrumental in the company's beginning, as "building modifications" and "procurement of critical production and quality control" equipment were "made possible through funding from the [World Bank's] International Development Agency, through Uganda Commercial Bank."[81] Initially, the company only "produce[d] a few drugs (e.g., cough syrup) and [planned] to produce eye drops, injectables and also cosmetics." Medipharm also "started producing ORS [oral rehydration salts] on an experimental basis in very small quantities."[82] In 1985, it only produced 1,000 packets, compared to the 1.8 million packets that were distributed in total in Uganda that year. This initial production was suspended in 1986, but it still piqued the interest of donors who were at this time promoting in Uganda the use of ORS as the basic treatment of diarrheal diseases among children.[83] The writer of a 1986 feasibility study was not convinced by Medipharm's capabilities or quality standards, and yet in 1988, Medipharm signed an agreement with UNICEF, the United States Agency for International Development (USAID), and the Program for Appropriate Technology in Health (PATH) for the production and distribution of ORS.[84] The program was not free; rather, the donors offered loans for the purchase of equipment, plant redesign, and marketing activities (SCRIP 1991b). However, PATH, which was involved in the project for five years, also provided training in production, distribution, and marketing.[85] By 1992, Medipharm's ORS total production capacity was 1,650,000 sachets, of which it sold around 800,000 to the Ugandan government, leaving the rest for sale in the private market (PATH 1992a). PATH reviews expressed concerns for both excess production capacity *and* low productivity (PATH 1992b). One of the challenges was leakage, as "Medipharm reported recurrent sales of the MOH public sector ORS packets in private shops and pharmacies" (PATH 1992b, 3). Partly as a result, Medipharm was losing money on its private brand (PATH 1992b). Low productivity—the estimated capacity utilization was 40 percent—was the result of absenteeism, adjustments to machines, unavailability of facilities, and power failures (PATH 1992c). Other concerns included the fact that PATH quality assurance policies were not implemented, even though the expected procedures were basic, as the training sessions described below clearly indicate (PATH 1992c, 2):

A one-day session was held to train Medipharm personnel in developing a production planning and inventory control system; three products were used as a model to plan 24 months of production and raw and packaging materials inventory. Medipharm has not yet developed a network of local, regional, and/or international sources of machinery spares parts and service/repair organizations. To achieve this objective, a visit to British-American Tobacco, which is one of the largest and most organized companies in Uganda, was arranged. As a result, local and regional sources were identified. After an evaluation was made of Medipharm's adherence to GMPs, several recommendations were made for improvement.

This initiative had characteristics that foreign aid in support of local pharmaceutical production followed later on: the creation of a potential market combined with technical transfer and monitoring of quality. (Later foreign assistance rarely came as loans and quality standards were more carefully monitored). The direct impact of this initiative on the firm cannot be fully evaluated because of insufficient data about Medipharm at the time. Nonetheless, for a small company, Medipharm did relatively well and avoided many of the challenges faced by other Ugandan pharmaceutical firms at the time.

To summarize, the emergence of a local pharmaceutical industry was delayed in Uganda in part due to the absence of nascent pharmacists-entrepreneurs (Kohli 2004), which was a result of lack of access to pharmacy education, lack of on-the-ground experience in the pharmaceutical field, and the severing of potential ties abroad that would have been able to compensate for the local scarcity. Hence, when the ration kits were introduced in the mid-1980s, there was no private pharmaceutical industry that could have benefited from a local component. Eventually, slowly, a pharmaceutical sector did emerge in Uganda, but initially this sector was even more vulnerable than the one that emerged in Tanzania. Some of the entrepreneurs in Uganda, among them Indian Ugandan returnees, did have educational background and/or experience that allowed them a basic foundation. Their companies continued to grow and became quite dominant in the sector later on. Others opened factories without such foundation, and these factories were less likely to remain operational. Notably, one of the small but relatively successful factories was an early beneficiary of foreign aid. Even those that stayed open, however, remained quite small, as I describe in the next section.

## The Ugandan Pharmaceutical Sector in the 1990s

When a DANIDA mission tried to evaluate local pharmaceutical manufacturers in Uganda in August 1990, they found little to report on:

> Little is known about their production capacity or of the quality and quantity of produced drugs. . . . Almost no information is available on [private] manufacturers. However, CMS has placed orders at one local manufacturer who failed to supply. Another manufacture has supplied a few items to JMS but the quality of these drugs has been questioned. [86]

Things developed in the following years, so that by 1994 a WHO mission learned that, "One of the manufacturers is in the last stages of finishing the construction of a new product facility. The other two are also in the process of renovating and expanding their production facilities" (WHO 1994a, 5). Although it remained extremely small, by the end of the decade, a private pharmaceutical sector could be said to exist, reportedly growing at almost four times the average rate for total industrial production.[87]

Based on the information we have from the end of the 1990s, it is clear that only few of the companies were of a notable size. The factory with the largest installed capacity was NEC Pharmaceuticals, which at full capacity could reportedly produce 400 million tablets (this was one-third of the capacity of TPI in Tanzania), 90 million capsules (this was more than Tanzania's total capacity), 200,000 liters of antibiotics and 192,000 liters of syrups per year, in addition to nine metric tons of creams and ointments and five metric tons of toothpaste per year (Muwanga 2002). This factory's production capacity was severely under-utilized, however (UNIDO 1997, 29). The other relatively large companies were Rene and KPI. In 1997, KPI had 200 employees. In contrast, UPL had 30 employees, and Medipharm had only 20 (UNIDO 1997, 29). Mavid, Kisakye, and Bychem were even smaller than Medipharm.

All these companies produced simple drugs, including simple antibiotics, analgesics and antipyretics, cough preparations, and antacids (WHO 1994a). KPI stood out as producing a relatively broad range of 110 drugs. Other than KPI, only UPL and Rene produced tablets and capsules. Medipharm, in addition to producing ORS, mostly manufactured "liquid pharmaceutical dosage forms (solutions for oral and external use, syrups, suspensions, etc.)." Mavid and Kisakye only produced solutions. Bychem produced linctus, suspensions, and liniment (UNIDO 1997, 29, Uganda Invest 2002).

As for quality standards, Uganda's first attempt to regulate drug quality standards was in 1952 (WHO 2002, 36), and in 1970, the *Pharmacy and Drugs Act No. 39* was enacted, "well in advance of similar legislation in east and west African countries." The 1970 law "brought under control the import, export, retail, manufacture of drugs and other related activities," and it "instituted machinery" for drug registration. However, most of the Act was not immediately implemented, partly due to vague regulation; and, in any case, the Act "could not be implemented without a large number of pharmacists, some with special training," which Uganda did not have.[88] The responsible agency at the time, the Office of Chief Pharmacist, had only two employees "that did everything." There was an approval process for imported drugs, but "there was no discretion—[they] stamped everything."[89] Other drug buyers in Uganda also had difficulty assuring quality of local products. "There is no quality control laboratory. . . . In case of drugs bought from local sources, JMS sends samples to the Netherlands for testing" (WHO 1994a). In 1993, Uganda passed a major new piece of drug regulatory legislation, the National Drug Authority Statute, which took time to implement and which I discuss in chapter 8.

In that legal context, even the more reputable pharmaceutical companies in Uganda did not follow quality standards. KPI, according to one interviewer, produced dozens of products, "but possibly with questionable quality." A 1986 review of Medipharm was critical. "The available space for production and storage is very limited and the overall planning of the factory seems impractical. Although the premises are new, they are hardly in line with GMP standards." Still, the same review also mentioned that, "the quality of drugs appears to be of primary importance to the company," that "an analytical and a microbiological laboratory [were] available," and that the "manufactured ORS [was] analyzed according to methods recommended by WHO/UNICEF (basic tests)."[90] Ten years later, after the foreign aid program already started, the review was even more cautiously positive. "The manufacturing premises . . . are kept clean and are continuously improved. The QC [quality control] laboratory seems to be working actively." Still, "Facilities, machinery and equipment are not qualified . . . and production processes are not validated" (UNIDO 1997, 29).

## Discussion

With the exception of a modest program supporting one small pharmaceutical firm, there was no foreign aid that benefited local pharmaceutical production in Uganda in the 1980s and 1990s. Indeed, it is hard to imagine that it would have changed the situation much under Amin, where the private sector was destroyed and the public sector overwhelmed to the point of paralysis, or during the civil unrest that followed. At the time, the state-owned pharmaceutical factories did poorly, if they operated at all, and none of the very small manufacturing facilities that had opened in the 1970s survived. Amin's decision to expel the commercial and industrial elite of the country, combined with the fact that there was no pharmacy school in Uganda until 1988 and only minimal opportunities to study abroad, meant that there were no pharmacists-entrepreneurs who could possibly take advantage of opportunities even if those were to exist. However, foreign aid would have made a difference during the recovery period starting in the late 1980s. The experience of Medipharm suggests as much. Yet the ration kits program that started in 1988 did not include a local component, and without foreign aid—and given the local conditions in place—the pharmaceutical industrial sector that emerged in the 1990s was as fragile as the one that emerged in Tanzania in the 1980s, and in some ways more so. Pharmacists-entrepreneurs who relied on know-how, experience, and ties abroad were here joined by entrepreneurs with financial capital. They were also joined by entrepreneurs, with neither knowledge nor funds. Many of these eventually closed.

Given the very basic state of local drug manufacturing in Uganda, it is hard to argue that donations of drugs had the effect of undermining the development of a local industry, as was more likely the case in Tanzania. Donations were nevertheless criticized, mostly for the conditions attached to the funds, which forced the Ugandan government to buy expansive drugs. One report explained: "Purchases from these bilateral transactions have to be made from the countries of the respective donors," which often were punitively expensive.[91] "The prices of brand-name drugs in the USA . . . are at least 5 times as expensive as their cheapest generic alternative, so that the actual available value for drugs provided . . . was substantially less than" what was given.[92] A similar issue—of brand-name drugs being substantially more expensive than generics—dominated the struggle over access to antiretrovirals (ARVs) and greatly shaped the characteristics of foreign aid in the 2000s. In the following chapters I discuss the effect of foreign aid on local pharmaceutical production in Kenya, Tanzania, and Uganda in the context of global donations of generic drugs.

# 6

# Kenya in the 2000s

## DEVELOPMENTAL FOREIGN AID (1)

And you have got to look at the period around 2000. . . . Things happened here. One, we had the TRIPS coming into effect, which raise[d] a lot of awareness on HIV and on malaria. Number two, we had Global Fund coming in place. Then number three, we had treatment guidelines changing. So these things brought a lot of pressure on the local industry.

—WILBERFORCE O. WANYANGA, A PHARMACEUTICAL QUALITY SYSTEMS
CONSULTANT, KENYA, DECEMBER 14, 2012

Quality standards were only of minimal concern in international discussions on local pharmaceutical production in the 1980s when locally owned pharmaceutical factories just opened in East Africa, but they became an increasingly important consideration starting in the 1990s. Due to public health concerns—and at a time that market liberalization led to increased imports of drugs from semi-regulated countries—Kenya, Tanzania, and Uganda all introduced, with the insistence and assistance of the World Health Organization (WHO) and other development agencies, legislation aimed to better regulate the manufacturing and distribution of drugs. Health considerations and political-economic realities often clash, however. For local pharmaceutical manufacturers in East Africa, who were competing over price with low-cost imports and with each other, quality—which would have increased the cost of production—was not a priority. Nor was it always a priority for their governments, which did not have the means, skills, or political will to enforce the quality standards they had put in place.

Because donors and development agencies were motivated by a different set of considerations, their decisions sometimes undercut the financial interests of local pharmaceutical producers in places like Kenya. One often-cited example of a potential clash between international development agencies and local manufacturers was treatment guidelines, including the decision by the Kenyan government in 2004 to adopt artemisinin-based combination therapy (ACT) as a first-line treatment for uncomplicated malaria, using artemether-lumefantrine (AL). At the time, no Kenyan manufacturer produced AL—and many, as a result, lost the malaria market that they had heavily relied on (Amin et al. 2007). According to one pharmacist, "[the] policy change to AL . . . messed up the local industry."[1] Because under the new treatment guidelines the only eligible ACT initially was Coartem, which was produced by the Swiss pharmaceutical company Novartis, at least one local producer blamed Novartis for the decision: "With their muscle, their drug, Coartem, became the drug of choice."[2] Tellingly, local producers also blamed development agencies. Because the decision followed WHO recommendations, the Kenyan government was blamed for "danc[ing] to the tune of the WHO."[3]

Another example of a potential clash between international agencies and local manufacturers was the way international agencies resolved the tension between drug cost and quality—by funding the purchase of drugs, either generic or brand-name, only as long as the drugs followed acceptable quality standards as certified by credible agencies, including the WHO prequalification (PQ) of Medicines Programme (chapter 1). When shortly after being established in 2002, the Global Fund to Fight AIDS, Tuberculosis and Malaria introduced this policy, both donors and recipient countries understood that it posed significant barriers to market entry (WHO 2009). In the debate over the use of the WHO PQ scheme by the Global Fund, an important concern for many recipients was, "What will this do to our local industry?"[4] The expectation was that stringent quality requirements would inhibit local production of drugs.[5]

In certain ways, this expectation proved accurate. The public market for antiretrovirals (ARVs) and ACTs in Kenya was almost entirely funded by the Global Fund, the US President's Emergency Plan for AIDS Relief (PEP-FAR), and the US President's Malaria Initiative (PMI)—and all of the ARVs and ACTs purchased with these funds were imported. Yet, I show in this chapter that international programs were critical in upgrading the practices of many local manufacturers: once the Global Fund, the German Technical Cooperation Agency (GTZ), and other donors got involved in the Kenyan drug market, local manufacturers began to produce a broader range of complex drugs, including ARVs and ACTs, and to invest in high quality standards—including standards that surpassed what was required by national laws. One local manufacturer,

Universal Corporation, got a drug prequalified by the WHO, and three local firms—Universal, Cosmos, and Regal—successfully passed inspections that certified that they were following European quality standards. Although other local companies failed to attain such certificates, in the course of trying to achieve them, they adopted better production practices. I argue that these changes were thanks to three resources that were not available locally and that foreign aid was able to provide—markets, monitoring, and mentoring. Markets created with donors' funding encouraged local manufacturers to produce new types of drugs; effective monitoring through stringent quality requirements assured that these local producers followed strict quality standards; and mentoring offered the technical know-how required for producing sophisticated drugs while meeting the required standards.

Chapter 3, on the emergence of a pharmaceutical sector in Kenya, concluded with a description of the sector in 1990. This chapter begins with a description of the sector twenty years later, in 2010. In the course of these two decades, much has changed. The sector became one of the largest pharmaceutical sectors in sub-Saharan Africa, consisting of around twenty companies, with an estimated market share of 28 percent; but the sector was also more differentiated—in regard to size, product complexity, and quality standards. The less sophisticated firms tended to be the newer ones, and, in that context, I describe the emergence of a new kind of a local pharmaceutical company— one that did not rely on ties abroad or political connections at home that had benefited the first generation of drug manufacturers back in the 1980s. In the remainder of the chapter, I focus on the larger pharmaceutical firms and describe the conditions that led them to invest in new products and higher quality standards. I show that this was based, in large part, on the companies' access to markets, monitoring, and mentoring—provided to them through foreign aid. At a time when the Kenyan government supported the local pharmaceutical industry only minimally and did not effectively enforce its quality regulations, the desire to access donors' markets, which were open only to quality-assured drugs, encouraged local manufacturers to invest in new drugs and improve their production practices. Similarly, technical know-how, which was not available locally, was provided by development agencies—through audits, workshops, and other forms of training. In chapter 3, I showed that in the 1980s, in addition to state support, ties abroad, which offered access to technical know-how, and social ties at home, which contributed to the local diffusion of that know-how, also helped with the emergence of a pharmaceutical sector in Kenya. In this chapter I argue that, by 2010, informal ties abroad became less useful as the industry grew more sophisticated; and while commercial relations with foreign companies contributed to some differentiation among the larger Kenyan companies, these connections did not affect the trajectory of the sector the way they did in Tanzania and Uganda, as I describe in the next two chapters. Still, the interest in mentoring was in part thanks to local networks, which helped diffuse awareness to quality standards, at times independently of the incentives offered.

In what follows, I first describe the Kenyan pharmaceutical sector as of 2010. I begin the analysis of the conditions that led at least some pharmaceutical companies in Kenya to invest in new drugs and better quality standards with the international context—specifically, the negotiations that led development agencies to give their support to local pharmaceutical production, in addition to drug donations and stringent quality standards. I then show that in a domestic context in which markets were small, quality enforcement weak, and technical know-how lacking, foreign aid—by promising markets, imposing monitoring, and offering mentoring—shaped the trajectory of the pharmaceutical sector in Kenya at the time. I conclude the chapter with a discussion of both the promises and the pitfalls of the foreign aid programs as experienced by Kenyan pharmaceutical firms.

## The Kenyan Pharmaceutical Sector in 2010: Old Patterns and New Practices

The trajectory of the pharmaceutical industry in Kenya from 1990 to 2010 should be examined in light of a challenging political-economic context, where the manufacturing industry overall remained relatively underdeveloped. In response to the debt crisis of the 1980s, in which many highly indebted developing countries were not able to service their international debt, the World Bank and the International Monetary Fund (IMF) provided "structural adjustment" lending aimed at market-liberalizing policy reforms (Frieden 2006). In Kenya, the economic and political reforms that started in the mid-1980s and intensified in the early-1990s included, as in many other countries, trade liberalization, exchange rate depreciation, privatization, elimination of exchange controls, and abolishment of price controls (Swamy 1994, Simonetti, Clark, and Wamae 2016). Although Kenya remained the most industrially developed country in East Africa, in the course of these transformations, the manufacturing share of its GDP increased only modestly—from an average of 11.95 percent in 1975–80 to an average of 13.36 percent in 2005–10.[6] Moreover, most manufacturing remained in the processing of agricultural products. Manufacturing firms continued to face serious challenges: structural adjustment reforms limited the extent to which manufacturing could be supported through industrial policies or other governmental measures and allowed for increased international competition, domestic and regional markets were small, the legal and regulatory frameworks were weak, and strategic management and technical skills were not available. In addition, manufacturers faced underdeveloped infrastructure, as well as costly, unstable supplies of energy and water; they had limited access to financial services, and they depended on imports for machinery, raw materials, and packaging materials (Anderson 2010, UNIDO 2010a, Hope 2011).

Local drug manufacturers experienced a similar set of challenges. Compared to the 1980s, the state was much less supportive of the sector at the same time that, as I describe in chapter 2, liberalization led to increased international competition from generic producers in the global South. The pharmaceutical sector nevertheless advanced since 1990 and was considered "a significant aspect of Kenya's industrial sector" and "a major force shaping the economics of medication use" (MoH Kenya 2003, 10). So even though the pharmaceutical sector contributed only about 2 percent of Manufacturing Value Added in the Kenyan economy as of 2008, and though the sector suffered from low capacity utilization (UNIDO 2010a, table 18), according to a number of indicators, it was doing quite well and was "the most well-established pharmaceutical manufacturing industry in the [East African] region" (MoI, MMS and UNIDO 2011). With twenty pharmaceutical companies, the sector was "at the forefront in the number of established [firms]" (Losse et al. 2007, 34).[7] Kenya was also one of the three largest local producers of medicine in sub-Saharan Africa, behind Nigeria but on par with Ghana, not counting South Africa where 70 percent of sub-Saharan Africa's pharmaceutical production was concentrated (IFC 2007, figure A3.2).[8] Local producers' market share in Kenya was estimated to be 28 percent (not including donor-funded purchases), which was much higher than that of local firms in either Tanzania or Uganda, both around 10–15 percent (UNIDO 2010a).[9]

The growth of the local pharmaceutical sector was in part reflection of the growth of the drug market in Kenya, including both government procurement and the private market—with more individuals paying for drugs out of pocket or with health insurance schemes. It was difficult to compete with imported drugs, especially generics from India (chapter 2), but local manufacturers were able to preserve a respectable market share in the private sector, where some local producers sold low-valued products that were of lesser interest to importers, whereas others successfully marketed branded generics. Local manufacturers also enjoyed better supply chain and distribution networks.[10]

Data on registered drugs, however, indicate a decline in the number of drugs registered by local producers and in their rate since 2000, as I also discuss in chapter 2. Between 1991 and 2000, local manufacturers registered 819 drugs, which was 23 percent of the 3,539 drugs registered during that period in total. Between 2001 and 2010, local manufacturers registered 751 new drugs, which was only 14 percent of the 5,289 drugs registered during that period in total. This decline could be partly attributed to the fact that that many of the larger Kenyan drug firms were already established and, therefore, kept selling the same drugs that they had been selling in the past, whereas the high rate of registration of imported drugs reflected a relatively high turnover of foreign companies. However, the decline in both the number and rate of drugs registered by local firms is also compatible with an assessment by the United Nations Industrial Development Organization (UNIDO) that "domestic sales [of local firms'] products remain stagnant or are even declining, and this at a time when the Kenyan market is growing" (UNIDO 2010a, 42).

This stagnation in the domestic market was offset by expansion into export markets—mostly to Tanzania and Uganda, but also to other Eastern and Southern African countries (MMS and MPHS 2010, UNIDO 2010a). Estimates suggest that at least one-third of the total annual turnover for local production was exports, and that the larger Kenyan pharmaceutical companies derived as much as half of their annual turnover from export sales (IFC 2007, 76, UNIDO 2010a, various interviews).

Kenyan manufacturers performed relatively well in the Tanzanian and Ugandan markets for a number of reasons. First, they established themselves in those countries early (chapter 3).[11] As the Kenyan pharmaceutical trade association described on its website: "Between the [19]70s and [19]80s—a period of turmoil and civil wars, skirmishes and political instability—the medical care needs in the neighboring countries were easily sourced here." Later, economic and political stability increased demand for drugs in those countries (UNIDO 2010a). Moreover, Kenyan producers benefited from the fact that the demand remained sufficiently small. When a market consisted of small volumes, importers from India could ship the products in one of two ways: either ship "less-than-container loads," which had proportionately higher freight rates than rates for full loads, or import in full-container loads, which meant waiting until a large enough order was put in place. In contrast, the neighboring Kenya could deliver smaller quantities faster, more frequently, and more cheaply. Some Kenyan exporters also offered more attractive supplier credit terms than Indian companies (UNIDO 2010a, Cardno 2011, 8, various interviews).[12]

In short, the Kenyan pharmaceutical sector remained the most successful in East Africa, and was able to grow and maintain a respectable market share at home and in neighboring countries. Not all firms in Kenya performed equally well, however. By 2010, Kenyan drug manufacturers were divided into three types of firms, based on their size, complexity of the medicines they produced, and level of investment in quality upgrading.

The first type included small firms that produced simple, often over-the-counter (OCT) products and that followed only minimal quality standards. Most of the firms in this category were relatively new and were opened by African Kenyan entrepreneurs, who did not always have available capital, political connections, or ties abroad. They did have pharmacy degree thanks to the opening of the first pharmacy school in Kenya at the University of Nairobi.[13] As "a critical mass of indigenous pharmacists" came out of the local pharmacy school, a number of them turned to entrepreneurship—with licensed pharmacists "climb[ing] up the chain," from retail, to wholesale, importation, and finally manufacturing.[14] For example, the founder of Sphinx, Sammy Opiyo, opened his manufacturing facility in 1996 after receiving a pharmacy degree from the University of Nairobi and then working in retail, dispensing, and industry.[15] Similarly, the founder of OssChemie, Njimia Daniel Wachira, received his pharmacy degree from the University of Nairobi and then worked in a small pharmacy for a number of years. He later opened his own retail store, Njimia, with money he had from selling his car. From retail he expanded to wholesale, importing, and then, in 2008, manufacturing.[16] Not all small companies were opened by locals, however. Medivet Products, for example, was opened by Indian nationals.

On the one hand, then, the ability to attain a pharmacy degree at home and to explore commercial opportunities with minimal capital enabled Kenyan entrepreneurs without ties abroad—the ties that had given access to know-how and otherwise benefited Indian Kenyan entrepreneurs since the 1980s—to open drug manufacturing facilities. On the other hand, lack of ties abroad, among other obstacles, meant that newer firms faced constraints that made growth particularly challenging. First, pharmacy education in Kenya was largely oriented toward clinical practice and academic knowledge and did not include industrial pharmacy (MMS and MPHS 2010, 45). A WHO official explained: "So they get . . . a lot of . . . chemistry and . . . other things. But if you look for skills [that] are needed for the local manufacturing, they don't get it."[17] Second, without ties abroad, these pharmacists did not have access to jobs in established manufacturing companies. Finally, as newcomers, they faced intense competition both from the more established companies at home and from imports, including imports of generics produced cheaply in the global South—at a time that, following the structural adjustment reforms, the state no longer offered much support to the industry.

For these reasons, the new companies normally remained small and "not sophisticated"—as of 2011, Medivet registered 43 drugs, Sphinx 27, and OssChemie and Skylight registered 11 drugs each.[18] UNIDO (2010a) reported that "some local companies are operating with one or part-time pharmacists, with untreated water from the municipal supply, or inadequate separation of air handling." Because many operated from rented facilities that were "clearly not built for that purpose," quality upgrading was challenging. According to one UNIDO official, if these pharmaceutical companies wanted to grow, they had "to start from scratch"—without the capital to do so.[19]

The companies included in the second category of Kenyan firms were doing better—although they were not all doing equally well. All of these companies were established in the 1980s. Over the years, they invested in the production of new drugs and, in principle, maintained local requirements of Good Manufacturing Practices (GMP)—but in other ways they "stayed in place."[20] One company that fell into this category was Dawa, the formerly state-owned pharmaceutical company that was privatized in 2004 and bought by Indian Kenyan investors, who had already owned an importing and distribution drug company, Medisel.[21] Another company was Biodeal. Both firms invested in the upgrading and expansion of their facilities through the replacement of some of the old machines and the addition of production lines (Medical Journal of Therapeutics Africa 2009, Nairobi Business Monthly 2015). Biodeal, at the time, expressed an interest in a new manufacturing plant in Thika that would allow for new types of drugs. Dawa reportedly made investments in improving the factory so that it followed local GMP standards of Kenya and other countries to which the company was exporting (Mulupi 2014b). However, both firms did not pass the Tanzanian audit and did not have drugs registered there.[22] Dawa, but not Biodeal, registered an ACT in 2010.

Another company that fell into the second category of firms and in some ways "stayed in place" was Elys Chemical Industries. On the one hand, Elys was one of the largest pharmaceutical firms in Kenya. It invested in the production of new drugs—it registered an ACT in 2011 and low-osmolarity oral rehydration salts (lo-ORS), which was the formulation recommended by the WHO to prevent and treat dehydration, in 2012 (CCMCentral 2013). Elys also participated in quality-upgrading initiatives—including subsidized training and auditing by European-qualified inspectors (see below). On the other hand, the company was in the same facilities since 1982, even if they were some upgrading and expansions later on. A more serious indication of the firm's minimal concern with quality standards was that in 2012, the Uganda's National Drugs Authority (NDA) found the firm to be noncompliant with the country's GMP requirements, ordered it to recall and destroy drugs in the market, and banned it from exporting to the country for eight months (Lubwama 2012).

In the final category of Kenyan firms were the Kenyan "Big Five"—Cosmos, Universal, Regal, Lab & Allied, and Beta Healthcare.[23] These were the most prominent pharmaceutical companies in Kenya. Although continuing to produce mostly noncomplex, cheap generic medicines that only required basic to moderate technological capabilities, these companies also advanced their manufacturing capabilities and produced new types of drugs, including ARVs and ACTs. These companies also followed high quality standards (UNIDO 2014, Simonetti et al. 2016).

Cosmos, Regal, and Lab & Allied, which opened in the 1980s (chapter 3), all remained family businesses—with directorship in all three firms held by the sons or nephews of the founders. Universal, which opened in 1996, was still managed and partly owned by the three original partners—Palu and Rajen Dhanani and the Finnish Pentti Keskitalo, who had previously worked for Orion in the Tanzania Pharmaceutical Industries (TPI) (chapter 4). In addition, 30 percent of the company's shares were owned by the government-owned Finnish Fund for Industrial Development (FinnFund) that provided financial support to Universal from early on (ACCI 2016). Beta Healthcare, which in the 1980s was the only firm owned by African Kenyans (chapter 3), was purchased in 2003 by the Indian Tanzanian Sumaria Group for $4 million. Sumaria also owned the Tanzanian pharmaceutical company Shelys Pharmaceuticals (Mhamba and Mbirigenda 2010). Both Shelys and the newly renamed Beta Healthcare International were later purchased by a large South African pharmaceutical company, Aspen Pharmacare.

As indicated by the number of employees and number of drugs registered (see table 6.1), all five companies were relatively large. One difference among the five firms was their market orientation—Regal and Beta Healthcare were both oriented toward the private market, whereas Cosmos, Universal, and Lab & Allied also invested in the public sector.[24] This partly explains why Regal and Beta Healthcare did not register ARVs and ACTs, which were available in Kenya mostly in the public sector. In contrast, Cosmos, Universal, and Lab & Allied were the first to learn how to produce ARVs (and they all registered ARVs in 2001–2). When Kenya adopted a new malaria policy in 2004 that followed WHO guidelines and recommended AL for the treatment of uncomplicated malaria, these three companies were also the first to learn how to produce and register AL. In another example of investment in new drugs that served the public sector, in 2013 Cosmos and Universal registered ORS-Zinc co-packaged products, as recommended by WHO (CCMCentral 2013).

The companies in this third category shifted away from old practices by investing in improved manufacturing practices. All five firms followed the GMP standards defined by Kenyan regulations and by regulations of the countries to which they were exporting (UNIDO 2010a, AUC and UNIDO 2012, various interviews). Moreover, Cosmos and Universal both tried to adopt the more restrictive WHO GMP standards. Whereas Cosmos significantly upgraded its quality standards in the process, the company failed to receive WHO PQ. Universal successfully passed the WHO audit and one of its drug was prequalified. In addition, all five companies, as well as Elys, participated in another quality-upgrading initiative: subsidized training to reach the quality level of two international instruments used in Europe—the Pharmaceutical Inspection Convention and Pharmaceutical Inspection Co-operation Scheme (PIC/S) (Losse et al. 2007). Cosmos, Universal, and Regal passed the PIC/S inspection and thereby stood out as the ones with "proven" quality standards.[25] Although Beta Healthcare and Lab & Allied did not attain the goal of successful inspection, they used the training to improve their procedures and to upgrade their quality standards in other ways. Lab & Allied, which had been previously implicated in particularly poor manufacturing standards, invested in upgrading and in the construction of an additional

TABLE 6.1. Characteristics of Kenya's top pharmaceutical companies, 2000s

| Firm | Drugs registered (2011) | No. of employees | New drugs | Quality |
|---|---|---|---|---|
| Cosmos | 312 | N/A | ARVs (2002); ACTs (2008) | WHO PQ; PIC/S (passed) |
| Universal | 166 | 133 (2003), 400 (2012) | ARVs (2001); ACTs (2008) | WHO PQ (passed); PIC/S (passed) |
| Regal | 107 | 380 | — | PIC/S (passed) |
| Lab & Allied | 264 | N/A | ARVs (2001); ACTs (2010) | PIC/S |
| Beta Healthcare | 25 | 344 | — | PIC/S |
| Elys | 107 | 200 | ACT (2011) | PIC/S |
| Dawa | 112 | 180 | ACT (2010) | — |
| Biodeal | 106 | N/A | — | — |

*Source:* Compiled by the author; for number of employees, see: interviews, UNIDO (2010a), FinnFund (2012).

*Note:* ARV = antiretroviral, ACT = artemisinin-based combination therapy, WHO PQ = World Health Organization prequalification, PIC/S = Pharmaceutical Inspection Convention and Pharmaceutical Inspection Cooperation Scheme.

facility (UNIDO 2010a, Juma 2011, Daily Nation 2015).[26] Beta Healthcare also upgraded its facilities in 2010, as part of "new drive to improve quality and efficiency."[27]

To summarize, by 2010, "the local pharmaceutical industry [in Kenya] grew in terms of . . . improvements in GMP compliance" (MMS and MPHS 2010, 18).[28] Still, there was "considerable disparity in the quality of facilities, equipment and personnel among local firms" (UNIDO 2010a). Whereas some companies continued to produce only simple drugs and did not fully follow local GMP standards, others learned how to produce complex drugs and how to maintain standards that went beyond what was required by the Kenyan law. A few were even able to formally meet international standards. Table 6.1 summarizes the characteristics of the two top categories of pharmaceutical companies in Kenya.

The only minimal interest in quality standards by some companies is easy to explain given lack of market mechanisms to enforce high quality and the weak regulatory conditions. More puzzling, therefore, is the decision of other companies to invest in quality upgrading. The first step in the analysis is understanding changes in the international context that allowed for a renewed interest in local pharmaceutical production in developing countries.

### How Pharmaceuticals Became "Development" (Again): The International Context

The debt crisis of the 1980s radically transformed the political-economic land-scape of many countries; it also changed politics at the international level. Developing countries' call for a New International Economic Order (NIEO) was summarily disregarded and replaced by US-led institutional and policy reforms. Global health policies came to echo the economic logic of the World Bank (Chorev 2012b). In the 1990s, developing countries also faced the cata-strophic reality of human immunodeficiency virus (HIV) and acquired immu-nodeficiency disease (AIDS). By 1999, AIDS was the number one killer in Africa—an estimated 33 million people were living with HIV, and 14 million people had died from AIDS since the start of the epidemic (WHO 1999). Health care systems in many poor countries were drastically weakened as a result of the World Bank's required budget cuts, which made fighting HIV/AIDS even more challenging than it would have been otherwise. Compounding the effect of inadequate health care services, the cost of anti-AIDS medicines was initially exorbitantly high. In early 2000, the price of ARV therapy for one patient for one year was $10,000–$12,000.[29]

Multinational pharmaceutical companies could charge such prices in part because of lack of competition enabled by intellectual property rights that were protected, at the global level, in the agreement on Trade-Related Aspects of Intellectual Property Rights (TRIPS). TRIPS, which was signed in 1994 under the auspices of the World Trade Organization (WTO), obligated all signato-ries to grant a lengthy patent protection to pharmaceutical products, making it legally difficult to produce generic versions of ARVs still under patent (see also chapters 1–2).

But the TRIPS agreement contained provisions describing permissible exceptions ("flexibilities") to the protection of intellectual property rights, and a number of developing countries, including South Africa, passed intellectual property laws with explicit references to the controversial exceptions that allowed them, under certain conditions, to locally produce or import generic versions of patented drugs. Multinational pharmaceutical companies' aggres-sive reaction against these laws and health activists' fight back tilted the bar-gaining leverage of the two sides of the dispute in an unexpected way. When forty multinational pharmaceutical companies tried to challenge in court the new law in South Africa, the global public outcry against "suing Nelson Mandela" caused a public relations disaster that significantly weakened the position of the multinational companies as well as the governments that advocated these companies' position (Chorev 2012a, 842). It was in that moment of enhanced bargaining leverage that developing countries attained formal declarations from

WTO members that affirmed countries' right to use flexibilities, among other concessions (Chorev 2012a).

Largely thanks to the production of generic ARVs, particularly in India, by 2002, the price of ARVs went dramatically down, to $300 per person per year.[30] Even with these much lower prices, most poor countries still did not have sufficient budgets to purchase these life-saving drugs. However, the moment of changed bargaining leverage also led rich countries—in attempts to demonstrate that TRIPS would not adversely affect access to drugs—to dramatically increase funding devoted to the purchasing of AIDS and other drugs, including both brand-name and generics (Chorev 2012a, 847). In East Africa, the agencies that provided funding for medicines were: the Global Fund to Fight AIDS, Tuberculosis and Malaria, an international financing institution that was established in 2002 to provide support to countries in their response to the three diseases (Chorev, Andia, and Ciplet 2011); the US PEPFAR, which was established in 2003; and the US PMI, which was established in 2005. These three institutions had mandates that went far beyond the provision of medicines, but treatment was central to all three programs. Although over time provision of ARVs and other drugs to people in poor countries became much less controversial, it is worth remembering that the Global Fund and subsequent programs emerged not long after it was still possible for the head of the US Agency for International Development (USAID) to oppose the provision of such drugs not only because of poor health care infrastructure, but also because Africans were allegedly incapable of following the complex ARV regimen (Herbert 2001).[31] Access to medicine became central to the global discussion on health *and* development beyond the Global Fund and US bilateral programs, as reflected in the many additional initiatives and declarations. New initiatives included Medicines for Malaria Venture, the Global Alliance for Vaccines and Immunization, Drugs for Neglected Diseases *initiative*, and Clinton Health Access Initiative (CHAI). Among the most important declarations was the UN Millennium Development Goals (MDGs); one of the eight goals was "combat HIV/AIDS, malaria and other diseases."[32]

Policies and programs in support of improved access to medicine were successfully negotiated, then, "in the shadow of power," as I discuss in chapter 1. At a moment in which multinational pharmaceutical companies were temporarily tamed, developing countries were able to loosen what were still demanding intellectual property obligations, by using the opportunities that were opened to them in that political context. Importantly, brand-name pharmaceutical companies did not give up the fight against the generic copying of their drugs. In addition to proclaiming the sanctity of intellectual property, multinational pharmaceutical firms used quality concerns to position their products as superior and to warn against the use of generics (Chorev 2015). The monitoring of quality standards through the WHO PQ scheme was in part a response to these claims. As with drug donations, here, too, positions and practices—of both recipients and donors—were a product of what was made possible by politics.

To understand the debates over quality, how they were resolved, and the effects they had, we need to remember that GMP standards are an integral part of pharmaceutical manufacturing—and all interested parties agree that local producers in developing countries must follow appropriate quality procedures or else the result would be an acceptance of "poor drugs" as good enough for poor people. When multinational pharmaceutical companies warned against poor quality standards, they effectively capitalized on those concerns. Even though quality drug requirements in most developing countries drew on WHO GMP guidelines, governments often loosened the standards to fit the local context, and enforcement was unreliable (Losse et al. 2007). Brand-name pharmaceutical companies therefore suggested that generic drugs produced in developing countries were not safe (Chorev 2015). Given the WHO's commitment to quality drugs, this was a genuine dilemma, including for international development agencies that procured generic drugs: Could they trust the quality of drugs produced in weak regulatory environments? The solution was the WHO PQ scheme, which was set up in 2001, and was designed to offer *credible* assessments—evaluations were conducted by international experts from stringent regulatory authorities—both of final products and of manufacturing sites.

WHO official Dr. Lembit Rägo credited the WHO PQ for making affordable drugs globally accessible. "Eight million people . . . could never have been treated without the prequalification program."[33] Indeed, by verifying the quality of generic drugs, the WHO played a critical role in weakening the allegations against generics made by brand-name companies, and it helped to legitimize the use of generic drugs produced in the developing world. According to another WHO official, Dr. Richard Laing, the WHO PQ scheme helped to eliminate the fear that "procuring quality-assured [generic] AIDS medicines was going to be difficult," because "the initial quality tests very quickly demonstrated it could be done."[34] The WHO PQ scheme did not simply verify quality; it arguably *oriented* generic producers toward quality manufacturing to begin with. According to Dr. Rägo, when manufacturers realized that they couldn't access the international drug market unless they assured the quality of their drugs, they invested in quality procedures.[35]

As was expected, the main beneficiaries of the PQ scheme were drug manufacturers in India—81 of the 121 ARVs that had been WHO-prequalified by October 2011 were manufactured in India. Speaking of Indian manufacturers in particular, Dr. Rägo claimed that if WHO PQ had not started when it did, Indian manufacturers would not be where they are today in regard to quality.[36] The impact spilled over from the prequalified drugs to the facility as a whole. "They produce in this unit not only the drug that they're interested [in prequalifying] but usually other drugs. So even if they don't get [other products] prequalified, they still must have [WHO] GMP."[37]

WHO PQ was not celebrated by everyone, however. Supporters of local pharmaceutical production suggested that international standards were too stringent and were going beyond what was necessary to ensure the safety of most drugs.[38] This was also the position of some local manufacturers in East Africa, who asserted that "the WHO puts too much emphasis on documents" and that "[local] GMP should be enough."[39]

Increased drug donations and international monitoring of quality standards both reflected increased interest in improved access to medicine as part of the global "development agenda." Unlike in the 1970s–1980s, however, that agenda did not initially lead to an interest in local pharmaceutical production in recipient countries. If anything, the opposite was the case. Given that it was cheaper for many poor countries to import ARVs and other drugs than to manufacture them locally, a public health perspective led to the argument that local drug manufacturing should not be supported and, specifically, that resources dedicated to the procurement of drugs should not be used to advance secondary priorities such as manufacturing capabilities. An influential 2005 report co-written by an expert on international health and by a WHO official, which was published as part of the World Bank's Health, Nutrition, and Population Discussion Paper Series, argued against investment in local pharmaceutical production for exactly those reasons. "In many parts of the world," the report concluded, "producing medicines domestically makes little economic sense" and may result in "less access to medicines" (Kaplan and Laing 2005, iii). For a while it seemed that this report could silence any support for local production. However, others countered the report's reasoning by emphasizing the danger of a country being entirely dependent on imports for essential commodities like drugs—especially when the conditions under which TRIPS allowed for generic production meant that drug manufacturers "[could] no longer automatically produce generic versions of newer, now patented, medications" (UNAIDS 2013, 5). There were also economic incentives to oppose the report, as recipient countries wanted Global Fund money to be spent locally. In that context, support for local pharmaceutical production in poor countries became part of the negotiations over how to avoid the effect that TRIPS would otherwise have on access to medicine in those countries. In time, developing countries did win a few political battles that opened the possibility for local pharmaceutical production in their countries.

In the negotiations over TRIPS, least developed countries (LDCs) were able to extend the time before they had to implement or enforce patent obligations with respect to pharmaceutical products, and later negotiations extended the original deadline. This meant that generic drugs that would have been difficult to get permission to produce in countries fully implementing TRIPS could still be produced in LDCs. Referring to the extended transition period for LDCs, the WTO stated on its website: "This is in recognition of their special requirements, their economic, financial and administrative constraints, and *the need for flexibility so that they can create a viable technological base.*"[40] A reiterative process helped institutionalize and prolong that exception (Chorev 2012a). As I describe in chapter 8, one Ugandan company was able to utilize the extended deadline. In support of that company, in 2016, "Uganda [was] leading the world's least developed countries . . . in the ongoing showdown talks at the WTO . . . where America remains the only powerful country still refusing to grant a permanent waiver on patents on medicines" (Barigaba 2015). Although poor countries have so far failed to achieve permanent waivers, they continue to get extensions, most recently until 2033 (WTO 2015).

In addition, development agencies became more tolerant of—and some even encouraged—supportive industrial policies by national governments.[41] The World Bank supported procurement preferences ("discounts") of 15 percent for local pharmaceutical producers in government tenders (Alexander and Fletcher 2012). UNIDO—at that time, in collaboration with the African Union—devised various business plans and roadmaps with the goal of strengthening African countries' "ability to produce high quality, affordable pharmaceuticals across all essential medicines" (AUC and UNIDO 2012). The Global Fund never a priori rejected the possibility of purchasing locally made drugs, but for a while it opposed the granting of preferences to local producers in tenders paid for by the Fund on the argument that, "the goal of the Global Fund is to ensure access, not economic development."[42] Later on, even the Global Fund softened its guidelines somewhat.[43] Other donors designated particular markets under certain conditions for specific local producers in East Africa with the explicit goal of contribution to local pharmaceutical production.

It might have helped that support for local pharmaceutical production, unlike the issues of intellectual property rights or quality standards, was not explicitly opposed by multinational pharmaceutical companies. Pharmaceutical companies within the European Union (EU) did not oppose programs in support of pharmaceutical production in poor countries because "the main product[s] in the portfolio of EU companies," such as cardiovascular, cancer, and diabetes, were "not on the list" of drugs that were to be produced.[44] The opposition of American drug companies, in turn, was somewhat weakened by the fact that the Europeans did not join their position. Although American companies reportedly tried to use their influence in various international development agencies, these attempts were countered by others, such as members of the public health, innovation, and intellectual property team at the WHO. Still, "local pharmaceutical production was never a battlefield," which was "why they put LPP [local pharmaceutical production] at the forefront."[45] That is, it was in part because multinational corporations did not care enough about the issue that pharmaceutical production became politically attractive and achievable for developing countries in the first place.

Technology transfer and other forms of mentoring were another way for development agencies to support local pharmaceutical production. Relying on Article 7 of TRIPS, which stated that, "the protection and enforcement of intellectual property rights should contribute to the promotion of technological innovation and to *the transfer and dissemination of technology*" (emphasis added), the WHO emphasized technology transfer in its *Global Strategy and Plan of Action on Public Health Innovation and Intellectual Property* (WHO 2011a), and both the WHO and UNIDO (with German funding) offered extensive trainings for local producers (WHO 2009, UNCTAD 2011b). In East Africa, the German Technical Cooperation Agency (GTZ), which was the implementing agency of the Federal Ministry for Economic Cooperation and Development (BMZ) in Germany, was particularly active in supporting efforts "to develop local capacities for the production and marketing of high-quality drug products at affordable prices" (GTZ 2009).[46] A number of these initiatives started too late to have an impact on the events described in this chapter (UNIDO 2014), but earlier initiatives, as I show below, made a big difference.

Although these technology transfer initiatives were western-led, active mobilization of recipient countries was at times required for international support. For example, in 2007, the Organization for Economic Co-operation and Development (OECD) held a high level forum on medicine for infectious diseases that produced an official document with references to pharmaceutical manufacturing plans for Africa and a statement in support of "developing countries-led efforts in strengthening their own health, local production and research systems . . . to ensure availability and accessibility of medicines, vaccines, diagnostics. . . ."[47] This document had no impact, however, and the process it was supposed to launch never came off the ground, until the Brazilian delegates effectively used the paper in WHO negotiations to defend the position of developing countries on the issue.[48]

To summarize, through contentious negotiations over TRIPS—in which the bargaining leverage of developing countries improved thanks to the tactical miscalculations of multinational pharmaceutical companies—what began as a particularly threatening agreement with little more than empty promises, was used by developing countries to improve their access to medicine, including through local pharmaceutical production. This, then, is how successful developing countries' priorities were constructed: they took advantage of existing political opportunities. AIDS became a priority disease—and the production of quality-assured drugs became one of the strategies to fight it—because political conditions made AIDS visible and poor countries then tried to make the most of the political situation.

## Local Production of Quality-Assured Drugs: Domestic and Foreign Influences

Domestic conditions in Kenya were not conducive to local pharmaceutical production. State support to the extent that it existed helped to sustain the sector
but did not help to upgrade it. Thanks to changed international circumstances,
however, foreign aid in the early 2000s offered three resources—the promise
of markets, the imposition of monitoring, and the provision of mentoring. These
three resources enticed Kenyan pharmaceutical manufacturers to invest in the
production of high-quality ARVs and ACTs and enabled some of them to do
so successfully.

### MARKETS

Kenyan drug producers relied on the private and the public markets, in addition to exports, as mentioned above. The increasing reliance on the private market was, in part, a reflection of this market's growth (WHO 2010, 25). The
private market was more attractive than the public market because it allowed
for marketing and branding, and because drug prices were generally higher
than when selling to the government (WHO 2006). The private market was
also more attractive because of important drawbacks of tenders conducted by
the government agency responsible for the procurement and distribution of
drugs, the Kenya Medical Supplies Authority (KEMSA). In addition to offering
only minimal profit margins, government tenders were uncertain, and for a
while were considered "dicey" (various interviews). (As I discuss in chapter 9,
KEMSA improved its reputation following reforms that started in 2008.) However, government tenders did have a number of advantages. One advantage was
that KEMSA was still the single largest buyer of drugs in the country, purchasing 30 percent of all prescription drugs in the domestic market (UNIDO
2010a). Another advantage was that because of the large scale of orders, the
profit was sizeable even with very low margins (various interviews). Some of
the larger firms then heavily relied on sales to KEMSA. Cosmos, for example,
mostly sold to the government (UNIDO 2010a); and KEMSA was a "major
local customer" for Universal (Mutegi 2011).

The Federation of Kenya Pharmaceutical Manufacturers (FKPM), the
trade association representing local manufacturers, lobbied for policies such
as a waiver of fees and duties to make local producers competitive in open
international tenders (i.e., tenders open to both local and foreign producers). More ambitiously, FKPM called for a price preference in government
tenders, as well as for a version of the so-called "Ghana list," in which the government would avoid importing drugs that local manufacturers could produce,
as was the case in Ghana (various interviews). FKPM's lobbying was often

opposed, however, by the better-resourced Kenya Association of Pharmaceutical Industry (KAPI), a group that represented the interests of drug importers and distributors—mostly multinational pharmaceutical companies and their local distributors.[49] Normally, then, FKPM had little influence on government policies. However, FKPM benefited from the changed international environment, which led the Kenyan government to introduce a number of supportive policies. (Interestingly, UNIDO's support was in part aimed at strengthening the pharmaceutical associations in Africa at the national and regional levels.)

State support included lower fees for drug registration, drug retention, and GMP factory inspection, as well as exemption from taxes and duties on active pharmaceutical ingredients, excipients (inactive substances), and packaging materials.[50] These exemptions partly compensated for the fact that there were no duties on imported prescription drugs (UNIDO 2010a). The government also introduced some policies to help local producers in tenders. For example, in tenders for the supply of Rural Health Kits (RHKs), which took up about 60 percent of KEMSA's procurement budget (UNIDO 2010a, 32), KEMSA no longer offered exclusivity to local producers (chapter 3), but it required that the bidders be manufacturers of about 50 percent of the products in the kit, which gave an advantage to locals who manufactured drugs based on what was on Kenya's Essential Drugs List (EDL). In 2007–2008, 10 out of 14 suppliers of RHKs were locally incorporated, including both local manufacturers and local importers. In addition, government tenders below a certain amount were reserved for local companies in open national tenders. This policy only had limited impact: in 2003, open national tenders were valued at only 5 percent of the total (MOH Kenya 2003, 13); and, as with RHKs, local distributors of imported drugs could also participate in these tenders. The government also supported local producers in open international tenders by dividing tenders, rather than giving the entire order to the lowest bidder, and then granting local manufacturers parts of these tenders. That was the case with the two tenders for ARVs that Cosmos won (see below). Finally, in 2005, the *Public Procurement and Disposal Act* allowed government procurement agencies, including KEMSA, to "grant a margin of preference of up to 15 percent in the evaluation of bids to candidates offering goods manufactured . . . in Kenya" (UNIDO 2010a).[51] It took several years before this policy was implemented in the pharmaceutical sector, but in 2010–11, two tenders included these local discounts (UNIDO 2010a). This last policy was enthusiastically endorsed by local producers. According to one Kenyan manufacturer, "locals get more products in government tenders because of the current preferential treatment . . . [Our share in government purchases] has never been higher!"[52]

Both the private and public domestic markets, then, offered a financial foundation for a local pharmaceutical sector, but given the modest demands and expectations of both markets, local manufacturers focused on simple, cheap drugs. That changed, however, when the government started to respond to the spread of HIV/AIDS in Kenya.

The HIV/AIDS epidemic in Kenya introduced a terrible shock to an already vulnerable health care system. At the epidemic's peak, Kenya had one of the highest HIV/AIDS infection rates in the world. In 1997, the estimated prevalence of HIV among adults aged 15 to 49 was 11.1 percent; by 2003, the rate was down, but still at 8.4 percent.[53] The rolling out of medicine was initially slow; the government started providing ARV therapy only in 2003 (NACC and NASCOP 2012). When the government introduced ARVs to the Kenyan market for the first time, the expectation was that all ARVs purchased by the Kenyan government, and later by donors, would be imported. In 2001–2002, however, Cosmos, Universal, and Lab & Allies had successfully registered ARVs with the Kenyan Pharmacy and Poisons Board (PPB)—meaning that PPB found that the drugs conformed to required standards of quality, safety, and efficacy and could be sold in Kenya (Osewe, Nkrumah, and Sackey 2008). In September 2003, Cosmos announced its plan to participate in a government tender (Kimani 2003). Cosmos' intention to produce ARVs would have made it the first sub-Saharan African firm outside of South Africa to do so, and it was acclaimed as a "bold move" that "put Kenya in the league of India and Brazil"—the two developing countries made famous by their local pharmaceutical capabilities (Okwembe 2004).

There was a complication, however, as Kenya had just passed its *Industrial Property Act, 2001*, in order to conform with TRIPS, and the drugs Cosmos had registered and intended to produce were under patent in Kenya (Okwembe 2004, Chorev 2015).[54] (The drug registration process does not consider issues such as violation of patents). According to Prakash Patel, the founder and chairman of Cosmos, this was part of what motivated his decision to participate in the government tender in the first place: he wanted Cosmos to be "the cat with the bell" that would expose the negative consequences of the patent system.[55]

As a first move, Cosmos asked the two patent holders of the drugs in question, GSK (for Lamivudine and Zidovudine) and Boehringer Ingelheim (for Nevirapine), for voluntary licensing, that is, for permission to produce generic versions of their drugs. The two companies ignored this initial request. Nevertheless, Cosmos went ahead; and in January 2004 the company won a tender to supply ARVs to the Kenyan government—a 30 percent component of a $1 million tender to kick-start Kenya's first public HIV/AIDS treatment initiative, making the need to resolve the patent issue more urgent. Under Kenya's law, the government could have issued compulsory licensing, which would have forced the patent holders to give other manufacturers a license to produce their drugs rather than relying on their voluntary permission. However, the Kenyan government was spared the decision of whether to confront the multinational companies, because—likely due to the possibility of compulsory licensing—GSK and Boehringer Ingelheim finally offered Cosmos voluntary licensing. Universal was similarly granted voluntary licensing from the two companies.[56] Cosmos and Universal could now produce and sell the ARVs they had registered. In spite of conditions that made competition challenging—for example, GSK and Boehringer Ingelheim both lowered their prices in Kenya—Cosmos won a 20 percent component of another ARV tender in 2005.[57]

As Patel later recalled, "then donors came in!"[58] Foreign aid brought opportunities by way of a much larger market for ARVs and ACTs, but aid also brought new challenges.

The provision of drugs through donations was nothing new, as we have seen (chapter 3), but the scope of it in response to AIDS was unprecedented. By 2006, foreign aid funded 52 percent of the total drug market in Kenya; in comparison, the government-funded public sector was only 9 percent and the private sector was 38 percent (MMS 2010, 2).[59] The Kenyan government provided only about 5–6 percent of the total funding of ARVs, mostly for cases of stock-outs, and the government's contribution to the total funding for malaria control in Kenya was only 0.5 percent (UNIDO 2010a, MoI, MMS and UNIDO 2011, 4). Instead, funding for HIV/AIDS, malarial and tuberculosis medications came mostly from the Global Fund, PEPFAR, and PMI. Between 2003 and 2010, the Global Fund disbursed a total of $297 million to Kenya (for all programs, not only the procurement of medicines).[60] In 2011, Kenya was granted $345 million, "one of the largest grants given to a country in a single [Global Fund] cycle" (Otieno 2011).[61] The budget of PEPFAR was even larger. In 2010 alone, total PEPFAR funding for Kenya was $547 million, out of which funding for the procurement of ARVs was $93 million.[62] That year, total PMI funding for Kenya was $40 million, out of which funding for the procurement of malaria drugs was $7.54 million (UNIDO 2010a).

In general, then, but particularly in regard to HIV/AIDS and malaria, donors spent large sums—both in relative and absolute term—on procuring drugs (UNIDO 2010a). It is difficult to overstate the role these funds played in improving access to medicine in Kenya. Where in 2003, only 5 percent of the people who needed ARVs were getting them, by 2016 that figure had grown to 64 percent, with more than one million patients receiving treatment.[63] Rate of access to ACTs was lower. In 2008, close to 8 million ACTs were distributed in Kenya (USAID 2011a, 123).

In the case of PEPFAR and PMI, the procurement and distribution of drugs was contracted to private companies or not-for-profit organizations. The Global Fund, in contrast, provided the funds to the government to use for the purchase of the needed medicine. Given the scarce resources available to Kenya's government, the provision of funds for the purchase of these drugs created a public drug market that did not exist before and arguably could not have existed otherwise.[64] (I refer to drug markets created by donors as "donor-funded markets," and distinguish it from the "public market" even if both markets were managed by the government.) As we have seen, a few local manufacturers had registered ARVs already in 2001–2002, and local manufacturers could potentially benefit from the much larger market that was created by donors. A Kenyan newspaper reported that Global Fund donations "encourage[d] more companies . . . to improve their competitiveness in international tenders to supply antiretroviral drugs" (Otieno 2011). In addition to the drugs that they had already registered, and in response to the new demand created by the Global Fund and other donors, Cosmos and Universal also registered triple fixed-dose combination therapies (i.e, drugs that include three active pharmaceutical ingredients combined in a single dosage form) in 2005 and 2007, respectively. They later registered ACTs.

However, when "donors came in," they did not just create markets. As the gatekeepers, they also set conditions for access to these new markets, including in regard to quality standards. The quality standards required by donors were significantly higher than the standards that had been required and enforced in Kenya at that time.

## MONITORING

The harm of consuming substandard drugs could be significant, yet quality assessment of pharmaceutical products requires laboratory examination that is not available to individual consumers or to drug providers such as pharmacies or hospitals. Consequently, market forces cannot be relied on to raise quality standards. Small firms are also deterred by the fact that quality assurance is a fixed cost, so the additional cost of production *per unit* is higher for them compared to larger firms. Additionally, scarcity of funds and lack of technical know-how makes upgrading challenging. Without market mechanisms to ensure quality, investment in producing better quality drugs is not economically rational (UNIDO 2010a, 51). In many countries, therefore, governments have regulations to ensure the quality of drugs. East African countries did not initially have that level of regulation, however—drug registration to ensure that drugs conform to required standards of quality started in Kenya in 1982, in Uganda in 1997, and in Tanzania only in 2000—and enforcement was lax. And "since nobody was checking," local drug manufacturers did not generally follow quality standards.[65] As for imported drugs, when the Kenyan government had previously bought drugs manufactured in developed countries (chapter 2), it could presumably rely on the home countries' regulations to assure the quality of its drugs. As I describe in chapter 3, some multinational pharmaceutical companies exploited the weak enforcement of quality standards to sell substandard or otherwise inappropriate drugs in under-regulated markets. In any event, this reliance on other countries' enforcement mechanisms could no longer suffice in the 1990s, when the liberalization of the drug market in Kenya led to the entry of drugs from semi-regulated countries. This created an urgent need to monitor the quality of drugs—and with foreign assistance, the Kenyan government introduced significant regulatory reforms in 1992–93, which included the restructuring of Kenya's PPB, and the launching of the National Quality Control Laboratory (NQCL).[66] A decade or so later, KEMSA was established to replace the Medical Supplies Coordinating Unit (MSCU; previously the Central Medical Stores, CMS).

The reforms initially led to only modest improvements in quality standards (Luoma et al. 2010). To begin with, the local GMP standards were low. Although the Kenyan regulations followed WHO guidelines, these were adapted to "local conditions," leading to "a marked difference" between the two.[67] According to UNIDO (2010a): "The bar is . . . set too low. Some firms that are GMP-certified by the regulatory body may not merit this status." There was also a consensus among local manufacturers and others that registration in Kenya was "relaxed" (Luoma et al. 2010, UNIDO 2010a). In interviews, commentators suggested that "the quality of registration is not great in Kenya" and lower than the rest of East Africa. One frustrated pharmacist complained that "everything under the sun is registered in Kenya." In addition, GMP inspection of manufacturing facilities—inspection of local manufacturers started in 1999 and inspection of foreign facilities started in 2004—suffered from significant shortcomings (Luoma et al. 2010).[68] To begin with, because the number of drugs registered in Kenya was quite large, the system was overwhelmed by the number of factories that had to be monitored. Additionally, there were very few GMP inspectors employed by PPB—there were only six in 2010—and these inspectors did not necessarily have the required skills or the experience (UNIDO 2010a, 45). As a result, "[the PPB's] resources and systems [were] simply not up to the regulatory burden" (UNIDO 2010a, 7). Others also hinted at instances of corruption (various interviews).

Enforcement was especially loose when it came to local producers. In a few cases, local firms had to take corrective measures following GMP inspections (Mutegi 2011b), but generally the experience of Kenyan producers was that GMP inspections were "tuned to" their needs, and that the expectations were sufficiently "flexible" so that one could walk around them. According to a number of manufacturers, inspectors only wanted to see "a basic minimum"— that they were "at least . . . trying"—and inspectors generally allowed for some violations as long as the end result was "fine." One manufacturer admitted that, "if we had to follow [the GMP standards 'by the book'], we wouldn't have passed" (various interviews). A UNIDO (2010a) report warned, "the result of very weak and ineffective regulation has been a flow of substandard medicines in the domestic market."

Improvements did take place over time. The number of inspectors increased, and inspectors were better trained. The frequency of inspections also increased and included surprise visits (PharmaAfrica 2012, various interviews). In addition to inspection of facilities, the quality control of the drugs themselves, either in the course of registration or post-marketing surveillance, also improved. First, the NQCL, which was set up in 1992 to support both the registration and the post-marketing surveillance functions, was initially a "very basic laboratory" but in 2008 received a WHO PQ.[69] According to one WHO official, "the prequalification process [of Kenya's NQCL] has led to improvement in the standards of [the] local regulators."[70] In addition, new guidelines that were introduced in 2010 raised the drug registration standards (GTZ 2009, MMS 2010, various interviews). Finally, the post-marketing surveillance department at PPB began to more frequently recall drugs that failed quality analysis, did not comply with labeling requirements, or were not registered. The department's action led to the closing down of at least one company, Gesto, "following repeated complaints on poor quality of its products" (Lifesaver 2011). These improvements notwithstanding, and given the level of national standards, even those local factories adequately following local GMP were not following the standards recommended by the WHO.

Following international standards, however, was necessary in order to access the new markets. PEPFAR required a US Food and Drug Administration (USFDA) approval, which was exceptionally stringent and expensive.[71] European donors required an auditing by European-qualified inspectors. The Global Fund, in addition to accepting "products registered by stringently-regulated authorities," such as the USFDA, also accepted "quality-assured products under the World Health Organization's prequalification scheme" (Global Fund 2012b).

As we have seen, drug manufacturers in India were the main target of the WHO PQ scheme. Drug manufacturers in East Africa were certainly *not* on anyone's mind when the WHO PQ initiative was launched. However, the promise of a "Global Fund market" that was conditioned on WHO GMP certification encouraged some Kenyan manufacturers to improve their standards. Other donor-funded markets with similar quality-assurance requirements had the same impact, as I describe below.

Not all drug manufacturers in Kenya responded in the same way. Because Kenyan drug manufacturers' interest in ARV production was initially in response to government tenders, they were not "worried" about quality at first.[72] To achieve WHO GMP, firms in Kenya would have had to upgrade their facilities or construct entirely new ones, which required significant financial resources and technical capabilities that local firms did not generally possess. It was also unclear whether companies would be able to recoup the financial investment—improved quality standards meant higher operational costs, which would have made production for all drugs manufactured in that facility more expensive and less competitive. Hence, when companies in Kenya learned that "to enter the big money of donor-funded programs, you need prequalification," many either did not try or gave up soon after attempting to achieve it.[73] Regal concluded that they "were not ready,"[74] while Lab & Allied similarly judged that WHO PQ was not for them.[75] In contrast, Cosmos and Universal did pursue WHO PQ.

Cosmos invested 200 million KSh (around $2.5 million) in the prequalification process, but eventually the firm faced difficulties that it was unable to resolve, mostly due to lack of local expertise. In addition, Cosmos "got overtaken by events": when a new ARV therapy regime recommended by the WHO substituted Zidovudine, which Cosmos had hoped to prequalify, with a different drug, Cosmos would have had to restart the entire PQ procedure, and it decided not to.[76]

Universal, like Cosmos, decided to apply for WHO PQ so it could "participate in international tenders" (FinnFund 2012, Mutegi 2011b). Universal's directors were also motivated by a sense of regional pride. Palu Dhanani describes how when he first consulted with the WHO, officials discounted his capabilities. He told me that, "they treat Africans as stupid"—and he "was almost kicked out of the WHO."[77] As a result, as a local consultant put it, Universal wanted "to show their muscle[s]" and prove WHO wrong.[78] In doing so, Universal had a number of advantages over Cosmos, including deeper pockets and easier access to technical know-how. Thanks to Finnish partner Pentti Keskitalo, Universal benefited, starting in 2005, from an investment by FinnFund, a subsidiary of the Finnish government that provided "long-term risk capital for profitable projects in developing countries that involve a Finnish interest" (FinnFund 2012). FinnFund, which later held 30 percent of the company's shares, in 2009 granted Universal $10 million of additional financing "to expand production and develop its operations towards quality certification by the WHO" (FinnFund 2009). Even with an easier access to funds, the high cost of certification meant that Universal could only pursue WHO PQ for one drug at a time, and they chose to submit the drug Lamozido, a combination of Zidovudine and Lamivudine (Mutegi 2011a), which at a time was "quite [a] lucrative" product. According to Dhanani, Lamozido "was reasonably profitable and the volumes were there as well."[79] In 2011, Universal became the first firm in Kenya to receive WHO PQ. This was a considerable achievement—it made Universal one of only three companies from sub-Saharan Africa to be granted WHO PQ certificate at that time; the others were Aspen Pharmacare from South Africa, and Quality Chemical Industries from Uganda.

This accomplishment confirmed both the willingness and ability of local manufacturers in semi-regulated environments to produce complex drugs and to invest in quality standards higher than what was locally required. The role of foreign aid here was clear. Development agencies provided an incentive to produce new drugs, and these agencies conditioned that access in a way that required Universal—and, as we will see, other local manufacturers as well—to follow more stringent quality standards. These conditions were not trivial, which explains Cosmos's frustration. Indeed, the experience of Cosmos and other companies in Kenya suggests that markets and monitoring may not be sufficient without access to technical know-how. Here, again, foreign aid played an important role.

## MENTORING

Successfully following WHO GMP required technical know-how that was not available in Kenya—due in part to a severe shortage of qualified technical personnel (UNIDO 2010a). I showed in chapter 3 that back in the 1980s, Kenyan drug manufacturers received access to technology thanks to ties abroad. Kenyans of Indian origin in particular benefited from educational and job opportunities abroad, as well as from informal connections with suppliers and manufacturers of drugs in India. To an extent, throughout the 1990s and 2000s, Indian Kenyan manufacturers continued to benefit from ties abroad; they often sent their sons and daughters to pharmacy schools abroad, although by then, more often to the UK and the US than to India, and they relied on community ties to hire Indian consultants. As we have seen, Universal was unique by having ties to Finland through a partner. By 2000, however, technological and political-economic transformations had diminished the importance of these ties. The increased level of sophistication of Kenyan pharmaceutical firms meant that informal chats could no longer be a sufficient form of learning. With globalization, ties abroad were available also without existing social or community ties. As a result, non-Indian Kenyan entrepreneurs were also able to hire Indian consultants if they had sufficient capital, whereas Indian Kenyans started to hire consulting firms from China and were as likely to buy raw materials from China as from India (various interviews). Some local pharmaceutical manufacturers in East Africa came to experience a new type of ties abroad through foreign direct investment (FDI)—the purchasing of existing drug companies (or the opening of new ones) by foreign interests. As we will see, FDI quite radically changed the Ugandan and Tanzanian pharmaceutical sectors (chapters 7–8), but Kenya was less affected by it. As of 2010, only one company, Beta Healthcare, was foreign-owned, and Beta Healthcare's practices remained similar to the practices of locally owned companies, such as Regal.[80] Universal at the time was partly owned by FinnFund, but this was a non-for-profit state-owned company, and FinnFund's support was not a commercial investment.

In Kenya, then, ties abroad were no longer a significant aspect of the sector's trajectory. Local networks at home did continue to play a role in the diffusion of information across the sector, albeit differently than the role they had played in the 1980s. In the 1980s, bounded solidarity among middleman minorities was the main foundation for diffusion. By the 2000s, this was the case among the largest companies, which were still mostly owned by Kenyans of Indian origin. However, with changes in the ethnic composition of the sector as a whole, the basis for diffusion changed as well. In addition to social relations, local networks were based on professional affinities (most owners were pharmacists) and geographical proximity (all factories were in Nairobi). The ties were institutionalized by the relatively active FKPM, whose members met every month or so at a social club.[81] Another difference was that in the 1980s, local networks led to diffusion of technical knowledge (chapter 3), but by 2010, knowledge was too complex to diffuse in this manner. Instead, conventions and ethos were diffused, so that if one company produced a new drug, opened a larger factory, or invested in quality standards, others considered doing the same.

Through the influence of these local networks, the issue of quality standards gained traction. Indeed, drug companies talked about the importance of quality standards almost independently of how well they followed them. Many local manufacturers talked about WHO GMP or WHO PQ as "benchmarks," and in boasting about their products, they referred to their drugs not only as the "most affordable" but also of "the best quality" (various interviews). One manufacturer proclaimed in the interview, "Quality products! No shortcuts!"

Given Kenya's limited access to technical know-how, foreign aid was instrumental. Just as development agencies created a market that provided incentives to produce new drugs, and that imposed conditions forcing adherence to higher quality standards, they also provided the means for local companies to produce these higher-quality drugs.

Mentoring was a central factor in Universal's success. To begin with, Universal received "hands on" assistance from the WHO even though technical guidance was not integral to the WHO PQ mission.[82] According to Dr. Rägo, "we have gone quite a long way to help them," with technical experts spending weeks "working with them in the unit, going through [everything] they do, coaching them."[83] In addition to the WHO's mentoring, the technical assistance provided by the GTZ was also central to Universal's accomplishments. As we have seen, Germany was an early supporter of pharmaceutical production in industrializing countries, which led to its funding of UNIDO's initiatives and also to an interest in providing direct technical support. The interest in East Africa, in particular, was motivated by a discussion at the German Standing Humanitarian Aid Committee over how to improve access to medicine in crisis-affected areas in the Democratic Republic of Congo (DRC) and the Sudan (Losse et al. 2007). The Committee supported procurement from East African drug manufacturers, but in order to use German funds, the medicine had to be of the same quality as required in Europe. The logic, then, was similar to the Global Fund's logic; a market was created, but quality conditions were attached to it. Unlike the Global Fund, in addition to monitoring the quality of drugs, GTZ also committed technical assistance for that purpose.[84] This was the context in which local manufacturers in East Africa were offered subsidized training to help them reach the quality levels of the PIC/S certification used in Europe (the companies paid for the improvements of their facilities) (Losse et al. 2007). Starting in 2005, this was a three-year project in which industrial pharmacists from Europe "walk[ed] [local manufacturers] through the whole process" so to bring them up to European standards.[85] By the end of the three-year period, participating manufacturers were audited. Those that passed received a certificate indicating that the factory was successfully audited by EU-accredited GMP inspectors. Universal was one of the Kenyan companies that enrolled in the PIC/S project. Universal's managing director gave GTZ much of the credit for his company's WHO PQ, saying they "trained our people how to build a dossier and how to build quality systems within the factory."[86] A pharmaceutical quality systems consultant from Kenya empathically agreed: "It is from PIC/S that Universal got WHO prequalification."[87] In turn, Cosmos did not make much progress with WHO PQ in part because the company "hit a lot of bottlenecks," and the WHO did not give them "the hands-on [training]" they needed. The same consultant complained, maybe unfairly, that, "They [WHO] just tell you, this is how you move, we come and inspect, and so forth. But it's for you to move there." Cosmos' experience with GTZ was different than the company's experience with the WHO. "In the PIC/S one, we are given the hands-on experience. . . . That was the big difference." The training involved not only the identification of concerns, but also how to solve them. "Inspectors tell you 'now you have done this, but your gap is here.' *Then they give you the way of how to fill that gap.*"[88]

In addition to Universal and Cosmos, four other companies in Kenya enrolled in the PIC/S project—Regal, Lab & Allied, Beta Healthcare, and Elys. All did so in the hope of obtaining access to new markets. As the managing director of Regal told me, "Of course there was a carrot dangled that the companies that go through this will get increase tender opportunities."[89] Universal, Cosmos, and Regal had successful inspections; the other three either dropped out or failed the audit.

Both with WHO PQ and PIC/S, failure to achieve the required standards did not necessarily mean failure to improve extant procedures. Local manufacturers in Kenya that went through the technical guidance and the audits learned what the international quality expectations were and started to follow at least some of the required steps. As the Kenyan pharmaceutical consultant insisted, "Not only was it a good experience, it made a [big] jump in the quality" of all the factories involved.[90]

In addition to aid from international development agencies, technology transfer was also offered by Roche, a multinational pharmaceutical company headquartered in Switzerland (WHO 2011b). This was one of the company's "corporate social responsibility" initiatives, which, as with other multinational pharmaceutical companies in the context of TRIPS, often focused on initiatives that meant to illustrate that stronger intellectual property rights would not have adverse effect on access to affordable medicine in poor countries. In 2006, Roche launched its AIDS Technology Transfer Initiative—offering local manufacturers in developing countries a voluntary licensing for its second-line ARV, Saquinavir. When the project began, forty-one companies from seventeen countries expressed interest in producing the drug.[91] After an audit for technological assessment, Roche signed a voluntary licensing agreement with thirteen companies (Roche n.d.a). In Kenya, the recipients were Cosmos, Universal, and Regal. If judged by the official objective, the experience failed as not one company of those receiving a license ended up registering or producing the drug. Kenyans were quite bitter about the process: "Piece of paper! Nothing came out of it!"[92] Because the drug was not in the WHO treatment guidelines in East Africa, it had no commercial value for local producers. Another frustration was the lack of mentoring: "We did not get any major training, maybe one visit or something."[93] In some ways, then, Roche served more as a useful indicator as to which factories in East Africa reached sufficiently high quality standards than as a factor in achieving that level of quality. Still, Roche's initiative had some value. We will see that this was the case especially in Uganda (chapter 8), but even in Kenya, a few local producers indicated that they had benefited from the audit: "Um, okay, the only thing we probably really learned [from the experience with Roche] was, of course, [the] inspection. [The information given to us in that inspection] was good for us."[94]

In addition to these initiatives, a number of development agencies offered technical transfer through general training programs, often at the regional level. The WHO, for example, hosted workshops on local production and offered regional training courses in quality management for both firms and regulators (Anderson 2010, WHO 2009, 2011d, various interviews). In 2005, UNIDO, with the financial support of the German government, launched a ten-year program to "increase the capacity of the local pharmaceutical sector in developing countries to supply safe, efficacious and affordable medicines" (UNIDO n.d.a). As part of that initiative, GTZ and UNIDO together established a regional certificate program in industrial pharmacy at the St. Luke's Foundation/Kilimanjaro School of Pharmacy in Moshi, Tanzania. For two years, UNIDO also teamed with the Muhimbili University of Health and Allied Sciences in Tanzania to offer a Master's of Pharmacy in Industrial Pharmacy (UNIDO n.d.a). UNIDO also provided technical and managerial assistance to firms on business plans, offered plant assessments (including assessing feasibility and economic viability of the production of quality medicines), and assisted firms in identifying potential partners for access to capital and/or technology (WHO 2011c). UNIDO asserted that "these training measures . . . are important contributions in pursuit of higher quality standards explicitly targeting international standards and WHO Prequalification" (UNIDO n.d.b). Kenyans have enthusiastically participated in the various UNIDO workshops. According to Häfele-Abah (2010), fifty-two personnel from ten different Kenyan manufacturing firms attended at least one of the training workshops. Häfele-Abah also found that participants had positive views of the experience—they credited the workshops for increasing their GMP awareness and for providing concrete ideas on what to implement in order to achieve and maintain GMP. According to one participant: "You can see the changes from where we used to be and where we are. . . . like the issues of validation, the issues of qualification. Initially issues like [standard operating procedures] . . . were not very well-known, but nowadays it is something which is well-known to everybody. So these trainings are very helpful" (Häfele-Abah 2010).

Development agencies, then, offered not only markets and monitoring, but also mentoring—either attached to specific markets, or independently of concrete opportunities. That mentoring shaped companies' extant practices as well as future plans. Lab & Allied, for example, withdrew from the GTZ training before completing the process, as the company came to realize that its factory was too old to move at the required pace; yet, according to the Kenyan pharmaceutical consultant, "When they pulled out, they went [back] to [the] drawing board and said, 'we want to build a facility that incorporates all these things we are talking of.'"[95] Other firms had similar experiences, "so all the companies you see in Kenya today, they are all the time on the rise."[96] Hence, by providing markets, monitoring, and mentoring, international development agencies helped with the transformation of the Kenyan pharmaceutical sector; firms came to produce more complex drugs and to follow higher quality standards. Foreign aid provided significant benefits for those that were able to take advantage of the opportunities offered and was instrumental in helping Kenyan pharmaceutical firms to move up the value chain. However, foreign aid also suffered from contradictions that are important to identify.

## The Promise—and Pitfalls—of Developmental Foreign Aid

By creating markets open only to quality-assured drugs, as well as by offering technical support for reaching the required quality standards, international development agencies paved a "high road" alternative for local drug manufacturers in Kenya. However, was this an attractive alternative for past practices? After all, not all the companies that invested in improving their quality standards received international certificates. Universal, which did receive WHO PQ, was still not able to sell its drugs to the Global Fund. A number of reasons prevented Universal from accessing the Global Fund market. According to Universal's managing director, "when we entered the program, there were very few prequalified products for [the] item we [chose] to qualify for; [and then] when we worked the prequalification, there were too many players."[97] Given the relatively high cost of production in Kenya, and with the Global Fund not allowing for preferences for local producers, Universal found it impossible to compete with WHO-prequalified manufacturers from India or China. Later on, the drug that Universal chose for certification was removed from the WHO's treatment guidelines. The market that helped trigger the interest in new drugs and quality upgrading, then, turned out to be mostly illusory. As Dr. Laing of WHO summarized, "of course [WHO PQ scheme] has turned out to be extremely problematic for the local industry. . . . Very few companies have been able to prequalify; and local companies that have prequalified haven't been able to win any Global Fund tenders."[98]

Yet, while both the WHO PQ and the PIC/S certificate did not bring "any return on investment per se," the production of new types of drugs and quality upgrading provided access to other markets.[99] Both Universal and Cosmos sold small orders of ARVs to the Kenyan government.[100] At least in one German-funded tender, Kenyan companies that passed the PIC/S audit won about 60 percent of the tender items (von Massow n.d.). Quality upgrading also improved companies' reputation in the private market, which helped with sales of their branded medicines. Most consequentially, WHO PQ and the PIC/S certificates "made a big difference" by assuring nongovernmental institutional buyers of the companies' high quality standards.[101] Universal, Cosmos, and Regal increased their sales to the faith-based Mission for Essential Drugs and Supplies (MEDS), which still provided medicine for a significant portion of all health facilities in Kenya and was known for its high quality standards. They could now also sell to international nongovernmental organizations (INGOs), including Médecins Sans Frontières (MSF), the International Committee of the Red Cross, and the German medical aid organization action medeor in Tanzania.[102] Some of these INGOs, in addition to testing the drugs they purchased, conducted audits and technical visits—adding mentoring to monitoring. Even USAID started to buy a few drugs from Universal, Cosmos, and Regal, and PEPFAR bought some drugs for AIDS-related opportunistic infections from local sources. To assure quality, they sampled the quality of each batch they bought.[103]

Additionally, Cosmos and Universal, in particular, continued to explore new products and additional markets, often with the support of donors. For example, as the WHO recommended the use of combined treatment of zinc and ORS for diarrhea in children, Universal worked with CHAI to develop co-packaged products. Universal also developed a chlorhexidine gel for umbilical cord care. Both products were sold to UNICEF (CCMCentral 2013, ACCI 2016). As Universal's director manager asserted, *"Because of [WHO PQ]*, we started getting orders from institutions like USAID and UNICEF" (ACCI 2016, emphasis added). Universal's growing reputation may have also been instrumental in its purchase by a foreign company. In 2016, one of the top Indian pharmaceutical firms, Strides Shasun, purchased a controlling 51 percent stake in Universal for a total of $14 million.[104] I discuss the implications of this purchase in chapter 9.

However, not all companies were able to take advantage of these opportunities, and those who did not benefit from foreign aid saw the condition of quality assurance as an entry barrier used to de facto exclude them, and they resented the WHO PQ requirement.[105] A local newspaper article stated: "Ironically, as more multinational pharmaceutical companies have agreed to give voluntary manufacturing licenses, a new hurdle—prequalification by the WHO—has emerged to block use of locally-manufactured generic ARVs by donor-supported treatment programs" (Kimani 2006). Even the Chairman of Cosmos maintained that, "GMP is a good concern. But [it] can be used as an economic weapon."[106] Indeed, in addition to the technical difficulties of attaining WHO PQ, the realization that the promised market was difficult to access turned other Kenyan companies against trying to achieve it. Lab & Allied cited the experience of Universal to claim that WHO PQ "provided no business opportunity."[107] When I asked a representative in South Africa about the possibility of Beta Healthcare producing prequalified drugs—because Aspen produced WHO-certified drugs in facilities in South Africa—I was told: "To get [PQ] you have to invest a lot and have to get the money back from consumers. [We] will have to increase prices. We saw other companies. They think it's a joke. WHO—they work on cheapest drugs. [Since we wouldn't be able to win any tenders, there is] no incentive for us to pay for upgrade."[108]

Finally, the trajectories of Universal, Cosmos, and Regal highlight an additional tension in the reliance on foreign aid for industrial development—the fact that training and other opportunities tend to benefit those who already do relatively well. Upgrading is a long, expensive, and risky process. Most factories in Kenya were already quite old, so they could not be simply modified to meet WHO requirements. As a WHO official admitted, "we can't coach those who are on the lowest level." As the official explained, "[We] can change only those who have at least reasonable facility because we [have very limited resources so we] can't build new facilities. So if the facility is total crap, it's hopeless."[109] The same initiatives and programs that benefited the "haves" did not reach the smallest companies, namely, those that had the most worrisome quality standards in the first place. Foreign aid, then, led to bifurcation, in which top companies had the opportunity to take the "high road," while the "low road" was still very much the only option for those without capital.

## Discussion

Back in the 1980s, the most consequential foreign aid involvement in local pharmaceutical production in Kenya was the ration kits program. The program had positive impact thanks to a supportive state that funded a local component reserved for local producers, and thanks to the presence of nascent entrepreneurs, who could take advantage of the opportunities provided by the ration kits due to access to the technical know-how that they had through ties abroad. In other words, although foreign aid was key for the emergence of a local pharmaceutical market in Kenya, it heavily relied on the state and on local actors for market and mentoring, respectively.

In this chapter, I showed that, by 2000, the state only offered a small market and minimal enforcement of quality standards, and the ties abroad and networks at home—while still important—could not offer the more complex technical know-how that was required by then. In turn, foreign aid provided markets, monitoring, and mentoring, which made it *developmental* foreign aid. Funds provided by international development agencies for the procurement and distribution of drugs for the treatment of AIDS, tuberculosis, malaria, and other diseases created an unprecedented demand. However, donors conditioned access to their funds on the monitoring of quality standards—which led those pharmaceutical companies interested in the new opportunities to produce new types of drugs and to improve the quality standards of the drugs they produced. Development agencies offered free or subsidized technical guidance that helped both with the production of new drugs and with the upgrading of quality procedures. The companies that took advantage of the opportunities provided by foreign aid—and that were able to overcome the technical challenges—benefited from their investment. Still, the challenges, and the risks, were not trivial. In the next chapter, I discuss the response of local pharmaceutical companies in Tanzania to similar opportunities.

# 7

# Tanzania in the 2000s

## DEVELOPMENTAL FOREIGN AID (2)

In 1990, the Tanzanian pharmaceutical sector was small and fragile, with two state-owned pharmaceutical companies, Keko Pharmaceutical Industries and Tanzania Pharmaceutical Industries (TPI), and four privately owned ones—all of them producing a limited range of simple products, as I describe in chapter 4. A decade or so later, the situation seemed more promising. Two of the private companies, Shelys Pharmaceuticals and Interchem Pharmaceuticals, as well as Keko and TPI, which had been privatized in 1997, improved their performances and were able to capture larger shares of the market. At its peak, the sector included eight pharmaceutical companies that reportedly captured as much as one-third of the local market. However, there were also challenges that made this success short-lived. By 2014, both the number of companies and their relative market shares had greatly declined—according to the director-general of Tanzania's Medical Stores Department (MSD), "only two of the six pharmaceutical plants in the country [were] operational" (Ubwani 2016). Another report highlighted the health implications of the situation (Wangwe et al. 2014):

> Tanzania is rapidly losing its pharmaceutical production capability. . . . The loss undermines Tanzania's medium-term security of supply of essential medicines. It threatens cumulative industrial and employment decline in one of Tanzania's few higher-skill sectors and in local suppliers, including plastics and packaging. It increases the trade deficit, and misses opportunities to exploit development synergies between health needs, health financing, and industrial growth.

The same report identified a number of factors that contributed to the decline, many of them similar to the challenges that Kenyan drug manufacturers also faced. One factor, for example, was increasing import price competition in a context of high local production costs. Another was the changed treatment guidelines of antimalarial drugs from sulphadoxine-pyrimethamine (SP), 90 percent of which had been sourced locally, to a new combination therapy, artemether-lumefantrine (AL), which local producers did not make (Wangwe et al. 2014). A third factor identified by the report—"costs of continuous upgrading to meet . . . regulatory pressures"—was unique to Tanzania. The report explained (Wangwe et al. 2014):

> All local firms are upgrading to meet . . . GMP guidelines. . . . TFDA [Tanzania Food and Drugs Authority] works actively with manufacturers to improve processes while ensuring safe current operation, inspecting local firms more frequently than overseas competitors. Continuous upgrading requires large investments in technology and staff training; support . . . for finance and access to technology is essential if upgrading is not to price firms out of local markets.

In this chapter, I describe the trajectory of Tanzanian drug companies in the decade following donors' increased funding of drugs in Tanzania, which started in 2005. The description challenges the impression of a pharmaceutical sector in crisis. No doubt, the Tanzanian pharmaceutical sector suffered from considerable weaknesses. The number of companies decreased, the sector was highly concentrated, and its market share certainly declined. Yet, most of the companies that closed down were small, and their closures implied a relative effective "weeding out" of poorly performing companies. The exception was the closing down of the second largest pharmaceutical company in Tanzania, TPI, which I describe below. Indeed, much of the decline in performance of the sector as a whole could be ascribed to TPI's fall. The large companies in Tanzania that stayed operational, however, invested in new products and in higher quality standards and in that way helped to improve the capabilities and reputation of the local sector. In short, although there was decline in quantity, there was also evident improvement in quality.

Investment in new products and in improved quality standards was in response to developmental foreign aid that, as was the case in Kenya, provided markets, mentoring, and monitoring. In Tanzania, markets that were promised by development agencies did not always rely on donors' funds but were created at the domestic level—through the generation of demand in the public and/ or the private sector. Mentoring, accordingly, focused not only on technical know-how, but on managerial and marketing support as well. Reliance on domestic markets, however, meant that access to markets could not be conditioned on World Health Organization (WHO) Good Manufacturing Practices

(GMP) or other international quality standards, as was the case in Kenya. Still, monitoring of quality standards was often a condition for receiving technology transfer. In addition, in Tanzania, the national regulatory authority, TFDA, enforced quality standards on local producers more effectively than the counterpart agencies in Kenya and Uganda, as Wangwe and colleagues (2014) also suggest. Although TFDA standards were not up to the WHO GMP standards, this relatively effective monitoring by the state partly solved the dilemma of creating a market that was not conditioned on WHO GMP; it also led to the closure of some of the local pharmaceutical firms, which helps to explain the low number of operating pharmaceutical facilities in Tanzania. In other words, the complementarity between developmental foreign aid on the one hand and state enforcement on the other was fundamental to Tanzania's experience—and it's what channeled some factories toward the "high road," while also blocking the "low road" in some cases.

In what follows, I first describe the Tanzanian pharmaceutical sector as of the early 2010s. Although some companies were small and did not maintain even local GMP standards, others had diversified their product range and maintained quality standards beyond what was required by law. In the rest of the chapter, I examine the conditions that led some companies to invest in new products and higher quality standards by looking at the access that local companies had to markets, monitoring, and mentoring. I show that in Tanzania, developmental foreign aid—this time, in interplay with domestic market opportunities and local monitoring—channeled Tanzanian pharmaceutical companies in new directions.

## The Tanzanian Pharmaceutical Sector in the 2010s

In the course of major political-economic reforms, the industrial sector in Tanzania faced a particularly challenging environment. A structural adjustment program (SAP) was initially resisted by President Nyerere—in 1979, the President asked the International Monetary Fund (IMF) Mission to leave the country after they had presented their demands to him (Edwards 2014, 136). Still, some tentative steps toward reform were taken in the early 1980s, and once Nyerere stepped down as President in 1985, Tanzania signed its first Standby Agreement with the IMF (Devarajan, Dollar, and Holmgren 2001). The reforms, which included major cuts in government spending and privatization, undermined many of President Nyerere's achievements, most notably, nearly universal primary education, a network of health centers within reach of most of the population, and rural water supplies (Benson 2001, Coulson 2013, 4–5). As for the economy, whereas gold mining and tourism, for example, did experience growth, manufacturing continued to suffer from structural bottlenecks in infrastructure, access to credit, and high costs of energy and communication

(Mans 2002, Coulson 2013). Sectors like pharmaceuticals additionally suffered from a lack of locally produced raw materials and a shortage of skilled human resources.[1] The share of manufacturing in GDP between 2005 and 2010 was only 7.58 percent, almost half that of Kenya during that time.[2]

In the 1990s, no new pharmaceutical companies opened in Tanzania, although the two state-owned pharmaceutical factories were privatized in 1997. In the 2000s, the older companies—Shelys, Interchem, Khanbhai Pharmaceuticals, Mansoor Daya Chemicals, the renamed Keko Pharmaceutical industries (1997), and TPI—were joined by three newer ones. Tanzansino United Pharmaceuticals opened in 2000, A. A. Pharmaceuticals opened in 2002, and Zenufa Laboratories opened in 2007. Khanbhai, Interchem, Tanzansino, and TPI later closed down, however. In addition, the market share of the few local producers that remained was low—only around 10–15 percent.[3]

Registration data give us another measure by which to assess the position of the local pharmaceutical sector and confirm the low and declining presence of locally produced drugs in the market. In 2012, local manufacturers had 214 drugs registered, which was around 6 percent of the 3,213 drugs that registered in total. As of June 2017, only 106 of 3,510 drugs—or around 3 percent—were registered by local manufacturers. Only three local companies—Shelys, Zenufa, and Keko—had their drugs registered that year. Even these three companies reduced the number of their registered drugs over time. The number of drugs registered by Shelys, for example, declined from 127 in 2012 to 53 in 2017.[4]

The decline in the number of manufacturing firms, in the local market share and in the number of registered local drugs, raised alarm bells among those supportive of local pharmaceutical production, as we have seen (Wangwe et al. 2014). Yet, an analysis of the companies that closed and why they closed and the practices of the companies that remained open depicts a more robust sector than the numbers on their own indicate. It is useful therefore to differentiate between a number of different types of local pharmaceutical firms based on size, production, and quality standards—and to look at their respective trajectories.

The first category includes Mansoor Daya, which opened in 1964, and A. A. Pharmaceuticals and Tanzansino, which were both founded after 2000. The three companies produced very simple drugs and were exceptionally small. None of the companies followed local GMP (MOHSW 2011). Mansoor Daya, which was the oldest drug firm in Tanzania, reportedly "got back in full swing" following the economic reforms—the company renovated its premises, expanded its activities, and acquired new machinery for manufacturing oral liquid formulations and tablets.[5] However, the firm still had only limited production capacity and suffered from limited technical know-how. One evaluation reported, for example, that, "although it has machinery for manufacturing pediatric formulations, the company lacks the technical knowledge for manufacturing them"

(MOHSW 2011, 9). The facility only manufactured paracetamol and aspirin and did not comply with GMP.[6] A. A. Pharmaceuticals was even smaller. It was established in 2002 by an African Tanzanian pharmacist; and with very basic infrastructure, it mostly produced creams/ointments and antiseptics (MOHSW 2011, Mwilongo 2011, Banda, Wangwe, and Mackintosh 2014).

The trajectory of Tanzansino is more surprising, given that it started as a $3 million joint venture between the Tanzanian and Chinese governments. The National Service of Tanzania (Suma JKT) provided 45 percent of the investment, and the New Technological Applications Center of northern China's Shangxi Province provided 55 percent of the investment.[7] The Chinese provided machinery and technical know-how and stationed seven to eight Chinese expatriates in the plant.[8] The collaboration was politically significant because it was seen as a signal of deepened bilateral economic cooperation between the two countries (People's Daily 2001). In the first few years of operation, Tanzansino was "quite famous, [and had a reputation for] good quality," even though it produced only a small number of drugs—antiworm medications and drugs for treating cholera and malaria.[9] In 2006, the factory stopped producing, however, possibly because the Shangxi Province lost interest in the enterprise. Not long after, in 2007, the Chinese shares were bought by the Holley Industrial Group—a Chinese industrial group that also owned Beijing Holley Cotec, which produced and exported to East Africa artemisinin-based therapies for malaria.[10] The purchase was reportedly motivated by the fact that the Chinese manufacturer was eligible for local preferences as a result.[11] The original plan was to produce antimalarials. However, change in national treatment guidelines that banned the use of artemisinin monotherapies, which was what Holley Cotec produced at the time, blocked that original plan. Possibly as a result, Holley Group only minimally renovated the factory, and when in 2008–2009 the factory started producing again, it only produced a few pain killers and anti-infectives (MOHSW 2011, UNDP 2016). By 2010, reportedly due to organizational problems among company shareholders, "all the Chinese left," and the factory stopped production.[12] At no point was the firm GMP compliant (MOHSW 2011).

The mid-range category includes two companies, Keko, which opened in 1975–76, and Interchem, which opened in 1987. In comparison to the smaller firms, their production included a broader range of basic medicines—including simple antibiotics, cough and cold preparations, painkillers, and simple antimalarials—and they were larger and produced a respectable share of the value of local production (Mhamba and Mbirigenda 2010, Mwilongo 2011, Chaudhuri, Mackintosh, and Mujinja 2010). In addition, they followed local GMP standards (MOHSW 2011). Interchem eventually closed, whereas Keko remained open and improved over time.

Interchem was sold to two African Tanzanian brothers soon after it had opened in 1987—Benjamin Mengi and his more successful sibling, Reginald

Mengi, who founded one of the largest industrial groups in East Africa, IPP (chapter 4). In 2004, majority shares of Interchem were bought by Mac Group, a diversified Indian Tanzanian group and, a couple of years later, by the National Investment Company Limited, and Benjamin Mengi and his wife Millie stayed on as minority shareholders (Sutton and Olomi 2012). Although Interchem started as a very small company, for a while it enjoyed a good reputation and by 2005 had 15 percent of the value of local production (East African 2008, UNDP 2016). Interchem was also one of the four companies—together with Shelys, TPI, and Keko—that received approval in the first round of local GMP inspections in 2005 (Losse, Schneider, and Spennemann 2007). However, the company acquired a $6 million loan, reportedly for expanding the existing tablets and capsule line and for establishing a new penicillin plant and a new line for the production of ARVs; and when it was not able to make back the payments, Interchem was placed under receivership and closed down in 2008 (East African 2008, Tibandebage et al. 2014, 47).

Keko, which was founded as a state company, was privatized in 1997—with 60 percent of its equity sold to local private investors and 40 percent remaining in the hands of the state—and renamed Keko Pharmaceutical Industries (1997).[13] According to one report, "the purchasers were a very energetic husband and wife team of indigenous Tanzanians," who had already owned and operated a drug importing and distribution firm, Diocare (Due, Temu, and Temu 1999). At the time they bought Keko, it was not operational, it was "highly leveraged," and it required additional investment "to enable upgrading of the machinery in order to comply with regulatory requirements" (World Bank 2010, 65). Reports suggest that the new owners made substantial investments—including "purchases of Indian-made equipment"—with the help of a $1.2 million loan. Nevertheless, in 2003, the factory had "a lot of obsolete equipment and facilities" and still needed "substantial upgrades and restructuring in order to be viable" (Summa Foundation 2003, 43). Some suggested that the company was "not doing well" due to management problems. The new owners did not have pharmaceutical backgrounds—and they might have been more interested in marketing than in manufacturing.[14] Others suggested that the private investors encountered unexpected debt and disputes with former employees, and the government, which still owned 40 percent of the shares, had not provided additional investment (Due et al. 1999). For a while, the company was only "open on and off."[15] As for quality standards, although in 2005, Keko's plant reached local GMP standards, in 2010, it was reported that Keko did not comply with GMP requirements "due to critical deficiencies" (MOHSW 2011, 10). Later on, things improved again. In 2013, it was reported that "Fabtech Technologies and Keko Pharmacy are finalizing talks on the envisaged renovation and expansion of [Keko] to state-of-art drug producing company" (Elinaza 2013). The same Indian company, with specialty in innovative turnkey solutions, had also worked with TPI in Arusha. As of 2017, Keko had successfully registered seven products at the TFDA, indicating that the company again received local GMP.

The final category of companies includes those that invested considerably to increase their capacity, diversify their product range, and upgrade their quality standards, at times going beyond what was required by Tanzanian regulations. Shelys, Zenufa, and TPI all did so, although a scandal later forced TPI to close.

Of the three companies, Shelys was the largest. Originally opened in 1981, Shelys was acquired by Sumaria Group in 1984, a diversified Indian Tanzanian group with interests in consumer goods, plastics and agro-processing (Shah 2009). (Sumaria later also purchased Beta Healthcare in Kenya, as I describe in chapter 6.) It was under the Sumaria Group that Shelys became a leading drug company in Tanzania. By 2009, Shelys had almost 60 percent of the value of local production (UNDP 2016). The company changed hands in 2008, when Aspen Pharmacare Holdings, a South African pharmaceutical company, acquired 60 percent of the share capital of Shelys Africa (which held shares of both Shelys and Beta Healthcare). In 2012, Aspen acquired the remaining 40 percent of Shelys Africa and became the sole owner of both Shelys and Beta Healthcare. Aspen was the largest generics manufacturer in the southern hemisphere and one of the top twenty generic manufacturers worldwide; it was also sub-Saharan Africa's first and largest generic manufacturer of antiretrovirals (ARVs).

Under Sumaria, Shelys invested in new products and planned to produce ARVs (Mhamba and Mbirigenda 2010). Once Aspen took over, Shelys focused instead on fast-moving items with high profit margins in the private sector, and the firm lost interest in drugs for the public sector, including ARVs; yet the company registered the antimalarial AL and was the first in sub-Saharan Africa to produce zinc treatment for diarrhea. Under both Sumaria and Aspen, Shelys followed local GMP standards and, with the technical support of German Technical Cooperative Agency (GTZ), successfully pursued a Pharmaceutical Inspection Convention and Pharmaceutical Inspection Co-operation Scheme (PIC/S) certificate that confirmed the company was following European quality standards. Shelys was also one of two firms in Tanzania (the other one was Zenufa) that successfully passed the audit that Roche conducted in preparation of offering voluntary licensing (on GTZ and Roche, see also chapter 6). A new factory that Shelys opened in 2006 was designed to be able to get a WHO prequalification (PQ) certificate, and Shelys planned to pursue WHO PQ for its zinc product (USAID 2008); in January 2010, a WHO GMP team that inspected Shelys' facility found only "not critical" deviations (MOHSW 2011). Still, in the years that followed, observers reported that quality standards in the factory fell short of original expectations.

A second reputable company in Tanzania was Zenufa Laboratories, which was established by four partners, all Ugandans of Indian origin, who before moving to Tanzania had a trading business in the Democratic Republic of

TABLE 7.1. Characteristics of Tanzania's pharmaceutical companies, 2000s

| Firm | Value of production (2004–2005) | Percentage of local production (annual average, 2004–2009) | No. of employees | Production capacity | Drugs registered (2017) |
|---|---|---|---|---|---|
| Shelys | $16 million | 60 | 330 | 6,500 million tablets; 2,160 million capsules; 108 million liquid orals; 18 million dry syrups | 53 |
| TPI | $6.65 million | 15.25 | 88 | N/A | |
| Interchem | $4.9 million | 15 (only 2004–2005) | N/A | N/A | |
| Keko | $3.686 million | 14 | 56 | 1,680 million tablets; 608 million capsules; 1.2 million dry syrup | 7 |
| Zenufa | [Not yet opened] | 5.5 (only 2007–2009) | N/A | 2,956 million tablets; 700 million capsules; million liquid orals; 30 million dry syrups | 30 |
| Mansoor Daya | $669,000 | 3.5 | 65 | 450 million tablets | |
| Tanzansino | $513,000 | 0.65 | 73 | 1 billion tablets | |
| A. A. Pharmaceuticals | $137,000 | 0.4 | N/A | N/A | |

*Source:* Compiled by the author; for value of production and % of local production, see UNDP (2016); for number of employees and production capacity, see MOHSW (2011).

the Congo. In Tanzania, they first had a company importing and distributing pharmaceutical products, and in 2007, they diversified to manufacturing.[16] Although much smaller than Shelys (UNDP 2016), Zenufa from early on emerged as an ambitious company interested in new products and high quality standards. Zenufa did not register ARVs, but it did produce zinc and artemisinin-based combination therapy (ACT). Zenufa met local GMP requirements (MOHSW 2011, 13) and pursued WHO PQ for its ACT.

TPI also for a time invested in new products and pursued high quality standards. Founded in 1980 as a state-owned company, TPI was privatized in 1997, with 60 percent of its equity sold to a consortium of local Tanzanian entrepreneurs, Pharmaceutical Investments Ltd., and 40 percent remaining government-owned. One of the private investors was Ramadhani Madabida, who became TPI's managing director, and was also the Chairman of the Dar es Salaam Region for Tanzania's ruling party, Chama Cha Mapinduzi or CCM (CCMCentral 2013). His wife Zarina Madabida was TPI deputy managing director and a shareholder in the company; she also held a Special Seat in Parliament as a member of CCM. In 2009, TPI was the second largest pharmaceutical firm in Tanzania, after Shelys (Wilson 2009). In addition to products such as aspirin, allergy and cough syrups, and medical kits, TPI started producing ACTs in 2003 and ARVs in 2005 (Losse et al. 2007, table 3, Chaudhuri et al. 2010). At the time, TPI followed local GMP standards (Mhamba and Mbirigenda 2010), but the company also built a new factory with the intention of following WHO GMP. However, in 2012, accusations of fraud led to the closure of both factories, as I describe below.

Table 7.1 shows different characteristics of the pharmaceutical companies in Tanzania. The origins of the newer companies reveal no common trajectory to becoming an entrepreneur in the pharmaceutical sector in Tanzania. Some companies were opened by pharmacists-entrepreneurs who were educated in Tanzania and had no ties abroad; other companies were opened by diversified commercial enterprises—either local, regional, or international. Firms that did relatively well shared a common experience, however. The remainder of the chapter describes the role foreign aid and domestic conditions played in the trajectory of these companies, through the provision of markets, mentoring, and monitoring.

## Local Production of Quality-Assured Drugs: Domestic and Foreign Influences

After liberalization, Tanzania struggled to preserve its socialist legacy of a relatively well-developed basic health care delivery system. Yet, as a WHO report put it: "It has been observed that SAPs have worsened the health . . . situation of communities" in Tanzania (WHO 1994b), with a high rate of HIV/AIDS making health care provision all the more challenging. In 1997, the estimated prevalence of human immunodeficiency virus (HIV) among adults aged 15 to 49 was 9.3 percent; in 2003, the estimated rate went down somewhat, to 7.9 percent.[17] The rolling out of ARVs was tragically slow. At the end of 2004, only 880 people received treatment through the public sector; an additional two thousand patients received treatment from private facilities and research projects (WHO 2007b). Together, this covered only 0.6 percent of those in need of treatment. With the help of foreign assistance, by 2016, an estimated 62 percent of those in need, or around 850 thousand people, were being reached—on par with both Kenya (64 percent) and Uganda (67 percent).[18]

The Tanzanian pharmaceutical sector in 2000 was not likely to contribute to the production of the needed drugs. As we have seen, most of the companies were small, and none possessed the technical know-how required for the production of ARVs. However, a number of factors made Tanzania an attractive site for foreign assistance—and the provision of markets, mentoring, and monitoring contributed to the upgrading of the top companies. To begin with, Tanzania was a Least Developed Country (LDC), and it was therefore exempt from having to implement or enforce patent obligations with respect to pharmaceutical products until 2016, which was later extended until 2021 and then 2033 (UNAIDS 2013, WTO 2015).[19] Consequently, Tanzania was considered a viable place for the production of newly developed drugs. As a former German colony, moreover, Tanzania was of particular interest to German development agencies, which, as I discuss in chapter 6, were especially involved in local pharmaceutical production in East Africa. Finally, Tanzania's enforcement of quality standards further encouraged allocation of aid to Tanzanian firms. In Tanzania, then, developmental foreign aid provided similar resources as in Kenya, including the offering of markets, mentoring, and monitoring. Yet, a heavier reliance on domestic markets in Tanzania led to mentoring that included guidance in marketing in addition to technical know-how, and this focus on domestic markets required monitoring that could not be based on international standards alone.

## MARKETS

The small size of the private drug market in Tanzania was a reflection of the economic position of the country: in 2004, with a population of 38 million, Tanzania had an estimated $345 GDP per capita (compared to $459 in Kenya).[20] Until 1997, moreover, commercial activity in the pharmaceutical field was limited, as the National Pharmaceutical Company (NAPCO) was the main agency responsible for the provision of drugs for the private sector (chapter 4). With liberalization, however, NAPCO was liquidated, and the market was open for privately owned retail pharmacies and wholesalers.

Imports from the global South accelerated as a result (chapter 2), although local drug producers had a number of advantages, at least in rural areas. First, local manufacturers had shorter supply chains; and, in rural areas, they had better private distribution networks (Mujinja et al. 2014). In referring to Shelys marketing strategies, an Aspen official in South Africa explained: "If you've got a good distribution infrastructure, then your product will get . . . as close to the end customer as possible, up to the rural areas, [to] people living far away from the main cities or main towns. [Therefore] . . . distribution is key for us. One of the things that we've invested a lot in . . . is to improve our distribution infrastructure."[21] A second advantage of local manufacturers was greater flexibility in their ability to respond to market needs. Third, the packets of locally produced medicine included information in Swahili, which increased both accessibility and trust of users (Mujinja et al. 2014). Relatedly, some of the locally produced items had brand recognition in shops (Mujinja et al. 2014). An Aspen official confirmed that: "Sales representation is another [key issue]. We've put a lot of sales reps on the ground just to make sure that health care professionals are aware of our products."[22] Finally, surveys showed that in rural areas there was no significant difference in the average price of medicine from Tanzania, Kenya, and India.[23] These advantages explain the relatively prominent presence of locally produced drugs in a survey of medicines in private drug shops in rural districts in Tanzania that took place in 2006. Of the medicine traced in the survey, 66 percent on average were from Tanzanian manufacturers, compared to 18 percent from Kenya and 11 percent from India (Chaudhuri et al. 2010, Mujinja et al. 2014). Still, given the poor purchasing power of the population in rural areas, this was a relatively small size of the drug market, and it was harder for Tanzanian companies to compete in the cities. Additionally, with the exception of Shelys, which in 2004–2005 exported 17 percent of its production, Tanzanian firms did not export their drugs (UNDP 2016, table 3).

As for the public sector, as in Kenya, the state tried to be supportive of local manufacturers, albeit with limited effect. The support was in spite of local manufacturers' minimal political influence. In 2012, the Tanzania Pharmaceutical Manufacturers Association (TPMA) had only four members: Keko, Mansoor Daya, TPI, and Zenufa (FEAPM 2012). Notably, Shelys was not a member. Geographically concentrated (Keko, Mansoor Daya, and Zenufa were in Dar es Salaam, and TPI was in Arusha), although without obvious social ties that brought them together, the four members met every two or three months, and they tried to reach a common position and be part of the policy-making process.[24] They were all also members of the larger and more influential Tanzania Association of Pharmaceutical Industry (TAPI), which represented those importing drugs and therefore held competing interests.

Although lacking political influence, local drug producers benefited from the cross-national diffusion of supportive policies—so that Tanzanian policies in the pharmaceutical field were similar to those of other developing countries. Hence, the state offered local drug producers some fiscal incentives. For example, there was no import duty on raw materials, packaging material, and machinery, and no value-added tax or excise for domestic formulations. Local manufacturers complained, however, that reimbursements were slow and that they had difficulties in obtaining exemption from duties for some imported inputs (Wangwe et al. 2014). These exemptions only partly countered the lack of duties on imported finished products. In addition, the TFDA charged lower fees from local producers for registration, retention, and GMP inspection (SADC 2009, Wilson 2009). Potentially more consequential were price incentives of 15 percent that the Tanzanian government granted for local drug producers. Unlike the enthusiastic endorsement of local producers when price incentives were introduced in Kenya (chapter 6), in Tanzania, local producers argued that the preferences have "not helped." The director-general of MSD, the agency conducting the tenders, countered that this was "a result of the low quantities" produced by local manufacturers (Ubwani 2016). In addition to price discounts, the government offered "a set of restricted tenders for local industry" (Wilson 2009). The amounts were not trivial—according to one estimate, national open tenders accounted for 10 percent of total public-sector procurement expenditures (SADC 2009, 19). Others argued that MSD could have made an even greater use of national tenders if there was greater national capacity to produce the drugs needed.[25]

In general, MSD seemed to have misgivings about most local producers, and the feelings were mutual. Local firms complained of delays in payments, lack of clear delivery dates, and failure to complete contracted purchases. Local firms also accused MSD for giving preference to imports by, for example, providing trade credit only to overseas suppliers (Printz et al. 2013). One study found that although the Tanzanian government was paying more for imports compared to local products, it applied much higher mark-ups on local products (135 percent) than on imports (65 percent), so that patients in public sector outlets were paying more for local products compared to imports (Ewen et al. 2017). In turn, MSD complained of quality and delivery problems from local producers (Wangwe et al. 2014, Ubwani 2016). A review concluded that, "a build-up of mutual mistrust has undermined local tendering" (Wangwe et al. 2014). In 2010, estimates suggested that about one-third of MSD's drug purchases were locally produced (Chaudhuri et al. 2010); toward the end of the decade, local producers' share of MSD medicine procurement was only around 20 percent (Ubwani 2016).

These challenges notwithstanding, MSD was still a major buyer for the larger local companies. In 2006–2007, TPI sold more than 40 percent of its production to MSD (a year later, this went up to 80 percent), Keko sold around 50 percent, and Shelys sold around one-third. Zenufa, which just opened in 2007, sold half of its production to MSD by 2011.[26] The public market was therefore undoubt-edly important. This market looked dramatically larger when donors began funding government's purchases of ARVs and ACTs.

In response to the HIV/AIDS epidemic in Tanzania, the national spending on medicine increased quite drastically. According to one estimate, in 2007, the size of the public drug market was five times larger than only one year earlier, due to the procurement of ARVs and, for malaria patients, ACTs (Häfele-Abah 2010, 14). This was made possible thanks to foreign aid. The Global Fund's first grant was in 2005. By 2010, it had provided $312 million for HIV/AIDS programs and $237 million for malaria programs (in both cases, not only for the procurement of medicine).[27] In 2014, the Global Fund accounted for about 70 percent of ARV procurement in Tanzania (Baran 2016). Funding in Tanza-nia by the US President's Emergency Plan for AIDS Relief (PEPFAR) began in 2005. In 2010, total PEPFAR funding for Tanzania was $355 million, out of which funding for the procurement of ARVs was $23 million.[28] The US President's Malaria Initiative (PMI) started distributing ACTs in Tanzania in 2006 and at the end of 2010, 4.9 million ACTs were distributed in Tanzania (USAID 2011a).

The Global Fund (but not PEPFAR or PMI) for a few years after providing its first grant to Tanzania relied on MSD for procurement.[29] That meant that in addition to purchasing ARVs and ACTs with the minimal budget provided by the government for that purpose (for drugs that follow local GMP), MSD also purchased ARVs and ACTS with funding provided to it by the Global Fund (only for drugs that followed WHO GMP). Procurement *through* the state made the Global Fund market visible, and potentially attainable, for the larger local manufacturers in Tanzania—TPI, Shelys, and Zenufa.

TPI went through a "modernization plan" following its partial privatization in 1997, which included "new design, good layout, separate penicillin production unit, new equipment, [and] new heating-ventilation-air-conditioning system" (UNIDO 1997, 11). The renovation was financed through small loans from inter-national development agencies, financial institutions, and—possibly because it was still partly state-owned—financial investments by public pension funds. As part of the upgrading, TPI implemented quality control measures that met local GMP standards. TPI was therefore in a relatively good position when mar-kets for new drugs were created (Losse et al. 2007, Wilson 2009). By 2009, TPI registered and produced three types of ACTs and four types of ARVs. Commenting on TPI's motives, a report remarked that "TPI is . . . . aware of the Global Fund . . . which might have influenced their decision to focus on drugs for these . . . diseases" (Losse et al. 2007, 24). Although never selling to the Global Fund, TPI was able to sell ARVs to MSD starting in 2007, lead-ing to a big increase in its share of government sales: from 40 percent of TPI's total sales in 2006 to double that one year later (UNDP 2016). When develop-ment agencies assisted TPI with the construction of a new factory, which was expected to follow WHO GMP (see below), the contractual arrangement still specified that the TPI would make ARVs available to the public health sector at low cost (PharmaAfrica 2011), implying that, in addition to the Global Fund market, the Tanzanian government remained another intended market.

Like TPI, Shelys too planned to produce ARVs and ACTs because "more donations" meant that "government business increased."[30] As one report suggested, "this [interest in new therapeutic areas] indicates that the company is geared towards the donor market, which will be in demand of drugs for these diseases in particular" (Losse et al. 2007, 21). Once Aspen took over from Sumaria, however, the company's orientation changed. Aspen's goal was to rationalize production by focusing on drugs that were the fastest selling and had the highest profit margins. Consequently, Shelys reduced the number of drugs it had registered, from 127 in 2012 to 53 in 2017. The focus was on branded generics aimed at the "emerging, growing middle class."[31] This orientation also meant a move away from government tenders, where profit margins were low. As an Aspen official explained, "the last thing you want to do is to compete with the cheaper generics from other countries."[32] Sales to MSD were accordingly reduced.[33] Consequently, many of the drugs that Shelys no longer retained on the Tanzania's registration list were essential drugs. An Aspen official confirmed that the move away from government tenders was "the main reason that we've cut down on the number of drugs that we've had."[34]

In line with this new orientation, Shelys abandoned its interest in the production of ARVs that it had registered (GTZ 2009). Yet Shelys continued to broaden its range of products, including in response to new donor markets.[35] One successful experience was the production of PedZinc, a zinc sulfate monohydrate tablet used in acute and chronic diarrhea. When Shelys first produced PedZinc in 2007, it was the first African-manufactured zinc treatment for diarrhea (USAID 2011b). Again, Shelys's interest in zinc was in response to foreign aid—this time an initiative of a USAID-funded Point-of-Use Water Disinfection and Zinc Treatment Project (POUZN) in collaboration with the Academy for Educational Development (AED). Unlike the Global Fund, which was not designed with the needs of local manufacturers in mind, or PIC/S, which mostly focused on technology transfer for quality upgrading, POUZN/AED paid particular attention to the question of demand and, therefore, suitable markets. Instead of promising a market that would rely on donations, this initiative relied on developing a domestic market, which had to be created. In the public sector, POUZN/AED was able to create a market by convincing the Tanzanian government, based on new WHO and UNICEF recommendations, to revise its national guidelines for treatment of diarrhea to include zinc therapy and a new low-osmolarity formulation of oral rehydration salts (lo-ORS). POUZN/AED also asked the government to add zinc and lo-ORS to its list of essential drugs, which the Tanzanian government did in November 2007.[36] POUZN/AED then helped convince TFDA to fast-track Shelys's registration of zinc (USAID 2011b, 7). In the private sector, POUZN/AED created a market by helping convince the government to approve zinc as an over-the-counter (OTC) medicine in 2009.

Zenufa was a lot smaller than Shelys, but it was new, modern, and had a "fantastic facility," so Zenufa, like Shelys, was recruited for the POUZN/AED program. As Zenufa was looking to compete with Shelys brands, they "were very excited" about the opportunity of producing zinc.[37] Zenufa was later also involved in the production of an antimalarial treatment with the support of the nonprofit drug research and development organization, Drugs for Neglected Diseases *initiative* (DNDi). In collaboration with the French pharmaceutical company Sanofi-Aventis, DNDi developed a fixed-dose combination of artesunate (AS) and amodiaquine (AQ), which simplified antimalarial treatment for children. In 2010, DNDi decided to transfer the technology to African manufacturers. After inspecting thirty-five companies, it short-listed three companies, and Zenufa was one of them. In 2016, Zenufa was able to successfully produce ASAQ.

Clearly, then, it was in response to market opportunities created by donors that some Tanzanian drug manufacturers developed an interest in producing a new range of products. Rather than donors encouraging local drug companies to produce drugs for internationally funded markets, which would require meeting WHO GMP and competition with Indian companies, some agencies steered Tanzanian companies toward the domestic market. However, this market had to be created, and POUZN/AED, in particular, was instrumental in creating it. Relying on domestic demand also came with an expanded scope of mentoring, as I describe next.

## MENTORING

Technical know-how was required for both the production of new drugs and for maintaining high quality standards. Inadequate training in pharmacy schools in Tanzania and few job opportunities meant that there was only minimal access to such technical know-how, however.[38] Some mentoring was provided by the TFDA, including GMP training workshops and consultations on the appropriate requirements during the construction of new manufacturing facilities (Losse et al. 2007, Wilson 2009). In addition, a few local pharmaceutical companies could rely on ties abroad to get access for technical know-how. Back in the 1980s, as I discuss in the first part of the book, ties abroad allowed mostly East Africans of Indian origin access to education, job experience, and links to suppliers and manufacturers of drugs. The reliance on connections abroad for technical know-how diminished somewhat with the opening of pharmacy schools and pharmaceutical factories in the region. In turn, as I discuss also in the case of

Kenya (chapter 6), globalization made access to knowledge abroad through commercial transactions easier, at the same time that the heightened sophistication of the required know-how meant that interpersonal ties alone were no long sufficient. The result was the leveling of connections with India—with Tanzanian companies relying on Indian expertise for their operations independently of who owned or managed the companies. Much of the technology for TPI's new factory, for example, was imported from India (IRIN News 2012), and consultation was also provided by an Indian company. Keko had an expert in quality assurance from India (MOHSW 2011, 10) and later reportedly hired the same Indian consulting company that had worked with TPI (Elinaza 2013). The CEOs of both Zenufa and Shelys were originally from India (Hermann 2013), and Zenufa hired an Indian company to put up new machines.[39]

Notwithstanding this access to technical know-how through private means, foreign aid was essential in offering invaluable mentoring. Technology transfer was provided not only to address the technical aspects of production, as in Kenya, but also, in the cases of Shelys and Zenufa, to assist with management and marketing.

TPI, however, was the main beneficiary of donors' mentoring and financial support. TPI learned how to produce ARVs and ACTs with the hands-on mentoring of action medeor, a German medical aid nongovernmental organization (NGO).[40] Action medeor's main organizational mission was providing generic drugs to developing countries at cost or by donation, but building local capacity was one of its goals. Starting in 2003, action medeor supported TPI in the manufacturing of ACTs for adults and pediatrics; and in 2005, action medeor supported TPI in producing ARVs (Mhamba and Mbirigenda 2010). For both projects, action medeor partnered with Dr. Krisana Kraisintu, formerly head of R&D of the state-owned Government Pharmaceutical Organization (GPO) in Thailand. Dr. Kraisintu served as a consultant for TPI—and, in that capacity, she provided the technical assistance for the production of two drugs that she had helped develop—one ACT (thaitanzunate), and one ARV (TT-VIR) (WHO 2009, 2011d). Although action medeor provided the technical know-how, TPI committed the funds to make the necessary renovations in the plant (Wilson 2009). The drugs produced in this factory were those bought by the Tanzanian government, as described above.

In addition to production of ARVs and ACTs in the existing factory, in December 2006, TPI embarked on an ambitious technology transfer project for construction of a new "greenfield WHO GMP-compliant manufacturing facility" in Arusha (Wilson 2009, 133). The plant was set to employ more than 140 people (Philemon 2011) with the capacity to serve a minimum of 100,000 patients, and with a reserve to triple that output (IRIN News 2012). This was a significant capacity—in Tanzania, in 2012, around 430,000 people living with HIV were receiving treatment.[41] Again, this could only be made possible with foreign support. TPI committed $963,000 and provided a plot for the construction, and action medeor contributed $660,000, yet the project was mostly funded by a European Union (EU) regional program, EU's Aid for Poverty-Related Diseases in Developing Countries, which contributed $6.6 million.[42] Given the technical challenges of the project, the construction was under the guidance of action medeor, and the finished factory was then to be transferred to a newly registered subsidiary company, TPI ARV Ltd., of TPI (Häfele-Abah 2010). Dr. Kraisintu again served as a technical consultant (Losse et al. 2007, WHO 2009). By the time TPI closed down, the factory was not yet fully operational.

Shelys, too, benefited from the mentoring of development agencies. Motivated by a promised market—to supply drugs to GTZ projects—Shelys participated in the program for attaining the PIC/S standards, which six pharmaceutical companies in Kenya had participated in earlier.[43] It was the only company in Tanzania to participate, and the company considered it a positive experience: "Shelys benefitted [from] regular inspections and trainings. After each inspection, the international inspectors who audit the production plant . . . using a regular cGMP [current Good Manufacturing Practices] checklist, hand over a list of issues that need to be improved in order to fulfill the standards" (Losse et al. 2007, 22). Shelys successfully passed the PIC/S inspection in 2008. Shelys was also successfully audited by Roche in 2008—as part of the Roche's initiative to offer voluntary licensing to companies to produce the second-line ARV saquinavir (chapter 6, Berger et al. 2010, table 7). Even though Shelys never went on to produce the drug, the company's CEO appreciated the experience: "The practical support that Roche has provided has been a great learning experience for my team, enabling us to make improvements to our entire technical and quality systems" (Roche 2008).

Shelys's production of PedZinc, as we have seen, involved the help of development agencies in creating a domestic market. POUZN/AED also helped Shelys with marketing in the private sector, both of PedZinc, which "was affordably priced . . . and attractively packaged" (USAID 2011b, 8), and with Shelys's brand of low-osmolarity oral rehydration therapy (lo-ORS), *SAVE*. For example, POUZN/AED helped Shelys "activate" wholesalers by providing 90 days of credit to each wholesaler for the first zinc supply to drug sellers (Goh and Pollak 2016). In addition, even though the reliance on domestic demand meant that there was no requirement to follow WHO GMP, mentoring involved upgrading of the company's quality standards. According to a POUZN report, "One of the chief incentives POUZN offered Shelys was technical assistance to achieve [WHO] GMP status" (USAID 2011b, 6). The know-how was provided, starting in 2007, by an India-based firm contracted by POUZN, CRMO Pharmatech. Shelys invested about $1 million to implement the recommended changes.

In turn, Zenufa benefited from mentoring from its very inception. When Zenufa opened—and without Sumaria's deep pockets and Aspen's expertise that helped Shelys—it entered a collaboration with the Belgian Investment Company for Developing Countries (BIO). BIO was a development finance institution that was established in 2001 by the Belgian Ministry of Development Cooperation and the private Belgian Corporation for International Investment (SBI/BMI) to support local companies in developing countries by granting them long-term financing at market conditions. BIO provided Zenufa a loan of $3.5 million over 8 years, which made Zenufa one of BIO's largest investments (BIO 2007). The loan came with "hands on" technology transfer—in regard to both manufacturing and management. According to BIO's report, "BIO was . . . involved at the technical level to validate and advise [Zenufa] on the technologies being used, and on the financial structuring of the project. BIO also persuaded [Zenufa] to adhere to corporate governance standards, more specifically by hiring an established auditing firm and appointing an independent director" (BIO 2007). Later on, Zenufa severed its relations with BIO; but, starting in 2008, POUZN/AED provided Zenufa the same kind of support it offered Shelys, including upgrading of operations and formulation, and marketing support.[44] DND*i*, in turn, helped Zenufa with the procurement of machines, the provision of raw materials for the stage of registration, as well as with local registration and WHO PQ—all in preparation for the production of ASAQ (DND*i* 2013).

Local pharmaceutical companies in Tanzania, then, received mentoring that went beyond the technical issues of production and quality standards and that included guidance on management and marketing. This training was often tailored to individual firms, which made the diffusion of knowledge across the sector secondary to the success of individual companies. One time, in response to "request of participants for more practical exposure," UNIDO and GTZ organized "an in-depth course with a focus on 'Qualification of equipment and validation of processes.'" The course, however, was held at the TPI premises. As a result, it "excluded technical personnel from other commercial manufacturing companies for reasons of competition" (Häfele-Abah 2010).

Normally, trainings by UNIDO, GTZ, and WHO were open and all companies were invited to attend. As we have seen in chapter 6, regional workshops took place in Tanzania, not Kenya or Uganda, making it easier for interested local manufacturers in Tanzania to participate (Häfele-Abah 2010). A manager of a Tanzanian drug manufacturing company had very positive things to say about the workshops (Häfele-Abah 2010, 70):

> The concept of GMP started [in Tanzania] only sometime in 1999. So it was really a new concept . . . [and] most of these pharmaceutical personnel [working in Tanzania] . . . did not have any practical experience. And they

didn't know much about the GMP . . . . So by . . . conducting these courses, they exposed the pharmaceutical personnel on the knowledge of the Good Manufacturing Practices, Good Laboratory Practice, Validation, Quality Assurance. . . . So they were very useful.

Another participant gave some of the credit to TFDA. He suggested that in Tanzania, "the environment for this capacity building initiative has been very conducive, since the newly created TFDA . . . was and is committed to set and enforce higher production standards" (Häfele-Abah 2010, 82). In other words, he suggested that the interest in the workshop was, in part, motivated by the fact that the TFDA began more stringent monitoring of the regulations in place, as I discuss below.

## MONITORING

A reform of drug regulations and their enforcement started in Tanzania in 2003. Following the reform, Tanzania "put significant efforts into its regulatory system" and improvement was seen as a result, even if "challenges remain[ed]" (Häfele-Abah 2010, 42). As part of the reforms, drug registration, GMP inspections, and post-marketing surveillance were under the responsibility of the newly created TFDA. The agency invested in premises and human resources (Häfele-Abah 2010), it was ISO 9001:2008 certified, and it ranked best among government institutions in Tanzania.[45] According to one evaluation, TFDA "appear[s] to be relatively strong" although the report also said that "it is obvious that there is still a lot to do" (Losse et al. 2007, 29).

As for TFDA monitoring of quality standards, one challenge was that GMP standards in Tanzania were lower than WHO GMP (Losse et al. 2007, Mhamba and Mbirigenda 2010). Back in 1997, a WHO report commented that there were "no cGMP guidelines and supplementary documents (to assist in the preparation of site master files, validation master files, etc.)," as a result of which "local manufacturers meet the legal requirements but not necessarily the internationally accepted minimum standards" (UNIDO 1997, 12). Even as standards became more stringent, local manufacturers in Tanzania, as was also the case in Kenya, were exempted from some of the more challenging requirements, such as the requirement for bioequivalence (BE) studies for registration (they were asked for comparative dissolution instead) (GTZ 2009). Still, the enforcement of standards through drug registration, factory inspections, and post-marketing surveillance improved over time.

Drug registration was required by law in the 1978 *Pharmaceuticals and Poisons Act*, but regulations were only put in place in 1990, and the process of registration started even later, in 1999, partly because the Pharmacy Board did not have the capacity to cope with registration documents (UNIDO 1997, 8,

Häfele-Abah 2010, 161, Mkumbwa 2013). Without registration, there was hardly any quality control of drugs (Chaudhuri et al. 2010), but the risk of substandard drugs flooding the country was relatively low when only the government procured drugs, using a list of allowed drugs.[46] In response to the influx of imported drugs by private hands following liberalization, registration finally started (MOHSW 2011), and TFDA developed the reputation of being the most stringent drug regulatory authority in East Africa (various interviews). Stringent, in part, because the TFDA was slower than the equivalent agencies in Kenya and Uganda—the average length of time for registration application was at least one year, "if you're lucky," as one interviewer complained. Still, the delay was also a sign of the agency "getting stricter and stricter," as reflected, for example, in the amount of information and later revisions asked for in the process.[47] In addition, Tanzania, like Kenya, had its Quality Control Laboratory prequalified by the WHO in 2011. However, again like Kenya, the TFDA did not use the laboratory for all registered drugs, but only sent samples of drugs in rare cases when there was contradictory information.[48]

The TFDA was considered relatively strict also in regard to GMP inspection. Earlier on, in 2000, none of the local manufacturers—including those that after inspection were allowed to stay open—met the GMP standards set by the Pharmacy Board (Center for Pharmaceutical Management 2003). The TFDA found it challenging to "adequately monitor even [local GMP] standards" later on (Mhamba and Mbirigenda 2010, 2). According to Chaudhuri and colleagues (2010), TFDA inspectors primarily checked whether the procedures mentioned in the product dossiers submitted by the manufacturers were followed; they did not check each product manufactured in the formulation plant, nor the raw materials sources. As a result, "There are manufacturers . . . who knowingly or unknowingly produce drugs that do not satisfy the quality requirements, and the drug control authorities . . . have [not] yet been able to prevent this" (Chaudhuri et al. 2010, 33). However, even as TFDA standards continued to fall short of international standards, these standards still forced local manufacturers to improve. In 2000, in a GMP inspection of 18 manufacturers in Kenya and 10 in Tanzania, the Pharmacy Board inspectorate approved only 10 of the 18 Kenyan facilities and ordered 3 Tanzanian plants to stop production.[49] After 2003, the TFDA conducted at least two regular audits a year at the local manufacturing sites (Häfele-Abah 2010, WHO and Global Fund n.d.); according to one local industrial pharmacist, TFDA inspections were "better" than under the Pharmacy Board, when "inspectors hardly knew what they were doing."[50] Others agreed (Chaudhuri et al. 2010):

> The TFDA's strengthening of the registration system based on plant inspection has substantially improved quality of privately-marketed drugs. Some of the international traders who used to get products manufactured from

India on contract basis disappeared. Both local and foreign manufacturers have been forced to upgrade.

Indeed, TFDA did not approve some of the Kenyan companies that passed inspection in Kenya—including Biodeal and Dawa.[51] TFDA was also stricter on local manufacturers than Kenya's PPB was on Kenyan manufacturers.

Stricter enforcement of drug registration and GMP inspection could have easily led to the closure of many drug companies in Tanzania. Although TFDA did close a number of facilities, in "trying not to kill the local industry," TFDA had policies in place that meant to allow local manufacturers to sell their drugs almost independently of their GMP.[52] Earlier on, TFDA provided local manufacturers a grace period, until 2010, to attain GMP requirements (Mwilongo 2011, 25). In addition, an amendment of TFDA's regulations provided special consideration in the registration process for locally produced products referred to as "provisional registration," and local companies that did not comply with GMP requirements could still market their products under special arrangement (MOHSW 2011, Mwilongo 2011). Nevertheless, the exceptional status created for local manufacturers indicated TFDA's refusal to simply provide undeserving GMP certificates for local manufacturers as a way to protect them. Rather, these were temporary exceptions—with the expectation that the companies would in time meet GMP certification requirements. As of 2017, only Shelys, Zenufa, and Keko—but none of the smaller companies—had drugs registered with the TFDA.

As a result of these policies, in Tanzania, more than in Kenya or Uganda, "quality control has been a key challenge faced by local manufacturers" (UNDP 2016). This "strengthened drug regulatory framework," in turn, was considered by development agencies "as an opportunity for enforcement of higher production standards on a *sustainable* basis" (Häfele-Abah 2010, 20, emphasis added). That is, TFDA's more stringent enforcement of standards on local manufacturers contributed to development agencies' interest in Tanzania as a country where it would be possible to encourage local production of new types of drugs under the condition of WHO GMP. Local manufacturers responded favorably, and the larger pharmaceutical companied did improve their quality standards, although, as of 2017, no company in Tanzania achieved WHO PQ.

Shelys under Sumaria was interested in donor markets, as we have seen, and therefore attentive to the conditions attached. "In order to comply with the increasing market demands *and international regulatory requirements*" (Losse et al. 2007, 22, emphasis added), in 2006, Shelys opened a new plant that was "built according to International Standards to meet the WHO-cGMP, US FDA [Food and Drug Administration] and European PIC/S guidelines" (Losse et al. 2007, 22). Under Aspen, the facility attained local GMP standards (MOHSW 2011), but Aspen's disinterest in the production of ARVs in Tanzania also meant

that Shelys did not pursue WHO PQ. Indeed, one reason for Shelys not to produce ARVs was the challenge of achieving an international certificate. According
to one Aspen official, "It's pointless having WHO pre-qualification in [Tanzania],
[if we can] get the products from South Africa *where the standard is there
already.*"[53] Aspen officials in South Africa argued that it made little sense to
try to achieve WHO PQ in a place like Tanzania: because of energy prices,
the need to import raw materials, and the need to import skilled workers who
required higher salaries, "local manufacturers would never be able to compete
[in the public market]."[54] In short, "we've realized [that] to try and slug it out
in the commoditized generic market . . . was quite an unattractive donor fund
business."[55] Nevertheless, when the WHO started PQ of zinc in 2008, Shelys
decided to take steps to get WHO PQ for its zinc product (USAID 2008). As
of December 2017, Shelys had not passed a WHO inspection.

Zenufa, with BIO's support, was "looking to become the first pharmaceuticals company in Tanzania to be cGMP certified by the WHO." The interest
in WHO PQ was again due to the promise of a donor market, as it "will enable
[Zenufa] to take part in international calls for tenders" (BIO 2007, 36). However, Zenufa soon thereafter decided not to pursue WHO PQ for either ARVs
or ACTs. In addition, as part of the POUZN/AED project, Zenufa produced
zinc not in tablets, as Shelys did, but in liquid form (syrup)—believing that
syrup would be more popular for young children and, because it was more
expensive, that it promised better profit margins. Because syrup was more
expensive, however, they could not sell it in the public sector, so Zenufa—
with the help of POUZN/AED—targeted the private market only.[56] The focus
on the private market meant that Zenufa did not need WHO PQ for zinc.
Still, with the consultation provided by BIO, Zenufa reportedly reached international production standards.[57] One indication of Zenufa's relatively high
standards was that in 2008, Zenufa passed the audit and signed an agreement
with Roche.[58]

Zenufa's reputation as a producer of quality products was somewhat shaken
in 2011, when, before the end of the five-year term, Zenufa decided to sever its
relations with BIO. The company paid BIO back the rest of its loan by taking
new loans from local banks. According to one of Zenufa's administrators, this
was because BIO exercised "too much supervising," which was manifested by
"a lot of restrictions," including on the amount of working capital and local
borrowing. The same interviewer also suggested that BIO "wanted too many
reports."[59] At around the same time, local pharmacists among others mentioned
that Zenufa was no longer as good as it used to be, and that the company was
"struggling" (various interviews). In the following years, however, the firm
recovered its reputation. The most significant sign was Zenufa's successful collaboration with DND*i*. Although "the journey was ridden with obstacles of a
technical, administrative and human nature," in 2016, DND*i* could declare that

Zenufa was "completely ready" to apply for WHO PQ for its ACT (SDC 2016). Another possible indication of Zenufa's recovery and success was that in 2016, Catalyst Principal Partners, a leading East African (Kenyan) private equity firm, acquired a controlling stake in the company.[60]

TPI's trajectory was even more volatile than Zenufa's, and it had a worse ending. Although TPI produced ARVs and ACTS, it could not participate in Global Fund tenders without WHO PQ, which the old factory did not have. The EU-funded new factory was supposed to follow WHO GMP, but before the new factory had a chance to become fully operational, a scandal forced the closing of both.

The scandal originated in an investigation in August 2012 in which the TFDA found "fake" ARV drug type TT-VIR 30 in a Tanzanian hospital, which, according to the TFDA, were sold to MSD by TPI (Saiboko and Tambwe 2012). There were multiple versions in regard to what exactly was the nature of TPI's violation. According to one version, the issue was that the label on the packet was different than the actual drug found in the packet. According to another, the problem was not only mislabeling, but also that the drugs were not in fact produced by TPI, but were produced abroad (possibly, in China or India), packed (secretly) by TPI, and then sold to MSD as if they were locally produced.[61] A third version maintained that drugs that were produced in order to check the machinery and had to be destroyed were instead sold by TPI (Saiboko and Tambwe 2012, various interviews). TFDA recalled the drugs and stopped the distribution of all drugs manufactured by the company. TPI consequently closed down.

TPI directors vehemently defended their company. Responding to the accusation of mislabeling, they claimed that the factory did not have the capacity to produce the drugs identified as theirs. According to the deputy director manager, Zarina Madabida, "we do not have the technology that can produce tablets in a round shape and in two colors; the product is simply not ours" (Saiboko and Tambwe 2012). Instead, Madabida claimed that the accusations were the doing of a syndicate aimed at tarnishing the company's image at a time that Tanzania's ruling party, CCM, was conducting internal elections, where both she and her husband were vying for various posts. Her claims seemed to have been vindicated by the fact that in May 2013, the Minister for Health and Social Welfare cleared TPI of any wrongdoing (Mugarula 2013). However, in February 2014, Ramadhani Madabida and five others were charged with supplying counterfeit drugs and obtaining money by false pretense and occasioning a loss to MSD (Kenyunko 2014). In 2015, Pharmaceutical Investment Ltd., the consortium through which the Madabidas and other investors owned 60 percent of TPI, went bankrupt (Tanzania Daily News 2015). In March 2017, Ramadhani Madabida was among twelve CCM members who were expelled from the party for "sabotage" (Nyanje 2017).

In spite of its peculiarities, the case of TPI demonstrates the effective monitoring by the Tanzanian government and the limits of monitoring by development agencies. Although the causes of TPI's ultimate fall are disputed, based on the information available, there is a consensus that TFDA not only acted in good faith, but also functioned competently, responding adequately to the facts available in the case. As for foreign aid, monitoring worked to the extent that the new factory was designed to be prequalified by the WHO, but aid clearly failed in maintaining quality standards if it was TPI that sold mislabeled or otherwise substandard drugs to MSD. I refer back to this point in chapter 9.

The scandal around TPI notwithstanding, monitoring by donors and by the state led, since 2000, to the upgrading of production facilities in Tanzania (IFC 2007, Losse et al. 2007, Thoithi et al. 2008, Chaudhuri et al. 2010, 9). As a result, INGOs, including not only action medeor but also the Red Cross, began to procure some drugs from local manufacturers; even USAID purchased local products "for a couple of million [dollar]s a year."[62] These buyers had their own auditing mechanisms, reinforcing as buyers the conditioned monitoring initially imposed by donors. For example, as a buyer, action medeor, in addition to GMP auditing, inspected all batches and did random testing using a WHO-prequalified laboratory (Mackintosh et al. 2016).

In turn, the case of Shelys demonstrates one way by which ties abroad (or foreign ownership more specifically), in addition to monitoring by the state and by development agencies, could impact quality standards. On the one hand, given its international reputation, Aspen had reasons to maintain high quality standards beyond what was required by local regulations. As one Aspen official explained: "Look, our quality standards are quite high, being part of a global organization. Over and above local laws and regulations, we also have *group-wide standards* that we need to maintain. . . . So when we first got in there [Tanzania], that was one of the first key items that we looked at and improved on. From a group perspective, there was work that needed to be and was done. . . . We ensure that we comply with local quality standards as well as the *group standards*."[63] Another Aspen official confirmed: "Obviously, the standard in East Africa is never going to be as high as it is in Germany. But if it's sorted down here and Germany's there, you'll get some type of an equalization effect . . . to an *Aspen standard*."[64] On the other hand, by focusing on the private market, Aspen changed Shelys' orientation toward *less* reliance on opportunities created by foreign aid—and therefore potentially less attentiveness to international quality requirements.

In short, quality standards were monitored in Tanzania by the state, by development agencies that provided mentoring, and by foreign investors and parent companies. This multiplicity of expectations meant that the larger pharmaceutical companies in Tanzania followed quality standards that were in line with local GMP standards and often aimed higher.

## Discussion

A USAID official in Tanzania offered a harsh critique of the local pharmaceutical sector, describing, as of 2013, a sector that was greatly behind current medical and technological developments:

> Local manufacturing capacity is a misnomer. Most local manufacturing capacity [are] for products we [USAID] don't need or old drugs off-patent that are not necessarily effective. Manufacturing in East Africa is 20 years behind China and India.

The same USAID official also commented on the high costs that production required.

> We work with [a name of a Tanzanian manufacturer]. [Each item] costs us $1 more than if we bought [it] from India. The only advantage for buying from them is that [it] cuts 8 weeks of shipping time. It's good as a backup in case of stock-out. Financially, it doesn't make sense to buy locally.[65]

Clearly, institutional buyers must have found it frustrating to work with some of the local pharmaceutical companies in Tanzania. At the same time, this grim depiction of the sector failed to mention that Shelys was the largest pharmaceutical company in East Africa and that the larger Tanzanian pharmaceutical companies followed high quality standards. This was, in large part, thanks to foreign aid initiatives.

The experience of the local pharmaceutical sector in Tanzania after 2000 resembles the experience of the sector in Kenya. In both cases, local manufacturers produced new drugs in response to markets created by donors, they invested in quality standards in response to donors' requirements, and they relied on donors' technical transfer to learn how to produce these new drugs following high quality standards. However, the differences between the two experiences are also important. One significant difference was that in Tanzania there was, in some cases, reliance on domestic markets rather than international markets and, as a result, greater dependence on domestic rather than on international monitoring.

As we have seen, in Tanzania, a few of the markets that donors created to support local pharmaceutical production did not rely on promised donations but on the development of local markets, either private or public. Although domestic markets were smaller than donor markets, they were less competitive and easier to enter. In cases in which the promised market was domestic, local producers were not required to follow WHO GMP. Because monitoring stayed in the realm of the state, local producers had only to follow local GMP, which required lower standards. (Institutional buyers such as NGOs, as we have seen, could enforce their own quality standards). The trade-off is clear: for the sake of a more accessible market, quality standards were potentially compromised. However, in Tanzania, the drug regulatory agency, TFDA, functioned relatively competently, which helped to block the "low road" alternative that was prevalent both in Kenya and Uganda. TFDA not only helped maintain the quality standards of the larger companies, but it also led to the closing down of noncomplying companies. In short, domestic monitoring in Tanzania functioned as a barrier to entry, one that was in part responsible for the decline of the pharmaceutical sector in Tanzania (Wangwe et al. 2014); but this should also be considered a *positive* barrier that prevented the functioning of companies that should not be manufacturing in the first place. The result was a pharmaceutical sector that was small but that, with the support of foreign aid, continued to develop.

# 8

## Uganda in the 2000s

### ENTREPRENEURSHIP WITH AND WITHOUT AID

A few months after a visit to Uganda, I received an email from one of the small local pharmaceutical companies I had interviewed:

> Currently we are in initial stages of our expansion program to construct a high-tech pharmaceuticals plant with production line including Capsulation, Tabulations, Veterinary medicine (Orals), at international, WHO standards. However, we are looking for development partners, like UNIDO, who can be able [to] support our initiative.

Two elements in this email are worth noting. First, the fact that a small company that manufactured very simple drugs claimed to be interested not only in expanding its range of products, but also in following "international, WHO [World Health Organization] standards," which were higher than the quality standards required by Ugandan law. Second, the company's impression that the best way to achieve that goal was with the support of "development partners, like UNIDO [United Nations Industrial Development Organization]." Unlike in Kenya and Tanzania, however, in Uganda, even the larger pharmaceutical companies, with one exception, did not follow the path of producing better quality drugs with the help of foreign aid. The pharmaceutical sector in Uganda had developed and improved since 1990 (chapter 5), but by the 2010s, it was still well behind Kenya and Tanzania. In this chapter, I show that the relatively unsophisticated state of the local pharmaceutical industry in Uganda was precisely due the absence of developmental foreign support.

In Kenya and Tanzania, newly created drug markets, international quality conditions, and technical transfer—all provided by international development agencies—were instrumental in transforming the local pharmaceutical sectors, both by triggering manufacturers' interest in a broader range of quality-assured drugs and by providing the means to pursue that interest. This was not the case in Uganda. The donors market was mostly inaccessible for local producers, and no tailored mentoring was offered to them. As a result, the local pharmaceutical sector in Uganda continued to mostly produce a limited range of simple drugs and to maintain minimal quality standards.

The exception was Quality Chemical Industries Ltd. (QCIL and since 2013, CiplaQCIL). QCIL opened in 2007 and was designed from its very inception to produce WHO-prequalified antiretrovirals (ARVs) and artemisinin-based combination therapies (ACTs). Foreign aid was critical for the development and trajectory of QCIL. The Global Fund market was one of the markets targeted by the company, and interest in that market led not only to an interest in producing complex drugs, but also in WHO quality assurance. However, similar to the case of the local component of ration kits in Kenya in the 1980s (chapter 3), the state offered critical support—here, it was in the form of years-long commitments to purchase the drugs produced by QCIL. Again, like the experience of local manufacturers in Kenya in the 1980s, technology transfer was thanks to ties abroad—this time, the fact that QCIL was a joint venture with one of the largest pharmaceutical companies in India, Cipla. QCIL was not only able to receive WHO prequalification (PQ), but, unlike Universal in Kenya (chapter 6), was also able to sell drugs to the Global Fund. Although the Kenyan government's support of Dawa in Kenya ultimately benefited other local drug companies as well, this was not the case in Uganda. QCIL's accomplishments, moreover, were marred by significant accusations and suspicions. Both these issues raise questions regarding the appropriateness of state support of one firm rather than the sector as a whole.

In what follows, I first describe the Ugandan pharmaceutical sector in the early 2010s. As in Kenya and Tanzania, the sector in Uganda was by then quite bifurcated, with a number of particularly small and vulnerable companies, and a few companies that were larger and more successful. I then show that the domestic conditions in Uganda provided only basic incentives and tools for the local sector to develop: the state did not offer substantial protection to pharmaceutical manufacturers other than to QCIL, and the enforcement of quality standards was minimal, as was the level of guidance. Although some local companies relied on ties abroad to access technical know-how not available locally, this did not lead to much investment in new products or to higher quality standards. Without donors' creation of potential markets and provision of mentoring, local pharmaceutical companies in Uganda did not grow or develop much. The exception was QCIL. I show how a combination of foreign investment, state support, and foreign aid led to the establishment of a thriving Ugandan company, albeit one causing criticisms and concerns.

## The Ugandan Pharmaceutical Sector in the 2010s

Uganda underwent its first structural adjustment program (SAP) in the early 1980s under President Milton Obote, but intensification of civil conflict from mid-1983 onwards undermined any stabilization efforts. In 1987, under President Yoweri Museveni, Uganda underwent its second SAP, which involved, as it did in other countries, widespread liberalization and privatization of the economy.[1] Although the economic reforms at that time emphasized agriculture as the engine of economic transformation, and focused on agro-processing (of cotton, coffee, sugarcane, and food crops) as the main industrial priority for the country (Okuku 2006, Obwona et al. 2014), the revival of other manufacturing sectors was also "high on the priority list," to be achieved through "the rehabilitation of the country's critical infrastructure and the encouragement of foreign investment, specifically by seeking to resolve the issue of dispossessed Asian properties" (Mbabazi and Mokhawa 2005, 135). Overall, though, the manufacturing sector played a peripheral role in Uganda's growth trajectory (Obwona et al. 2014, 10). The share of manufacturing in GDP between 1975 and 1980 was 5.10 percent. That share was 7.86 percent between 2005 and 2010—on par with Tanzania, but almost half that of Kenya.[2] The bulk of manufacturing firms in Uganda still operated on a small-scale, with most firms employing thirty-five persons or less, and with low capacity utilization (Livingstone 1998, Siggel and Ssemogerere 2004, Okuku 2006).

The challenges facing industrial production in general and pharmaceutical production in particular were similar to the challenges in Tanzania and Kenya, including inadequate, intermittent, and costly electricity and water supply, and poor transport network. Ugandan industrialists also had little or no access to credit, and they faced the additional challenge of being in a land-locked country, depending on port services in Kenya and Tanzania (UNCTAD 2001, Mohamed 2009, Klissas et al. 2010, UNIDO 2010b). This was particularly difficult for the local pharmaceutical sector, which relied heavily on imports, not only for equipment and spare parts, but also for all active pharmaceutical ingredients and excipients and most primary packaging material (UNIDO 2010b, UNCTAD 2011a).[3] The local pharmaceutical sector also suffered from lack of skilled personnel, since Ugandan pharmacy schools did not qualify a sufficient number of pharmacists, and because training in Uganda remained clinically oriented with little attention to the field of industrial pharmacy.[4]

Given these challenges, most local pharmaceutical companies remained under-developed. Although the number of drug manufacturing facilities increased over the years "from two large manufacturing plants registered in the mid-1990s to eleven" in 2010 (CEHURD 2013, 2), three of these firms later closed, and the estimated local market share was 10 percent (MoH Uganda 2002, 40, Uganda Invest 2002, UNIDO 2010b, UNCTAD 2011a), which was not trivial "compared to almost none before 1993" but still very small (African Confidential 2013). Registration data confirm the minimal presence and activity of Ugandan drug manufacturers. In 2012, only 143 of 3,380 registered drugs, or a little more than 4 percent, were local (chapter 2). The industry employed only 1,216 people in total as of 2010 (UNIDO 2011b). In terms of its size, the Ugandan drug sector resembled the Tanzanian sector, but in terms of the drugs produced and quality standards maintained, it was quite behind. Pharmaceutical production in Uganda mostly stayed in "an early stage of development" in terms of both product capacities and quality standards (MoH Uganda 2002, 40, WHO 2002, Klissas et al. 2010).

There were still important differences among drug companies, however. The small- and medium-scale manufacturers produced very basic products such as simple antibiotics, antiseptics, and painkillers and did not necessarily follow local quality standards (UNIDO 2011b). These included not only old companies, but also new ones, suggesting that the opportunity structures did not change much over the years. Three of these companies closed. A second category of companies included three larger ones: Kampala Pharmaceutical Industries (1996) (KPI), Rene Industries, and Abacus Parenterals Drugs Ltd. (ADPL or Abacus). These were the kind of companies that in Kenya and Tanzania attempted to produce new products and upgrade their quality standards. In Uganda, however, although maintaining local GMP and registering new types of drugs, these companies did not increase much the technical sophistication of their manufacturing process and did not invest in quality upgrading. Finally, a third type of companies includes only one firm, CiplaQCIL, which produced WHO-prequalified ARVs and ACTs, as well as Hepatitis B medicines. Table 8.1 summarizes the characteristics of the local pharmaceutical sector in Uganda.

The smaller pharmaceutical firms in Uganda included Medipharm (EA), Kisakye Industries, Sev Pharmaceuticals, Kwality Afro-Asia, and three that closed down—Uganda Pharmaceuticals (1996) (UPL), Mavid, and Bychem. These firms were untouched by the post-2000 developments that affected many larger drug manufacturers in the region. Often, the founders had pharmacy degrees or some experience in the pharmaceutical sector, and many of the manufacturing facilities were attached to "an associated [drug] wholesale operation" (MoH Uganda 2002, 40). Medipharm—which opened in 1982 and early on benefited from an oral rehydration salts (ORS) project in collaboration with the United States Agency for International Development (USAID), the United Nations International Children's Fund (UNICEF), and the Program for Appropriate Technology in Health (PATH) (chapter 5)—was the largest

TABLE 8.1. Characteristics of Uganda's pharmaceutical companies, 2000s

| Firm | Turnover (2008) | No. of employees | Production capacity | Drugs registered (2017) |
|---|---|---|---|---|
| QCIL | N/A | 300 | 100 million tablets a month | 9 |
| KPI | $6.6 million | 275–300 | 10 million large-volume parenterals per year | 60 |
| Rene | N/A | 250–300 | N/A | 76 |
| Abacus | N/A | 300–350 | N/A | 27 |
| UPL | N/A | 60 | 120 million tablets; 30 million containers of capsules; 250,000 bottles of wet syrup; and 40,000 bottles of dry syrup *per month* | |
| Medipharm | $2.1 million | 50 | N/A | 18 |
| Mavid | N/A | 52 | N/A | |
| Kwality Afro-Asia | $300,000 | 35–45 | 300,000 bottles *per month* | 6 |
| Kisakye | $230,000 | 40 | N/A | |
| Sev | $255,000 | 25–30 | N/A | 10 |
| Bychem | N/A | N/A | N/A | |

*Source:* Compiled by the author; for turnover, number of employees, and capacity, see UNIDO (2010b).

and most successful of these small companies. When the company met with financial difficulties due to a loan it found difficult to repay, the African Ugandan founders sold 51 percent of the company to Kulal International, a Kenyan pharmaceutical distribution company in Nairobi that was owned by M. O. Ogalo, an African Kenyan who became the director of Medipharm, and Robert Glenie, who was originally from the UK. Business stayed steady since then.[5] Kisakye, which opened in 1999, was founded by Kitumba Benjamin Benson, an African Ugandan entrepreneur with a "diploma in medicine," who had previously owned pharmacies and wholesalers.[6] Unlike Medipharm, Kisakye's founder maintained full ownership of the firm. Sev, in turn, was opened by an African Ugandan couple. Both attended pharmacy school in Russia with a scholarship from the Soviet government in the late 1980s. After an internship in Mulago hospital in Kampala, they opened a retail pharmacy in the suburbs. They felt, however, like "shopkeepers" and moved to drug manufacturing in 2004.[7] Finally, Kwality Afro-Asia, which opened in 2007, was founded by three Indian investors, who had lived in Uganda for more than ten years (UNIDO

2010b), and since the 1990s, had owned a drug wholesaler and importer company, Pell Pharma.

These companies produced a limited range of products. Medipharm produced simple drugs, including cough syrups, antimalarials, analgesic, antibacterials, ORS, and antihistamines.[8] Kisakye, Sev, and Kwality Afro-Asia only produced oral liquid and external liquid preparation.[9] All of their products were over-the-counter (OTC) and were sold only in the private sector. These manufacturers did not export their products, although Kwality Afro-Asia reported that "others" from Congo, Rwanda, Burundi, and South Sudan "come and buy" very small orders.[10]

The production processes in these factories were particularly basic, with almost no opportunity for upgrading, even though most companies by 2012 moved from manual to semi- or fully-automated processes (UNIDO 2010b). Kisakye, for example, was originally located in the trading center of Kampala, on the very busy William Street, which limited the possibility of expansion. As a result, Kisakye faced both financial and regulatory challenges, and the factory did not operate for six months after it was "advised" to close by the National Drug Authority (NDA). The company later opened new premises, but, according to the owner, he "messed up" with a loan for machines he didn't have sufficient capital to install.[11] Sev's facilities, in turn, were located on the outskirts of Kampala, not in an industrial zone, and they occupied part of the second and third floors of a building. Again, therefore, no upgrading was possible without relocation.[12] Kwality Afro-Asia was also located in a mostly residential neighborhood on the outskirts of Kampala, and it occupied the first floor of what was otherwise an office building. As a result, expansion and quality upgrading were technically challenging. Medipharm was doing much better, but it still failed the audit offered by Roche as part of its offering of voluntary licenses for the production of a second-line ARV—indicating that it was not suitable for the production of quality-assured drugs (chapter 5). This is not to say that the companies were not interested in quality. For example, Kwality Afro-Asia sent its pharmacist in-chief to India for two weeks to learn the quality assurance system.[13] However, lack of capital and skills meant that only Medipharm and Kwality Afro-Asia followed local GMP.

Three other companies closed down—UPL, Mavid, and Bychem. Of these three, the decision to close down UPL, which was one of the largest companies at the time, had the greatest impact on the sector.[14] Founded as a state-owned company, UPL was privatized in 1996 and sold to the Dawda Group for $1.5 million (Mugunga 2016).[15] Dawda, a large Indian Kenyan group of companies, started doing business in Uganda in 1990. In addition to large industrial enterprises, Dawda owned pharmacies and was the wholesale agent of a number of Indian pharmaceutical companies.[16] At UPL, Dawda invested in new machinery, and the company was able to expand its capacity and range of products (Kukunda 2001, UNIDO 2010b). Quality standards, however, were poor in the late 1990s, partly because "the manufacturing premises were constructed at least twenty years ago" (UNIDO 1997, 29–30), and stayed poor later on. One of the challenges, again, was location—the plant was at the center of Jinja, and as an NDA official mentioned in talking about UPL: "You can't have a factory in the center of town! Manufacturing of drugs creates a lot of dust!"[17] One former pharmaceutical manufacturer stated (off the record) that UPL "wasn't a professional factory. Cottage industry. No GMP standards." In 2003, Dawda sold 70 percent of its UPL shares to Libyan investors, who eventually closed UPL in 2010 (Kakamwa 2010). In interviews, a number of reasons were offered for the new investors' decision to close down the factory. Some said that the business was not profitable or that the investors were more interested in a different company that they bought from Dawda as part of the same purchase, the food processing firm Britania. Others suggested that UPL collapsed partly because the NDA asked for practices that the company did not follow, so it "couldn't keep up with regulation" (various interviews); however, one NDA official insisted that UPL's closing had "nothing to do with quality issues."[18]

In addition to these small and clearly fragile firms, Uganda also had four large pharmaceutical companies—KPI, Rene, Abacus, and CiplaQCIL. Of the estimated 1,216 people employed by the local pharmaceutical industry in 2010, 83 percent worked for these large-scale manufacturers (UNIDO 2010b), and these firms had around 80 percent of the drugs registered by local manufacturers. With the exception of CiplaQCIL, however, Uganda's large companies experienced only relatively modest broadening of product categories, and they only minimally invested in quality upgrading.

Four years after it was founded by Aziz Damani (chapter 5), KPI was sold to the Industrial Promotion Services (IPS) for around $5 million in 1996 (Pharma Letter 1996). IPS was part of the Aga Khan Development Network (AKDN)—a group of private, nondenominational, international development agencies that was founded by the Aga Khan, the spiritual leader of the Ismaili community.[19] Most of the agencies in the AKDN were concerned with social and cultural issues and were nonprofits, but the Aga Khan Fund for Economic Development, which included IPS, was for profit. Not having experience in the pharmaceutical sector, when IPS bought KPI, it partnered with Kopran Pharma, a company from India that served as the technology partner. Later, IPS bought out Kopran Pharma and became the sole owner of KPI. In 2003, IPS hired as the KPI managing director an Ismaili originally from Uganda, Nazeem Mohamed, who had received biochemistry and marketing degrees from the UK and worked for many years in a large number of multinational pharmaceutical companies across Europe and the US before returning to Uganda to take the KPI position.[20]

In spite of the IPS backing, KPI was a modest enterprise, and the factory did not go through any major investments. Still, the company grew over time, and by 2010 it was one of the largest drug manufacturers in Uganda. The company focused on branded generics of the same types commonly produced in East Africa, including pain killers, simple antibiotics, cough and cold syrups, creams, ointments, allergy products, and simple antimalarials. However, KPI also "recognized that the disease pattern in Uganda is continuously changing and lifestyle diseases . . . were on the rise," so in 2008, the company launched a new line of treatment for diabetes, and in 2009, it launched antihypertensive products "to meet the new demand" (CEHURD 2013, 12–13). Like other KPI products, these were "part of the essential products lists" (Saez 2014). Indeed, the firm relied quite heavily on selling essential medicines to the public sector. In 2012, for example, half of KPI's sales were to the National Medical Stores (NMS). KPI also exported to South Sudan, Rwanda, and Tanzania.[21] Although KPI was the first Ugandan company to locally launch an ACT called Duact (artesunate-amodiaquine), it never produced or tried to prequalify it.[22] It did not register or produce ARVs either. As for quality, KPI's standards improved over time, but it did not go beyond what was required by Ugandan law. Back in 1997, the firm received a lukewarm evaluation from a UNIDO consultant: "KPI . . . would benefit from regular cGMP self-inspections and corrective measures for continuous improvement" (UNIDO 1997). A decade later, KPI failed the Roche audit as its facility was found unsuitable for the production of second-line ARVs. Thus, KPI was a major voice among local companies that decried what they considered an over-emphasis on quality assurance. KPI's managing director insisted that, "we are continually improving our quality standards, but between quality and price there is a balance" (Saez 2014). Still, the company maintained local GMP. Similarly to Shelys (chapter 7), at stake was the reputation not only of the local company, but its parent company as well, and the company pharmacist insisted that "Aga Khan doesn't compromise on quality."[23]

Rene was as large as KPI and had similarly modest ambitions. The company, started in 1988, stayed in the hands of the original founders, Rishi and Meera Vadodaria (chapter 5). The owners' daughters, one of whom pursued an advanced pharmacy degree abroad, later were also involved in the company— one as the finance director and the other as the operations director. The facility grew over time from having 60–65 workers at the beginning to 250–300 by 2010.[24] Rene produced a broad range of simple products, including pain killers, antibacterials, and ORS (Ewen et al. 2017) in the form of oral liquid, capsules, and tablets (UNIDO 2010b). Like KPI, the public sector was central for Rene, with 60 percent of the company's sales going to the Ugandan government, 35 percent to the private market in Uganda, and 5 percent to exports to Congo, Sudan, Burundi, and Rwanda. Rene did not export to Kenya or Tanzania.[25] In

2010, Rene registered, but did not produce, an ACT (AL).[26] Rene also did not produce ARVs. As for quality, Rene's pharmacist described the owners "up to date with quality stuff" and mentioned that Rishi Vadodaria provided him a "checklist" every year for additional, step-by-step improvements.[27] Although this description suggests interest in quality, it also reveals the low level of sophistication with which it was pursued. When Roche audited the factory, the inspectors concluded that Rene would need a different plant to produce ARVs. Yet, Rene was successfully audited by the Red Cross in 2010, and Uganda's Joint Medical Store (JMS) bought drugs from them in case of stock-outs.

Abacus was different from KPI and Rene. It was new—it opened in 2009— and started with a large investment of $25 million. The company was established by the Kiboko Group, which was founded in 1992 in Uganda by four Indian investors. Kiboko initially specialized in the distribution of roofing sheets but soon expanded to the distribution of other goods, including pharmaceuticals. It opened a pharmaceutical import business called Abacus Pharma in 1995.[28] Following a common trajectory, the investors then added a manufacturing facility to their enterprise by opening Abacus Parenterals Drugs Ltd. in 2009. As its name suggests, the company specialized in the manufacturing of parenterals— that is, in medicines administered intravenously or by injection, not by oral intake. In order to take advantage of economies of scale and in attempt to dominate the East African market, the company continued to increase its capacity.[29] Abacus participated in government and hospital tenders and sold in the private sector, and it exported to other markets, mostly to the land-locked neighboring countries, Rwanda and South Sudan. Abacus had drugs registered in Tanzania and in Kenya, although in Kenya in 2012 they mostly sold in the towns bordering Uganda.[30] Because of its specialization, and independently of its level of sophistication or quality standards, there were clear limits to the extent the company could broaden its range of products, and Abacus was never involved with development agencies. The company followed local GMP standards.[31]

Given the large capital invested, Abacus symbolized for some "a new age in the Ugandan pharmacy sector."[32] So did QCIL—which was in a category of its own. Unlike the other three large companies in Uganda, QCIL, which opened in 2007, explicitly and from its very inception oriented itself toward the donors markets. Like Abacus, it started as the expansion of a drug importing company, Quality Chemicals Limited (QCL), but in this case, as I describe in detail below, the Ugandan firm entered a joint venture with one of the largest and most reputable multinational pharmaceutical companies in India, Cipla (chapter 2). With an investment of $38 million, it was much larger than the average East African drug factory—the original factory "could . . . produce about as much as the next three largest local factories combined" (Klissas et al. 2010, UNCTAD 2011a). With an additional investment of $40 million, the factory later expanded, with plans to provide all the ARVs and ACTs needed in the "entire East African market" (BBC 2012). It only registered a few drugs in Uganda, but these were ARVs, ACTs, and, later, Hepatitis B medicines (Uganda Business News 2017). QCIL registered four drugs (one antimalarial, three anti-retrovirals) in Kenya in 2017. It passed the audits of a number of international agencies, and, as of 2017, it was the only factory in Uganda that had drugs prequalified by the WHO. It sold its drugs initially to the Ugandan government, through an agreement that committed the government to buy medicine in the value of $30 million (later, $40 million) a year. Later, it also sold drugs to other African governments, directly or through the Global Fund. In short, QCIL was the one company in East Africa that was able to achieve the goal that many other companies initially set out to achieve when they invested in quality standards. In the next section, I show that the unique trajectory of QCIL was thanks to support it received both from the Ugandan government and international development agencies. In turn, lack of foreign aid to compensate for lack of state support and other domestic conditions contributed to the trajectory of the other local pharmaceutical companies in Uganda.

## Local Production of Drugs without Markets, Mentoring, or Monitoring (and One Exception)

Even with the political stability that ensued after the National Resistance Movement (NRM) seized power in 1986, the health indicators in Uganda continued to be poor in the 1990s. In particular, the government spent insufficient funds on basic health care inputs in rural areas, including medicines, health workers' salaries, and health center maintenance. Even though the number of health facilities in Uganda increased by 400 percent since 1972, in 1993 still only 49 percent of the population lived within 5 km (or about one hour's walking distance) of a health facility (WHO 2006). Like Kenya and Tanzania, moreover, Uganda suffered from a high rate of HIV/AIDS. In 1997, the estimated prevalence of HIV among adults aged 15 to 49 was 10.9 percent; in 2003, the estimated rate decreased to 8.2 percent.[33] However, Uganda was one of the first African countries to respond aggressively to the HIV/AIDS epidemic, especially in regard to measures aimed at preventing HIV transmission (WHO 2003, 2). The Ugandan government also embarked early on, in 1998, in an effort to provide access to ARV therapy, first in collaboration with the Joint United Nations Programme on HIV/AIDS (UNAIDS) and later with the support of the WHO. By the end of 2000, however, these efforts resulted in only about one thousand Ugandans on ARV therapy with an estimated 60,000 to 90,000 in need of the medication. With radical reductions in drug prices (chapter 2, WHO 2003, 11), in 2004 the government announced a five-year pilot program to provide free treatment to people living with HIV/AIDS (Losse, Schneider, and Spennemann 2007). Initial drugs roll out was still fairly slow, however. By 2006,

24 percent of adults in need of antiretroviral treatment were receiving drugs (Uganda Law Reform Commission 2011, 34). However, by 2016, the number was up to 67 percent.[34]

Development agencies' response to AIDS in Uganda was similar to their response in Kenya or Tanzania. But because in Uganda the Global Fund did not work with the NMS, the government agency responsible for procurement and distribution of drugs to the public sector, and because development agencies did not seek out local manufacturers with targeted projects for drug production, drug donations did not turn into promised markets for local producers. Development agencies also did not offer the targeted mentoring that they offered Tanzanian companies (chapter 7). Without the presence of donor market incentives, monitoring of quality standards did not come into play. Without foreign aid, it was only domestic conditions that shaped the trajectory of the pharmaceutical sector, keeping local drug production relatively underdeveloped, with the exception of QCIL.

## CIPLAQCIL: INDIAN KNOW-HOW, UGANDAN MARKET, AND INTERNATIONAL MONITORING

QCIL was oriented toward the donors market from the start. With technical support from Cipla and financial and political support from the Ugandan government, the company was able to produce WHO-prequalified ARVs and ACTs and sell them to the government and to the Global Fund.

The company's unique opportunities were thanks to its relatively privileged position in Uganda. Like many other pharmaceutical companies in the region, the enterprise started with a trading company that imported and distributed generic drugs and moved to manufacturing only later, while maintaining its importing business. The original company, QCL, was established in 1997 by six investors—four African Ugandans, one Kenyan European, and one Irishman.[35] The partners' interest in drug manufacturing arose when they saw a unique opportunity in the new ARV and ACT markets created by donors, in a context in which Uganda as a Least Developed Country (LDC) was exempt from some provisions of the Trade-Related Aspects of Intellectual Property Rights (TRIPS) agreement, which allowed it to produce on-patent drugs until 2016 (later, 2033).[36]

Uganda, however, did not have the technology needed for the production of quality-assured ARVs and ACTs. QCL therefore looked for a "reputable" foreign "technology partner."[37] One of the pharmaceutical companies that QCL worked with was the Indian pharmaceutical firm Cipla, which made history by being the first generic pharmaceutical company that offered to produce cheap generic ARVs (chapter 2). With the support of the Ugandan government, as I describe below, QCL approached Cipla, and the two companies agreed to establish a joint venture, Quality Chemical Industries Ltd., with Cipla having a foreign equity share of 38.55 percent and QCL having a local equity of 61.45 percent (UNCTAD 2011a). In 2013, Cipla acquired additional shares and became the majority shareholder. QCIL accordingly changed its name to Cipla Quality Chemical Industries Ltd., or CiplaQCIL.[38]

Cipla's investment in pharmaceutical production in Uganda was consistent with Cipla's new strategy of greater involvement in emerging markets.[39] However, Cipla wouldn't have risked investment in Uganda without some assurances, which the local investors were not able to provide on their own. So before presenting an offer to Cipla, QCL secured the support of the Ugandan Government. Indeed, when the investors came to India to meet Cipla's founder and chairman, Yusuf Hamied, the Ugandan Minister of Health and Vice President, Gilbert Bukenya, joined them. The government was reportedly motivated by "the importance of self-sustainable [drug] industry."[40] Close relationships between QCL and the Ugandan political leadership, including President Museveni, might have also helped (see below). Off the record, many commented that, QCL owners had "good friends in the government," including the President.

The incentives offered to Cipla by the government were substantial and included: (a) Financing some of QCL's capital investment in the new company through a low-interest loan; (b) Providing land where the plant was to be built;[41] (c) Guaranteeing access to roads, power supply, and clean water; (d) Paying the salaries of Cipla's pharmaceutical experts to train local staff; (e) Granting a ten-year tax holiday on corporate income tax; and finally, (f) Agreeing to procure medicine from the plant worth $30 million per year for a period of seven years.[42] The promise to procure medicine in the value of $30 million a year—in 2012, this commitment was increased to $40 million a year and extended to 2019—was notable. The government allocated additional sums to its existing health budget for that purpose, thereby tripling the government allocation for essential medicines at the time (UNIDO 2010b).[43] It was a substantial commitment even when compared to the budgets of international donors—in 2015, the Ugandan government, the Global Fund, and the US President's Emergency Plan for AIDS Relief (PEPFAR) all together spent a total of $140 million towards treatment of AIDS patients (Khisa 2015). According to a United Nations Conference on Trade and Development (UNCTAD) report: "The efforts of [the Ugandan] government . . . were critical to secure this deal, as Quality Chemicals alone would never have been able to offer the type of assurances and financial assistance needed for Cipla to agree to manufacture . . . in Uganda." The report added that, "the combination of these incentives makes the joint venture virtually cost and risk free for Cipla" (UNCTAD 2011b, 46).

In October 2007, QCIL opened its $38 million state-of-the-art "modern glass and concrete" facility on the outskirts of Kampala (Klissas et al. 2010, 16,

Kafeero 2013). The large factory was built according to Cipla design and standards. All drug formulations—originally, these were only ARVs and ACTs—were from Cipla, and QCIL was manufacturing not under its own name, but "under license" from Cipla. Although not formally managing the plant, Cipla seconded a dozen people to the factory, including professionals for quality control and quality assurance.[44] With such technical support, manufacturing standards at QCIL were as high as Cipla factories in India, and the QCIL facility was successfully certified by the International Committee of Red Cross, and Drugs for Neglected Diseases *initiative* (DNDi).[45] However, the most important certificate for the company was a WHO PQ—without which QCIL would not have been able to participate in Global Fund tenders. This proved to be important also for President Museveni. According to a local pharmacist, "the President wanted a WHO prequalified plant!" By 2010, WHO PQ also proved to be somewhat urgent, as QCIL was interested in providing ACTs for the two-year Affordable Medicines Facility—malaria (AMFm) Program—the Global Fund program that subsidized producers of ACTs selling in the private sector (chapter 6)—which was to be launched in Uganda starting in 2011. The AMFm application by Uganda was deliberately delayed as the President's Office did not want to apply unless QCIL was involved, whereas QCIL could not participate without WHO PQ, which it did not yet have.[46] After some negotiations, the WHO agreed to fast-track QCIL's application. In June 2010, the WHO prequalified QCIL, under license from Cipla, for ARV lamivudine-nevirapine-zidovudine fixed dose tablet preparation; and in December that year, the WHO prequalified QCIL for antimalarial fixed dose combination of artemether-lumefantrine (AL). QCIL was the first African manufacturer to receive WHO PQ to manufacture an ACT. This was, no doubt, thanks to Cipla's involvement. Some criticized the PQ process as "rushed," however, and disapprovingly mentioned the "out of balance" pressure put on the WHO by the Ugandan President (various interviews).

WHO PQ allowed QCIL to venture to new markets—to the private Ugandan market through the AMFm, but also to other Global Fund programs and public markets.[47] For example, the company supplied ACTs for NMS in Uganda and for the Kenya Medical Supplies Authority (KEMSA) in Kenya.[48] By 2016, 54 percent of the company's sales were to the Ugandan government, while ACTs sold to Global Fund programs accounted for an additional 22 percent of the sales, and the remaining 24 percent were to other sub-Saharan African governments.[49]

Indeed, from early on, QCIL had an interest in exporting drugs across all of East and Central Africa (Klissas et al. 2010); and by 2017, the company's products were distributed in eight sub-Saharan African countries—directly or by the Global Fund (Uganda Business News 2017). In some cases, it was through government-to-government arrangements. For example, following a request by the government of Uganda from the Government of Rwanda to consider granting QCIL access to Rwanda's drug market, the two governments signed a bilateral trade and investment framework agreement on pharmaceutical products in 2014 in which QCIL also committed to work with Rwanda to build a plant to manufacture essential drugs other than those manufactured in Kampala (MOTI 2014). In 2012, the Ugandan and Kenyan governments started negotiating a bilateral framework agreement on health and medicine. Kenya, which depended exclusively on donor funding for its malaria and AIDS programs, was reportedly willing to create a $28 million fund in its budget for purchases of medicine from QCIL. Four years later, however, "this has not yet come to fruition." Among other obstacles, "Kenya . . . challenged the price of drugs from Cipla Quality Chemicals, which were 25 percent to 30 percent higher than the minimum prices, rendering them uncompetitive" (Khisa 2015, Nakaweesi 2016).

Even in expanding to new markets, then, CiplaQCIL heavily depended on the support of the Ugandan government. This support led to bitter debates in Uganda and among global public health experts, as some found it excessive and in conflict with public health interests. Most contentious was the fact that the price the Ugandan government paid for locally produced drugs was higher than it would have paid for imported drugs, due to the permitted 15 percent mark-up for local manufacturers. In defending the agreement, QCIL officials described it as an example of industrial policy that also functioned as health policy. According to one of the Ugandan investors, "the government of Uganda came in because, although this was a private-led investment, it was going to address social issues, it was going to address problems that were a catastrophe to the country, people were dying of malaria, people were dying of HIV/AIDS" (BBC 2012). Such an industrial policy could presumably only work if the government agreed to absorb higher prices of drugs. The chairman of Cipla, Yusuf Hamied, justified this position when describing his meeting with the Vice President of Uganda when the two met in India:

> I said, we believe that a country should be self-reliant and self-sufficient . . . But a country has to pay a price for that. If you put up a factory [in Uganda] . . . you can't compete in a tender on AIDS [drugs] with China and India. So don't even try. But to be self-reliant, you have to pay a price. So if in the tender the price is, say, one dollar, and your factory can supply you at two dollars, for argument's sake, you should accept. And they [the President and Vice President of Uganda] were wise enough to accept that.[50]

In other words, rather than an arbitrary mark-up to enrich the company at the expense of the government, as this was viewed by critics, the price supposedly reflected the company's cost of production, and was therefore a necessary condition if the government wanted to support local manufacturing of drugs.

Critics, however, saw these as special favors for one company—especially given the relative neglect of other firms in the same sector. As one international nongovernmental organization (INGO) official in Uganda asked, "Why prioritize *this* company?" Some public health experts argued that the funds would be better spent on cheaper drugs. "And when they pay so much more for each drug, there aren't enough drugs available."[51] QCIL's drugs *were* expensive, with estimates suggesting that they were 1.5 to 2 times more expensive than the same drugs purchased internationally (various interviews). In addition to the principled criticisms described above, there were more severe accusations against NMS officials of "corruption, abuse of office, misappropriation, illicit enrichment, plunder and wastage of government resources . . . *in complicity with QCIL*" (East African Court of Justice 2015). In December 2011, the Acting Inspector General of Government reported that, as of 2010, only 16 percent of drugs delivered by QCIL to NMS were manufactured in Uganda, with the rest imported from India, and that the 15 percent mark-up that was supposed to be applied by QCIL only for drugs manufactured locally was also applied to the drugs NMS purchased from India *through* QCIL. This meant that between December 2009 and October 2010, NMS paid $17.8 million more than it should have to QCIL (ACCU 2013, IRIN News 2013). QCIL denied the allegations. The case was weakened by the fact that the whistle-blower who led to the charges was a representative of an Indian pharmaceutical company that had been supplying ARVs and ACTs to the Ugandan government and could therefore be seen as motivated by business rivalry. Although these accusations were not resolved, new accusations surfaced—that CiplaQCIL was offering NMS drugs at prices that were 36 percent higher than the prevailing global market prices and therefore higher than the statutory 15 percent local content advantage. CiplaQCIL did not deny selling drugs to NMS at prices higher than it charged on the export market, but it blamed the Ugandan government. The company explained that it sold the same drugs at cheaper prices to outside markets other than Uganda because it had to find ways of using the excess capacity of the factory caused, according to the company, by the government's failure to buy all medicine produced by Cipla as the government had committed to in their agreement (Nassaka 2016).

In sum, CiplaQCIL stood out in Uganda as the one company that was able to take advantage of the market for new drugs—it was not only able to convince the government to *create* a market for it, but it was also the only East African company that participated in Global Fund programs. From a public health perspective, the guaranteed purchases of more expensive drugs were problematic. From an industrial perspective—but also from the point of view of those concerned with a country's dependence on others for the medicine it needs—this was a remarkable achievement.

Whereas CiplaQCIL bears similarities with the Tanzania Pharmaceutical Industries (TPI) in Tanzania—both had tight connections with the government and both were accused of misconduct—in regard to the factors that affected its development, CiplaQCIL's experience may be most similar to the experience of the state-owned pharmaceutical company Dawa in Kenya back in the 1980s (chapter 3). In both cases, foreign aid (ration kits in the case of Dawa; Global Fund funding in the case of QCIL) allowed for state support (a local component in the case of Dawa; guaranteed annual procurement in the case of QCIL). In both cases, technical knowledge was achieved not with the support of foreign aid (or the state), but through ties abroad. An important difference was quality monitoring in the case of QCIL, due to foreign aid involvement, but not in the case of Dawa. In turn, the success of Dawa spilled over to other private companies in Kenya. That was not the case in Uganda—and other manufacturers suffered not only from the neglect of the government, but the neglect of development agencies as well, as I describe in the next section.

## MARKETS

With liberalization reforms in the late 1990s, a private drug market was established in Uganda (UNIDO 1997). However, local manufacturers had only a few advantages over imported drugs in this market—the most significant one was that because Uganda was a land-locked country, importation could be lengthy and costly. A report from 2010 describes the length and costs of shipping drugs first from India to the port in Kenya and then from Kenya to Uganda (Klissas et al. 2010):

> To ship a typical 40-foot freight container of drugs and medical supplies from Bangalore [in India] to Mombasa [in Kenya]—about 3,000 miles—costs $800–$1,200 . . . and takes about seven to nine days. To move the same container overland the 600 miles from Mombasa to Kampala [in Uganda] costs $3,000–$3,600 and takes . . . 10–14 days.

In spite of the high shipping costs, the private drug market in Uganda was dominated by imports (chapter 2). The faith-based JMS similarly bought only 10 percent of drugs from local producers.[52] Ugandan manufacturers also only minimally exported to neighboring countries—mainly to the neighboring countries of the Democratic Republic of Congo (DRC), Rwanda, Southern Sudan, and Tanzania (UNIDO 2010b, 11). Only Abacus and QCIL had drugs registered in Kenya.

As for the public sector, with the exception of the government's unprecedented support of QCIL, the government's policies in support of local pharmaceutical production were similar to the basic ones offered in Kenya and

Tanzania, and these were not always effectively implemented. The government's attention to the plight of local manufacturers, to the extent it existed, was more a reflection of an international context relatively supportive of drug production in developing countries (chapter 6) and less the doing of the Ugandan Pharmaceutical Manufacturers Association (UPMA). UPMA was only established in the early 2000s, and the association was not a "robust" or "vibrant" organization (various interviews). Contributing to the sector's political weakness was the fact that whereas all local manufacturers were members of the UPMA (FEAPM 2012), many were also members of the Uganda Pharmaceutical Promoters Association (UPPA), which—as the lobbying group for importers—was more influential than UPMA and had interests that competed with those of local manufacturers.[53] Hence, one report suggested that the UPMA was "fairly active in lobbying the government and in trying to coordinate member actions" (Klissas et al. 2010), but other reports stated that, with only quarterly meetings, "the UPMA is just a tea party which does not help their members and performs no action" (CEHURD 2013, 14). The smaller companies felt particularly marginalized: "The big manufacturers look at us like children." Still, the UPMA had a formalized list of requests, including a 20 percent local price discount in the entire region and a partial ban of products that were manufactured locally. Although success was "limited" (UNIDO 2010b), the UPMA was considered instrumental in the government allowing locally manufactured pharmaceuticals a 15 percent preferential price margin in NMS procurements.

In addition to the preferential price margin, other policies to support local pharmaceutical production included exemption for local manufacturers from all taxes on raw materials and exemption from import duty tax on machinery (MoH Uganda 2011a). Local manufacturers complained that the reimbursement process was cumbersome and unpredictable, however (UNIDO 2011b). In addition, the NDA charged local manufacturers lower fees for registration, inspection, and other services, whereas all imported pharmaceuticals were charged a service fee of 2 percent of the Freight on Board (FOB) value (various interviews, MoH Uganda 2011a). The Ugandan government did not make much use of more consequential policies that would have allowed local manufacturers to more successfully compete in public tenders. The preferential price margin was introduced only in 2012 (CEHURD 2013). The government only minimally used national ("restricted domestic") tenders (various interviews).

Independently of the effectiveness of the policies in place, local manufacturers had quite a negative perception of the agency responsible for procurement of drugs to the public sector (Klissas et al. 2010). NMS was meant to replace the Central Medical Stores (CMS) in 1996, but soon after the NMS was established, a massive decentralization reform following the adoption of a new Constitution in 1995 meant that most of the health budget marked for the procurement of medicine was distributed through the local governments rather than through NMS, which handled only 20 percent of the national medicines budget.[54] Even with this limited mandate, NMS was perceived as "run down," unreliable, inconsistent, and very slow, as orders got delayed or even lost, and bills were not paid (Klissas et al. 2010). In 2009—in response to public outrage over widespread stock-outs of even the most basic drugs and supplies at health facilities—the government "recentralized" procurement, and NMS received control over 100 percent of the drug procurement budget (Governance 2011, Klissas et al. 2010). After recentralization, official assessments and reports continued to strongly criticize NMS performance (Auditor General 2010, 32, Governance 2011), although some were understanding of the fact that the institutional capabilities at NMS were overwhelmed by the sudden and substantial increase in budget and drug quantities that it was meant to manage (Governance 2011). Although accusations of corruption were common (various interviews), a report written for the Swedish Embassy in Uganda concluded: "There is no evidence suggesting grand scale corruption . . . [but i]nstead, continued inefficiencies, many of which could presumably be attributed to lack of adequate implementation of rules and lack of proper technical expertise" (Governance 2011).

In spite of these various challenges, which meant that much of what was produced locally was "taken up by William Street" and sold in the private market (Klissas et al. 2010), KPI, Rene, and Abacus still relied quite heavily on public procurement, as we have seen. The experience of Abacus is quite instructive in regard to the opportunities and obstacles that local manufacturers faced in Uganda as the plant was specifically designed for the local market.[55]

When Abacus decided to open a drug manufacturing facility, it specifically looked for products that could be competitive in the Ugandan market. Hence, the investors looked for products that were not already made by other local manufacturers and that could also compete with imported drugs. The company thus decided to focus on parenterals, including intravenous fluids and vials of sterile water for injections and eye drops, because parenterals were heavy and therefore more costly to ship, which gave a cost advantage to local producers (Sempijja 2009, UNIDO 2010b). An initial investment of $25 million was obtained from savings, commercial loans, as well as from government-backed low-interest loans, and funds from the World Bank's International Finance Corporation (IFC) and the African Development Bank. In 2010, Abacus also received a $9 million investment from the AfricInvest Fund II, a private equity investor based in Tunisia, with funds given by the Commonwealth Development Corporation, the private equity arm of the UK Department of International Development (PEI 2014).[56] With the original funds, the company built a thirty-six-acre plant outside Kampala. Impressively, within the first five months of production, Abacus was able to lower the price of intravenous infusions in

Uganda by 30 percent (Fischer, Jenkes, and Kibira 2014, UNIDO 2010b). Competitors responded by reducing the price of imports to similar levels, but Abacus was still able to gain control over 60 percent of the local market.[57]

Abacus's focus on parenterals made the company unsuitable for the donors drug market. However, this did not have to be the case with KPI and Rene, two other large and GMP-compliant companies. Yet, foreign aid in Uganda did not have the same effect that it had on local pharmaceutical firms in Kenya or Tanzania, even though Uganda relied as heavily on foreign donations for the procurement of anti-AIDS and antimalarial drugs. From 2003 to 2010, the Global Fund disbursed a total of $101 million for HIV/AIDS programs in Uganda (including all programs, not only treatment) and $152 million for malaria programs.[58] PEPFAR's contribution for the procurement of ARVs in 2010 was $45 million.[59] The US President's Malaria Initiative (PMI) started distributing ACTs in Uganda in 2006. By 2008, PMI helped deliver almost 11.3 million treatment courses of ACT (USAID 2011a). In 2006–2007, the contribution from these global initiatives for programs for malaria, HIV/AIDS, tuberculosis, vaccines, and reproductive health commodities amounted to 60 percent of the total that was spent in Uganda (UNIDO 2010b).

In Kenya, the donors market was made visible partly by the fact that an ARVs market initially created by the Kenyan government and that was of interest to local producers was threatened by the Global Fund. Deprived of a more accessible market, local producers like Cosmos and Universal sought entry to the new, even if more demanding, market (chapter 6). In Tanzania, markets were made accessible mostly through company-specific initiatives (chapter 7). In Uganda, in contrast, new markets were perceived as much more inaccessible for a number of reasons. First, the Global Fund did not trust the government procurement agency and therefore although some warehousing and distribution of Global Fund drugs operated through the NMS, procurement did not.[60] Second, for reasons I describe below, there were no targeted or tailored drug markets created for individual companies, as was the case in Tanzania. This meant not only lack of markets, but also lack of monitoring and lack of mentoring.

## MONITORING

The Ugandan agency responsible for monitoring the quality of drug production through drug registration, GMP inspections and post-marketing surveillance, the National Drug Authority (NDA), faced both financial and political obstacles over the years (WHO 2002).[61] Reports warned that lack of sufficient resources hindered "efforts aimed at staff skills development, technology transfer, and purchase of equipment," which, in turn, inhibited the "improvement of NDA's regulatory capacity" and its enforcement capabilities (UNIDO 2010b,

41). In addition, the semi-autonomous status of the NDA did not shield it from political intrigues and volatile leadership.[62]

The NDA also suffered from technical deficiencies. The local GMP standards were a looser version of WHO standards, adjusted to better fit local needs, as was also the case in Kenya and Tanzania.[63] More stringent standards would have been impossible to enforce in any event. For example, while bioequivalence (BE) studies were required for HIV/AIDS, antimalarials and antituberculosis products, a report remarked that, "it could not be ascertained as who is evaluating the BE data dossiers submitted . . . to NDA before marketing authorization" (GTZ 2009). In general, testing at the National Drugs Quality Control Laboratory (NDQCL) was mandatory only in a number of exceptions, and evaluation of drug quality in the process of registration, which was enforced since 1997, was based on documentary evidence and physical inspection only.[64] Unlike the laboratory facilities in Kenya and Tanzania, the NDQCL was not prequalified by the WHO: it had limited facilities, insufficient number of staff, and inadequate equipment and laboratory space (Auditor General 2010, Agaba et al. 2013, Fischer et al. 2014).

Views vary in regard to NDA's drug registration and GMP inspection of factories. The general consensus in regard to registration was that with credible procedures (Losse, Schneider, and Spennemann 2007) and committed personnel (Klissas et al. 2010), the registration process was "slow but good."[65] So while local manufacturers and importers complained of delays—according to one respondent, "it takes years to register"—they also referred to NDA as "the most stringent authority" (various interviews).

This stringency was not applied to GMP inspections of local facilities. Over the years, the NDA did enforce some minimal standards that occasionally led to the temporary closing of local manufacturers.[66] One explanation for the decision of KPI's founder to sell the company, for example, was that once the NDA came into the picture in 1996, he could no longer operate with the low standards he had followed (various interviews). Because of "GMP issues," NDA forced a temporary closure of UPL in 2006; and, of Kisakye in 2011.[67] Still, an NDA official in the inspection department maintained that permanent closing of UPL, Bychem, and Mavid "had nothing to do with quality issues."[68] Indeed, the NDA inspection unit had serious capacity limits—as of 2010, it operated at about 50 percent of its human resource capacity (Agaba et al. 2013)—which made it impossible to inspect all of the local and foreign facilities requiring inspection.[69] Unlike foreign manufacturers that were inspected at most every three years, locals were inspected at least once a year (MoH Uganda 2011a)—but inspection of local facilities was lenient, especially of the less sophisticated companies. A local manufacturer told me that the NDA treated them "like babies"—they made minimal demands in attempt to help them grow.[70] An NDA official confirmed that, "[the local pharmaceutical] sector is young so [NDA] tries to help them improve."[71] A local manufacturer, quoted in a 2013 report, confirmed the lax attitude of NDA (CEHURD 2013, 13):

> Every year NDA does annual inspection for compliance of local producers, however they never act on the findings of the inspection. If you asked for inspection reports, you will find that firms which failed the inspection still have licenses and have not been disqualified. This negates the whole purpose and puts into discredit the local manufacturing sector since inspection and approval mechanisms are not effectively being implemented.

With minimal enforcement of quality standards on local manufacturers by the responsible state agency, international monitoring could have led to significant quality upgrading. However, without the offering of targeted markets and/or tailored training, development agencies could not require quality upgrading as a condition for their assistance, which they did in Kenya and Tanzania. As a result, international monitoring, with the exception of CiplaQCIL, had no presence in Uganda. We should not discount the technical difficulties that local manufacturers would have faced if such attempts in quality upgrading would have taken place—many factories, for example, used facilities that were not originally meant for pharmaceutical production, so they could never be prequalified by the WHO.[72] Yet, in Kenya and Tanzania foreign aid helped improve quality standards even if they did not reach the international standards, an effort that did not take place in Uganda.

## MENTORING

By 2010, the local pharmaceutical sector in Uganda included a broad range of investors: African Ugandans, Indian Ugandans (including returnees), African Kenyans, Indian Kenyans, and a number of investors from outside the region, mostly from India, but also Libya. Given the plurality of investors, social relations played an insignificant role in the diffusion of knowledge across the sector—as compared to Kenya, for example (chapter 6). Even the attention given to the meteoric rise of QCIL had little influence on the practices of other companies—again, as compared to the influence Cosmos and Universal's practices had on the pharmaceutical sector in Kenya. Although small companies in Uganda did envision expansion with the help of development agencies, as I described in the introduction of this chapter, no other company in Uganda invested in quality upgrading in imitation of QCIL.

Technology transfer by private means, then, still happened solely through ties abroad. Indeed, with the exception of Kwality Afro-Asia (a company with ties abroad that remained small), ties abroad set apart the more successful firms from the less successful. With the exception of CiplaQCIL (owned by African

Ugandans), in general ties abroad seemed easier for East Africans of Indian origin to establish. As in the 1990s, connections with India provided access to know-how not available locally (chapter 5). Rene, for example, continued to buy machines and to hire skilled workers from India.[73] As mentioned earlier, when IPS bought KPI, they partnered with the Indian company Kopran Pharma for technical know-how. KPI also hired quality control experts from India, although Aga Khan's commitment to local training led to a change in these practices, and by 2012, the firm had only one Indian national employed full-time.[74] Abacus, which was owned by Indians of the Jain community, hired thirteen expatriates from India, many of whom were Jain.[75] Similarly, KPI recruited as managing director Nazeem Mohamed, who belonged to the Ismaili community. Of course, technical transfer was fundamental, as we have seen, for the joint venture between Cipla and QCL.

In addition to technical transfer through ties abroad, drug manufacturers in Uganda received some mentoring from the NDA, which provided cGMP trainings for local pharmaceutical manufacturers one or two times a year (Auditor General 2010, UNIDO 2010b). Local manufacturers also found NDA's GMP inspections to be helpful in improving their practices; according to a UNIDO (2010b) report, NDA audits "provide an opportunity to offer free cGMP advice to the local pharmaceutical industry." One Chief Inspector who was at the NDA in 2007 was mentioned as particularly helpful in "pushing local manufacturers to comply with GMP norms." "Every year there was inspection of GMP. He prepared a list of: critical, major, and minor issues. Then [he marked for each issue, whether the factory was] conforming/nonconforming. We had to eliminate the critical and the major issues."[76]

At most, however, the NDA could help local manufacturers reach the minimal requirements that the regulatory agency enforced. Mentoring by foreign aid, too, was marginal to the experience of drug producers in Uganda. Although local manufacturers were invited to participate in the training provided by the German Technical Cooperation Agency (GTZ) and UNIDO in Arusha, Tanzania (chapter 6), only one Ugandan company, KPI, attended the workshops, compared to eight manufacturing companies from Tanzania and ten from Kenya.[77] In addition, development agencies did not provide technology transfer in Uganda, as they did in Kenya and Tanzania. UNIDO and GTZ, for example, did not pursue Pharmaceutical Inspection Convention and Pharmaceutical Inspection Co-operation Scheme (PIC/S) training in Uganda. Development agencies did not offer a targeted mentoring for the production of specific drugs, as they did in Tanzania.[78]

Lack of mentoring was quite surprising given that, with Uganda's political and economic stability after 1986, the country was the "darling" of the donor community. Uganda was also temporarily exempted from some TRIPS provisions—a consideration that encouraged support of local pharmaceutical production in Tanzania (chapter 7) and motivated the joint venture between QCL and Cipla. Indeed, an initial interest in Uganda did exist, as UNIDO chose Uganda as one of the countries to conduct an exploratory report on strengthening the local production of essential generic drugs in developing and least developed countries (UNIDO 2010b, iii). In the case of UNIDO and GTZ, at least, the decision not to invest in Uganda was based on the evaluation that the pharmaceutical firms in Uganda did not meet the minimal conditions that would have allowed them to successfully absorb the guidance given to them.[79] Poor capabilities were confirmed in the DND*i* inspection of Ugandan factories for a possible technology transfer for the production of ASAQ and in the audits conducted as part of Roche's AIDS Technology Transfer Initiative (chapter 6). Ugandan companies failed both types of audits.

Surprisingly, interviews suggest that Roche's audits were more positively received in Uganda than in Kenya or Tanzania—possibly reflecting the dire state of mentoring and technology transfer in the country, considering how basic some of these audit reports were. As I describe in chapter 6, in 2008, Roche offered a free one-day technical assessment, or "mini-audit," of companies that expressed interest in the initiative. According to a Roche official, they were "basically checking if the technology is around and in which manufacturing . . . environment do they operate." "In other words, [is it] a garage, [is it following] acceptable standard[s]," etc.[80] Following the assessment, Roche inspectors provided the companies with detailed written reports of their technical assessment and put genuine effort into making these reports intelligible, independently of whether the company passed or failed the audit. In one case, for example, they attached photos to the various descriptions. An excerpt from another report illustrates the basic but detailed level of the recommendations (Roche n.d.b):

- The personnel access from the outside to the clean room should be organized through a two-step changing room providing proper gowning, e.g., a simple change from street shoes to slippers is not appropriate.
- The clean room should only contain the equipment and tools required for the product to be produced.
- Equipment and tools should have a clear status 'clean' or 'to be cleaned.'
- Clean equipment and tools should be protected and stored in order to ensure their cleanliness.

The same report, however, also made generic recommendations, such as, "the existing documentation should be reviewed and structured to comply with cGMP." Reports on factories with higher quality standards, like Medipharm and KPI, were necessarily more complex, and managers in these companies too found the audit reports useful; and some said that they had used them as roadmaps for future improvements.[81]

Development agencies, then, only minimally offered mentoring that could compensate for the lack of access to technical know-how in Uganda and for the inability of most local drug manufacturers to get access to foreign technology through the private market.

To summarize, domestic conditions in Uganda, including minimal market opportunities and lack of access to technical know-how, were unfavorable to the development of a pharmaceutical sector that would invest in quality standards beyond what was enforced by the NDA. These conditions were not substantively different from the conditions in Kenya or Tanzania—but without support of development agencies, Ugandan pharmaceutical companies were not able to broaden the type of their products and improve their quality standards in the way that some companies in Kenya and Tanzania were able to. The exception to that characterization—CiplaQCIL—was the one company that was able to heavily rely on the state and ties abroad, but also on foreign aid, in the form of both markets and monitoring.

## Discussion

Back in the 1980s, Kenyan pharmaceutical companies were able to participate in the ration kits program thanks to a local component of the program. That scheme was not available for local manufacturers in Tanzania or Uganda. In Tanzania at the time, development agencies did not support a local component because they did not trust the ability of the Tanzanian state to successfully implement the scheme. As we have seen in chapter 7, the relations between donors and the drug regulatory authority in Tanzania improved over the years, and donors invested in local pharmaceutical production in Tanzania in the 2000s partly because they trusted the state to complement their work. In Uganda in the 1980s–1990s, development agencies opposed a local component because they did not trust the capabilities of local manufacturers to produce the necessary drugs. This concern with local manufacturers' capacity to absorb foreign assistance has continued, so that also in the 2000s international development agencies were reluctant to offer support to the Ugandan pharmaceutical sector, in stark contrast to their involvement in Kenya and, especially, Tanzania during the same period of time.

In Uganda, therefore, the only donor market was the one created by the Global Fund, accessible only in the unique case of CiplaQCIL—and without adequate mentoring, local producers did not have the capabilities or incentives to change their strategies and invest in new products or in higher quality standards. As a result, local pharmaceutical firms in Uganda continued to produce mostly simple drugs. CiplaQCIL was doing much better but was fragile for a different reason—including its heavy dependence on personal ties to the state. One informant questioned the sustainability of the company by asking what would happen to the company once Museveni is no longer the President. I offer a more general discussion of the role of the state—and what implications this has on foreign aid—in the concluding chapter.

# 9

# Foreign Aid and the State

State sovereignty—the principle that states should have the right to govern without exogenous interference—has never been fully practiced (Krasner 1999). The notion that there are defined boundaries between the state and external political influences seems nowadays especially easy to dismiss. Many external authorities—including other governments, international governmental organizations, international nongovernment organizations, and multinational corporations—shape the state and its policies. As social scientists have long argued, actors outside the state develop scripts that governments then internalize as their own (Meyer and Rowan 1977), and they use threats or concessions to impose policies that are less welcomed (Simmons, Dobbin, and Garrett 2006). Not only state policies but also state institutions themselves are a product of exogenous influences, as I discuss below. This is particularly easy to observe in formerly colonized, poor countries in the periphery of the world system. No example in recent decades has made this more obvious than the structural adjustment programs used by the World Bank and the International Monetary Fund to thoroughly transform entire political and economic systems (Babb 2013). Clearly, then, if we are to understand domestic, political, or economic developments, we cannot ignore international influences. This book is concerned not with all foreign interventions, but with what falls under the category of foreign aid—namely, interventions that are officially aimed to support development in the recipient country. It is fair to condemn—in the name of sovereignty, democracy, or justice—many forms of international interventions. Although foreign aid is supposedly unique because it purports to serve the needs of the recipient country, many have questioned the motivations behind foreign aid, and many more have asserted that—putting motivation aside—the outcomes themselves are hardly beneficial. In an attempt to contribute to this important debate, this book is concerned with the extent to which foreign aid is or is not effective.

However, to ask "is foreign aid effective?"—which is how much of the literature on foreign aid addresses the matter, as I discuss in chapter 1—is akin to asking, "Is the state effective?" The literature on the developmental state has contributed greatly to the debate on development not only by insisting that the state "matters" to development, but also by identifying what policies make the state effective, and by analyzing the conditions under which a state becomes "developmental" in the first place (Amsden 1989, Evans 1995). This book takes its cue from that literature and asks similar questions in regard to foreign aid: What interventions make foreign aid effective? Under what conditions does foreign aid become developmental in the first place?

Based on the experiences of local pharmaceutical manufacturers in Kenya, Tanzania, and Uganda from the 1980s to the 2010s, this book offers a number of conclusions. First, foreign aid matters to development. Foreign assistance helped with the emergence of a local pharmaceutical sector in Kenya in the 1980s and with the upgrading of local pharmaceutical sectors in Kenya and Tanzania in the 2000s. Without foreign assistance, emergence was limited and delayed in Tanzania and Uganda in the 1980s and upgrading of the sector did not take place in Uganda in the 2000s. Second, the types of interventions that make foreign aid effective include the provision of three resources: markets, monitoring, and mentoring. Through the creation of markets and imposition of conditions, foreign aid offered *incentives* to produce quality-assured products. Through technical transfer, foreign aid provided *means* to learn how to produce such products. Aid that offers these three resources functions as developmental foreign aid. Third, foreign aid is not simply imposed by development agencies and donors on passive recipients. Rather, it reflects the conditions of possibility at the international level within which recipient countries construct and make their demands. Fourth, also at the stage of implementation, foreign aid is hardly an external imposition that can act independently of the existing political-economic conditions in place. Foreign aid complements local opportunities.

Of the six cases analyzed in the book, two cases—Kenya and Tanzania, both after 2000—exemplify instances in which developmental foreign aid led to the upgrading of the local pharmaceutical sector. In both cases, foreign aid precipitated change in the practices of local pharmaceutical manufacturers by opening up for local pharmaceutical producers the possibility of new markets if they followed international Good Manufacturing Practices (GMP), and by offering technical support required for the production of new drugs and for reaching a higher level of quality standards.

In Kenya, the first market that attracted the attention of local producers was created by the Global Fund, which, together with US bilateral support, was largely responsible for the improved availability of antiretrovirals (ARVs) and artemisinin-based combination therapies (ACTs) in Kenya after 2003. To get access to the Global Fund market, producers needed their drugs to be prequalified by the World Health Organization (WHO). Some Kenyan companies upgraded quality standards to receive WHO prequalification (PQ); others, with the help of the German Technical Cooperation Agency (GTZ), upgraded quality standards to European standards. Given lack of local know-how, Kenyan manufacturers relied on technical assistance from the WHO, GTZ, the United Nations Industrial Development Organization (UNIDO), and others. Many local pharmaceutical companies in Kenya transformed as a result of such efforts—producing drugs that they had not produced before and following quality standards higher than the standards they had followed until then. Although no Kenyan company ended up selling to the Global Fund, quality upgrading gave local pharmaceutical companies access to other new markets, such as international nongovernmental humanitarian organizations, which had been reluctant to buy locally produced drugs before that time.

The Tanzanian pharmaceutical sector after 2000 was smaller and weaker than the Kenyan one, but in Tanzania, too, companies produced new drugs and improved quality standards with foreign assistance. Developmental foreign aid in Tanzania was more "hands on" than in Kenya, with most upgrading occurring as a result of projects in which mentoring was specifically tailored for individual companies and included, in addition to technical know-how, also managerial and marketing support. Tailored mentoring in Tanzania at times came with the setting up of a domestic market, which reflected a (deserved) trust in and reliance on Tanzanian regulatory authorities rather than only on international schemes.

Kenya in the 1980s is a third case in which foreign aid contributed to the local pharmaceutical sector. In this case, aid was not developmental in the sense of providing all three elements of markets, monitoring, and mentoring. Rather, the most important contribution of foreign aid was to trigger state action in support of local pharmaceutical production—through industrial policies as well as through a "reserved market" as part of the ration kits program. The absence of mentoring meant that only entrepreneurs with access to technical know-how—mostly, through ties abroad—were able to take advantage of the opportunities provided through the ration kits.

The experience of CiplaQCIL in Uganda in the 2000s, which is unique in many ways, is similar to the case of Kenya in the 1980s in terms of the complimentary roles played by foreign aid, the state, and ties abroad. Also in the case of CiplaQCIL, foreign aid was instrumental in triggering state support. Guaranteed purchases by the state, combined with the promise of a Global Fund market, allowed for the establishment of the joint venture. Technical know-how, again as in Kenya in the 1980s, was not provided by foreign aid and was accessed through ties abroad. Foreign aid was critical for the emergence and success of CiplaQCIL in other ways: because CiplaQCIL relied on Global Fund purchases, in contrast to Kenyan firms in the 1980s, it had to adhere to the condition of WHO PQ, which was key to the high level of quality standards that the company has maintained.

The other three case studies—Tanzania and Uganda in the 1980s and Uganda after 2000 (with the exception of CiplaQCIL)—show the likely fate of local pharmaceutical production without foreign assistance. In Tanzania and Uganda in the 1980s, reliance only on local resources led to the emergence of a small and fragile pharmaceutical sector in both countries. The Ugandan pharmaceutical sector in the 2000, excepting CiplaQCIL, also remained underdeveloped.

———

Although this book focuses on the production of quality-assured drugs, the lessons are applicable to aid in support of other manufacturing sectors, as well as to the provision of commodities or services—which is a major aspect of international development agencies' response during relief operations or humanitarian crises.

In regard to promoting industrial production, although the pharmaceutical sector is in some ways unique, there is nothing about the measures used to promote pharmaceutical production that cannot be applied effectively to other industrial sectors. As for *markets*, one feature that made it presumably easier to create a market in support of the pharmaceutical sector through donations is that the drugs in question were provided through the public sector. However, there are many other commodities, including essential commodities, that are provided, or could be easily provided, through the public sector. More importantly, there are numerous ways for donations to create or enlarge a private market as well, as demonstrated in the Affordable Medicines Facility–malaria (AMFm), in which the Global Fund subsidized producers of drugs that sold in the private sector. As for *monitoring*, emphasis on quality is an integral part of any industrial upgrading, not only drugs, and monitoring could apply to other standards—including performance standards or labor or environmental standards. Also in other industrial sectors, it will often be hard for producers to meet the conditions without technical guidance by way of *mentoring*. In short, by creating market opportunities for products with specifications that producers are taught how to follow, developmental foreign aid can be effective not only in improving the quality of locally produced drugs, but also in improving, for example, fair pay in privately owned textiles factories or in rice harvests of smallholder farmers.[1]

Significantly, the findings should apply not only to manufacturing of commodities but their distribution as well. This is important, given the preference today for humanitarian over economic aid, as I discuss in chapter 1. In the field of global health, for example, foreign aid supports not only the procurement of drugs, but their distribution as well, and donors fund major initiatives for the distribution of vaccines, bed-nets, condoms, and many other essential goods, including food for human immunodeficiency virus (HIV)-positive patients. As with manufacturing, distribution is challenging in countries with weak state capabilities. Some international organizations are seeking to improve delivery through means that echo my focus on markets and monitoring, including performance-based financing schemes, where donors provide funds on the basis of results. In such programs, funds (which in the context here are akin to markets in the industrial sector) are distributed incrementally, and subsequent installments of funds depend on the achievement of certain benchmarks with earlier installments—in a vaccination program, for example, the benchmark may be a certain number of children vaccinated (Chorev, Andia, and Ciplet 2011). As the executive director of the Global Fund from 2007 to 2012, Michel Kazatchkine, stated, to assure performance, "all funds are released incrementally based on demonstrated results against targets we have jointly agreed [on] with the countries."[2] In other types of performance-based financing, providers may be offered financial incentives for the provision of a defined set of services—health care workers, for example, may be offered a bonus payment for each delivery (Grover, Bauhoff, and Friedman 2018). Schemes that prioritize merit, however, carry the risk of abandoning exactly those countries or institutions with the greatest need (Chorev et al. 2011). Hence, foreign aid programs that involve performance-based conditions need to work not by excluding poor performers, but by making sure that their performances improve. For that, mentoring is particularly important. In their work on cash-for-delivery, Birdsall et al. (2012, 19) call for "a hands-off approach, emphasizing the power of incentives rather than guidance or interference," but they also make it clear that they do not object to technical assistance, as long as it is the recipient's choice. Birdsall and her collaborators reason that "such demand-driven technical assistance has a greater chance of being useful to recipients, and because they selected it, they are more likely to apply it" (24). In countries with scarce know-how, it is reasonable to expect that technical assistance will be both welcomed and useful.

———

This book suggests that foreign aid interventions were instrumental to the emergence and upgrading of pharmaceutical manufacturing facilities in East Africa—and that developmental foreign aid could have similar impact in other industrial or nonindustrial sectors as well. Still, also in the pharmaceutical field, the outcomes did not escape a number of challenges and contradictions.

One significant contradiction stems from aid allocation. Foreign aid is dictated by a number of considerations, including political and strategic considerations of the donors, the needs of the recipients, and also the potential capacity of recipients to effectively absorb aid.[3] When absorption capacity is considered, aid tends to serve those with extant capabilities and resources (e.g., Alesina and Dollar 2000, Briggs 2017). In that way, aid may reproduce inequities among countries.[4] Indeed, differences in the nature of drug donations and other forms of foreign assistance in Kenya, Tanzania, and Uganda discussed in this book were in part in response to domestic conditions, including the perceived absorption capacity of either the state or the local industry. Although all three countries received ration kits in the 1980s, only in Kenya did the ration kit program include a local component, because perceived lack of state capacity in Tanzania and lack of manufacturing capabilities in Uganda ruled out that option. In the 2000s, development agencies did not offer technology transfer in Uganda in part because of concern that local firms would not be able to successfully absorb the know-how. Consequently, aid in support of the pharmaceutical sectors benefited exactly those countries that already did better on their own.

Donors' tendency to serve those who already have capabilities and resources also leads to inequities among firms—aid in the 2000s benefited the better-off firms in each country, including firms with political connections. In turn, the smallest firms did not receive support. Serving the better-positioned firms could be interpreted positively as "picking winners" (Rodrik 2008) if not for two additional challenges—the first challenge is that the "have nots" (in this case, firms with poor quality standards) did not die out. Because international monitoring was voluntary, and because national monitoring was normally lax, ignoring the conditions imposed by foreign aid did not generally have the effect of weeding out those pharmaceutical firms that, from a public health perspective and possibly from an economic perspective as well, should have been closed.

A second challenge is that the "winners" did not necessarily win. Because these were international tenders, there was no guarantee that a local company, rather than a foreign manufacturer, would be the one benefiting from the tenders. No Kenyan company, for example, ended up benefiting from the Global Fund funding given to the Kenyan government. This is related to the fact, discussed in chapter 1, that monitoring in this case—the condition of quality standards—allowed for upgrading without improved competitiveness. Kenyan companies that improved their quality standards found alternative markets to sell their drugs, but this does not change the fundamental tension of investment in better products when these products are not competitive in international markets at the same time that consumers in the local market cannot afford them.

In addition to these inherent contradictions, other tensions stemmed from the fact that developmental foreign aid is still dependent on local conditions, including state capacity. On the one hand, the provision of markets, monitoring, and mentoring by international development agencies is much more interventionist than alternative forms of aid. For example, even as the Global Fund abides by the principle of "country ownership" by offering funds based on state-led applications, these funds are provided within certain parameters decided by the Global Fund and the WHO, not by the applying countries. With little fanfare, the WHO has made itself an alternative regulatory body responsible for the evaluation of quality practices of pharmaceutical producers, superseding the regulatory bodies in the countries where these factories are located. (As we have seen, national regulations are themselves influenced by WHO recommendations and guidelines.) Mentoring is similarly interventionist in offering guidance as to how to reach standards developed elsewhere. On the other hand, greater interventionism does not make developmental foreign aid any less dependent on local conditions. This dependence explains one of the contradictions of foreign aid mentioned above—that foreign aid is likely to help those countries that are relatively less in need of support.

This dependence, in turn, leads to the question of whether foreign aid could help improve the local conditions that need to be in place in order for foreign aid to then be effective. Specifically, given the importance of state capacity, can foreign aid stimulate state capacity building? Although there are obvious challenges, in the following section I describe what I find to be convincing indications that domestic pharmaceutical regulation and the enforcement of that regulation by state agencies significantly increased thanks to foreign support. I then assess the possibility of foreign aid bypassing the state, as one way of avoiding reliance on state capacity, and conclude against such a solution. Finally, I discuss recent acquisitions of local pharmaceutical firms in East Africa by foreign companies and suggest that foreign ownership makes the role of the state even more indispensable.

## State Capacity Building

State capacity is important beyond the question of foreign aid allocation or effectiveness—as it is a basic condition for a functioning governance (Evans 1995, Kohli 2004). Like the effect of foreign aid on development more generally, which I discuss in chapter 1, the effect of aid on state functioning is highly contested (Wright and Winters 2010). Critics have argued that foreign aid is responsible, for example, for inefficient public spending, bloated and corrupt bureaucracies, and increased rent seeking (Burnside and Dollar 2000, Remmer

2004). Aid may alter states negatively in more mundane ways: relying on the state to administer aid may overwhelm existing state capacities, as was the case early on with agencies distributing donated ARVs, and foreign funding may alter states' existing priorities rather than merely adding to them or supporting existing ones, as with the prioritization of access to medicine over health-system strengthening (Epstein 2015, Greene 2015). Foreign aid can undermine the state also indirectly, through an "internal brain drain," in which civil servants leave the state to work with aid agencies or donors-funded nongovernmental organizations (Bristol 2008). Others, however, argued that a "political aid curse" is not inevitable (Altincekic and Bearce 2014, Bermeo 2016, Prasad and Nickow 2016) and that foreign aid could have a positive impact on issues such as the quality of democratic governance (Goldsmith 2003, Dunning 2004, Wright 2009, Krasner and Weinstein 2014).

The effect of foreign assistance aimed specifically at capacity building— through direct technical assistance provided by "flying-in experts" or the training of locals (Collier 2007, 112)—has been similarly debated. Although scholars have reported on "a growing consensus . . . that [the efficacy and effectiveness of technical assistance] . . . has largely been a failure" (Riddell 2007, 203), others suggested that technical assistance has been reasonably successful (Collier 2007, Krasner and Weinstein 2014) and even the otherwise very critical Easterly and Williamson (2011) accept that, "Technical assistance can be well-done and productive in some cases."

In Kenya, Tanzania, and Uganda, foreign influences altered state policies and programs in the pharmaceutical field to an extraordinary degree. Many regulations, treatment guidelines, and procedures in the field of public health in these countries have been minor deviations from WHO guidelines and recommendations; and the regulatory agencies responsible for drug registration, GMP inspection, and post-marketing surveillance, which were established in the early 1990s—the Kenyan Pharmacy and Poisons Board (PPB), the Tanzania Food and Drugs Authority (TFDA), and the Ugandan National Drug Authority (NDA)—were all supported by foreign aid. One WHO official described the organization's influence in Uganda in the following way: "The WHO is the main technical adviser for NDA. We train their inspectorate staff, we help in preparing guidelines and tools for medicines inspection and assessment, and we also assist in capacity building for the laboratory and quality control staff. *The NDA would not exist without WHO*" (Agaba et al. 2013, emphasis added). Technical assistance from other donors included, for example, a UK-sponsored project, Medicines Transparency Alliance (MeTA), which, among other initiatives, helped post the list of registered drugs on the NDA website. Development agencies also helped with the recruitment or training of staff. For example, the first people working at the Ugandan NDA were elected (and paid for) by the

Dutch International Development Agency (DANIDA).[5] Due to such "executive selection," in the first few years, DANIDA was reportedly able to recruit and rely on a group of enthusiastic, committed local employees.[6] DANIDA also brought a British pharmacist to help NDA to "achieve its mandate."[7] Years later, in the early 2000s, the WHO PQ Program launched a project of rotational fellowships, in which personnel from developing countries were posted at the WHO for three months, where they "participated in a wide range of prequalification activities and were provided with a complete set of the WHO norms and standards that underpin prequalification."[8] A WHO official commented, "it's a fantastic thing . . . that has terrific impact."[9] As of 2016, Tanzania had five and Uganda had four rotational fellows (WHO 2016). The first rotational fellow from Tanzania, Hiiti Sello, who completed his rotation in 2007, became the TFDA director general in 2011.[10]

Even more than the drug regulatory agencies, donors invested in capacity-building in the agencies responsible for the procurement, warehousing, and distribution of drugs—the Kenya Medical Supplies Authority (KEMSA), Tanzania's Medical Stores Department (MSD), and Uganda's National Medical Stores (NMS). With foreign assistance, KEMSA was established in 2000 to replace the Medical Supplies Coordinating Unit. For almost a decade, KEMSA was viewed as an "ungainly and bureaucratic agency unable to fully deliver on its mandate" (Yadav 2014). Harsh evaluations from that time referred to "inadequate human resource capacity and skill sets, lack of necessary systems, poorly maintained and limited access to adequate operating facilities, [and] sub-optimal financial resources for capitalization, operations and maintenance" (Johnson et al. 2008). Starting in 2008, reforms "to transfer needed skills to KEMSA staff" (Global Fund 2012c) were initiated by the World Bank's Health Sector Support Program, USAID's [United States Agency for International Development] KEMSA Support Program, the WHO, and the Global Fund. Among the reforms identified as responsible for the later improvements were the recruitment of "leadership talent" (interestingly defined as "people with strong commercial sector experience in the healthcare, financing and logistics industries and not civil servants or career bureaucrats"), greater transparency of procurement contracts, and a more appropriate legal framework that provided KEMSA greater political and financial autonomy, allowed a higher salary scale for staff, and required better governance structure (Yadav 2014).[11] Follow-up evaluations concluded that the reforms led to a "tremendous transformation" (FEAPM 2012, 67). "KEMSA . . . has shown sustained improvements in performance, accountability and transparency" (Yadav 2014) leading to "marked improvements . . . in the public-sector supply of essential medicines" (WHO 2010, 25). Local manufacturers and distributors also noted a difference. By 2012, KEMSA was seen as professionally run, tenders were considered rational and fair, and payments were said to be more reliable (various interviews). Donors, in turn, showed their confidence by expanding KEMSA's authority over funds.[12] After the reforms, the Global Fund, the World Bank, DANIDA, the German KfW Development Bank, the African Development Bank, and even USAID let KEMSA do for some products the entire cycle of procurement, warehousing, and distribution.[13]

Not all agencies were as welcoming to foreign meddling as KEMSA. In Uganda, NMS replaced the Central Medical Stores (CMS) in 1996, with heavy financial and technical support from DANIDA.[14] Yet, it was only after the government reversed its decision to decentralize the procurement of drugs in 2009 that NMS received control over 100 percent of the drug procurement budget. Given the political debates over recentralization, "NMS [general manager] would be especially concerned about disclosing information on less-than-optimal outcomes or inefficient procedures that could potentially be used as evidence to generate pressures to revert the [recentralization] policy decision" (Governance 2011). Likely as a result, the NMS refused any technical assistance that would have required disclosure of its "internal procedures and performance indicators" and did not collaborate with development partners, including, for example, Securing Ugandans' Right to Essential Medicines (SURE)—a USAID-funded $39-million program that was aimed at "assisting the Government of Uganda . . . to strengthen the national pharmaceutical supply system." SURE developed such bad relations with NMS that the director of SURE could not enter the agency's building.[15]

In short, although a systematic comparison of state capacity building initiatives and their outcomes is beyond the scope of this book, the anecdotal evidence that we do have suggests that not all technical assistance programs are successful or sustainable in the long-run, but also that there are cases in which state capacity building is fruitful.[16] This is critical to note when we consider whether, rather than relying on a state with weak state capacity or putting efforts into state capacity-building that may not succeed, foreign aid may be better off bypassing the state altogether, as I discuss next.

## Against Bypassing the State

Although developmental foreign aid still relies on the state, it arguably does not need to. In Kenya and Tanzania after 2000, the Global Fund market functioned through the state procurement agency, but the more targeted markets did not. Working with the state made the Global Fund market visible, but a similar arrangement could have been conducted with nonstate agencies just as successfully. Monitoring relied on international rather than national standards and was based on convincing local manufacturers to comply with expectations beyond what was required from them by state law. Mentoring was rarely coordinated with states.

As an alternative to building state capacity, therefore, we may ask whether developmental foreign aid could replace or, less dramatically, bypass the state. Ironically, skeptics of foreign aid like William Easterly are more likely to offer solutions that bypass the state and consequently increase the scope of aid involvement, whereas advocates of foreign aid like Jeffrey Sachs seem more comfortable with the idea of foreign aid relying on collaboration with the state. Interestingly, donor governments are divided according to similar ideological lines. Dietrich (2016) finds that donor governments whose political economies emphasize market-based delivery systems (such as the US, UK, and Australia) are more likely to pursue "bypass tactics" in poorly governed countries. Donor countries with less market-oriented delivery systems (such as Japan, South Korea, France, and Germany) bypass less and emphasize a more active role of the state in development. International governmental organizations, although responsive to US models, do often work with governments. The different approaches taken by the US-funded President's Emergency Plan for AIDS Relief (PEPFAR) and the Global Fund demonstrate these divergent models. Together, these two institutions have been responsible for the provision of most ARVs in Kenya, Tanzania, and Uganda since the early 2000s—but PEPFAR managed its entire operation, including procurement, warehousing, and distribution, in parallel to government agencies, whereas the Global Fund generally preferred to work with state agencies (although at times state mismanagement led the Global Fund to transfer responsibilities elsewhere or even withdraw funds altogether).[17]

In studies on foreign aid, the debate over which practice is preferable sets two considerations—efficiency and state capacity—as competing priorities. So whereas Moss, Pettersson, and van de Walle (2008, 263) emphasize the "politicized and patrimonialized" allocation of goods when working with the state, Reinikka (2008) is concerned with aid agencies' undermining the state. As Dietrich (2016, 68, emphasis added) concisely summarizes: "Bypass tactics under conditions of bad governance emphasize *efficiency gains* in aid delivery through the use of market-type mechanisms. 'Hands-on' government-to-government aid delivery emphasizes the importance of *continued state engagement and capacity building in aid delivery* under similar conditions." The case of local pharmaceutical production in East Africa offers additional reasons to support "continued state engagement."

One reason to support the state is that of sustainability. PEPFAR's practices do not pave the way to a possible future in which its services may no longer be needed. In contrast, when the Global Fund or other donors focus on making sure the state appropriately procures, warehouses, and distributes the drugs for which these donors are paying, their efforts may help to improve the handling of drugs bought by the state itself as well and point toward a future in which the state can fulfil these functions on its own.

Another consideration is particularly important for developmental foreign aid. The monitoring offered to local pharmaceutical companies by international agencies was voluntary. It could have been mandatory if it were to be imposed by the state—but that would have brought up all the existing challenges of laws in under-regulated markets, including loose standards and poor enforcement, which monitoring through foreign aid is aimed to resolve. Because it was voluntary, companies could choose not to comply. Those companies that did not choose to comply with international standards were left under the purview of the state. This is one of the contradictions mentioned above—developmental foreign aid has no means to weed out those that do not follow even minimal standards. For that task, the state is needed.

Finally, confining the discussion only to the question of efficiency versus capacity-building may lead, as Morgan and Orloff (2017, 18) warn, to a "conceptual blurring such that all forms of power are viewed as equivalent." Morgan and Orloff refer to public versus private power, but the same logic applies to national versus international power. I mentioned earlier the very loose boundaries between the state and external political influences, especially in developing countries, yet formal legal sovereignty "remains a defining feature of what it is to be a state" (Morgan and Orloff 2017, 18), which sets the state apart from competing local and foreign entities. The principles of sovereignty grant legitimacy to the state, legitimacy on which providers of foreign aid cannot rely. One recent illustration of mistrust in providers of foreign aid was during the Ebola epidemic in West Africa, where locals accused foreign health workers for spreading the virus (Nossiter 2014). In the pharmaceutical field in East Africa, local producers often referred to state policies that did not favor them—such as new treatment guidelines banning the simple antimalarial drugs or the imposition of higher quality standards—as coming from the WHO or multinational pharmaceutical companies, precisely as a way to question these policies' legitimacy (various interviews). There are instances, of course, in which foreign aid is trusted—foreign aid may even be more trusted than the state. However, when the state *is* legitimate, foreign aid could gain legitimacy by channeling its actions through the state, exactly because this implies that aid agencies do not give up on the state but rather respect and support state sovereignty.

## A Future of Denationalization?

National laws and international monitoring are not the only sources of regulation or the only means of enforcing specific practices. Companies with a global market may follow practices that go beyond what is required by national law—due to pressure to follow laws of *other* governments. In East Africa, no pharmaceutical company sells outside the regional market—but a few companies are owned by multinational pharmaceutical companies that do have an international market. These include Shelys and Beta Healthcare, which are owned by the South African company Aspen, and CiplaQCIL, which is owned by the Indian company Cipla.

Shelys and CiplaQCIL represent two trajectories that companies with a global orientation may take in response to opportunities provided by developmental foreign aid (there may be other responses). Thanks to access to resources and technical know-how, CiplaQCIL was not in need of mentoring through foreign aid, but otherwise the company responded to developmental foreign aid in a way similar to other local manufacturers such as Universal or Cosmos in Kenya: it focused on the new market of ARVs and ACTs and invited international monitoring of its quality standards. Shelys, in contrast, showed less interest in the donors market. Having the resources and human skills for branding and marketing, it focused instead on the private market, particularly for the middle-class. Although there were other local companies, like Regal in Kenya, that followed similar strategies, Shelys stood out in its determined focus on the most profitable, fast-moving products. One result that is of consequence to public health was Shelys's lessened focus on essential medicines. In addition, rejecting the markets offered by development agencies also meant that Shelys for a while rejected the monitoring that came with foreign aid. (It later welcomed it for zinc.) Shelys claimed to follow quality standards that were higher than what was required by law. Specifically, the Tanzanian factory reportedly followed an "Aspen standard"—an informal company standard that, although uneven across the factories in different countries, was still sufficiently high.[18] The decision to stay above a certain minimum in *all markets* was motivated by the fear that poorly made drugs in Tanzania could potentially affect the company's reputation in places like Germany, where much higher quality standards are required, even if drugs produced in Tanzania would never be sold in Germany. Self-regulation, as we saw in regard to western pharmaceutical companies in the 1980s, is not always effective, however, and some suggested that Shelys was neglecting its commitment to quality.

In short, local companies that were owned by multinational pharmaceutical firms had different approaches to donors markets, which influenced both the type of drugs that they produced and the quality standards that they maintained: although these local companies were arguably better equipped to take advantage of foreign aid, they were also better positioned to take advantage of other opportunities, including in the private market, making it easier for them to ignore the incentives and therefore the conditions that came with foreign aid.

Additional acquisitions of pharmaceutical companies in East Africa by foreign investors since 2016 signals a growing interest in the pharmaceutical sector in the region. This is partly due to the emerging perception of Africa as a "growing market," including for branded generics.[19] According to one Aspen official: "African consumers now, they can start affording brands. So that's our primary consideration."[20] Arguably, this is also partly due to developmental foreign aid that, by enabling upgrading, made local pharmaceutical firms more attractive to foreign investors. Indeed, for many investors, purchasing an existing company was more attractive than establishing an entirely new one because, as another Aspen official explained: "It just made sense to have something that was there already, with the infrastructure, with the products that they have available, and the fact that they've got the necessary approvals for manufacturing and selling in those markets."[21]

In the most notable acquisition, in 2016 the Indian pharmaceutical company Strides Shasun bought a controlling stake in Universal. Strides Shasun at the time already had fourteen manufacturing facilities (five in India, two in Europe, and seven in Africa); and signaling the high reputation of the company, six of the factories were approved by the United States Food and Drug Administration (USFDA).[22] Like CiplaQCIL, Strides Shasun was motivated by the advantages of producing in Africa, especially as both local governments and donors became more willing to support local production. According to a 2016 Strides Shasun press release, "Strides Shasun plans to transfer several strategic institutional products to this facility [in Kenya] as *[donor and] government procurement agencies have a preference for 'Made in Africa' products*" (emphasis added; see also Economic Times 2016).

Other investments did not involve the acquisition of existing companies. In 2018, Square Pharmaceuticals, one of the major drug companies in Bangladesh, announced its decision to build an entirely new pharmaceutical factory in Kenya. With an initial investment of $25 million, the plant will be large—it is reportedly designed to manufacture 2 billion tablets and capsules and 60 million bottles of liquid formulations. Although reports mention that the plant will be producing essential drugs without specifying a plan to produce donors-funded drugs, they also mention that, "the products will be pre-qualified through World Health Organization and supplied throughout Africa in the long run" (Daily Star 2018, Hossain 2018).

Given the lack of financial resources and technical know-how in East Africa, a common sentiment is that, "the best option for local industry . . . is to conclude strategic partnerships or joint ventures with pharma players in more developed countries" (UNIDO 2011a, 6). Historically, there were "very few initiatives between developed and developing country [pharmaceutical] firms happening . . . on a purely commercial basis" (WHO 2009, 23). Today there seems to be a greater interest, especially from the global South, in industrial opportunities in African countries, including in the pharmaceutical sector. From the perspective of developmental foreign aid, the rise of companies with access to technical know-how and credible strategies as of how to reach markets is both a relief and a challenge. The relief is that these companies do not have to rely on donors to succeed. The challenge is that companies that choose not to rely on the markets offered by foreign aid are also free of the conditions imposed by donors. Monitoring, in that case, remains in the hands of the state. Although other considerations, such as international reputation, may lead to the maintenance of adequate quality standards, it is not a good idea to rely exclusively on the self-regulation of multinational companies. We saw that in the 1980s, when multinational pharmaceutical companies sold drugs in poor countries that they could not sell in regulated markets (chapter 3); and although the easy diffusion of information nowadays makes it more likely that abuse in one market would be revealed and affect a company's reputation in other markets, effective laws are still more potent deterrents. There are other reasons to worry about the effect investment by multinational pharmaceutical companies would have on the pharmaceutical markets in East Africa. In Uganda, government support of local production has been focused only on CiplaQCIL, excluding all the other companies from the Global Fund market. In Tanzania, Shelys today controls more than 60 percent of the local market share, potentially creating a local monopoly. (Of course, it still has to compete with imported drugs.) A new wave of foreign investment, therefore, makes state capacity—to monitor quality and to regulate competition—not less but possibly even more urgent.

————

Is foreign aid effective? The experience of local pharmaceutical production in Kenya, Tanzania, and Uganda since the 1980s offers cautious optimism. On the one hand, much depends on local conditions. The state, in particular, is a constitutive force that cannot be ignored when inquiring about conditions for development. Entrepreneurs, too, play a critical role. In the pharmaceutical field, entrepreneurs' access to technical know-how was necessary for state policies and foreign aid to make a difference. However, foreign aid could offer incentives and means to channel entrepreneurs—and, as I suggest in this chapter, also the state—in a productive direction. In East Africa, first the emergence and then the upgrading of local pharmaceutical manufacturing was often thanks to foreign aid that created demand for new drugs, specified terms for the kind of drugs donors might buy, and offered guidance as of how to produce those drugs and how to meet the attached conditions. Foreign aid could not and should not replace the state. However, it *should* act in a way that is compatible with a (developmental) state—offering the types of incentives and tools that the experience of developmental states suggest are effective.

As a way to conclude, it is worth repeating that much is at stake. It is not only that developmental foreign aid may assist with the development of a recipient sector, but that, conversely, without developmental components, foreign aid may be undermining a country's well-being. Food aid in the 1950s and the 1960s contributed to agricultural underdevelopment in formerly self-sufficient agrarian societies (Friedmann 1982), and a second-hand clothing market, partly in the form of donations, is blamed for the inability of some countries to (re) develop their textiles and clothing industries (de Freytas-Tamura 2017). In the pharmaceutical sector, I showed that drug donations in Tanzania in the 1980s potentially undermined the emergence of local pharmaceutical production and that, more recently, the free provision of antimalarials (combined with new treatment guidelines) decreased the market opportunities of local producers in all three countries. The solution cannot be to avoid aid altogether. Inefficiencies and potential distortions cannot be a reason to stop providing food, clothing, or appropriate medicine for people in need. Rather, inefficiencies and potential distortions should force donors to look for ways by which their donations provide for urgent needs at the same time that they also contribute to longer-term development. This book offers at least one way by which this could be achieved.

# NOTES

## Chapter 1. Foreign Aid in Comparative-Historical Perspective

1. Local production refers to the production of medicines in a given country. A pharmaceutical firm is "locally owned" when it is owned (or partly owned, in cases of joint ventures) by locals (citizens or residents).

2. Although state capacity and private entrepreneurship are themselves products of nonlocal conditions, in this book, I refer to both as "local" or "domestic" given their institutional presence at the domestic level.

3. The terms "Indians" or "Asians" in East Africa refer to people who originated from the Indian subcontinent before the partition in 1947.

4. On the history of foreign aid, see Frank and Baird (1975), Lancaster (2007), Riddell (2007).

5. I consider as foreign aid both official development assistance (ODA), which is the aid measured by the Organization for Economic Co-operation and Development (OECD), and non-ODA. Most quantitative analyses only rely on the ODA data.

6. For helpful reviews on the debate, see Radelet (2006), Lancaster (2007), Wright and Winters (2010). See Prasad and Nickow (2016) for a careful consideration of the "aid curse."

7. On the positive impact on foreign aid, see Bräutigam and Knack (2004), Kosack and Tobin (2006), Finkel, Pérez-Liñán, and Seligson (2007), Savun and Tirone (2012).

8. See Addison, Mavrotas, and McGillivray (2005), Bourguignon and Sundberg (2007), Wright and Winters (2010), Asongu and Nwachukwu (2017), but see Doucouliagos and Paldam (2011).

9. In economics and political science, some researchers consequently turned to randomized controlled trials (RCTs) (e.g., Duflo and Kremer 2008). Critics of RCTs point both at methodological limitations (Deaton 2010) and practical implications, including the worry that RCTs produce little more than policy manuals, which are based on interventions designed with feasibility constraints in mind (Ravallion 2009, Picciotto 2012, Viterna and Robertson 2015, Adams 2016). A different response to the inconclusive results of macro-level analysis, in line with the study here, was a move to sector-specific studies (Gopalan and Rajan 2016).

10. Between 1953 and 1960, US aid to South Korea amounted to some 10 percent of the latter's gross national product (GNP) per year (Amsden 1989, Kohli 2004). During the 1950s in Taiwan, economic aid equaled about 6 percent of GNP (Wade 1990).

11. Amsden (1989, 47, 142), Wade (1990, 83–4), Kohli (2004, 73–4), but see Amsden (1985, 90–1). Both Amsden (1989) and Kohli (2004, 74) suggest that the relative ineffectiveness of US aid was due to the *type of economic policies* that the US imposed, which in Korea were aimed at maintaining minimal consumption rather than at rebuilding the economy. For a positive reading of the effect of aid on South Korea, see Prasad and Nickow (2016).

12. Amsden (2001) rightly notes, however, that not all industrial policies work well for all sectors, as shown by the positive effect price controls had on the Indian pharmaceutical industry but its negative effect on the steel industry in the same country.

13. http://www.un.org/millenniumgoals/, accessed Dec.4, 2018.

14. UNDP, "Development Cooperation, Tanzania: Corrigendum to 1989 Report," Nov. 1991, C17/372/2, WHO Archives.

15. http://www.oecd.org/statistics/datalab/oda-recipient-sector.htm, accessed Jan. 7, 2018.

16. http://www.un.org/sustainabledevelopment/sustainable-development-goals/, accessed Dec. 4, 2018.

17. Japan gave 35 percent of its aid for Africa in these categories; South Korea gave 47 percent. One reason that some new donors invest their aid in industrial production is the positive experiences that they had as aid recipients themselves (Stallings and Kim 2017, 25–26).

18. On upgrading in the apparel and textiles sectors, see Gereffi and Memedovic (2003).

19. I make a similar argument in my analysis of "reactive diffusion," where I suggest that countries in the global South do not simply accept global norms but alter them in the course of their diffusion (Chorev 2012a).

20. I borrow the phrase from the literature on the "bargaining in the shadow of the law" (Mnookin and Kornhauser 1979, Steinberg 2002). Powell (1999) uses the phrase in a somewhat similar manner in his own study of international conflicts.

21. See also Lall (1992, 113–14), who similarly focuses on incentives (including "sufficient selective *protection*"), institutions (that facilitate the working of markets, including information, services, and *standards*), and *capabilities* (including the launching of physical environment, the provision of human capital, and the undertaking of technological effort).

22. "Tender" is the term used to describe invitation to bids in East Africa and many international organizations.

23. See also Dore (1986), Lall and Pietrobell (2002), Sanjaya (2004). On the role of invention and innovation in development, see Breznitz and Murphree (2011), who similarly suggest that innovation is not necessary for sustainable growth in a global economy in which processes of production are fragmented.

24. On the role of local context in shaping international influences, see, for example, Brenner and Theodore (2002), Fourcade and Babb (2002), Hanley, King, and János (2002), Prasad (2006), Chorev (2012a), Evans and Sewell (2013), Çakmaklı et al. (2017).

25. "Good" institutions include state capacity or democracy (Kosack 2003, but see Bourguignon and Sundberg 2007); "good" policies include economic policies that are important for growth (Burnside and Dollar 2000, but see Easterly, Levine, and Roodman 2004) or appropriate spending priorities (Mosley, Hudson, and Verschoor 2004, Gomanee et al. 2005).

26. Not all state agencies in the same country are similarly capable, so it is important to consider the capacity of the relevant agencies rather than the government as a whole (McDonnell 2017).

27. The literature on the neo-developmental state has been more explicitly focused on the making of entrepreneurs (ÓRiain 2004a, Breznitz and Murphree 2011; see also Amsden and Chu 2003).

28. The essentialist characterizations that have been used in explaining the contribution of Indian Kenyans to the Kenyan economy (e.g., Himbara 1994) have been rightly criticized. Most critiques addressed the issue by claiming that Indians' contribution to the Kenyan economy has been overstated, not by rejecting the explanation to their dominance. More recent investigations do focus on structural characteristics (e.g., Biggs, Raturi, and Srivastava 1996, Fafchamps 2000, Vandenberg 2003), but like the literature on middleman minorities more generally (see notes 31–32 below), they investigate domestic rather than international ties, which is the main focus here.

29. See Amin (1974), Evans (1976, 37–38), Evans (1979, 37–38), Portes (1997), Chibber (2005), Moran (2006), Kosack and Tobin (2006).

30. See ÓRiain (2004a), Saxenian (2007), Nee and Opper (2012), Hillmann (2013), Samila and Sorenson (2017), Kwon, Heflin, and Ruef (2013).

31. Although the literature often analyzes the middleman minorities' position in trade and commerce, where they tend to concentrate, it is also the case that second and third generations tend to move to manufacturing (Cardoso 1967, Bonacich 1973).

32. The literature on middleman minorities also considers the transnational links of ethnic communities, but it focuses on relations of exchange (goods, money) rather than other forms of connections, such as information (Portes and Zhou 1992, Portes, Guarnizo, and Haller 2002).

33. Today, Kenya's GDP per capita is $1,455 (population 48 million), compared to Tanzania's $879 GDP per capita (population 55 million) and Uganda's $615 GDP per capita (population 41 million) (https://data.worldbank.org, accessed Aug. 4, 2018).

34. Because the information on individual pharmaceutical companies I describe in this book is at times publicly available, it is both impossible and unnecessary to hide the identity of the companies in question. For similar reasons, with their consent, I do not hide the identity of the individuals I interviewed. I do not reveal the identity of an individual, however, in cases in which the comment is potentially sensitive.

35. "Local Pharmaceutical Manufacturing: Problems and Opportunities," Apr. 23, 1990, KEN018, MedNet, WHO Archives, p. 5; World Bank (1990). By comparison, already a decade earlier, the locally produced share of the pharmaceutical market in Egypt and India was 80 percent and 94.4 percent, respectively (UNCTC 1979).

36. "Local Pharmaceutical Manufacturing"; World Bank (1990).

37. "Local Pharmaceutical Manufacturing"; World Bank (1990); Center for Pharmaceutical Management (2003).

38. In 2008, the contributions of the pharmaceutical sectors in Kenya and Uganda were estimated to be, respectively, 0.2 percent and 0.18 percent of GDP (UNIDO 2010a, 2010b). There are no equivalent estimates for the pharmaceutical sector in Tanzania (Losse, Schneider, and Spennemann 2007). In India, by comparison, the pharmaceutical sector's contribution to GDP was 2 percent (Akhtar 2013).

## Chapter 2. Global Pharmaceuticals and East Africa

1. This estimate includes both nonbranded and branded generics, which explains why it is much higher than estimates that count only nonbranded generics (WHO 2004, 35, Chaudhuri 2005, 12–13).

2. API is any substance used in the manufacture of a pharmaceutical dosage form that is biologically *active* and produces the drug's effect; excipient, which in addition to API is the other core component of a drug, is a chemically *inactive* substance that helps with the delivery of the medication. Strictly speaking, when API production is not part of the drug making process, as is the case in East Africa, factories are formulators rather than manufacturers (Owino 1985, 151–66, WHO 2007a, Klissas et al. 2010, UNCTAD 2011b, figure 1).

3. Interview with Dr. P. V. Appaji, executive director, Pharmaceutical Export Promotion Council of India (Pharmexcil), India, Jan. 3, 2012.

4. Good Manufacturing Practices (GMP) include, for example, standards and procedures for storing of inputs at the correct temperature and humidity and in the correct containers, cleaning and upkeep of machines, keeping the areas dedicated to formulation sterile, and requiring special clothing and gear when staff enter these areas. GMP is one part of a comprehensive system of Quality Assurance (QA), which also covers procedures to assure safety and efficacy. However, safety and efficacy testing is required for originator drugs, not generic equivalents (WHO 1995a, 2007a, UNCTAD 2011b; interview with Jurgen Reinhardt, senior industrial development officer, UNIDO, July 11, 2013).

5. Brand-name pharmaceutical companies also sell substandard drugs. In the early 1980s, for example, multinational companies were found to be selling expired and mislabeled drugs in developing countries (chapter 3).

6. Kenya was under British rule from 1895 to independence in 1963. The Tanganyika territory, which was earlier part of German East Africa, was administered by the British between 1916 and 1961. After independence, Tanganyika and Zanzibar formed Tanzania. Uganda was a protectorate of the British Empire from 1894 to 1962.

7. Interview with George Masafu, Kenya, Dec. 22, 2012; interview with Vijai Maini, managing director, Surgipharm, Kenya, June 19, 2012.

8. On western medicine in colonial East Africa, see Beck (1971, 1981), Iliffe (1998), Baronov (2008). For a critique, see Ferguson (1980), Turshen (1984), Comaroff (1993), Anderson (2014).

9. Foreign subsidiaries in Kenya included: Glaxo East Africa (UK), Wellcome Kenya (UK), Boots Co. of Kenya (UK), Infusion Kenya (subsidiary of Hoechst, FRG), Sterling Products Int'l (US), Beecham of Kenya (UK), Nicholas Kiwi (K) (Australia), Howse and McGeorge (UK) and Chemafric (Thoithi et al. 2008). They still mostly produced consumer products (e.g., Glaxo), or cosmetic and toiletry (e.g., Boots). At their peak, the largest factories—Glaxo, Boots, and Sterling— each employed 150–250 workers (UNCTC 1984, tables H.1, H.4, Owino 1985, table 3.3, Ikiara 1995).

10. M. A. Attisso, "Present Situation Regarding Pharmacy and Drugs in Kenya," Aug. 12, 1971, AFR/PHARM/5, WHO Archives, p. 9.

11. P. E. Christensen and P. Nissen, "The Medical Supply System in Uganda," Danish Red Cross, Jan. 1980, WHO Archives, p. 19.

12. See Barker and Wield (1978, 321–31); also G. Osuide, "Manufacture and Quality Control of Drugs and Training of Personnel in Uganda," Jan. 11, 1973, AFR/PHARM/9, WHO Archives.

13. Interview with Maini, Surgipharm, Kenya, Dec. 21, 2012.

14. Interview with Dhirendra Shah, managing director, Biodeal, Kenya, May 30, 2012; interview with Ashok Patel, chairman, Elys Chemical Industries, Kenya, June 15, 2012.

15. Interview with Maini, Surgipharm Kenya, Dec. 21, 2012.

16. M. A. Attisso, "Present Situation Regarding Pharmacy and Drugs in Tanzania," Feb. 17, 1972, AFR/PHARM/7, WHO Archives, p. 9 and M. A. Attisso, "Present Situation Regarding Pharmacy and Drugs in Tanzania," Apr. 26, 1972, AFR/PHARM/8, WHO Archives, p. 14.

17. John Korn, "The Drug Situation in Tanzania," DANIDA, May 1981, TAN004, WHO Archives, p. 22.

18. Korn, "The Drug Situation in Tanzania."

19. Most left in the mid to late 1990s. Partly, this was a consequence of a wave of mergers in the industry, which led to the closing of many factories. In addition, companies moved production facilities to other countries because Kenya had relatively high cost of manufacturing, excess capacity, and increasingly stricter regulation (Simonetti, Clark, and Wamae 2016, 34; *East African* 1999).

20. Generics were encouraged by other government policies as well. For example, the Kenya National Drug Policy 1994 stated that, "prescribers will be encouraged to prescribe by generic name and use the Essential Drugs Concept." However, the law did not *require* the prescribing of medicines by generic name, and it did not oblige the dispensing of generic medicine (MMS and MPHS 2009, 13). This was possibly due to opposition of manufacturers and importers of brand-name drugs, represented by the Kenya Association of Pharmaceutical Industry (KAPI) and guided by the Geneva-based International Federation of Pharmaceutical Manufacturers and Associations (IFPMA). KAPI used the common argument that "quality and safety and efficacy [come] before price" (interview with George Masafu, pharmacist, Kenya, Dec. 22, 2012).

21. Interview with Gopakumar Nair, India, Dec. 24, 2011.

22. Other state policies were aimed to encourage subsidiaries of foreign pharmaceutical companies to locally produce not only final formulations, but also bulk drugs, which required more

complex technology and high-technology drugs. This was done by conditioning the level of foreign equity on what was produced. These policies did not prove effective, however—most foreign companies settled for reduced equity holdings, or they left India. See UNCTC (1984), Chaudhuri (2005), Horner (2013); interview with Nair, India, Dec. 24, 2011; interview with Raghu Cidambi, India, Jan. 4, 2012.

23. Interview with Neeraj Verma, Macleods, India, Dec. 27, 2011; interview with Salama Pharmaceuticals, Tanzania, Mar.21, 2013.

24. Interview with William M. K. Mwatu, GSK, Kenya, Dec. 11, 2012.

25. See Horner (2013); also interview with Jubilant Pharma, India, Dec. 19, 2011.

26. Interview with Mugo Dawa, production supervisor, Dawa, Kenya, Dec. 10, 2012.

27. Interview with Rogers Atebe, pharmacist, Regal Pharmaceuticals, Kenya, June 5, 2012.

28. Interview with Manesh Patel, managing director, Lab & Allied, Kenya, May 18, 2012.

29. Interview with Maini, Surgipharm, Kenya, Dec. 21, 2012.

30. It should be mentioned that an earlier increase in imports of drugs in developing countries (still mostly imported from the West) slowed down after the second oil price shock in 1979, the ensuing slower economic growth, and the debt crisis a few years later. Whereas between 1970 and 1980 the average annual growth rate in drug imports in developing countries was 29.8 percent, between 1980 and 1984 it decreased by 1.3 percent (WHO 1988, 25–26). Both Tanzania and Uganda suffered from severe shortage of drugs due to lack of foreign currency (chapters 4, 5).

31. Interview with Mwatu, GSK, Kenya, Dec. 11, 2012; also, interview with M. Patel, Lab & Allied, Kenya, May 18, 2012.

32. Interview with Yusuf Sinare, chair, Tanzania Association of Pharmaceutical Industry (TAPI), Tanzania, Mar. 26, 2013.

33. Interview with Mwatu, GSK, Kenya, May 28, 2012.

34. Interview with Jubilant Pharma, India, Dec. 19, 2011.

35. Interview with Sinare, TAPI, Tanzania, Mar. 26, 2013.

36. Interview with M. Patel, Lab & Allied, Kenya, Dec. 20, 2012.

37. Interview with Maini, Surgipharm, Kenya, Dec. 21, 2012.

38. Interview with Atebe, Regal, Kenya, June 5, 2012.

39. Interview with Pharmacy and Poisons Board (PPB), Kenya, June 14, 2012.

40. Interview with Mission for Essential Drugs and Supplies (MEDS), Kenya, June 7, 2012. A substandard drug is a drug of poor quality, caused by poor manufacturing practices, poor transportation techniques or poor storage facilities. A counterfeit drug is a product that intends to look like a specified drug (e.g., Advil) and as if it is manufactured by a specific company (e.g., Pfizer) even though it is not manufactured by that company. Counterfeit drugs are often, though not always, substandard, whereas many substandard drugs are not counterfeits (Chorev 2015).

41. Some unlicensed outlets operated without a licensed pharmacist; others, however, operated by licensed pharmacists who opened more than one facility without licensing each of them. Interview with Masafu, Kenya, Dec. 22, 2012; interview with Paul Mwaniki, chairman, Pharmaceutical Society of Kenya (PSK), Kenya, May 19, 2012; BroadReach Healthcare (2011). In addition, there was a reason for the Kenyan authorities to turn a blind eye. In referring to the issue of unlicensed shops, one assessment permitted that "the standard of services and quality of medicines sold cannot be verified," but also noted that "these outlets provide services to populations that would otherwise lack access to medicines" (Luoma et al. 2010, 56).

42. See Peterson (2014) for the impact of the structural adjustment programs (SAPs) on pharmacies, local pharmaceutical production, and access to medicine in Nigeria. Peterson (2012, 232) emphasizes "the excess of counterfeits, illegal drug markets, self-medication, and drug-labeling problems" and largely ignores the role that imported drugs played in improving access to affordable, high quality medicine.

43. Interview with Mwatu, GSK, Kenya, May 28, 2012.

44. Elsewhere I explain why other frequently cited estimates of the rate of counterfeit drugs in Kenya, which are extremely high, are unreliable (Chorev 2015).

45. Interview with Marion Biotech, Kenya, June 5, 2012.

46. The larger market share over time reflects both the growing gap in the prices of brand-name and generic drugs, as well as a growing middle-class in Kenya that could afford brand names. Notably, when locally produced drugs are included, only 40 percent of all drugs by value came from the global North, whereas 32 percent were imported from the global South, and an additional 28 percent were locally produced (UNIDO 2010a, 42).

47. See UNIDO (2010a); also interview with Moses Mwangi, chair, KAPI, Kenya, May 18, 2012.

48. Data on registered drugs in Kenya were collected from various issues of the *Kenya Gazette* (1982–92) and from a list of registered drugs that was published online by Kenya's PPB in 2012. The registration data at the time listed all registered drugs, including drugs that were not later retained—which means that it captured the drug market as it was the year of registration, independently of whether the drugs continued to be sold later on. (PPB later changed this practice and began to post online only the list of retained drugs.) It is important to appreciate the limits of registration data. The data say nothing about the value or volume of the drugs registered. Still, it is useful for measuring the *activity* of individual companies, and local producers often referred to the number of drugs they have registered as an indication of their overall success.

49. "Assessment of the Use of the WHO Certification Scheme in Tanzania," WHO Mission, TAN040A, 27–30 Apr. 1993, WHO Archives; UNIDO (1997).

50. The second largest importer was Kenya, with 25.4 percent of total imports; the US was third with 6.7 percent of total imports; China was sixth, with only 3.9 percent (UNDP 2016).

51. Data on registered drugs in Tanzania were obtained from the Tanzania Food and Drugs Authority (TFDA) in 2012. The registration data listed both retained and expired drugs, but I kept only the data for retained drugs—which means that the data only capture drugs that continued to be registered in Tanzania in 2012. For similar use of Tanzania's registration data, see Mhamba and Mbirigenda (2010), Chaudhuri, Mackintosh, and Mujinja (2010), UNDP (2016).

52. Interview with National Medical Stores (NMS), Uganda, Jan. 7, 2013.

53. Data on registered drugs in Uganda were obtained from the Uganda National Drug Authority (NDA) in 2012. The registration data capture only retained drugs—which means that it includes only drugs that were retained as of 2012.

54. Interview with Anastasia Ngumbi, Kenya, Dec. 13, 2012.

55. Interview with Mwaniki, PSK, Kenya, May 19, 2012; interview with Rakesh Vinayak, Surgipharm, May 21, 2012.

56. At the time, Indian drug firms, with the support of the Indian government, put great efforts to improve the reputation of their drugs. For example, African regulatory authorities were invited to India to visit the plants and see that they conform with international quality standards (SCRIP 2003; interview with Neeraj Verma, Macleods, India, Dec. 27, 2011).

57. On what counts as "new drugs," see Sampat and Shadlen (2015).

58. See Horner (2013, 18) and Chaudhuri, Park, and Gopakumar (2010); also interview with K. M. Gopakumar, Third World Network, India, Dec. 13, 2011.

59. Interview with Kajal Bhardwaj, Médecins Sans Frontières (MSF), India, Dec. 19, 2011.

60. Interview with Sunil Panicker, Clinton Health Access Initiative (CHAI), India, Dec. 23, 2011.

61. http://www.gmp-compliance.org/gmp-news/fda-publishes-list-of-gmp-facilities-producing-for-the-us-market-generic-drug-products-and-apis, accessed Aug. 5, 2018.

62. A few Indian pharmaceutical companies also suffered from serious setbacks in regard to quality compliance, however (Harris 2014, Kazmin 2015).

63. 214 Indian companies registered drugs in Kenya between 1982 and 2005. 120 of these companies did not register a new drug after 2005. In turn, 120 other Indian companies registered drugs in Kenya for the first time since 2005. As for the companies with no new registered drugs after 2005, this does not mean that they did not continue selling the drugs already registered. It only means that they did not introduce new drugs to the market.

64. It is less informative to look at Kenya's registration list because it includes drugs that are no longer retained. Still, of the 334 Indian companies that had drugs registered in Kenya by 2011, only 94 companies—or 28 percent—were in one of the other four lists. Yet, these companies were the ones that registered most of the drugs (in part because they were around for longer). Of 3,829 Indian drugs that were registered in Kenya, 2,238 drugs—or 58 percent—were by reputed companies. The larger rate of nonreputable Indian companies in Kenya compared to Uganda confirms the reputation of the registration process in Kenya as relatively loose, as well as the interest among smaller Indian manufacturers in the Kenyan market more than in the Ugandan market.

65. In the 1980s, there were 20 major Indian manufacturers of drugs and more than 1,200 licensed small-scale manufacturers (UNCTC 1984, 54). Over the years, the "first tier" grew, but the sector continued to be decentralized. In 1995, there were 200 large and 8,000 small manufacturers (WHO 1995, 27). Greene (2007, table 1) divides the sector into 100 large firms, around 200 mid-size firms, and the "smallest" 5,700 firms.

66. Interview with Jubilant Pharma, India, Dec. 19, 2011; interview with Verma, Macleods, India, Dec. 27, 2011.

67. Interview with Yusuf Hamied, chairman, Cipla, India, Jan. 11, 2012.

68. See Patwardhan (2007); also interview with Hamied, Cipla, India, Jan. 11, 2012.

69. Interview with Phanindra Reddy, Hetero, India, Jan. 4, 2012.

70. Interview with Reddy, Hetero, India, Jan. 4, 2012. In Uganda, in 2017, 60 percent of the 34 drugs registered by Hetero were antiretrovirals (ARVs), compared with 30 percent of the 79 drugs registered by Cipla.

71. Indian drugs in the US and Europe are not sold as brands; in Africa, Indian drug companies do sell branded generics, which allows higher profits than nonbranded generics (interview with Brian Tempest, former CEO, Ranbaxy, India, Dec. 12, 2011; interview with Jubilant Pharma, India, Dec. 19, 2011).

72. Interview with Anselme Sahabo, Eris, Uganda, Jan. 9, 2013.

73. Interview with Surgipharm, Uganda, Jan. 9, 2013.

74. See Chaudhuri (2005) and Harris (2014); also interview with Nair, India, Dec. 30, 2011; interview with Panicker, CHAI, India, Dec. 23, 2011.

75. Korn, "The Drug Situation in Tanzania."

76. Both the WHO and the USFDA were involved in guiding GMP standards in China to more closely resemble international standards. For the US, helping the Chinese improve its GMP standards and enforcement was a way to "offset inadequate . . . inspections" of the USFDA in foreign countries. "Essentially, the FDA is outsourcing its regulatory power to other countries" (Liu 2012, 4; see also Bumpas and Betsch 2009).

77. Interview with Guilin, China, Oct. 15, 2013; interview with NMS, Uganda, Jan. 7, 2013.

78. Unlike with final formulations, China caught up with India in exporting bulk drugs and is today the world's largest export of APIs. In 2009, APIs accounted for 84 percent of China's pharmaceutical exports (Bumpas and Betsch 2009). However, API producers in China were behind producers in India in regard to quality standards. As of 2017, 107 sites in India were WHO prequalified, compared with 40 sites in China. They were also somewhat behind in regard to USFDA approval. 238 API sites in India received USFDA approval, compared with 166 in China (http://www.gmp-compliance.org/gmp-news/fda-publishes-list-of-gmp-facilities-producing-for-the-us-market-generic-drug-products-and-apis, accessed Aug. 8, 2018).

79. Interview with Alex Zheng, Global Pharma Service, China, Oct. 27, 2003.

80. Interview with Dawa, Kenya, Dec. 11, 2012; interview with Surgipharm, Uganda, Jan. 9, 2013.

81. http://www.gmp-compliance.org/gmp-news/fda-publishes-list-of-gmp-facilities -producing-for-the-us-market-generic-drug-products-and-apis, accessed Aug. 5, 2018.

82. The Chinese pharmaceutical sector has also been trying to break into the innovator drug market. Research and Development (R&D) has been encouraged by the Chinese government refocus on innovation (Grace 2004, Deng and Kaitin 2004, Festel et al. 2005) and was reinforced by the opening of small start-up companies by "returnees," who had worked in multinational pharmaceutical companies abroad (Pefile et al. 2005, Shen 2008, Ward 2016). Some Indian pharmaceutical sectors also increased their R&D budget. However, "Indian pharmaceutical firms are yet to prove their competence in innovating new products" (Chaudhuri 2013, 129).

83. Interview with Guilin, China, Oct. 15, 2013.

84. Guilin initially worked with the French pharmaceutical company Sanofi on the development and production of the drug. In 2008, Guilin also collaborated with Medicines for Malaria Venture (MMV)—an NGO that focuses on funding and providing technical support for the development of new malaria drugs—for the development and WHO-prequalifying of an injectable artesunate for treatment of severe malaria (interview with Holley Pharm, Tanzania, Mar. 30, 2013; see also https://www.mmv.org/access/products-projects/artesun-injectable-artesunate, accessed Aug. 7, 2018).

85. Interview with Holley Pharm, Tanzania, Mar. 30, 2013.

86. As I explain in chapter 6, the procurement of antimalarial drugs for the public sector in East Africa heavily relied on funds provided by donors, and these funds could only be used to procure drugs that were prequalified by the WHO or other stringent authorities.

87. Interview with David Ekau, pharmacist, Uganda, Jan. 4, 2013.

88. Part of the challenge was the fact that the drug is an innovator drug rather than a generic, which means that the company has to go through the complete process of drug approval (including showing not only quality, but also safety and efficacy) without having the necessary skills and facilities to do so.

89. On "China in Africa," see, for example, Alden (2005), Broadman (2007), Mohan and Power (2008), Bräutigam (2009). On "India in Africa," see Broadman (2007), Narlikar (2010).

90. China's general presence in Kenya, Tanzania, and Uganda is relatively modest compared with its presence in other countries that are richer in natural resources. In Zimbabwe, between 2005 and 2013, China's share of foreign investment was 82 percent. During those years, China's share of foreign investment was 28 percent in Uganda, 19 percent in Tanzania, and 7 percent in Kenya (Aisch, Keller, and Lai 2015). As for foreign aid, with the exception of relatively trivial donations of antimalarial drugs, neither India nor China had any direct effect on access to medicine in East Africa through aid (Freeman and Boynton 2011, Huang 2013).

## Chapter 3. Kenya in the 1980s: International Origins of Local Production

1. "Local Pharmaceutical Manufacturing: Problems and Opportunities," Apr. 23, 1990, KEN018, MedNet, WHO Archives, p. 5.

2. The firms that opened between 1979 and 1985 include: Laboratory & Allied Equipment (also known as Lab & Allied), Regal Pharmaceuticals, Elys Chemical Industries, Cosmos, Didy Pharmaceutical, Mac's Pharmaceutical, Pac's Laboratories, Pharmaceutical Manufacturing Company (PMC), and Pharmaceutical Products. Another company, Beta Healthcare, was a take-over

of an existing foreign subsidiary. Biodeal Pharmaceuticals opened in 1989, and Universal Corporation opened in 1996.

3. Interview with Ashok Patel, chairman, Elys Chemical Industries, Nairobi, Kenya, June 15, 2012.

4. The terms "African Kenyans" or "indigenous Africans" are used here to refer to indigenous Africans in Kenya. The term "Indian Kenyans" is used here to refer to Kenyans who originated from the Indian subcontinent before the partition in 1947. "Asians" is used when I quote from interviews or secondary literature.

5. "Local Pharmaceutical Manufacturing: Problems and Opportunities."

6. UN General Assembly, Sixth Special Session, May 1, 1974, A/RES/S-6/3201.

7. I describe the World Health Organization (WHO) response to the New International Economic Order (NIEO) in detail in Chorev (2012b).

8. The Primary Health Care (PHC) approach heavily criticized the costly high-technology, urban-based, and curative care that led to skewed resource allocation. Accordingly, the WHO rejected its traditional emphasis on vertical interventions and called for health care services to be provided at the community level, with the goal of *universal* provision of the most *essential* ("basic") services at *affordable* cost. UNICEF, "The National Programme on Essential Drugs: Plan of Operations and Plans of Action, 1988–1990," TAN018, Mar. 1986, WHO Library; see also Chorev (2012b, 66–79) and Greene (2015).

9. "Prophylactic and Therapeutic Substances: Report by the Director-General," 1975, A28/11, Pan American Health Organization (PAHO) Library.

10. "Background Document for Reference and Use at the Technical Discussions on 'National Policies and Practices in Regard to Medicinal Products, and Related International Problems,'" 1978, A31/Technical Discussions/1, PAHO Library.

11. WHO Document EB69/SR/15, Jan. 1982, WHO Library.

12. "Record of Meeting of Commonwealth Representatives. Prior to the Thirty-First World Health Assembly. Geneva, 7 May 1978," RG25, vol. 14977, file 46–4-WHO-1, part 7, Canada National Archives.

13. WHO Document EB61/SR/2, 1978, WHO Library.

14. "Guidelines and Recommendations for the Establishment of a Low Cost Pharmaceutical Formulation Plant in Developing Countries," 1980, DPM/80.2, WHO Archives, p. 5.

15. "Draft Prepared by UAR Delegation to the Symposium on Industrial Development in Africa," Cairo, 27 Jan.-10. Feb. 1966, Annex VII, N 80/440/3, WHO Archives.

16. "Guidelines and Recommendations for the Establishment of a Low Cost Pharmaceutical Formulation Plant in Developing Countries."

17. "Draft Prepared by UAR Delegation to the Symposium on Industrial Development in Africa"; see also letter from Dr. L. Bernard, WHO Assistant Director-General to Dr. A. E. Brown, WHO Liaison Officer with ECA, Apr. 24, 1967, N72/372/2, WHO Archives.

18. Fifth Summit Conference of Heads of State or Government of the Non-Aligned Movement, Colombo, Sri Lanka. 16–19 Aug. 1976.

19. See Lall (1978), UNCTC (1979), Mamdani (1992), and WHO (2009); also interview with Dr. Zafar Mirza, WHO, Switzerland, June 25, 2013.

20. See, for example, "III International Conference. Transfer and Development of Technology in the Developing Countries Under Favorable Conditions in the Pharmaceutical Industry," Belgrade, Yugoslavia, June 1979: Final Report with Conclusions and Recommendations, P5/86/43, WHO Archives.

21. "Guidelines and Recommendations for the Establishment of a Low Cost Pharmaceutical Formulation Plant in Developing Countries."

22. "Establishment of Pharmaceutical Production in Developing Countries. Report by the Director-General," 5 Apr. 1971, A24/A/5, WHO Archives; "WHO Statement Made to the UNIDO Industrial Development Board," 25 May 1971, N80/418/2, WHO Archives.

23. Even more than locally produced drugs, the WHO paid attention to the quality of imported drugs. Programs developed by the WHO included a certification scheme and (together with UNICEF) group bulk purchasing schemes. However, by the mid-1980s, bulk purchasing was abandoned. As I discuss in chapter 4, UNICEF instead increased the capacity of the UNICEF Supplies Division, which supported the ration kits programs.

24. WHO Document EB63/SR/21, 1979, WHO Library.

25. WHO Document EB66/SR/2, 1980, WHO Library.

26. Regional Office for the Western Pacific, Meeting of Working Group on the Regional Aspects of Drug Policies and Management, Mar. 1978, WPR/DPM/78.8, WHO Library.

27. UNIDO, First Consultation on the Pharmaceutical Industry, Lisbon, Portugal, 1–5 Dec. 1980, WHO Archives; see also Foster (1986).

28. WHO Document EB69/SR/13, 1982, WHO Library.

29. WHO Document EB66/SR/2, 1980, WHO Library. Correspondence from the late 1970s already hints at deflated interest among WHO officials. For example, discussions in 1979 between UNIDO and the WHO in regard to potential collaboration in the areas of "manufacturing and control of pharmaceuticals" suggested a minor role for the WHO. Although UNIDO was still to "focus on the definition and implementation of industrial production policies, including pharmaceutical production," among the "areas . . . considered for joint implementation," there was no mentioning of local production of pharmaceuticals. "UNIDO/WHO Strategy Paper on Manufacturing and Control of Pharmaceuticals," 8 Jan. 1980, N80/36/2, WHO Archives.

30. "DAP Comments on ACC Task Force Project Proposal No. 3," 24 May 1984, WHO Library.

31. "Summary of Progress in the WHO Action Programme on Essential Drugs [DAP] and Vaccines," Apr. 1985, WHO Archives.

32. DAP, "Report of A Workshop on Essential Drugs: New Management System of Drug Supplies to Rural Health Facilities in Kenya, Nairobi, Kenya, 4–9 Dec. 1983," DAP/84.2, KEN001B, MedNet, WHO Archives; see also UNCTC (1984); interview with Mugo Dawa, production supervisor, Dawa, Kenya, Dec. 10, 2012,

33. Others mentioned, however, that technical support came from the multinational pharmaceutical company Beecham and that the Yugoslav company only provided raw materials.

34. One of the Dawa investors, Njenga Karume, who by the time of his death in 2012 was among the wealthiest individuals in the country, personifies the tight link in Kenya at the time between political ties and economic success. Back in the early 1950s, Karume entered the business of transporting timber; and less than a decade later, he obtained the coveted distribution rights of East African Breweries (EAB) products in the Kiambu District, which he then extended into a transport business. His move into production on a large scale began after independence, when he made investments in saw milling, tea processing, and shoe manufacturing. Karume was a close friend of President Kenyatta, and his political connections not only helped his business expansion, but also enabled him to consolidate a powerful political base. In 1971, Karume was appointed chairman of the Gikuyu (Kikuyo), Embu and Meru Association (GEMA), which became the main arm of Kenyan industrial capital and spearheaded the move of indigenous capital into production (Swainson 1977).

35. Many have highlighted the low performance of state-owned enterprises (SOE) in developing countries (Swamy 1994). However, Grosh (1991) provides considerable evidence of managerial competence and efficiency in Kenya's SOEs through the mid-1980s. She finds that, "about half of the firms have performed well throughout the period." She adds that many problems have been observed only since 1978, and were due to the tighter economic conditions in that period. To

blame poor public enterprise performance for causing the crisis, she suggests, may be to reverse cause and effect. Rather, poor performance might have been the result of undercapitalization and foreign exchange shortage.

36. "Tour Notes of Dr. B. B. Gaitondé, RA/HLS, on his Visit to Kenya for Participation in WHO IR Workshop on Essential Drugs, Nairobi, 6–10 Dec. 1982," E19/445/3 KEN, WHO Archives.

37. Interview with Dawa, Kenya, Dec. 10, 2012.

38. Even this could only be done within limits. Foreign support—quite extensive in the public health realm—often required that drugs be purchased in the country providing the aid (interview with Vijai Maini, managing director, Surgipharm, Kenya, Dec. 21, 2012).

39. This system started in Kenya in the early 1970s, in the context of a balance of payment crisis to facilitate the Department of Trade and Supplies' task of banning the importation of products that competed with those produced locally. The difficulty of knowing which sizes and grades of products were locally available led the department to pass on the decision to the domestic firms themselves (Hopcraft 1979, Fahnbulleh 2006, Mwega and Ndung'u 2008, 355).

40. "DAP Comments on ACC Task Force Project Proposal No. 3."

41. "An Evaluation of WHO's Action Programme on Essential Drugs," 1989, s21279en, WHO Library, p. 1.

42. "An Evaluation of WHO's Action Programme on Essential Drugs," pp. 23, 32.

43. In contrast to East Africa, "Francophone Africa has, for the most part, been unreceptive to the essential drugs concept," possibly because countries that could convert their local currencies to the French franc did not feel "the drain on foreign exchange." ("An Evaluation of WHO's Action Programme on Essential Drugs," p. 22.)

44. See Moore (1982); see also Gerald Moore, "Pharmaceuticals in Kenya Government Health Care: Action Programme on Essential Drugs," 1987, KEN009A, MedNet, WHO Archives.

45. Kenya became the first country to launch the ration kits program mostly because one of the originators of the program, Dr. Gerald D. Moore, was in Nairobi at the time—first as a DANIDA advisor and later as a WHO consultant. Indeed, "the WHO was not initially involved" in the ration kits program, but "the publicity value together with the recruitment to WHO/DAP of one of the key individuals in the programme [Gerald D. Moore], brought it under WHO's fold." Also important for WHO support was the involvement of the DAP director Dr. Ernst Lauridsen. According to a WHO official, Dr. Lauridsen "got access, which at the time was secret, to the UNICEF Procurement Price List. And . . . he was able to show . . . that the prices [for drugs] UNICEF was [paying for] their own projects were about one-third to one-fifth of the global market price." This made drugs seem much more affordable. "And so, he [Dr. Lauridsen], with . . . Gerald Moore, came up with this idea of [ration] kits." ("An Evaluation of WHO's Action Programme on Essential Drugs," p. 43; see also interview with Dr. Richard Laing, WHO, Switzerland, June 21, 2013.)

46. See Moore (1982); see also "Drugs for Rural Health Care in Kenya. Report from the First Workshop on Essential Drugs. Nairobi, Kenya. 6–10 Dec. 1982," DAP/83.4, WHO Archives, p. 3.

47. See Haak and Hogerzeil (1995); see also DAP, "Report of A Workshop on Essential Drugs."

48. Gerald Moore, "Travel Report Summary," July 7, 1987, E19/445/3 KEN, KEN007, MedNet, WHO Archives.

49. See Moore (1982); Moore, "Pharmaceuticals in Kenya Government Health Care"; Report from G. D. Moore, WHO, to S. Kanani, DDMS, "Strengthening the Management of Drug Supplies to Rural Health Facilities," Nov. 28, 1979, E19/445/3 KEN, WHO Archives; "An Evaluation of WHO's Action Programme on Essential Drugs," p. 32.

50. "An Evaluation of WHO's Action Programme on Essential Drugs," p. 39.

51. Bryan Pearson, "Kenya: Financial Constraints Dominate Health Debate," E19/445/3 KEN, WHO Archives.

52. "An Evaluation of WHO's Action Programme on Essential Drugs," p. 43; Haak and Hoger-zeil (1991, 40).

53. "Pharmaceuticals in Kenya Government Health Care."

54. "An Evaluation of WHO's Action Programme on Essential Drugs," p. 32, emphasis added.

55. ASU, "Proposed New Management System of Drug Supplies for Rural Health Facilities," Apr. 1980, E19/445/3 KEN, No. 1, WHO Archives, p. 5.

56. DAP, "Report of A Workshop on Essential Drugs; WHO, "Towards a National Drug Policy for Kenya. Report of a Mission to Kenya," 17–24 Apr. 1990, KEN030, WHO Archives.

57. "Report of A Workshop on Essential Drugs"; Gerald Moore, "Travel Report Summary," July 7, 1987, E19/445/3 KEN, KEN007, MedNet, WHO Archives.

58. ASU, "Proposed New Management System of Drug Supplies for Rural Health Facilities."

59. ASU, "Proposed New Management System of Drug Supplies for Rural Health Facilities."

60. Report from G. D. Moore, WHO, to J. Maneno, ASU. "Strengthening of Rural Health Facilities—Role of Local Industry in Preparing Ration Kits," n.d., E19/445/3 KEN, No. 1, WHO Archives.

61. ASU, "Proposed New Management System of Drug Supplies for Rural Health Facilities."

62. Interview with Wilberforce O. Wanyanga, consultant, PharmQ, Kenya, Dec. 14, 2012.

63. Report from Moore to Maneno, "Strengthening of Rural Health Facilities."

64. Report from Moore to Kanani, "Strengthening the Management of Drug Supplies to Rural Health Facilities."

65. DAP, "Report of A Workshop on Essential Drugs."

66. Moore, "Travel Report Summary."

67. This also indicates the extraordinary marketing efforts of multinational companies in the pharmaceutical field, as discussed above.

68. DAP, "Report of A Workshop on Essential Drugs."

69. The impact was greater on local producers than foreign subsidiaries that were able to overcome such barriers by manipulating transfer prices of raw materials imported from their parent companies ("Local Pharmaceutical Manufacturing: Problems and Opportunities"; UNCTC 1984).

70. "Local Pharmaceutical Manufacturing: Problems and Opportunities," p. 2.

71. Interview with Mugo Dawa, production supervisor, Dawa, Kenya, Dec. 10, 2012.

72. Interview with Dhirendra Shah, managing director, Biodeal, Kenya, May 30, 2012.

73. Interview with Manesh Patel, managing director, Lab & Allied, Kenya, Dec. 20, 2012.

74. Interview with M. Patel, Lab & Allied, Kenya, May 18, 2012; interview with George Masafu, pharmacist, Kenya, Dec. 22, 2012.

75. Interview with Palu Dhanani, managing director, Universal, Kenya, May 18, 2012.

76. Interview with M. Patel, Lab & Allied, Kenya, May 18, 2012.

77. Later reports mentioned that the list of exempted raw materials was not regularly updated, and that the procedure required paperwork which made it costly ("Towards a National Drug Policy for Kenya"; "Local Pharmaceutical Manufacturing: Problems and Opportunities").

78. Interview with M. Patel, Lab & Allied, Kenya, May 18, 2012; interview with Maureen Nafule, consultant, Kenya, Dec. 14, 2012.

79. Jenny Bryan, "Kenya Stops the Drugs From Going Astray,"1981, E19/445/3 KEN, No. 2, WHO Archives.

80. Bryan, "Kenya Stops the Drugs from Going Astray."

81. Interview with Wanyanga, PharmaQ, Kenya, Dec. 14, 2012.

82. https://directory.africa-business.com/business/075b24119a/LABORATORY-AND-ALLIED-LIMITED, accessed May 6, 2018.

83. DAP, "Report of A Workshop on Essential Drugs."

84. https://directory.africa-business.com/business/075b24119a/LABORATORY-AND -ALLIED-LIMITED, accessed May 6, 2018.

85. Moore, "Pharmaceuticals in Kenya Government Health Care by Gerald Moore"; Action Programme on Essential Drugs. WHO. Geneva." 1987. MedNet. KEN009A. WHO Archives.

86. Moore, "Pharmaceuticals in Kenya Government Health Care."

87. From G. D. Moore to Dr. J. Maneno. "Summary Report. Rural Health Drugs' Supply System, 1981–1984." Mar. 15, 1984, MIS/17/3/24 Vol 7, E19/445/3 KEN No. 2, WHO Archives.

88. Moore, "Pharmaceuticals in Kenya Government Health Care."

89. The decision in 1986 to centralize the procurement for church medical institutions under MEDS was encouraged by a WHO feasibility study and was in response to economic and administrative challenges—including the cessation of government support to faith-based health services in the early 1980s ("MEDS. Mission for Essential Drugs and Supplies. Semi-Annual Report. Jan–June 30, 1988." KEN014, MedNet, WHO Archives; Gerald Moore, "Travel Report Summary," 27 June 1989, E19/445/3 AF, KEN023, MedNet, WHO Archives; interview with MEDS, Kenya, June 7, 2012; WHO 2010).

90. Interview with Prakash K. Patel, chairman, Cosmos, Kenya, June 8, 2012; interview with Dhirendra Shah, managing director, Biodeal, Kenya, May 30, 2012; interview with A. Patel, Elys, Kenya, June 15, 2012.

91. "MEDS. Mission for Essential Drugs and Supplies. Semi-Annual Report. Jan–June 30, 1988."

92. Interview with Wanyanga, PharmaQ, Kenya, May 29, 2012; interview with Rohin Vora, managing director, Regal, Kenya, June 5, 2012.

93. Moore, "Pharmaceuticals in Kenya Government Health Care."

94. Interview with Wanyanga, PharmaQ, Kenya, Dec. 14, 2012.

95. Interview with Vora, Regal, Kenya, June 5, 2012. Mamdani (1983, 98) notes that goods imported to Uganda from Kenya often came from British companies. One of the ten largest Kenyan companies to whom Uganda was indebted in 1979 was Pfizer Labs Ltd., a German pharmaceutical subsidiary.

96. "Local Pharmaceutical Manufacturing: Problems and Opportunities."

97. Interview with Wanyanga, PharmaQ, Kenya, May 29, 2012.

98. The original company that later became Beta Healthcare, Kenya Overseas Ltd., was founded by a trader from India in 1939. Initially a trading company, it later opened an official manufacturing unit. In the 1970s, the firm was purchased by the large UK retail company, Boots, and renamed Boots Company of Kenya Limited. At its peak in the 1970s, Boots was the largest cosmetic and toiletry firm in Kenya, with a turnover 2.5 times larger than Glaxo's and with 200 employees. In the 1980s, like other foreign subsidiaries of pharmaceutical companies at the time (chapter 2), Boots left Kenya and the company—now called Beta Healthcare Ltd.—was sold to African owners. Among the new owners were family members of Jomo Kenyatta, Kenya's former president, including his son, Uhuru Kenyatta. The company was quite successful during that time; and in 2003, it was sold to Sumaria, an Indian Tanzanian Group, and later to a multinational South African pharmaceutical company, Aspen Pharmacare (Eglin 1979, 129; interviews with Nelson Odhimabo, pharmacist, Beta Healthcare, Kenya, June 7 and Dec. 18, 2012; interview with Hitesh Upreti, chief marketing officer, Shelys, Tanzania, Mar. 21, 2013; see chapter 6).

99. Many Indians who did not get Kenyan citizenship, and some who did become citizens, left the country. Between 1962 and 1969, it is estimated that 50,000 Indians, or 28 percent of the Indian population in Kenya, left. Among those most likely to leave were public employees, whereas traders were more likely to stay (Ghai and Ghai 1971, Bharati 1972, Aiyar 2015).

100. Interview with P. K. Patel, Cosmos, Kenya, June 8, 2012.

101. Interview with Vijai Maini, managing director, Surgipharm, Kenya, Dec. 21, 2012.

102. This came at a time of some improved access to pharmacy education in Kenya (see below). Still, Masafu suggested that many of these pharmacies were opened not by registered pharmacists, but by "nurses, just businessmen, and just quacks" (interview with Masafu, Kenya, Dec. 22, 2012).

103. The role of Indian Kenyans in Kenya's industrialization was only implicit in the "Kenya debate" between those giving the credit for Kenya's impressive economic growth after independence to an emerging African capitalist class supported by the state and largely independent of foreign capital, and those informed by dependence theory and insisting that it was still benefiting foreign capital (Kaplinsky 1979a, 1980, Leys 1978, 1980, Swainson 1980, 1987). Later, the question of Indians triggered a "second Kenya debate" (Himbara 1994, Fafchamps et al. 1994).

104. One exception was Universal, where the original two partners had no formal pharmacy education. However, through commercial relations with a Finnish pharmaceutical company, Orion-yhtymä Oy, they met Pentti Keskitalo, an experienced pharmacist, who joined them as a partner. Here, then, a different type of ties abroad compensated for lack of technical knowledge.

105. Makerere College in Kampala, Uganda, which was first opened in 1922 (it started as a government-sponsored vocational and professional training institution) was for a long while the region's only college. The Royal College of Nairobi in Kenya opened in 1956, and the University College of Dar es Salaam in Tanzania opened in 1961. After independence, all three colleges terminated the affiliation they had with the University of London, and each institution became a constituent college of a newly established unit, the University of East Africa. This conglomerate was disbanded in 1970 (Goldthorpe 1965, Ssekamwa 1997, Byaruhanga 2013). Indians were not admitted to Makerere College until 1952; and by the end of the 1950s, there were only 69 Indians and Goans of the 881 students in residence. Indians fared better in the Royal Technical College in Kenya (Goldthorpe 1965, 13).

106. Interviews with wholesalers of pharmaceutical products who did not go into manufacturing suggest that they had a similar trajectory, including the pursuit of pharmacy degree abroad.

107. Interview with Ashok Patel, chairman, Elys Chemical Industries, Kenya, June 15, 2012.

108. Before 1974, training had been available only for compounders, dispensers, and later pharmacy assistants and technicians—all at the Kenya Medical Training College, which was established in 1927. The school in the University of Nairobi remained the only pharmacy school in Kenya until 2009.

109. Interview with Dr. Lembit Rägo, WHO, Switzerland, June 21, 2013.

110. This was the experience of many drug importers and distributors, not only manufacturers.

111. Interview with A. Patel, Elys, Kenya, June 15, 2012.

112. Interview with Vora, Regal, Kenya, June 5, 2012.

113. Interview with M. Patel, Lab & Allied, Kenya, May 18, 2012.

114. Interview with A. Patel, Elys, Kenya, Dec. 17, 2012.

115. On information traveling from abroad through commercial channels, see chapter 1.

116. Interview with P. K. Patel, Cosmos, Kenya, June 8, 2012.

117. Interview with A. Patel, Elys, Kenya, June 15, 2012.

118. Interview with A. Patel, Elys, Kenya, Dec. 17, 2012.

119. Interview with M. Patel, Lab & Allied, Kenya, May 18, 2012.

120. Interview with P. K. Patel, Cosmos, Kenya, June 8, 2012.

121. Interview with Sarah Vugigi, quality assurance manager, Elys, Kenya, May 28, 2012.

122. Interview with A. Patel, Elys, Kenya, June 15, 2012.

123. "Local Pharmaceutical Manufacturing: Problems and Opportunities"; interview with A. Patel, Elys, Kenya, June 15, 2012; interview with Shah, Biodeal, Kenya, May 30, 2012.

124. UNCTC (1984, 174).

125. "Local Pharmaceutical Manufacturing: Problems and Opportunities," p. 2.

126. http://www.regalpharmaceuticals.com/index.php/regalabout, accessed May 20, 2018.

127. Interview with M. Patel, Lab & Allied, Kenya, Dec. 20, 2012.

128. Capacity is calculated for 200 working days, two shifts. This increased capacity led to concerns regarding capacity utilization. An external report estimated a relatively high utilization of 70 percent ("An Evaluation of WHO's Action Programme on Essential Drugs," p. 32), but another estimated the level of installed capacity to be 40 percent ("Local Pharmaceutical Manufacturing: Problems and Opportunities," p. 2). Low utilization makes the product more expensive, in addition to lowering revenues. The reports do not differentiate between locally owned and foreign factories.

129. On registration data in Kenya, see chapter 2.

130. This estimate includes foreign subsidiaries. "Local Pharmaceutical Manufacturing: Problems and Opportunities."

131. Locally owned firms and foreign subsidiaries together registered 387 drugs from 1982 to 1990. Combined, then, local drug companies in Kenya registered 24 percent of the drugs listed (see chapter 2). Locally owned firms registered 66 percent of these local drugs. From 1991 and 2000, locally owned drugs made 95 percent of all registered local drugs. This increase was both due to the growing capacity of locally owned companies and because many foreign subsidiaries had left and those that stayed were not likely to register new drugs.

132. Interview with Masafu, Kenya, Dec. 22, 2012.

133. This was an amendment to the main law governing the pharmaceutical market in Kenya since 1957, the *Pharmacy and Poisons Act (Cap. 244)*. Cap. 244 also established the Pharmacy and Poisons Board (PPB), the agency responsible for ensuring the quality, safety, and efficacy of pharmaceutical products and services (WHO 1995, Luoma et al. 2010, UNIDO 2010a).

134. In addition, registration does not provide a guarantee of the product's efficacy, safety, or quality for subsequent shipments, which requires post-marketing surveillance.

135. Interview with Maini, Surgipharm, Kenya, Dec. 21, 2012.

136. Interview with Maini, Surgipharm, Kenya, Dec. 21, 2012.

137. "An Evaluation of WHO's Action Programme on Essential Drugs," p. 32.

138. "Local Pharmaceutical Manufacturing: Problems and Opportunities," p. 2.

## Chapter 4. Tanzania in the 1980s: The Limits of Limited Aid

1. Interview with Mansoor Daya, chairman, Mansoor Daya Chemicals, Tanzania, Mar. 20, 2013. Tanganyika was under German colonial rule until after World War I, when the League of Nations gave it as a mandate to the British. The United Republic of Tanzania was established in 1964 with the union of Tanganyika, which had received independence in 1961, and the island of Zanzibar, which was a British protectorate from 1890 until 1963.

2. A third pharmaceutical plant, Zanzibar Pharmaceutical Industries (ZPI), opened in Zanzibar in the early 1970s. Given the complicated administrative relations between mainland Tanzania and Zanzibar—e.g., Zanzibar has its own registration rules—Zanzibar is not part of the analysis.

3. Gaspar K. Munishi and H. Halfani, "The Essential Drug Programme in Tanzania: Management and Policy Implications and Impacts," Nov. 1989, TAN027, WHO Archives, pp. 12B–13B; Coulson (2013).

4. Gaspar K. Munishi, Immanuel K. Bavu, and Philip Hiza, "An Analysis of Tanzania's Health Policy in the Context of the National Essential Drugs Programme. A Research Proposal," 1987, TAN017, WHO Archives, p. 3.

5. The Arusha Declaration and TANU's Policy on Socialism and Self-Reliance, 1967, TANU, Dar es Salaam.

6. This was a significantly higher proportion than in most African countries, although many health facilities were reportedly of poor quality (Iliffe 1998, 203).

7. A focus on "basic needs" challenged the common understanding of "development" that reduced it to economic growth. Instead, development was to focus on satisfying the basic needs of the entire population, including primary consumption of goods (food, clothing, shelter), services (water, health, education, transport), and employment. Primary Health Care (PHC) was an actualization of the basic needs approach in the realm of health (Chorev 2012a).

8. Munishi and Halfani, "The Essential Drug Programme in Tanzania," p. 15.

9. UNICEF, "Supply of Essential Drugs—Rural Health Services in the United Republic of Tanzania. Programme Plan of Operations and Plans of Action," Dar es Salaam, 31 May 1983, TAN004, Appendix I, WHO Library, p. 3.

10. UNICEF, "Supply of Essential Drugs—Rural Health Services in the United Republic of Tanzania"; Coulson (2013, 252–53).

11. Munishi and Halfani, "The Essential Drug Programme in Tanzania," p. 20.

12. UNICEF, "Supply of Essential Drugs—Rural Health Services in the United Republic of Tanzania," p. 2.

13. Munishi and Halfani, "The Essential Drug Programme in Tanzania," pp. 19–20.

14. UNICEF, "Supply of Essential Drugs—Rural Health Services in the United Republic of Tanzania," p. 3.

15. Later on, Tanzania's Essential Drugs Programme (EDP) was seen as suffering from "democratic deficit" because the Programme Management Committee representatives were only from UNICEF, WHO, DANIDA, and the MoH Headquarters, leading to an "anomaly in the EDP's management situation in which . . . expected cooperants are not involved democratically in the initiation and implementation of such a spanning policy." UNICEF, in particular, "was criticized for managing the EDP more or less from its own offices initially and later on using its programme officers located in the MoH, but still responsible to UNICEF" (UNICEF, "Supply of Essential Drugs—Rural Health Services in the United Republic of Tanzania," p. 2; Munishi and Halfani, "The Essential Drug Programme in Tanzania," pp. 20, 34, 37).

16. Munishi and Halfani, "The Essential Drug Programme in Tanzania," pp. 20–21.

17. Munishi and Halfani, "The Essential Drug Programme in Tanzania."

18. M. A. Attisso, "Present Situation Regarding Pharmacy and Drugs in Tanzania," Feb. 17, 1972, AFR/PHARM/7, WHO Archives, p. 11.

19. "Report of the WHO/DANIDA/FINNIDA Joint Mission on Local Pharmaceutical Production in the United Republic of Tanzania," Apr. 1988, TAN021, WHO Archives, p. 5.

20. UNICEF, "Supply of Essential Drugs—Rural Health Services in the United Republic of Tanzania," p. 7.

21. Interview with William M. K. Mwatu, GSK, Kenya, Dec. 11, 2012; Kaplinsky (1979b).

22. The performance of parastatals in Tanzania has been generally weak (Barker et al. 1986, 186–88), although a sympathetic report by the International Labor Organization (ILO) cited raw material shortage and machine breakdown as the main problems, rather than mismanagement or corruption. The problems cited by the ILO, in turn, were due to the fact that through foreign partners, parastatals often used highly sophisticated technology that was difficult to fix or replace (Barker et al. 1986, 124). On joint ventures in Tanzania, see Coulson (2013) and Lofchie (2014).

23. The Ministry of Industries and Trade has changed its name (and portfolio) over the years, including to the Ministry of Industries, Trade and Industries, Trade and Industry, and Industry and Trade (Munish and Halfani, "The Essential Drug Programme in Tanzania," p. 68).

24. John Korn, "The Drug Situation in Tanzania," DANDIA, May 1981, TAN004, WHO Archives, p. 9.

25. Korn, "The Drug Situation in Tanzania," p. 9.

26. UNCTAD, "Technology policies in the pharmaceutical sector in the United Republic of Tanzania," TAN002, WHO Archives, p. vii; "Report of the WHO/DANIDA/FINNIDA Joint Mission on Local Pharmaceutical Production in the United Republic of Tanzania," Apr. 1988, TAN021, WHO Archives, p. 8.

27. The report also congratulated the National Development Corporation (NDC) for choosing a loan from the East African Development Bank over a loan from the Government of Finland that would have tied the funds to purchases of equipment from Finland (UNCTAD, "Technology policies in the pharmaceutical sector in the United Republic of Tanzania," p. 23). This loan would later prove difficult to return.

28. World Bank (1990). One of the experts sent by Orion to Tanzania later became a partner in the Kenyan pharmaceutical company Universal (chapters 3, 6).

29. M. J. Bhatt, "National Health Planning in Tanzania. Report on a mission. 1 August 1973–28 April 1974," 24 July 1974, AFR/PHA/126, WHO Archives, p. 7; "Report of the WHO/DANIDA/FINNIDA Joint Mission on Local Pharmaceutical Production in the United Republic of Tanzania," p. 5.

30. Korn, "The Drug Situation in Tanzania," p. 10.

31. UNCTAD, "Technology policies in the pharmaceutical sector in the United Republic of Tanzania."

32. DANIDA, "Tanzania. Essential Drugs Programme. Joint Evaluation Report," Mar. 1985, TAN008, WHO Archives, p. 27.

33. Korn, "The Drug Situation in Tanzania," p. 9; interview with Romuald Mbwasi, chief pharmacist, Ministry of Health, Tanzania, Mar. 28, 2013.

34. The economic crisis was not the doing of Tanzania's industrial policy, although the reliance on imported capital goods increased the vulnerability of local industries in many developing economies (Frieden 2006). In the years after the Arusha Declaration, industrial activity in Tanzania grew steadily and remained high (Barker et al. 1986, 93–94; Mwase and Ndulu 2008, 446), and the manufacturing sector's contribution to GDP rose from 4 percent at independence to a peak of 12 percent in 1977 (Ndulu and Semboja 1995, 167). Between 1980 and 1986, by contrast, Tanzania saw a *minus* 2.4% per annum change in industrial output (Stewart, Lall, and Wangwe 1992, 14–15).

35. UNDP, "United Republic of Tanzania. Resident Coordinator's Report 1984," Mar. 1984, Dar es Salaam, C17/372/2TAN, WHO Archives, pp. 5–6.

36. Korn, "The Drug Situation in Tanzania," p. 8.

37. E. Lauridsen, "The Drug Situation in Tanzania II. A Follow-up Report," Oct. 1981, TAN004, WHO Archives, p. 2.

38. Munishi and Halfani, "The Essential Drug Programme in Tanzania."

39. Government of the United Republic of Tanzania and UNICEF, "Support to the National Programme on Essential Drugs. Plans of Action. 1991–1993," Oct. 1989, TAN025A, WHO Archives, p. 9.

40. "Report of the WHO/DANIDA/FINNIDA Joint Mission on Local Pharmaceutical Production in the United Republic of Tanzania," p. 12.

41. Lauridsen, "The Drug Situation in Tanzania II. A Follow-up Report," pp. 3–4.

42. Lauridsen, "The Drug Situation in Tanzania II. A Follow-up Report," p. 4.

43. UNICEF, "The National Programme on Essential Drugs. Plan of Operations and Plans of Action. 1988–1990," Mar. 1986, TAN018, Archives, p. 42.

44. Munishi and Halfani, "The Essential Drug Programme in Tanzania."

45. It took some time for the essential drugs list to fully "govern the procurement of drugs." An early visit to the CMS storage and distribution facilities revealed that, "Several essential drugs

were missing on the shelves. . . . Other drugs, essentials as well as nonessentials, were in stock in quantities so large that their use before deterioration was quite unlikely" (Korn, "The Drug Situation in Tanzania," p. 22).

46. "Report of the WHO/DANIDA/FINNIDA Joint Mission on Local Pharmaceutical Production in the United Republic of Tanzania," pp. 8, 16–17.

47. Korn, "The Drug Situation in Tanzania," pp. 27–28.

48. Korn, "The Drug Situation in Tanzania," pp. 27–28.

49. "Report of the WHO/DANIDA/FINNIDA Joint Mission on Local Pharmaceutical Production in the United Republic of Tanzania," p. 8.

50. Munish and Halfani, "The Essential Drug Programme in Tanzania," p. 44.

51. "Report of the WHO/DANIDA/FINNIDA Joint Mission on Local Pharmaceutical Production in the United Republic of Tanzania," p. 16.

52. Munishi and Halfani, "The Essential Drug Programme in Tanzania," p. 60.

53. The public sector as a whole supplied an estimated 50.5 percent of the country's supply at the time. "United Republic of Tanzania. National Drug Policy. Programme of Collaboration. 1992–1993," Report from a WHO/DAP mission. 8–14 Nov. 1992, TAN039, WHO Archives, p. 3.

54. Korn, "The Drug Situation in Tanzania," pp. 23–24.

55. UNICEF, "Supply of Essential Drugs—Rural Health Services in the United Republic of Tanzania," p. 3.

56. "An Evaluation of WHO's Action Programme on Essential Drugs," 1989, s21279en, WHO Library, p. 43.

57. "An Evaluation of WHO's Action Programme on Essential Drugs," p. 17.

58. "An Evaluation of WHO's Action Programme on Essential Drugs," p. 17; Munishi and Halfani, "The Essential Drug Programme in Tanzania: Management and Policy Implications and Impacts."

59. "An Evaluation of WHO's Action Programme on Essential Drugs," p. 39.

60. Munishi and Halfani, "The Essential Drug Programme in Tanzania."

61. Munishi and Halfani, "The Essential Drug Programme in Tanzania.".

62. Tanzania rather than Kenya became the common model. Even though "Objections to kits being supplied by UNIPAC were expressed by some countries," after Tanzania, "Most of the countries using kits . . . import[ed] the major part of their kits from Europe, often from UNIPAC" ("An Evaluation of WHO's Action Programme on Essential Drugs," p. 33).

63. Korn, "The Drug Situation in Tanzania," p. 8.

64. This was not the case in regard to the two privately owned companies that existed at the time, Mansoor Daya and Khanbhai (UNCTAD, "Technology policies in the pharmaceutical sector in the United Republic of Tanzania.")

65. Korn, "The Drug Situation in Tanzania," p. 8.

66. Munishi and Halfani, "The Essential Drug Programme in Tanzania," p. 91.

67. H.W.A. den Besten and J.J.M. van Haperen, "Drug Distribution in Tanzania. Draft," Dec. 1990, TAN030, WHO Archives, p. 28.

68. This is not to underestimate the challenges that local drugs manufacturers faced at the time, including not only shortages of raw materials, but also shortage of fuel; and in the case of Keko, the unavailability of spare parts for the Chinese manufacturing machines.

69. Korn, "The Drug Situation in Tanzania," p. 13.

70. "An Evaluation of WHO's Action Programme on Essential Drugs," p. 33.

71. Munishi and Halfani, "The Essential Drug Programme in Tanzania."

72. "An Evaluation of WHO's Action Programme on Essential Drugs," p. 23.

73. Indeed, one concern regarding Tanzania's EDP was that it failed to strengthen state capabilities ("Report of the WHO/DANIDA/FINNIDA Joint Mission on Local Pharmaceutical

Production in the United Republic of Tanzania"; Munish and Halfani, "The Essential Drug Programme in Tanzania: Management and Policy Implications and Impacts," pp. 2, 76–80).

74. Munishi and Halfani, "The Essential Drug Programme in Tanzania," p. 59.

75. Another reason to support local packing was that, "it is important to design the supply and packing system in a way that stimulates gradual national take-over" (Korn, "The Drug Situation in Tanzania.")

76. DANIDA, "Tanzania. The National Programme on Essential Drugs. Phase II. An Appraisal Report Prepared by a DANIDA Mission," 23 Oct.-11 Nov. 1986, TAN012, WHO Archives, pp. 23, 38.

77. "Tanzania. The National Programme on Essential Drugs. Phase II."

78. Den Besten and van Haperen, "Drug Distribution in Tanzania. Draft."

79. "An Evaluation of WHO's Action Programme on Essential Drugs," p. 23.

80. Den Besten and van Haperen, "Drug Distribution in Tanzania. Draft."

81. Korn, "The Drug Situation in Tanzania," p. 12.

82. Munishi and Halfani, "The Essential Drug Programme in Tanzania," p. 68.

83. Munishi and Halfani, "The Essential Drug Programme in Tanzania," p. 9.

84. Korn, "The Drug Situation in Tanzania," p. 13.

85. Munishi and Halfani, "The Essential Drug Programme in Tanzania," p. 70.

86. Attisso, "Present Situation Regarding Pharmacy and Drugs in Tanzania," p. 10.

87. Korn, "The Drug Situation in Tanzania," pp. 10, 36.

88. But see Hopkins (1971) and Aminzade (2013) on education of the Tanzanian elite. It should be noted that Indians were generally blocked from attending Makerere College.

89. There was one local school that trained auxiliary pharmacists (Attisso, "Present Situation Regarding Pharmacy and Drugs in Tanzania," p. 6).

90. Interview with Romuald Mbwasi, chief pharmacist, MoH, Tanzania, Mar. 28, 2013.

91. Attisso, "Present Situation Regarding Pharmacy and Drugs in Tanzania," p. 6. This estimate, which is based on registration, may be slightly exaggerated. Another review, from 1973, cites only 34 registered pharmacists, including 7 "national" and 27 "non-nationals" (i.e., Europeans and Indians who did not get Tanzanian citizenship) (R. B. Salama, "Pharmacy Programme (B/Pharm) at the University of Dar es Salaam: Report on a Mission. 27 Aug.–23 Nov. 1974," 1975, AFR/PHARM/14, WHO Archives, p. 1). A third estimate, based on the local directory, suggests that in 1972 there were only 27 pharmacists in Tanzania (the same survey shows 144 pharmacists in Kenya and 52 in Uganda) (Gregory 1993, 226).

92. University College of Dar es Salaam was opened eight weeks before Independence, in Oct. 1961. From 1963 to 1970 the college was part of the University of East Africa, that included units also in Kenya and Uganda. In July 1970, the University was disbanded, and the college changed its name to the University of Dar es Salaam (chapter 3). In 1976, the Department of Pharmacy, which was originally in the Faculty of Medicine, was upgraded to a Division of Pharmaceutical Sciences of the Muhimbili Medical Centre. It later became the School of Pharmacy and part of the renamed Muhimbili University of Health and Allied Sciences (MUHAS) (Attisso, "Present Situation Regarding Pharmacy and Drugs in Tanzania," p. 6; Salama "Pharmacy Programme (B/Pharm) at the University of Dar es Salaam," p. 1; Mkony 2012).

93. R. Sutila, "Hospital Based Production of Pharmaceuticals in Tanzania," June 1987, TAN016, WHO Archives.

94. In addition, the British hired educated Indians to "fill the middle rungs of the East African Civil Service" (Nagar 1996, 63).

95. The total population at the time was around 11 million, including around 17,000 Europeans, and 30,000 Arabs (Rweyemamu 1973, 1).

96. The prevalence of Tanzanians of Indian origin in commerce and industry does not mean that they maintained the economic dominance that they had enjoyed under colonialism, but, rather, is indicative of the fact that Africans in Tanzania, as was also the case in Kenya, commonly established an economic foundation through the state rather than through the private market.

97. The State Trading Corporation (STC) absorbed the Cooperative Supply Association of Tanganyika Ltd. (COSATA), a parastatal company that was established in 1962 as a wholesaler to the consumer cooperatives (Gregory 1993, 83–85). There were also policies that explicitly targeted Tanzanians of Indian origin. The nationalization of commercial buildings in 1971, for example, led to a widespread confiscation of Indian-owned rental property. Later on, during the economic crisis of the 1980s, the government's "anti-economic saboteur" campaign led to the arrest of more than four thousand people, the majority of whom were Indian Tanzanian merchants accused of hoarding, although some were African managers of state-owned trading companies (Lofchie 2014, 34–35).

98. Attisso, "Present Situation Regarding Pharmacy and Drugs in Tanzania," p. 12.

99. Korn, "The Drug Situation in Tanzania," pp. 27–28.

100. Interview with Yusuf Sinare, chair, Tanzania Association of Pharmaceutical Industry, Tanzania, Mar. 26, 2013; "Report of the WHO/DANIDA/FINNIDA Joint Mission on Local Pharmaceutical Production in the United Republic of Tanzania," p. 5; "United Republic of Tanzania. National Drug Policy. Programme of Collaboration. 1992–1993," Report from a WHO/DAP Mission, 8–14 Nov. 1992, TAN039, WHO Archives, p. 3.

101. Mr. Mansoor Daya, the founder, had the distinction of being the first registered pharmacist in Tanzania (Interview with Mansoor Daya, chairman, Mansoor Daya, Tanzania, Mar. 20, 2013).

102. As we have seen, industry was limited in Tanganyika by British colonial opposition and Kenya's dominance. Still, there was some manufacturing activity during the colonial era, with the earliest industries, owned by Indians, dating back to the end of the nineteenth century. Between World War I and World War II, some Indians who were involved in handling produce continued as merchants and wholesalers while opening small-scale processing plants. These industries were usually family enterprises requiring little capital and small overhead. By the end of colonial rule, Indian manufacturers controlled most of the small and medium enterprises, but they could still not expand into large industries (Honey 1974, 61, Barker et al. 1986, 43–46, Coulson 2013, 111).

103. Interview with Mansoor Daya, Tanzania, Mar. 20, 2013.

104. http://www.bashirkhanbhai.co.uk/cv.htm, accessed September 2, 2018.

105. Bashir Khanbhai then moved back to the UK and was for a while a successful politician—he was the UK Conservative Member of the European Parliament (Eastern Region). He was later deselected by his party, however, due to an expenses scandal (Evans-Pritchard 2004).

106. UNICEF, "Supply of Essential Drugs—Rural Health Services in the United Republic of Tanzania."

107. Indians in Tanzania who did not have enough capital for investment in larger industries later shifted their investment patterns from partnerships among family members to inter-family and inter-territorial partnerships, often with Indians in Kenya and Uganda (Coulson 2013, 207).

108. By 2009, 14 percent of Sumaria's revenue was from Shelys. An additional 7 percent was from Beta Healthcare, the Kenyan pharmaceutical firm that was also owned by Sumaria (Shah 2009, figures 3.3, 3.4).

109. Korn, "The Drug Situation in Tanzania."

110. Munishi and Halfani, "The Essential Drug Programme in Tanzania," p. 48

111. "An Evaluation of WHO's Action Programme on Essential Drugs."

112. Munishi and Halfani, "The Essential Drug Programme in Tanzania," p. 24.

113. "Local Pharmaceutical Manufacturing: Problems and Opportunities," p. 2; World Bank (1990, 105–106).

114. Registration in Tanzania started in 1999, so registration data cannot be used for the 1990s.

115. DAP, "Report of A Workshop on Essential Drugs"; World Bank (1990, 105–106).

116. Interview with Mansoor Daya, Tanzania, Mar. 20, 2013.

117. The long-term debt included servicing of the $2 million loan that had been granted by the East African Development Bank in the late 1980s. This took up 30 percent of TPI's sales earnings ("Report of the WHO/DANIDA/FINNIDA Joint Mission on Local Pharmaceutical Production in the United Republic of Tanzania," p. 22).

118. Until the late 1970s, the two texts that constituted the legal basis for quality control in Tanzania—*The Food and Drugs Act* of 1947 and the *Pharmacy and Poisons Ordinance* of 1959—simply described to what standards drugs must conform; they did not provide for any systematic control or monitoring of those standards (Attisso, "Present Situation Regarding Pharmacy and Drugs in Tanzania," p. 14).

119. They eventually passed in 1990 (WHO 1995a).

120. Munishi and Halfani, "The Essential Drug Programme in Tanzania"; Bjorn Melgaard, "Essential Drugs Programme in Tanzania Mainland. Final Progress Report," 1 May 1990, TAN029, WHO Archives, p. 18.

121. Munishi and Halfani, "The Essential Drug Programme in Tanzania," p. 72.

122. Munishi and Halfani, "The Essential Drug Programme in Tanzania," p. 61.

123. UNCTAD, "Technology policies in the pharmaceutical sector in the United Republic of Tanzania," p. 18.

124. UNCTAD, "Technology policies in the pharmaceutical sector in the United Republic of Tanzania," pp. 18–19; World Bank (1990, 105).

125. Munishi and Halfani, "The Essential Drug Programme in Tanzania," pp. 69–70.

126. World Bank (1990, 105); also, "Report of the WHO/DANIDA/FINNIDA Joint Mission on Local Pharmaceutical Production in the United Republic of Tanzania," p. 12.

127. UNICEF, "Supply of Essential Drugs—Rural Health Services in the United Republic of Tanzania"; DANIDA, "Tanzania. Essential Drugs Programme. Joint Evaluation Report," p. 26.

128. "Report of the WHO/DANIDA/FINNIDA Joint Mission on Local Pharmaceutical Production in the United Republic of Tanzania," pp. 9–10.

129. "Report of the WHO/DANIDA/FINNIDA Joint Mission on Local Pharmaceutical Production in the United Republic of Tanzania," p. 3, emphasis added.

## Chapter 5. Uganda in the 1980s and 1990s: The Missing Entrepreneurs

1. "Strategic Framework for Drug Supplies to the National Health Service in Uganda 1990–2000," Jan. 1989, UGA015A, WHO Archives, p. 3.

2. The Ugandan Protectorate was established in 1894. Uganda became independent in 1962.

3. G. Osuide, "Manufacture and Quality Control of Drugs and Training of Personnel in Uganda," Jan. 11, 1973, AFR/PHARM/9, WHO Archives, p. 30.

4. MOH/UNICEF/Danish Red Cross, "Proposal for Essential Drugs Programme," Kampala, July 1984, E19/445/3 AF no. 2, WHO Archives, p. 2.

5. M. Mburu, "Managing Essential Drug Supplies to Rural Health Centres by UNICEF Uganda 1981–1986: Evaluation Report," Apr. 1984, UGA005, WHO Archives, p. 5.

6. Danish Red Cross, "Uganda Essential Drugs Management Programme: Plan of Operation 1988–1990, Phase 2," UGA014, WHO Archives, p. 5.

7. Mburu, "Managing Essential Drug Supplies to Rural Health Centres by UNICEF Uganda 1981–1986," p. 4.

8. Joint Medical Store, "'A Painful Cure to a Healthy Situation': Mission Report on Joint Medical Store Uganda," 23–30 Jan. 1984, UGA003, WHO Archives, p. 8.

9. Danish Red Cross, "Uganda Essential Drugs Management Programme," p. 5.

10. According to a report prepared in 1984, Uganda's population at the time, of about 14 million people, was served by a network of 76 hospitals, 170 health centers, and around 450 smaller health units. There was a health unit within 10 km of 57 percent of the population, compared to 93 percent in Tanzania at the time (MOH/UNICEF/Danish Red Cross, "Proposal for Essential Drugs Programme," p. 1).

11. P. E. Christensen and P. Nissen, "The Medical Supply System in Uganda," Danish Red Cross, Jan. 1980, UGA001, WHO Archives, p. 17.

12. MOH/UNICEF/Danish Red Cross, "Proposal for Essential Drugs Programme," p. 2.

13. Christensen and Nissen, "The Medical Supply System in Uganda," p. 17.

14. Danish Red Cross, "Uganda Essential Drugs Management Programme," p. 2.

15. MOH/UNICEF/Danish Red Cross, "Proposal for Essential Drugs Programme," p. 4

16. Mburu, "Managing Essential Drug Supplies to Rural Health Centres by UNICEF Uganda 1981–1986. Evaluation Report," p. 8.

17. Mburu, "Managing Essential Drug Supplies to Rural Health Centres by UNICEF Uganda 1981–1986," pp. 8, 11.

18. The Joint Medical Store (JMS) was established in 1979 as a medical relief supply agency that was jointly owned by the Uganda Catholic Medical Bureau and the Uganda Protestant Medical Bureau (Danish Red Cross, "Uganda Essential Drugs Management Programme"; WHO 1994a).

19. "Strategic Framework for Drug Supplies to the National Health Service in Uganda 1990–2000," p. 2.

20. Uganda used one type of kit for all levels of care (Haak and Hogerzeil 1995).

21. "Strategic Framework for Drug Supplies to the National Health Service in Uganda 1990–2000," p. 1.

22. Vincent Habiyambere, "Pilot Project to Improve Access to HIV/AIDS-Related Drugs, Exploratory Visit: The Pharmaceutical Sector," Jan. 1997, UGA043, WHO Archives, p. 6.

23. "Strategic Framework for Drug Supplies to the National Health Service in Uganda 1990–2000," p. 2.

24. "Strategic Framework for Drug Supplies to the National Health Service in Uganda 1990–2000," p. 2.

25. "Strategic Framework for Drug Supplies to the National Health Service in Uganda 1990–2000," p. 3.

26. MOH/UNICEF/Danish Red Cross, "Proposal for Essential Drugs Programme," p. 2.

27. When in response, Britain cancelled all aid to Uganda, Amin nationalized forty-one foreign-owned firms, of which fifteen were British (Mamdani 1983, 65). In 1975, more foreign businesses were expropriated. British technicians and managers were also expelled.

28. Osuide, "Manufacture and Quality Control of Drugs and Training of Personnel in Uganda," p. 26.

29. Osuide, "Manufacture and Quality Control of Drugs and Training of Personnel in Uganda," p. 41.

30. In the early 1970s, the Central Medical Stores (CMS) and the government hospitals carried out very basic production of mixtures and solutions for external use and of intravenous infusion and other sterile solutions. These facilities were not appropriate for the production of other pharmaceutical products (Osuide, "Manufacture and Quality Control of Drugs and Training of Personnel in Uganda," p. 30; M. A. Attisso, "Present Situation Regarding Pharmacy and Drugs in Uganda," Apr. 26, 1972, AFR/PHARM/8, WHO Archives).

31. Osuide, "Manufacture and Quality Control of Drugs and Training of Personnel in Uganda," p. 30; M. A. Attisso, "Present Situation Regarding Pharmacy and Drugs in Uganda," Apr. 26, 1972, AFR/PHARM/8, WHO Archives.

32. Osuide, "Manufacture and Quality Control of Drugs and Training of Personnel in Uganda," p. 41.

33. Osuide, "Manufacture and Quality Control of Drugs and Training of Personnel in Uganda," pp. 41–42.

34. Interview with Ajith Prasad, UPL, Uganda, Jan. 12, 2013.

35. Christensen and Nissen, "The Medical Supply System in Uganda," p. 6.

36. Christensen and Nissen, "The Medical Supply System in Uganda," p. 6.

37. A private company, Opa Laboratories, existed in Ninja since the 1950s (see below). It is likely that the Uganda Pharmaceuticals Ltd. (UPL) facility in Jinja, Opa, was the same factory, which had been nationalized (H. Faust, "Travel Report Summary to Review Feasibility of Establishing Local Production of ORS," World Health Organization, Sept. 1, 1987, UGA012, WHO Archives, p. 3).

38. Faust, "Travel Report Summary to Review Feasibility of Establishing Local Production of ORS."

39. A few references indicate a possible collaboration between Uganda and the Palestinian Liberation Organization (PLO). According to Mamdani (1983), the PLO agreed to build a pharmaceutical factory to be financed by the Afro-Arab Investment and Contracting Company in Kampala in 1977. Shweiki (2014) mentions a pharmaceutical factory in Uganda jointly owned by the Ugandan government and the Factories of the Sons of the Palestinian Martyrs Organization.

40. Ironically, the Amin regime found alternative skilled personnel in India, Pakistan, and Bangladesh. According to Mamdani (1976), Amin first attempted to get technical assistance from Germany and Japan, but spare parts for the machinery used in many factories, as well as technicians who could work those machines, could only be found in the Indian subcontinent.

41. Faust, "Travel Report Summary to Review Feasibility of Establishing Local Production of ORS," p. 3.

42. D. K. Raditapole, "Report on Assessment of the Feasibility of Local Drug Production for Church Related Health Institutions—Uganda," Christian Medical Commission, Switzerland, UGA010, WHO Archives.

43. Faust, "Travel Report Summary to Review Feasibility of Establishing Local Production of ORS," p. 3.

44. Raditapole, "Report on Assessment of the Feasibility of Local Drug Production for Church Related Health Institutions—Uganda."

45. The more basic production at CMS fared slightly better, thanks to foreign assistance. According to a Danish report from 1980, "A certain degree of production of medicaments . . . is taken care of by the CMS," but due to the lack of raw materials, tins, and bottles, the production in the nonsterile department had almost stopped (Christensen and Nissen, "The Medical Supply System in Uganda," p. 21). The situation looked somewhat rosier after the mid-1980s. One report stated that "there is a considerable amount of production of IV fluids at hospital level and also at the Central Medical Stores in Kampala." This was achieved thanks to "assistance from Denmark" (Raditapole, "Report on Assessment of the Feasibility of Local Drug Production for Church Related Health Institutions—Uganda," p. 3; Edith Kaufman, "Establishment of a National Drug Control Laboratory in Uganda," Feasibility Study, German Pharmaceutical Health Fund, 1991, UGA020, WHO Archives, p. 2; WHO 1994a).

46. Raditapole, "Report on Assessment of the Feasibility of Local Drug Production for Church Related Health Institutions—Uganda," p. 4.

47. Interview with Prasad, UPL, Uganda, Jan. 12, 2013.

48. The Tanzanian military, too, invested in a pharmaceutical factory (chapter 7).

49. DANIDA, "Review cum Appraisal of the Uganda Essential Drugs Management Programme: Final Draft Report Prepared by a DANIDA Mission Visiting Uganda from 28 May to 16 June 1990," Aug. 1990, UGA016, WHO Archives, par. 1.4.5.

50. Attisso, "Present Situation Regarding Pharmacy and Drugs in Uganda," p. 15; Osuide, "Manufacture and Quality Control of Drugs and Training of Personnel in Uganda," p. 30.

51. Osuide, "Manufacture and Quality Control of Drugs and Training of Personnel in Uganda," p. 15.

52. "Osuide, "Manufacture and Quality Control of Drugs and Training of Personnel in Uganda," p. 30. A 1972 WHO report mentions six manufacturing establishments, but without naming them (Attisso, "Present Situation Regarding Pharmacy and Drugs in Uganda," p. 17).

53. "Osuide, "Manufacture and Quality Control of Drugs and Training of Personnel in Uganda," p. 31.

54. "Osuide, "Manufacture and Quality Control of Drugs and Training of Personnel in Uganda," p. 30.

55. "Osuide, "Manufacture and Quality Control of Drugs and Training of Personnel in Uganda," pp. 15–16.

56. "Osuide, "Manufacture and Quality Control of Drugs and Training of Personnel in Uganda," p. 31.

57. "Osuide, "Manufacture and Quality Control of Drugs and Training of Personnel in Uganda," pp. 31–31.

58. "Osuide, "Manufacture and Quality Control of Drugs and Training of Personnel in Uganda," p. 30.

59. Danish Red Cross, "Uganda Essential Drugs Management Programme, Plan of Operation 1988–1990, Phase 2," p. 3.

60. "Mission Report on Joint Medical Store Uganda," pp. 11–12.

61. Indians could also utilize community financial resources (Mamdani 1976, 83). The situation improved after independence. For example, the number of African students attending senior secondary schools rose from about 3,000 in 1958 to 40,000 in 1970 (Jørgensen 1981, 240). Still, in 1977, only 48.5 percent of all children of primary school age were enrolled in government-aided schools; and only about 20 percent of the children who completed primary school could proceed to post-primary institutions (Kajubi 1985, 16).

62. Uganda had a school for training auxiliary pharmacists (Attisso, "Present Situation Regarding Pharmacy and Drugs in Uganda").

63. Osuide, "Manufacture and quality control of drugs and training of personnel in Uganda," pp. 26, 77.

64. Osuide, "Manufacture and quality control of drugs and training of personnel in Uganda," p. 77. Interviews suggest that Africans attended pharmacy schools in the USSR, India, Cuba, and Kenya on government fellowships.

65. Osuide, "Manufacture and quality control of drugs and training of personnel in Uganda," p. 25.

66. Attisso, "Present Situation Regarding Pharmacy and Drugs in Uganda," p. 6. This number, which is based on registration, may be an over-estimation. An estimate based on the local directory suggests that in 1972 there were 52 pharmacists (4 African, 32 Indian, and 16 European) (Gregory 1993, 226).

67. Unlike other countries in the region, however, in Uganda a pharmacist could work in more than one pharmacy, so there could be more registered pharmacies than licensed pharmacists (WHO 1994a).

68. Attisso, "Present Situation Regarding Pharmacy and Drugs in Uganda," p. 17.

69. Christensen and Nissen, "The Medical Supply System in Uganda."

70. The (second) government of Milton Obote passed the *Expropriated Properties Act* in 1982, which provided for the return of properties and businesses expropriated during 1972–73 to former owners (Okuku 2006, 150). Continuing instability initially precluded the return of all but a few of the exiles, however. President Museveni later actively wooed Ugandan Indians abroad, with somewhat greater success than his predecessor. In the end, only about 5,000 returned to stay, but these included many with substantial assets (UNCTAD 2001, 18). Some major investors who returned preferred to still be identified as foreign investors.

71. Interview with Kwality Afro-Asia, Uganda, Jan. 4, 2013.

72. Interview with Abacus, Uganda, Jan. 14, 2013.

73. Interview w Anselme Sahabo, Eris, Uganda, Jan. 9, 2013.

74. Interview with Aziz Damani, Gittoes, Uganda, Jan. 16, 2013.

75. Interview with Shakti G. Monpara, production manager, Rene, Uganda, Jan. 5. 2013; interview with Prasad, UPL, Uganda, Jan. 12, 2013.

76. Kaufman, "Establishment of A National Drug Control Laboratory in Uganda."

77. Reports indicate the existence of additional manufacturing companies that operated in the 1980s and 1990s, but they all closed, and there is no reliable information about them. These include: UCIL Laboratories, Duse Pharmaceuticals, Equator Pharmacy, and Medical Products Use ("Mission Report on Joint Medical Store Uganda," p. 11; see also UNIDO 1997, WHO 1997, 32, UNCTAD 2001, 37).

78. Drug shops are limited in the type of drugs they can sell compared with pharmacies.

79. Interview with Kitumba Benjamin Benson, managing director, Kisakye, Uganda, Jan. 18, 2013.

80. DANIDA, "Review cum Appraisal of the Uganda Essential Drugs Management Programme."

81. Interview with M. O. Ogalo, managing director, Medipharm, Uganda, Jan. 11, 2013; http://medipharm.co.ug/?page_id=221, accessed Jan. 3, 2018.

82. Faust, "Travel Report Summary. To Review Feasibility of Establishing Local Production of ORS."

83. In 1983, UNIDO commissioned a detailed feasibility study for local production of ORS in Uganda. At the time, only UPL's factory in Kampala was considered appropriate, but it required a construction of a new production unit, and the idea was not pursued (Faust, "Travel Report Summary to Review Feasibility of Establishing Local Production of ORS").

84. Faust, "Travel Report Summary to Review Feasibility of Establishing Local Production of ORS"; SCRIP (1991b).

85. DANIDA, "Review cum Appraisal of the Uganda Essential Drugs Management Programme"; interview with Ogalo, Medipharm, Uganda, Jan. 11, 2013.

86. DANIDA, "Review cum Appraisal of the Uganda Essential Drugs Management Programme."

87. During the same period the value of imports also quadrupled, which suggests that, although the market share of local producers did not grow, they were at least able to protect their share in a context of growing competition (UNCTAD 2001, Haakonsson 2009b, 508).

88. Osuide, "Manufacture and quality control of drugs and training of personnel in Uganda," p. 2.

89. Interview with Otim, Jan. 8, 2013.

90. Faust, "Travel Report Summary to Review Feasibility of Establishing Local Production of ORS."

91. "Mission Report on Joint Medical Store Uganda," p. 11.

92. "Mission Report on Joint Medical Store Uganda," p. 13.

## Chapter 6. Kenya in the 2000s: Developmental Foreign Aid (1)

1. Interview with Sarah Vugigi, quality assurance manager, Elys, Kenya, May 28, 2012.

2. In 2007, the Indian company Ajanta began producing a generic version of Coartem.

3. Interview with Ashok Patel, chairman, Elys, Kenya, June 15, 2012.

4. Interview with Dr. Richard Laing, WHO, Switzerland, June 21, 2013.

5. Local producers were even more alarmed by the Global Fund program, the Affordable Medicines Facility—malaria (AMFm), which intervened in the *private* market, where treatment guidelines were less effectively enforced and, therefore, where local producers could still sell their antimalarial drugs. The AMFm—a two-year pilot-program that the Global Fund launched in 2010 in eight countries, including Kenya—subsidized producers of quality-assured artemisin-based combination therapies (ACTs) (Arrow et al. 2012). In order to be eligible to supply ACTs under the AMFm, drugs had to be WHO-prequalified or approved by a stringent drug regulatory authority, so local manufacturers were excluded. One local manufacturers asserted, "[the] so-called donors destroyed the local pharmaceutical industry." A more empathetic local pharmacist concluded, "[AMFm] is good for Kenyans, harmful for the industry."

6. As of 2005, the largest contributor to Kenya's GDP was the service sector (63% of GDP, with tourism being the dominant segment), followed by agriculture (24% of GDP); 50 percent of Kenya's revenue was from exports, especially of tea, horticultural produce, and coffee; see UNIDO (2010a), https://data.worldbank.org/indicator/NV.IND.MANF.ZS?locations=TZ-KE-UG, accessed 20 May 2018.

7. In 2010, forty-two companies were officially *registered* as local pharmaceutical manufacturers in Kenya (UNIDO 2010a). However, not all registered firms produced drugs, and they did not all produce human drugs. To offer a more accurate number of firms relevant to this study, I removed manufacturers of animal products, of chemicals, and of nonmedical products. I also removed wholesalers, pharmacies, and pharmaceutical manufacturers that did not produce locally, as well as research institutions. Those that remained on the list are: Beta Healthcare International, Biodeal Laboratories, Comet Healthcare, Concepts (Africa), Cosmos, Dawa, Didy Pharmaceuticals, Elys Chemical Industries, GSK, Lab & Allied, Mac's Pharmaceuticals, Medivet Products, Novelty Manufacturing, OssChemie, Pharmaceutical Manufacturing Company (PMC), Regal, Skylight Chemicals, Sphinx Pharmaceuticals, Stedam Pharma Manufacturing, and Universal Corporation.

8. In the absence of credible data, estimates of market value vary. UNIDO (2010a) estimated that the value of sales by local producers for the domestic market in 2008 was $67 million (of a total overturn for local production of approximately US $103 million, with the rest coming from exports). The World Bank's International Finance Corporation (2007) estimated that in 2006 Kenya produced drugs for the local market in the value of $56 million, compared with a value of $12 million in Tanzania, and $9 million in Uganda.

9. In the absence of credible data, estimates of market share vary, from as low as 10 percent (AFRO 2005) to as high as 30–35 percent (Losse et al. 2007). UNIDO's estimate is the most credible and the one most often cited (e.g., MMS and MPHS 2010).

10. Interview with Dawa, Kenya, Dec. 11, 2012; interview with Lab & Allied, Kenya, May 18, 2012; interview with Nazir Ally, sub-Saharan Africa regional executive, Aspen Pharmacare, South Africa, Jan. 28, 2014.

11. Kenyan manufacturers supplied approximately 8 percent of the total drugs in Tanzania (FEAPM 2012, 68). According to registration data, as of 2012, Kenyan drugs made 7 percent of the drugs registered in Tanzania and 8 percent of the drugs registered in Uganda (chapter 2, tables 2.4, 2.6).

12. One concern regarding the future viability of the Kenyan pharmaceutical sector was therefore that, as the Tanzanian and Ugandan markets grow, Kenya's relative advantage vis-à-vis India

and China would diminish. "[An] increased volume of demand will make it far more commercially viable for importers . . . to buy full-container loads of medicines directly from China or India" (UNIDO 2010a, 43).

13. The first cohort, which graduated in 1978, was of twenty-four students. The size of the graduating class has increased somewhat since then, with an average of thirty-nine graduating a year. This was for a long time the only training facility for pharmacists in Kenya. In 2009–10, Kenyatta University and two private universities began to offer degree courses in pharmacy (MMS and MPHS 2010, 46).

14. Although still not meeting the needs of the population (UNIDO 2010a, MMS and MPHS 2010), the number of pharmacists grew in Kenya—from an estimated 144 pharmacists in 1972 (Gregory 1993) to 719 registered pharmacists in 1996 (Gazette Notice No. 5009, June 1996) and 2,295 by 2010 (MMS and MPHS 2010).

15. Interview with Sammy Opiyo, Sphinx Pharmaceuticals, Kenya, May 24, 2012.

16. Interview with Njimia Wachira, Njimia Pharmacy, Kenya, Dec. 17, 2012.

17. Interview with Dr. Lembit Rägo, WHO, Switzerland, June 21, 2013. The mismatch between the curriculum in the local pharmacy school and the needs of industrial pharmacy partly explains why, even after the school opened, owners of larger local manufacturers sent their own sons and daughters to pharmacy schools abroad and often hired pharmacists who were educated abroad.

18. Interview with Wilberforce O. Wanyanga, consultant, PharmaQ, Kenya, May 29, 2012.

19. Interview with UNIDO, Austria, July 11, 2013.

20. Interview with Wanyanga, PharmaQ, Kenya, May 29, 2012.

21. In 2001, Dawa failed to pay a debt to the National Bank of Kenya and went through receivership and bankruptcy and was later offered for sale. Dawa's difficulties stemmed from growing competition, including from "newly established local manufacturers" (Gazette Notice No. 2727, June 9, 1989, p. 781), at a time that the company lost state support and, according to some interviews, was poorly managed. The sale of Dawa, in 2004, to a company that already imported and distributed drugs resembled the pattern of the past—of pharmacists-entrepreneurs moving from trading to manufacturing (one of the investors was a US-trained pharmacist). However, this time, the pharmaceutical manufacturing firm was integrated into a larger diversified group, with enterprises spanning across health care and real estate. A potential conflict emerged as Medisel imported products that competed directly with Dawa's products. Indeed, some suggested that in buying Dawa, the new owners at least initially had less interest in the manufacturing capabilities of the firm than in the list of drugs registered under its name. Allegedly, the company contracted out the manufacturing of drugs registered under Dawa's name to producers outside of Kenya. Still, reports suggest that "Dawa weathered the storms and has come out strong" (Mulupi 2014b). The company realized a high growth rate through improved operations and focus on exports (Mulupi 2014a, Nairobi Business Monthly 2015; interview with Dawa, Kenya, Dec. 11, 2012; interview with Maureen Kinyua, quality assurance manager, Dawa, Kenya, May 26, 2012; interview with Mugo Dawa, production supervisor, Dawa, Kenya, Dec. 10, 2012).

22. Interview with Tanzania Food and Drugs Authority (TFDA), Tanzania, Mar. 19, 2012.

23. Interview with Wanyanga, PharmaQ, Kenya, May 29, 2012.

24. Interview with Wilberforce O. Wanyanga, PharmaQ, Kenya, Dec. 14, 2012; Mhamba and Mbirigenda (2010).

25. Interview with Wanyanga, PharmaQ, Kenya, Dec. 14, 2012.

26. According to a number of interviews, the Kenya Medical Supplies Authority (KEMSA), the government agency responsible for the procurement and distribution of drugs, found in the Lab & Allied warehouses evidence for systematic "product failures," including drugs that were expired and moldy. When KEMSA blacklisted Lab & Allied in 2005 it reportedly "shook up" the company and led it to change its ways, as indicated by the decision to move to a new factory.

27. Interview by Ben Bradlow with Nazir Ally, sub-Saharan Africa regional executive, Aspen Pharmacare, South Africa, July 27, 2015.

28. Based on drug samples collected between 2001 and 2005, one study found that, "In contrast to previous years when failure rates of over 20% were recorded . . . the overall rate of failure to comply with quality specifications was 6.1%, comprising of 8.7% locally manufactured and 4.5% imported drugs" (Thoithi et al. 2008). A 2003 WHO study of antimalarials found no consistent quality differences between locally produced and imported products (IFC 2007); and in a later WHO review of antimalarials in Kenya, "only two of 24 ACT samples tested failed and all [19] SP samples were found to be compliant" (WHO 2011d).

29. http://data.unaids.org/publications/fact-sheets04/fs_treatment_en.pdf, accessed 20 May 2018.

30. http://data.unaids.org/publications/fact-sheets04/fs_treatment_en.pdf, accessed 20 May 2018.

31. This focus in the global public health field on vertical (disease-specific) health programs, and the subsequent focus of donors on funding for the procurement of drugs, has also led to some important criticisms, however. Particularly contentious is the overwhelming prioritization of HIV/AIDS. For example, of the $14.5 billion development assistance for health in 2007 for which project-level information was available, $5.1 billion was for HIV/AIDS (Ravishankar et al. 2009). Although the impressive resources invested in the fight against HIV/AIDS have been praised by many, critics of the medicalizing or "pharmaceuticalization" of public health view the funding spent on antiretrovirals (ARVs) as a crystallization of new inequalities (Biehl 2008, Greene 2015, Packard 2016). Some are deeply worried about the neglect of national health systems (Greene 2015, Epstein 2015), the importance of which the recent Ebola pandemic clearly confirmed (Lakoff 2017).

32. http://www.un.org/millenniumgoals/aids.shtml, accessed 20 May 2018.

33. Interview with Rägo, WHO, Switzerland, June 21, 2013.

34. Interview with Dr. Richard Laing, WHO, Switzerland, June 21, 2013.

35. Interview with Rägo, WHO, Switzerland, June 21, 2013.

36. Interview with Rägo, WHO, Switzerland, June 21, 2013.

37. Interview with Rägo, WHO, Switzerland, June 21, 2013.

38. Brhlikova, Harper, and Pollock (2007), Abbott and Dukes (2009, 91), Light, Lexchin, and Darrow (2013). Although the WHO Good Manufacturing Practices (GMP) is considered the appropriate level of quality standards, UNIDO, which initially supported the goal of mentoring drug manufacturers in developing countries so that they could achieve that standard, later developed a different strategy, while still "agreeing on the WHO standards." First, UNIDO's new position was holistic (rather than drug-specific), shifting from anti-HIV and antimalarial drugs to all essential medicines. Second, UNIDO's focus moved from (the drug-specific) WHO prequalification to GMP quality requirements for all medicines produced in any given facility. This, according to UNIDO, would allow for all companies to eventually comply, rather than a fortunate few. Third, UNIDO began to tolerate incremental change (Interview with UNIDO, Austria, July 11, 2013). This was heavily criticized by Dr. Rägo: "[UNIDO] are [now] trying to also work with some inspectors and [are] trying to do some sort of *elementary GMP*." Blaming UNIDO for being willing to "quietly lower the standards," he argued that, "Even in Africa in the longer term, it's a dead duck solution." He continued: "Because . . . the world develops, and to try to . . . have some sort of a lower standard, for me it's crazy, in the twenty-first century, it's crazy!" (Interview with Rägo, WHO, Switzerland, June 21, 2013).

39. Interview with Kinyua, Dawa, Kenya, May 26, 2012; interview with P. K. Patel, Cosmos, Kenya, June 8, 2012.

40. https://www.wto.org/english/tratop_e/trips_e/ldc_e.htm, accessed 2 Dec. 2018; emphasis added.

41. Interview with UNIDO, Austria, July 11, 2013; interview with Dr. Zafar Mirza, WHO, Switzerland, June 25, 2013.

42. Interview with Global Fund, Switzerland, June 24, 2013.

43. In the Global Fund's 2012 *Guide to Global Fund Policies on Procurement and Supply Management of Health Products* (Global Fund 2012a) it was made clear that, "national preference in procurement decisions is not acceptable to the Global Fund." By 2017, however, the Fund changed its policy somewhat. In the revised *Guide to Global Fund Policies on Procurement and Supply Management of Health Products* (Global Fund 2017), an exemption was made: "National or domestic preference in procurement decisions is not acceptable to the Global Fund, except if mandatory under applicable laws."

44. We should not overestimate the indifference of European pharmaceutical companies, however. When German funding for local pharmaceutical production was eventually cut in 2018, I was told that it was because the "head of division at the ministry [is now] from the liberal party and [they are] friends with multinational pharmaceutical companies." Possibly, then, the relative lack of clout at the German Ministry for Economic Cooperation and Development helped to influence the position of the German pharmaceutical companies (Interview with Frank Schmiedchen, BMZ official, Germany, July 31, 2018).

45. Interview with Schmiedchen, BMZ, Germany, July 31, 2018.

46. Germany, which has a large pharmaceutical industry, supported the Agreement on Trade-Related Aspects of Intellectual Property Rights (TRIPS). Still, understanding that TRIPS would likely have an adverse impact on the price of drugs in poor countries, BMZ from early on promoted local pharmaceutical production. Particularly central to the promotion of these initiatives was Frank Schmiedchen, who was described by a colleague as "a left-wing social democrat," and "an individual thinker with his own political ideas" (interview with GIZ official, Germany, June 13, 2018). Schmiedchen said that his proposals promoting local pharmaceutical production were in the spirit of the Federation of German Scientists, which is committed to "responsible science" (interview with Schmiedchen, BMZ, Germany, July 31, 2018). (In 2011, GTZ merged with other agencies to form the German Development Agency, GIZ).

47. https://www.oecd.org/pcd/38845838.pdf, accessed 3 Dec. 2018.

48. Interview with Schmiedchen, BMZ, Germany, July 31, 2018.

49. Interview with Moses Mwangi, chair, KAPI, Kenya, May 18, 2012.

50. MMS and MPHS 2010; interview with Ahmed I. Mohamed, PPB, Kenya, May 29, 2012.

51. The law allowed up to 10 percent discount to importers registered as local Kenyan companies.

52. Interview with Daniel M. Karimi, OssChemie, Kenya, May 30, 2012.

53. http://aidsinfo.unaids.org/, accessed 3 Dec. 2018.

54. In general, however, the issue of patent protection—including negotiations over the Industrial Property Act and related laws—was of minimal interest for local producers in Kenya, because they normally produced off-patent medicine, either because the patent expired or was never sought (UNIDO 2010a, Chorev 2015).

55. Interview with P. K. Patel, Cosmos, Kenya, June 8, 2012.

56. Interview with P. K. Patel, Cosmos, Kenya, June 8, 2012; interview with Wanyanga, PharmaQ, Kenya, May 29, 2012; see also Okwembe (2004) and UNIDO (2010a); on the politics of compulsory and voluntary licenses, see Chorev (2012a).

57. Interview with Abdinasir Amin, ICF, Kenya, May 29, 2012; see also Osewe, Nkrumah, and Sackey (2008).

58. Interview with P. K. Patel, Cosmos, Kenya, June 8, 2012.

59. There are other estimates of the size of the Kenyan drug market, e.g., UNIDO (2010a).

60. It is difficult to quantify the Global Fund funding on an annualized basis because it approves funding in rounds, which are typically multi-year allocations. https://www.theglobalfund.org/en /portfolio/country/?k=013e944b-94da-41e1-90d1-b22b4f87f1cc&loc=KEN, accessed 3 Dec. 2018.

61. In 2008, after an audit revealed "suboptimal" performance, including unmet targets and mismanagement of funds (Global Fund 2012b), some disbursements to Kenya were suspended, and Kenya's applications in 2008 and 2009 were rejected (East African 2010, UNIDO 2010a).

62. https://data.pepfar.net/country/funding?country=Kenya&country=Tanzania&country =Uganda&year=2010, accessed 3 Dec. 2018.

63. http://aidsinfo.unaids.org/, accessed 3 Dec. 2018.

64. Some health activists consider heavy dependence on foreign aid "a dangerous situation," and they call governments to devote more of their own funds on health and medicines. It is possible that the Kenyan government would have devoted the necessary funds for the provision of ARVs and ACTs if not for the available donations, but it is also quite unlikely given a tight budget and other pressing priorities. The Ugandan government devoted $30 million a year for the purchasing of local ARVs and ACTs, but under unique circumstances, which I discuss in chapter 8.

65. UNIDO (2010a); Interview with Maureen Nafule, consultant, Kenya, Dec. 14, 2012; interview with Laing, WHO, Switzerland, June 21, 2013.

66. WHO (1995), MoH Kenya (2003), MMS and MPHS (2010), Luoma et al. (2010); interview with George Masafu, pharmacist, Kenya, Dec. 22, 2012.

67. Interview with Manesh Patel, managing director, Lab & Allied, Kenya, Dec. 20, 2012.

68. The introduction of inspection to the registration process was in accordance to WHO guidelines. A Pharmacy and Poisons Board (PPB) official also mentioned that by then, "Uganda and Tanzania were already doing it. [We] didn't want them to come to inspect us. Looks bad!"

69. Interview with Masafu, Kenya, Dec. 22, 2012; interview with NQCL, Kenya, Dec. 13, 2012.

70. Interview with Laing, WHO, Switzerland, June 21, 2013.

71. The US President's Emergency Plan for AIDS Relief (PEPFAR) initially only procured brand-name drugs, but pressures led the policy to change in 2004. By 2008, PEPFAR spent 57 percent of its procurement budget for ARVs on generic drugs. Additionally, in response to criticisms, the US government instituted an expedited and cheaper USFDA approval process for the procurement of drugs. This approval did not allow these drugs to be distributed in the US.

72. Interview with Wanyanga, PharmaQ, Kenya, May 29, 2012.

73. Fred Siyoi, PPB, PSK annual meeting, June 1, 2012.

74. Interview with Rohin Vora, managing director, Regal, Kenya, Dec. 14, 2012.

75. Interview with M. Patel, Lab & Allied, Kenya, Dec. 20, 2012.

76. Interview with Wanyanga, PharmaQ, Kenya, Dec. 14, 2012.

77. Interview with Palu Dhanani, managing director, Universal, Kenya, May 18, 2012.

78. Interview with Wanyanga, PharmaQ, Kenya, Dec. 14, 2012.

79. Interview with Dhanani, Universal, Kenya, Dec. 10, 2012.

80. Interview with Nelson Odhimabo, pharmacist, Beta Healthcare, Kenya, June 7, 2012.

81. In a meeting I attended, representatives of eight firms participated. Of the eight, six were among the more established companies (they also held the leadership positions, including the Chairman and Vice Chairman), but two of the eight were new and small. I was told that around ten to twelve of the sixteen to eighteen members of the Federation of Kenya Pharmaceutical Manufacturers (FKPM) were active on a regular basis. Another frequent participant was Wilberforce Wanyanga, who after obtaining a pharmacy degree from the University of Nairobi in 1981 and working for years in the government and the private pharmaceutical sector, set up a consultancy firm, PharmaQ, which provided training and consultation in quality management systems. Among

other roles, Wanyanga served as a UNIDO consultant. As such, he served as a constant, and quite effective, voice in Kenya in favor of quality upgrading.

82. Interview with Rägo, WHO, Switzerland, June 21, 2013.

83. Interview with Rägo, WHO, Switzerland, June 21, 2013.

84. BEGECA, a private company that was supported by the German government to procure goods and drugs for noncommercial, social, development-oriented institutions in the developing world, was contracted to implement the projects (von Massow n.d.).

85. Interview with Wanyanga, PharmaQ, Kenya, Dec. 14, 2012.

86. Interview with Dhanani, Universal, Kenya, Dec. 10, 2012.

87. Interview with Wanyanga, PharmaQ, Kenya, Dec. 14, 2012.

88. Interview with Wanyanga, PharmaQ, Kenya, Dec. 14, 2012.

89. Interview with Vora, Regal, Kenya, Dec. 14, 2012.

90. Interview with Wanyanga, PharmaQ, Kenya, Dec. 14, 2012.

91. Interview with Luc Schnitzler and Esfandiar Ardalan, Global Alliance, Roche, Switzerland, June 19, 2013, Roche (n.d.).

92. Interview with Wanyanga, PharmaQ, Kenya, Dec. 14, 2012.

93. Interview with Dhanani, Universal, Kenya, Dec. 10, 2012.

94. Interview with Vora, Regal, Kenya, Dec. 14, 2012.

95. Interview with Wanyanga, PharmaQ, Kenya, May 29, 2012; interview with Lab & Allied, Kenya, May 18, 2012.

96. Interview with Wanyanga, PharmaQ, Kenya, May 29, 2012.

97. Interview with Dhanani, Universal, Kenya, Dec. 10, 2012.

98. Interview with Laing, Switzerland, June 21, 2013.

99. Interview with Dhanani, Universal, Kenya, Dec. 10, 2012.

100. Osewe, Nkrumah, and Sackey (2008), UNIDO (2010a), Ligami (2012), interview with Dhanani, Kenya, May 18, 2012,

101. Interview with Vora, Regal, Kenya, Dec. 14, 2012.

102. Interview with Dhanani, Universal, Kenya, Dec. 10, 2012; interview with M. Patel, Lab & Allied, Kenya, May 18, 2012; interview with Mission for Essential Drugs and Supplies (MEDS), Kenya, June 7, 2012.

103. Interview with Vora, Regal, Kenya, June 5, 2012; interview with KenyaPharma, Kenya, May 31, 2012.

104. At around the same time FinnFund exited the company (ACCI 2016, FinnFund 2016).

105. Interview with K. M. Gopakumar, Third World Network, India, Dec. 13, 2011.

106. Interview with P. K. Patel, Cosmos, Kenya, June 8, 2012.

107. Interview with Lab & Allied, Dec. 15, 2012.

108. Interview with Nazir Ally, sub-Saharan Africa regional executive, Aspen Pharmacare, South Africa, Jan. 28, 2014.

109. Interview with Rägo, WHO, Switzerland, June 21, 2013.

## Chapter 7. Tanzania in the 2000s: Developmental Foreign Aid (2)

1. Losse, Schneider, and Spennemann (2007), Wilson (2009), Chaudhuri, Mackintosh, and Mujinja (2010), Wangwe et al. (2014).

2. The most prominent industrial sectors were food products, textiles, beverages, and tobacco products; https://data.worldbank.org/indicator/NV.IND.MANF.ZS?locations=TZ-KE-UG, accessed 20 May 2018.

3. In the absence of credible data, estimates of both market value and relative market share vary widely. For example, IFC (2007) estimates that in 2006, Tanzania produced drugs in the value of $12 million; another estimate, however, suggests that the value of the market that year was almost double that, $23.7 million (UNDP 2016, 4). As for relative market share over time, although some estimate the market share in 2007 to be low, at around 10 percent (Losse et al. 2007), other estimates suggest that the local market share was much higher, as high as one-third of the market (Center for Pharmaceutical Management 2003, 24, UNDP 2016, 4, Chaudhuri et al. 2010, 7, Mhamba and Mbirigenda 2010, 9). Yet, these higher estimates relied on under-estimation of the value of imports "as the Pharmacy Board does not get figures from all ports of entry" (Center for Pharmaceutical Management 2003, 22). Reports and interviewers agree on the estimated market share as of 2014 (Tibandebage et al. 2014, Wangwe et al. 2014a, Tambwe 2015, Sambo 2016; interview with TFDA, Tanzania, Mar. 19, 2012; interview with MSD, Tanzania, Mar. 27, 2013).

4. Data on registered drugs in Tanzania as of 2012 were obtained from the Tanzania Food and Drugs Authority (TFDA) (chapter 2). Data on registered drugs in Tanzania as of June 2017 were obtained from the TFDA website (https://tfda.go.tz/portal/registered-products, accessed June 12, 2017).

5. Interview with Mansoor Daya, chairman, Mansoor Daya Chemicals, Tanzania, Mar. 20, 2013, MOHSW (2011).

6. Interview with Daya, Mansoor Daya, Tanzania, Mar. 20, 2013; Mwilongo (2011).

7. People's Daily (2001), Bräutigam (2009, 71–72); interview with Tanzansino, Tanzania, Mar. 22, 2012.

8. Interview with Holley Pharm, Tanzania, Mar. 29, 2012.

9. Interview with Holley Pharm, Tanzania, Mar. 29, 2012.

10. Interview with Tanzansino, Tanzania, Mar. 22, 2012; Banda, Wangwe, and Mackintosh (2014), chapter 2.

11. Interview with Holley Pharm, Tanzania, Mar. 29, 2012; Bräutigam (2009).

12. Interviews with Holley Pharm, Tanzania, Mar. 25 and 29, 2013; MOHSW (2011).

13. The process of privatization in Tanzania, which started in 1990, was initially very slow, due to the fierce opposition of the parastatals' senior managers—many of whom were prominent members of the ruling party, CCM. From 1994 to 1998, Tanzania divested about 150 of the 385 public enterprises initially held (World Bank 1999). In the following years, most parastatal enterprises in the industrial and commercial sectors were privatized, as well as key infrastructure enterprises such as energy and water. Privatization intensified ethnic tensions in the country—as a perceived "Asianization" of the economy became a major political issue, with some calling for "indigenization," to make sure that Africans would have control over businesses (Mans 2002, Edwards 2014, 160–92). In the pharmaceutical sector, both Keko and Tanzania Pharmaceutical Industries (TPI) were sold to African Tanzanians. (In the case of TPI, as we will see, some of the private investors were connected to CCM).

14. Interview with Pyramid Pharma, Tanzania, Mar. 20, 2012; interview with Romuald Mbwasi, chief pharmacist, Ministry of Health, Tanzania, Mar. 28, 2013; interview with UNIDO, Tanzania, Mar. 26, 2012.

15. Interview with Bahari Pharmacy, Tanzania, Mar. 20, 2012.

16. Interview with Zenufa, Tanzania, Mar. 19, 2012.

17. http://aidsinfo.unaids.org/, accessed 3 Dec. 2018.

18. http://aidsinfo.unaids.org/, accessed 3 Dec. 2018.

19. UNAIDS (2013), https://www.wto.org/english/news_e/news25_e/trip_06nov15_e.htm.

20. https://data.worldbank.org/indicator/NY.GDP.PCAP.CD?end=2016&locations=TZ -KE&start=2004, accessed 20 May 2018.

21. Interview by Ben Bradlow with Nazir Ally, sub-Saharan Africa regional executive, Aspen Pharmacare, South Africa, July 27, 2015.

22. Interview by Bradlow with Ally, Aspen, South Africa, July 27, 2015.

23. Mackintosh and Mujinja (2008). Given that production cost was generally higher in Tanzania than in India (Wilson 2009), Tanzanian producers must have relied on particularly low profit margins.

24. Interview with Daya, Mansoor Daya, Tanzania, Mar. 20, 2013.

25. Interview with Hitesh Upreti, chief marketing officer, Shelys, Tanzania, Mar. 21, 2013.

26. Interview with Zenufa, Tanzania, Mar. 19, 2012, UNDP (2016).

27. https://www.theglobalfund.org/en/portfolio/country/?loc=TZA&k=19a42508-b05c-4128-a2ed-ff5eea6af30d, accessed 3 Dec. 2018.

28. https://data.pepfar.net/country/funding?country=Kenya&country=Tanzania&country=Uganda&year=2010, accessed 12 June 2018.

29. Interview with MSD, Tanzania, Mar. 21, 2013. More than in many other Sub-Saharan African countries, in Tanzania, donors directed some of the largest health financing to the government, suggesting confidence in the country's governance. From 1997 until 2002, 90 percent of total external funding was channeled through Tanzania's public sector. By comparison, Kenya and Uganda received substantially less public-sector financing: 60 percent and 45 percent, respectively (Wilson 2009, 141).

30. Interview with Upreti, Shelys, Tanzania, Mar. 21, 2013.

31. Interview by Ben Bradlow with Stavros Nicolaou, senior executive, Aspen Pharmacare, South Africa, July 26, 2015.

32. Interview by Bradlow with Ally, Aspen, South Africa, July 27, 2015.

33. Interview with Shelys Pharmaceuticals, Tanzania, Mar. 27, 2013.

34. Interview by Bradlow with Ally, Aspen, South Africa, July 27, 2015.

35. Shelys produced new antibiotics, and it produced an antimalarial artemether-lumefantrine (AL), branded as Co-Malafin, for the private sector (http://www.actwatch.info/databases/antimalarial_survey_data/results, accessed 3 June 2018). However, when the Global Fund introduced the Affordable Medicines Facility—malaria (AMFm), a scheme of subsidizing producers of quality-assured artemisinin-based combination therapy (ACTs) sold in the private market, the price of the brand-name anitmalarial produced by Novartis went down drastically, and "nothing came out of" Shelys's plan (Interview with Shelys, Tanzania, March 27, 2013). More generally, as in Kenya, the introduction of ACTs as first-line recommended treatment in 2006, followed by the AMFm in 2011, had significant impact on local producers, who lost a large share of their antimalarial market as a result (AMFm Independent Evaluation Team 2012, Wangwe et al. 2014a).

36. Point-of-Use Water Disinfection and Zince Treatment Prokect (POUZN) and UNICEF provided the government with the initial supply, which was purchased from the main producer at the time, Nutriset, a European company.

37. Interview with Bongo Mgeni, Population Services International (PSI), Tanzania, Mar. 27, 2012.

38. In addition to the School of Pharmacy that opened in Muhimbili University of Health and Allied Sciences (MUHAS) in 1974, new pharmacy schools were established at St. John's University of Tanzania and at the Catholic University of Health and Allied Sciences. All pharmacy schools were focused on producing community and hospital pharmacists, not industrial pharmacists. One university in Tanzania offered a Master's degree in industrial pharmacy (MOHSW 2009), and St. Luke Foundation in Moshi and the Research and Development Laboratory under action medeor at MUHAS School of pharmacy offered diploma and continued pharmacy education in industrial pharmacy, respectively. The majority of the students attending industrial pharmacy courses at these places, however, came not from Tanzania but from Kenya, Uganda, and other neighboring countries (Häfele-Abah 2010, Mwilongo 2011).

39. Interview with Zenufa, Tanzania, Mar. 19, 2012. At the same time, there was a growing expectation in Tanzania to hire locals, specifically indigenous Africans. Under Sumaria, the skilled

workers at Shelys, including not only in the pharmacy realm, but also in finance, marketing, and so on, were mainly Indian and British expatriates. Already, then, this was seen by the firm's management as a "major problem" (Losse et al. 2007). This reportedly changed under Aspen, which "promoted the locals" (interview with Shelys, Tanzania, Mar. 27, 2013). "The factory manager is a local Tanzanian. But he [received training] from a South African that was [in Tanzania] for two years. . . . Our entire philosophy is to try and up-skill the local people as far as possible. So that's what we've done there. So we've taken someone with good potential, given him the necessary tools, and now he's doing his job appropriately" (interview by Bradlow with Ally, Aspen, South Africa, July 27, 2015).

40. In 2015, more than 50 percent of action medeor funding came from the German government, including from GIZ.

41. http://aidsinfo.unaids.org/, accessed 3 Dec. 2018.

42. WHO (2011c), IRIN News (2012); interview with action medeor, Tanzania, Mar. 22, 2012.

43. Chapter 6, Losse et al. (2007), Häfele-Abah (2010); interview with Shelys Pharmaceuticals, Tanzania, Mar. 27, 2013.

44. Interview with Mgeni, PSI, Tanzania, Mar. 27, 2012.

45. Interview with TFDA, Tanzania, Mar. 19, 2012. ISO 9001:2008 is a standard developed by the International Organization for Standardization that specified requirements for a quality management system where an organization "needs to demonstrate its ability to consistently provide product that meets customer and applicable statutory and regulatory requirements" (https://www.iso.org/standard/46486.html, accessed 3 Dec. 2018).

46. Interview with TFDA, Tanzania, Mar. 19, 2012.

47. Interview with Vora, Regal, Kenya, Dec. 14, 2012.

48. Interview with TFDA, Tanzania, Mar. 19, 2012

49. These included Khanbhai Pharmaceuticals and two other manufacturers, one called Afya Laboratories, which most likely was a distributor/wholesaler with an informal manufacturing facility, and another called Elychem (Center for Pharmaceutical Management 2003).

50. Interview with Shelys, Tanzania, Mar. 27, 2013.

51. Interview with TFDA, Tanzania, Mar. 19, 2012; interview with Dawa, Kenya, May 26, 2012.

52. Interview with Tanzansino, Tanzania, Mar. 22, 2012.

53. Interview by Bradlow with Ally, South Africa, July 27, 2015, emphasis added.

54. Interview with Upreti, Tanzania, Mar. 21, 2013.

55. Interview by Bradlow with Nicolaou, Aspen, South Africa, July 26, 2015. Shelys employees held a critical view of the international "establishment" and the commercial interests behind multiple and renewable certificates. In the context of renewing their Pharmaceutical Inspection Convention and Pharmaceutical Inspection Co-operation Scheme (PIC/S) certificate, they described a particularly insistent European consultant who pushed for audits according to his own schedule and irrespective of Shelys' readiness and who charged them handsomely for his time and for the time of another consultant he pressed them to hire (Interview with Shelys, Tanzania, Mar. 27, 2013).

56. Interview with Mgeni, PSI, Tanzania, Mar. 27, 2012, USAID (2008, 2011a).

57. Interview with action medeor, Tanzania, Mar. 22, 2012.

58. As with other companies, although Zenufa found the auditing with Roche to be a "good experience," it didn't lead to anything (interview with Zenufa, Tanzania, Mar. 19, 2012; Roche 2008, Berger et al. 2010).

59. Interview with Zenufa, Tanzania, Mar. 19, 2012.

60. The acquisition of Zenufa was Catalyst's second investment in the health care sector after acquiring in 2014 the Kenyan Mimosa Pharmacy (later rebranded "Goodlife Pharmacy"), a leading pharmacy retail chain with high quality outlets across the region. (Later that year, Catalyst

Principal Partners sold its stake in Goodlife Pharmacy to LeapFrog Investments, another private equity investment company) (Dorbian 2016, Mwiti 2016).

61. The contracting out could be motivated by lower costs (it was cheaper to produce abroad) but also by lack of capacity—if the company received orders that it did not have sufficient capacity to fulfill on time.

62. Interview with USAID, Tanzania, Mar. 22, 2012; interview with Zenufa, Tanzania, Mar. 19, 2012.

63. Interview by Bradlow with Ally, Aspen, South Africa, July 27, 2015, emphasis added.

64. Interview by Bradlow with Nicolaou, Aspen, South Africa, July 26, 2015, emphasis added.

65. Interview with USAID, Tanzania, Mar. 22, 2012.

## Chapter 8. Uganda in the 2000s:
## Entrepreneurship with and without Aid

1. On structural adjustment reforms in Uganda, see: Livingstone (1998), Siggel and Ssemogerere (2004), Akampumuza (2005, 61), Mbabazi and Mokhawa (2005, 134), Okuku (2006).

2. https://data.worldbank.org/indicator/NV.IND.MANF.ZS?locations=TZ-KE-UG, accessed 20 May 2018.

3. Primary packaging is the packaging that touches the drug. Secondary packaging was locally produced.

4. WHO 2002, Klissas et al. 2010, UNIDO 2010b; interview with SURE, Uganda, January 15, 2013. In addition to the School of Pharmacy at Makerere University, which started operation in 1988, two departments of pharmacy opened after 2000, at Mbarara University of Science and Technology and at the School of Health Sciences at Kampala International University (UNIDO 2010b, table 7). The number of graduates in Uganda increased as a result from ten–twelve to around fifty–sixty pharmacists a year. There were around 450 licensed pharmacists and 500 pharmaceutical technicians and assistants in 2010 (MOH Uganda 2011a).

5. Ogalo had a similar trajectory to other Kenyan entrepreneurs in the pharmaceutical sector (chapter 3). He received a pharmacy degree from Nairobi University in 1980. After graduation, he worked for a government hospital and then moved to the private sector, where he first worked in a retail pharmacy and then joined the multinational firm Howse and McGeorge. He joined Kulal International in 1999. Interview with M. O. Ogalo, managing director, Medipharm, Uganda, Jan. 11, 2013, UNIDO (2010b).

6. Chapter 5; interview with Kitumba Benson, managing director, Kisakye, Uganda, Jan. 18, 2013.

7. Interview with Sev Pharmaceuticals, Uganda, Jan. 10, 2013.

8. UNIDO (2010b), http://medipharm.co.ug/?page_id=227, accessed Jan. 3, 2018. ORS production provided 15 percent of the Medipharm's revenue.

9. UNIDO (2010b); interview with Benson, Kisakye, Uganda, Jan. 18, 2013.

10. Interview with Benson, Kisakye, Uganda, Jan. 18, 2013.

11. UNIDO 2010b; interview with Benson, Kisakye, Uganda, Jan. 18, 2013; interview with National Drug Authority (NDA), Uganda, Jan. 11, 2013.

12. UNIDO (2010b); interview with Sev, Uganda, Jan. 10, 2013.

13. Interview with Kwality Afro-Asia, Uganda, Jan. 4, 2013.

14. There is no information regarding Bychem's decision to close. Mavid most likely closed due to a business dispute with one of its suppliers, a Pakistani company called Royal Group, which evolved into a dispute between Mavid and the owner of Bychem (chapter 5, Observer 2009, UNIDO 2010b, Kaaya 2014).

15. When the National Resistance Movement (NRM) seized power in 1986, the government inherited around 146 state-owned enterprises, which employed more than 30,000 people, accounting for more than one quarter of total employment in the formal sector, and generated about 10 percent of GDP. Some of these enterprises performed poorly, with low productivity, high losses, and rising debts (Reinikka and Collier 2001, Ddumba-Ssentamu and Mugume 2001, 9–10, Tangri and Mwenda 2001). Pressed by the International Monetary Fund (IMF) and the World Bank, the Ugandan government eventually privatized many of these companies. The process of privatization was harshly criticized, including for the fact that many companies were sold not to indigenous Africans, but to foreign investors and especially Indians previously from Uganda or otherwise from East Africa (Tangri and Mwenda 2001, 118, Roberts 2005, 126, 130–31, Kibikyo 2008). Out of a total of 74 enterprises sold between 1992 and 2000 (others were liquidated), 41 went to local buyers (55%), 27 to foreign buyers (37%), and 6 to joint ventures (8%). However, the value of enterprises bought by foreigners was 187 billion Uganda shilling (UGX) ($93.5 million) whereas the value of enterprises bought by locals was only 40 billion UGX ($19.8 million) (Livingstone 1998, 45–46, Ddumba-Ssentamu and Mugume 2001, Kibikyo 2008).

16. Interview with Ajith Prasad, UPL, Uganda, Jan. 12, 2013; interview with Kwality Uganda, Jan. 4, 2013.

17. Interview with Frances Otim, NDA and Astra, Uganda. Jan. 8, 2013.

18. Interview with NDA, Uganda, Jan. 11, 2013.

19. Under colonialism, a prominent Ismaili community originally from India developed in East Africa, especially in Tanganyika. The Industrial Promotion Services (IPS) was founded in 1963, in Tanzania by Aga Khan and two other Ismaili enterprises, the Diamond Jubilee Insurance Company and the Diamond Jubilee Investment Trust, with the goal of helping local Ismailis to form partnerships with the state or with foreign capital to invest in manufacturing.

20. Interviews with KPI, Uganda, Jan. 12 and 18, 2013; Saez 2014.

21. Registration data from Kenya and Tanzania (chapter 2) show that KPI had five drugs registered in Tanzania as of 2012. It registered one drug—an analgesic—in Kenya, in 2004, but it had no drugs registered in Kenya in 2017 (interview with KPI, Uganda, Jan. 18, 2013; Saez 2014).

22. Kalyango (2006); http://kpi.co.ug/company-history/, accessed 20 May 2018; http://www.actwatch.info/duactkamapala-pharmaceutical-industries1996ltd, accessed 3 June 2018.

23. Interview with Sarkar Tapan Kumar, pharmacist, KPI, Uganda, Jan. 15, 2013.

24. Interview with Shakti G. Monpara, production manager, Rene, Uganda, Jan. 5. 2013.

25. Interview with Monpara, Rene, Uganda, Jan. 5. 2013.

26. http://www.actwatch.info/lumarenrene-industries-ltd, accessed 3 June 2018.

27. Interview with Monpara, Uganda, Jan. 5. 2013.

28. Interview with Harish Shah, Abacus Parenteral Drugs, Uganda, Jan. 14, 2013; PEI (2014).

29. Interview with Shekhar Srvastava, Abacus Parenteral Drugs, Uganda, Jan. 14, 2013.

30. Registration data from Kenya and Tanzania (chapter 2) show that Abacus had nine drugs registered in Tanzania as of 2012. It registered five products in Kenya, in 2010–11, and it had fifteen registered products in Kenya as of 2017. Interviews with Abacus Parenteral Drugs, Uganda, Jan. 5 and 14, 2013; CEHURD (2013).

31. Interview with NDA, Uganda, Jan. 11, 2013.

32. Interview with NDA, Uganda, Jan. 11, 2013.

33. http://aidsinfo.unaids.org/, accessed 3 Dec. 2018.

34. http://aidsinfo.unaids.org/, accessed 3 Dec. 2018.

35. The four Ugandans were Francis X. Kitaka, Emmanuel Katongole, Frederick Mutebi Kitaka, and George Baguma, the Kenyan was Edward Martin, and the Irish investor was Randall Tierney. Francis X. Kitaka is known as the first bio-chemist in Uganda and had a solid background in the pharmacy business. He worked for the multinational pharmaceutical company Wellcome, and

when the company pulled its distribution business out of Uganda in the 1970s, Kitaka, Martin, and Tierney took over; they renamed it Cooper Uganda Limited. Interview with Quality Chemicals Ltd., Uganda, Jan.y 8, 2013, BBC (2012).

36. Chapter 2; interview with QCIL, Uganda, Jan. 9, 2013; WHO (2011e).

37. Interview with QCL, Uganda, Jan. 8, 2013.

38. In 2013, Cipla's wholly-owned subsidiary, Meditab Holdings, acquired an additional 14.5 percent stake in QCIL, for $15 million. Together with the original shares, Cipla then held a 51.05 percent stake in QCIL. In 2015, Cipla acquired a 51 percent equity stake in the trading company, QCL, for $26 million. Because QCL owned a 22.05 percent equity stake in CiplaQCIL at the time, Cipla's effective holding in CiplaQCIL rose up to 62.3 percent. The other shares of QCIL were owned by two private equity investors, the South-African-based Capitalworks (14.4%) and TLG Capital, a UK firm specializing in emerging markets (12.5%) (Interview with QCL, Uganda, Jan. 8, 2013; Verma 2015).

39. So was Cipla's later investment in the parent distribution company, QCL. Historically, Cipla's international expansion followed a "hands off" model, in which it mostly relied on local distributors, in addition to selling mostly in the public sector. Starting in the 2010s, the company sought greater control over its business; and it developed greater interest in the private market. According to Nevin Bradford, CEO of CiplaQCIL, QCL "provide[d] Cipla with a platform to expand its non-tender private market reach in Uganda." This expansion was to rely mostly on drugs produced in India. "Cipla from India has 2,000 products. Here in Uganda, we certainly intend to expand what we offer." However, it came with an intention to also manufacture new types of drugs locally. "CiplaQCIL is currently expanding its portfolio to manufacture medicines for tropical diseases such as sleeping sickness, worm infestations and hepatitis C" (http://www.cipla.com/en/uganda.html, accessed 22 May 2018; interview with Salama Pharmaceuticals, Tanzania, Mar. 21, 2012).

40. Interview with SURE, Uganda, Jan. 15, 2013.

41. The land was not given to the company for free, but critics mentioned that to calculate the shares given to the government in return to the land it was valued based on its value prior to the manufacturing company putting any investment in it, instead of evaluating it based on the much higher value of the land once the factory was there.

42. Interview with SURE, Uganda, Jan. 16, 2013; interview with QCIL, Uganda, Jan. 9, 2013; see also Klissas et al. (2010), UNIDO (2010b), BBC (2012).

43. Many criticized the government's decision as wasteful, whereas others saw it as a positive turn in the direction of the Ugandan government using its own resources for the procurement of drugs rather than relying on donations (various interviews).

44. Interview with QCIL, Uganda, Jan. 9, 2013; interview with Nevin Bradford, Cipla, Tanzania, Mar. 15, 2013; interview with Yusuf Hamied, chairman, Cipla, India, Jan. 11, 2012; see also Klissas et al. (2010).

45. Interview with Bradford, Cipla, Tanzania, Mar. 15, 2013; Klissas et al. (2010); http://www .ciplaqcil.co.ug/, accessed 22 May 2018.

46. This was harshly criticized by many observers, who asked: Why prevent millions of dollars coming to the country for the sake of one manufacturing company? (Various interviews).

47. Given the kind of drugs it produced, QCIL had limited opportunities in the private market. Still, in 2009, QCIL began selling to Joint Medical Store (JMS) in Uganda, and it developed a small private market business in Zambia and South Sudan. Interview with Quality Chemical Industries Ltd., Uganda, Jan. 9, 2013; see also Nakaweesi (2016).

48. http://portfolio.theglobalfund.org/ReportLibrary/AMFm/Summary.aspx, accessed 3 Dec. 2018.

49. The Ugandan government "fought tooth and nail" to make the Global Fund buy ARVs from QCIL. However, because QCIL "[could not] compete in the [international] ARVs market,"

it couldn't win an open tender, and the Global Fund refused to let the Ugandan government use Global Fund funds without a tender. Interview with QCL, Uganda, Jan. 8, 2013; interview with Global Fund, Switzerland, June 24, 2013; Uganda Business News (2017).

50. Interview with Hamied, Cipla, India, Jan. 11, 2012.

51. Interview with SURE, Uganda, Jan. 15, 2013; interview with Hanif Nazer Ali, DANIDA, Tanzania, Mar. 27, 2013.

52. Interview with JMS, Uganda, Jan. 14, 2013

53. Interview with Surgipharm, Uganda, Jan. 9, 2013; interview with Prasad, UPL, Uganda, Jan. 12, 2013.

54. Interviews with National Medical Stores (NMS), Uganda, Jan. 7, 2013.

55. http://www.kibokogroup.com/our-companies/abacus-parenteral-drugs/, accessed May 29, 2018.

56. Sempijja (2009); interviews with Abacus Parenteral Drugs, Uganda, Jan. 14, 2013. Loans from the World Bank's IFC and the African Development Bank and the investment by AfricInvest Fund II fall under the category of foreign aid. However, in this case, these funds did not involve markets, monitoring, or mentoring.

57. Interviews with Abacus Parenteral Drugs, Uganda, Jan. 14, 2013; interview with Harley's, Uganda, Jan. 8, 2013, UNIDO (2010b).

58. MoH Uganda (2011b), https://www.theglobalfund.org/en/portfolio/country/?loc=UGA&k =9e8b8568-adaa-4b26-af09-da5b112c51e7, accessed 3 Dec. 2018.

59. That year the general PEPFAR funding for treatment (not only ARVs) was $83 million, and total PEPFAR funding was $277 million. https://data.pepfar.net/country/funding?country =Kenya&country=Tanzania&country=Uganda&year=2010, accessed 3 Dec. 2018.

60. Not only procurement, but also the distribution of Global Fund ARVs in Uganda mostly bypassed the state, as the Global Fund relied instead on the non-for-profit sector (various interviews, Governance 2011, MoH Uganda 2011b). In addition, following a major embezzlement scandal, Uganda's Global Fund money was almost entirely cut off from 2005 to 2009 (Croke 2011, 188–89).

61. In the conclusion of the book, I discuss the capacity-building efforts of DANIDA and the WHO that started from the very inception of NDA and NMS in 1994.

62. The first NDA Executive Secretary, Abbas Kabogo, who started his position in 1995, was "pushed out" due to a "small scandal"—he was charged with abuse of office and importation of illegal drugs. John Lule, who replaced Kabogo in 1999, was prosecuted in 2003 for authorizing the importation of drugs of a blacklisted Chinese factory. The case was later withdrawn and Lule was allowed to return to office. The third Executive Secretary, Apollo Muhairwe, was able to avoid scandals and lasted two terms, from 2003 to 2011. He was later hired as an Operations Office at the World Bank office in Uganda. The fourth, Gordon Ssematiko, also served two terms, from 2011 till 2017, although conflicts over his appointment led the Minister of Health to suspend the entire NDA board. In 2017, after allegations of corruption, he was replaced by Donah Kusemererwa (Allio 2003, Mukisa 2005, Naturinda and Mugerwa 2011, Kasujja 2016).

63. Interview with NDA, Uganda, Jan. 11, 2013.

64. Interview with NDA, Uganda, Jan. 11, 2013.

65. Interview with Prasad, UPL, Uganda, Jan. 12, 2013.

66. Interview with NDA, Uganda, Jan. 11, 2013.

67. Interview with NDA, Uganda, Jan. 11, 2013. Post-marketing surveillance also yielded some punitive actions. In 2012, a special inspection of the premises of the Kenyan pharmaceutical company Elys Chemicals Industries in Kampala found the company to be non-compliant, and NDA banned Elys products from Uganda for eight months (Lubwama 2012, Agaba et al. 2013).

68. Interview with NDA, Uganda, Jan. 11, 2013.

69. The NDA did not inspect companies that sold in high-regulatory markets: these companies were asked to only submit a desk review, but they still paid fees. At the same time, the NDA introduced unannounced GMP inspections of manufacturing facilities. In 2012, as a result of one such unannounced visit, triggered by complaints from doctors, a popular India-based drug manufacturer, Flamingo Pharmaceuticals Limited, was found noncompliant and lost its license to market its drugs in Uganda (Agaba et al. 2013, various interviews).

70. Interview with Sev, Uganda, Jan. 10, 2013; GTZ (2009).

71. Interview with NDA, Uganda, Jan. 11, 2013.

72. Interview with Nazeem Mohamed, general manager and CEO, KPI, Uganda, Jan. 18, 2013; interview with Monpara, Rene, Uganda, Jan. 5. 2013.

73. Interview with Monpara, Rene, Uganda, Jan. 5. 2013.

74. Interview with Kumar, KPI, Uganda, Jan. 15, 2013.

75. Interview with Abacus, Uganda, Jan. 14, 2013.

76. Interview with Prasad, UPL, Uganda, Jan. 12, 2013.

77. Interview with Nazeem, KPI, Uganda, Jan. 12, 2013; Häfele-Abah (2010).

78. In one case in which a development agency did suggest a targeted project for a local pharmaceutical firm, the incentives were reportedly not sufficiently attractive. In that case, KPI was approached by the WHO for building a new facility for producing vaccines. The WHO promised technological help, but KPI decided against the initiative due to concern that, without guaranteed markets, which the WHO did not offer, they would not be able to sell the products (interview with Nazeem, KPI, Uganda, Jan. 12, 2013).

79. Interview with UNIDO, Austria, July 11, 2013.

80. Interview with Luc Schnitzler and Esfandiar Ardalan, Global Alliance, Roche, Switzerland, June 19, 2013.

81. Interview with Ogalo, Medipharm, Uganda, Jan. 11, 2013; interview with Nazeem, KPI, Uganda, Jan. 12, 2013.

## Chapter 9. Foreign Aid and the State

1. Although not about foreign aid, the analysis of Locke, Amengual and Mangla (2009) on voluntary compliance programs, similarly emphasizes the role of audits (monitoring) and technical assistance (mentoring) in improving working conditions and labor rights.

2. http://english.ohmynews.com/articleview/article_view.asp?menu=c10400&no=382131&rel_no=1, accessed 12 Dec. 2018.

3. On strategic considerations in foreign aid allocation, see Burnside and Dollar (2000), Claessens, Cassimon, and Van Campenhout (2009), De Mesquita and Smith (2009), Wright and Winters (2010, 63); but see Kevlihan, DeRouen Jr., and Biglaiser (2014). On local conditions, see Hout (2002), Bermeo (2008), Dietrich (2013).

4. In contrast, aid on the basis of need may address rather than reproduce inequities. Importantly, development assistance for health (DAH) seems to correspond to countries' health needs. Lee and Lim (2014) found that when the health status of a recipient country deteriorates, the total value of health aid to the country increases, and Ravishankar et al. (2009) found that DAH was positively correlated with burden of disease. These findings are consistent with the fact that donors responded to severe shortages of drugs in Kenya, Tanzania, and Uganda.

5. Interview with David Ekau, pharmacist, Uganda, Jan. 15, 2013.

6. Interview with Ekau, Uganda, Jan. 15, 2013; see also McDonnell (2017).

7. Interview with Frances Otim, National Drug Authority (NDA) and Astra, Uganda. Jan. 8, 2013.

8. https://extranet.who.int/prequal/about/success-stories/who-rotational-fellowships-platform-learning-and-collaboration, accessed 12 June 2018; WHO (2016).

9. Interview with Dr. Lembit Rägo, WHO, Switzerland, June 21, 2013.

10. Although WHO officials seemed to believe in their ability to transform fellows' "norms and standards" in the course of three months, they also realized that they could not fully protect "their guys" from the larger political system in which they function. A WHO official described the challenges in that way: "But there is one little trick. Can they implement what they have learned? And the answer, in many cases is no." Interview with Rägo, WHO, Switzerland, June 21, 2013.

11. In her analysis of conditional subsidies, Amsden (2001) observes that conditions that could be easily monitored permitted not only supervision of the manufacturers, but also supervision of the *supervisors*—because it was no longer as easy to grant subsidies to undeserving companies. In that way, it minimized government failure. By restricting state discretion, a few of the reforms mentioned above, such as transparency of contracts, had a similar effect.

12. Interview with Crown Agents, Uganda, May 18, 2012; interview with USAID, Kenya, Dec. 18, 2012.

13. Interviews with KEMSA, Kenya, June 4, 6 and 19; interview with National Empowerment Network of People living with HIV/AIDS in Kenya (NEPHAK), Kenya, June 4, 2012; interview with USAID, Kenya, Dec. 18, 2012; UNIDO (2010a), FEAPM (2012), NACC and NASCOP (2012), Kilonzo (2015).

14. Vincent Habiyambere, "Pilot Project to Improve Access to HIV/AIDS-Related drugs: Exploratory Visit. The Pharmaceutical Sector," Jan.1997, UGA043, WHO Archives; interview with Otim, NDA and Astra, Uganda. Jan. 8, 2013; WHO (1994a), WHO (1995b), UNIDO (1997), WHO (2002).

15. Interviews with SURE, Uganda, Jan. 15 and 16, 2013; interview with USAID, Uganda, Jan. 17, 2012; interview with Surgipharm (Uganda), Uganda, Jan. 9, 2013; SURE (2012).

16. For a careful discussion on the impact of PEPFAR and Global Fund on health system strengthening in Tanzania and Uganda, see Croke (2011).

17. This is only in regard to the management of the procurement and distribution of drugs. In other realms, the Global Fund is inclusive of non-state actors (Chorev, Andia and Ciplet 2011).

18. Interview by Ben Bradlow with Stavros Nicolaou, senior executive, Aspen Pharmacare, South Africa, July 26, 2015.

19. Interview by Ben Bradlow with Nazir Ally, sub-Saharan Africa regional executive, Aspen Pharmacare, South Africa, July 27, 2015.

20. Interview by Ben Bradlow with Nicolaou, Aspen, South Africa, July 26, 2015.

21. Interview by Ben Bradlow with Ally, Aspen, South Africa, July 27, 2015.

22. FinnFund (2016), ACCI (2016), http://ucl.co.ke/partners/, accessed 12 June 2018.

# REFERENCES

Abbott, Frederick M., and Graham Dukes. 2009. *Global pharmaceutical policy: Ensuring medicines for tomorrow's world*. Cheltenham: Edward Elgar.

ACCI. 2016. Universal Corporation: A Kenyan pharmaceutical manufacturing company. Cameroon: African Center for Competitive Intelligence.

ACCU. 2013. Call to government to recover UGX 44.5 billion lost through breach of contract by Quality Chemicals Industries Ltd. Ntinda: Anti Corruption Coalition Uganda.

Adams, Vincanne. 2016. *Metrics: What counts in global health*. Durham: Duke University Press.

Addison, Tony, George Mavrotas, and Mark McGillivray. 2005. "Development assistance and development finance: Evidence and global policy agendas." *Journal of International Development* 17(6):819–36.

African Confidential. 2013. "NDA's contribution to Uganda at 20," Feb. 26.

AFRO. 2005. Local production of essential medicines, including antiretrorivrals: Issues, challenges and perspectives in the African region (Report of the Regional Director). Brazaville: WHO Regional Committeee for Africa.

Agaba, Amon Ganafa, Jonans Tusiimire, Petra Sevcikova, Jude Murison, Karen Maigetter, and Allyson Pollock. 2013. Implementation and enforcement of Good Manufacturing Practice (GMP) regulations in Uganda: Implications for access to quality medicines. Unpublished manuscript.

Aggarwal, Aradhna. 2004. Strategic approach to strengthening the international competitiveness in knowledge based industries: The Indian pharmaceutical industry (RIS Discussion Paper). New Delhi: Research and Information System for the Non-Aligned and Other Developing Countries

Aisch, Gregor, Josh Keller, and K. K. Rebecca Lai. 2015. "The world according to China." *New York Times*, July 24.

Aiyar, Sana. 2015. *Indians in Kenya: The politics of diaspora*. Cambridge, MA: Harvard Univ. Press.

Akampumuza, James. 2005. "Uganda's institutional framework for development since colonialism: Challenges of a developmental state." In *The potentiality of 'developmental states' in Africa*, ed. Pamela Mbabazi and Ian Taylor, 57–78. Dakar: Council for the Development of Social Science Research in Africa.

Akhtar, Gulshan. 2013. "Indian pharmaceutical industry: An overview." *IOSR Journal of Humanities and Social Science* 13(3):51–66.

Alden, Chris. 2005. "China in Africa." *Survival* 47(3):147–64.

Alesina, Alberto, and David Dollar. 2000. "Who gives foreign aid to whom and why?" *Journal of Economic Growth* 5(1):33–63.

Alexander, Myrna, and Charles III Fletcher. 2012. "The use and impact of the Bank's policy of domestic preferences." In *Review of World Bank Procurement Policies and Procedures* (Background Paper).

Allio, Emmy. 2003. "Uganda: Spotlight: National Drug Authority bosses back in office." *New Vision*, Jan. 6.

Altincekic, Ceren, and David H Bearce. 2014. "Why there should be no political foreign aid curse." *World Development* 64(C):18–32.

AMFm Independent Evaluation Team. 2012. Independent evaluation of phase 1 of the Affordable Medicines Facility—malaria (AMFm): Final report. Calverton, Maryland and London: ICF International and London School of Hygiene and Tropical Medicine.

Amin, Abdinasir A., Dejan Zurovac, Beth B. Kangwana, Joanne Greenfield, Dorothy N. Otieno, Willis S. Akhwale, and Robert W. Snow. 2007. "The challenges of changing national malaria drug policy to artemisinin-based combinations in Kenya." *Malaria Journal* 6(1):72.

Amin, Samir. 1974. "Accumulation and development: A theoretical model." *Review of African Political Economy* 1(1):9–26.

Aminzade, Ronald. 2013. *Race, nation, and citizenship in postcolonial Africa: The case of Tanzania.* Cambridge: Cambridge Univ. Press.

Amsden, Alice. 1985. "The state and Taiwan's economic development." In *Bringing the state back in*, ed. Peter B. Evans, Dietrich Rueschemeyer, and Theda Skocpol, 78–106. Cambridge: Cambridge Univ. Press.

Amsden, Alice H. 1986. "The direction of trade—past and present—and the 'learning effects' of exports to different directions." *Journal of Development Economics* 23(2):249–74.

Amsden, Alice H. 1989. *Asia's next giant: Late industrialization in South Korea.* Oxford: Oxford Univ. Press.

Amsden, Alice H. 2001. *The rise of "the rest": Challenges to the west from late-industrializing economies.* Oxford: Oxford Univ. Press.

Amsden, Alice H, and Wan-wen Chu. 2003. *Beyond late development: Taiwan's upgrading policies.* Cambridge, MA: MIT Press.

Amutabi, Maurice N. 2006. *The NGO Factor in Africa.* New York: Taylor & Francis.

Anand Rathi Research. 2010. Indian pharma: Global healing. Anand Rathii Financial Services.

Anderson, Tatum. 2010. "Tide turns for drug manufacturing in Africa." *Lancet* 375(9726):1597–98.

Anderson, Warwick. 2014. "Making global health history: The postcolonial worldliness of biomedicine." *Social History of Medicine* 27(2):372–84.

Andia, Tatiana, and Nitsan Chorev. 2017. "Making knowledge legitimate: Transnational advocacy networks' campaigns against tobacco, infant formula and pharmaceuticals." *Global Networks* 17(2):255–80.

Andreoni, Antonio, and Ha-Joon Chang. 2016. "Bringing production and employment back into development: Alice Amsden's legacy for a new developmentalist agenda." *Cambridge Journal of Regions, Economy and Society* 10(1):173–87.

Arrow, Kenneth J., Patricia M. Danzon, Hellen Gelband, Dean Jamison, Ramanan Laxminarayan, Anne Mills, Germano Mwabu, Claire Panosian, Richard Peto, and Nicholas J. White. 2012. "The Affordable Medicines Facility—malaria: Killing it slowly." *Lancet* 380(9857):1889–90.

Asongu, Simplice A., and Jacinta C. Nwachukwu. 2017. "Foreign aid and inclusive development: Updated evidence from Africa, 2005–2012." *Social Science Quarterly* 98(1):282–98.

AUC and UNIDO. 2012. Pharmaceutical manufacturing plan for Africa: Business plan. Addis Ababa and Vienna: African Union Commission and United Nations Industrial Development Organization.

Auditor General. 2010. Annual report of the Auditor General for the year ended 30 June 2010. Republic of Uganda, Office of the Auditor General.

Babb, Sarah. 2013. "The Washington Consensus as transnational policy paradigm: Its origins, trajectory and likely successor." *Review of International Political Economy* 20(2):268–97.

Baliamoune-Lutz, Mina, and George Mavrotas. 2009. "Aid effectiveness: Looking at the aid–social capital–growth nexus." *Review of Development Economics* 13(3):510–25.

Banda, Geoffrey, Samuel Wangwe, and Maureen Mackintosh. 2014. "Making medicines in Africa: An historical political economy overview." In *Making medicines in Africa*, ed. Maureen

Mackintosh, Geoffrey Banda, Watu Wamae and Paula Tibandebage, 7–24. London: Palgrave Macmillan.

Banerjee, Abhijit V, and Ruimin He. 2008. "Making aid work." In *Reinventing foreign aid*, ed. William Easterly, 47–92. Cambridge, MA: MIT Press.

Baran, Charlie. 2016. "Tanzania will use its HIV grant extension to cover costs of ARVs through to the end of 2017." *Global Fund Observer Newsletter*, Aug. 17.

Barigaba, Julius. 2015. "Uganda leads push for permanent waiver on drug patents." *East African*, Nov. 9.

Barkan, Joel D. 2004. "Kenya after Moi." *Foreign Affairs* 83(1):87–100.

Barker, Carol, Malur R Bhagavan, Peter Von Collande, and David Wield. 1986. *African industrialisation: Technology and change in Tanzania*. Aldershot: Gower Press.

Barker, Carol, and David Wield. 1978. "Notes on international firms in Tanzania." *Utafiti* 3 (2):316–41.

Baronov, David. 2008. *The African transformation of western medicine and the dynamics of global cultural exchange*. Philadelphia: Temple Univ. Press.

BBC. 2012. "Making drugs into profit in Uganda," 9 Apr.

Beck, Ann. 1971. "The role of medicine in German East Africa." *Bulletin of the History of Medicine* 45(2):170–78.

Beck, Ann. 1981. *Medicine, tradition, and development in Kenya and Tanzania, 1920–1970*. Waltham: Crossroads Press.

Benson, John S. 2001. "The impact of privatization on access in Tanzania." *Social Science & Medicine* 52(12):1903–15.

Berger, M., J. Murugi, E. Buch, I. Jsselmuiden, C. M. Moran, J. Guzman, M. Devlin, and B. Kubata. 2010. Strengthening pharmaceutical innovation in Africa. Geneva and Midrand: Council on Health Research for Development (COHRED) and New Partnership for Africa's Development (NEPAD).

Bermeo, Sarah Blodgett. 2008. *Foreign aid, foreign policy, and strategic development*. Princeton: Princeton Univ. Press.

Bermeo, Sarah Blodgett. 2016. "Aid is not oil: Donor utility, heterogeneous aid, and the aid-democratization relationship." *International Organization* 70(1):1–32.

Bharati, Agehananda. 1972. *The Asians in East Africa: Jayhind and Uhuru*. Chicago: Nelson-Hall Co.

Biehl, João. 2008. "Drugs for all: The future of global AIDS treatment." *Medical Anthropology* 27(2):99–105.

Biggs, Tyler, Mayank Raturi, and Pradeep Srivastava. 1996. Enforcement of contracts in an African credit market: Working capital financing in Kenyan manufacturing (RPED Discussion Papers). Washington, DC: World Bank.

Bigsten, Arne, and Steve Kayizzi-Mugerwa. 2001. Is Uganda an emerging economy? A report for the OECD project "Emerging Africa" (Research Report No 118). Uppsala: Nordiska Afrikainstitutet.

BIO. 2007. Annual Report. Brussels: Belgian Investment Company for Developing Countries.

Birdsall, Nancy, William D Savedoff, Ayah Mahgoub, and Katherine Vyborny. 2012. *Cash on delivery: A new approach to foreign aid*. Washington, DC: Center for Global Development Books.

Bonacich, Edna. 1973. "A theory of middleman minorities." *American Sociological Review* 38(5):583–94.

Bornschier, Volker, Christopher Chase-Dunn, and Richard Rubinson. 1978. "Cross-national evidence of the effects of foreign investment and aid on economic growth and inequality: A survey of findings and a reanalysis." *American journal of Sociology* 84(3):651–83.

Bourguignon, François, and Mark Sundberg. 2007. "Aid effectiveness: Opening the black box." *American Economic Review* 97(2):316–21.

Bräutigam, Deborah. 2009. *The dragon's gift: The real story of China in Africa*. Oxford: Oxford Univ. Press.

Bräutigam, Deborah A, and Stephen Knack. 2004. "Foreign aid, institutions, and governance in sub-Saharan Africa." *Economic Development and Cultural Change* 52(2):255–85.

Brenner, Neil, and Nik Theodore. 2002. "Cities and the geographies of 'actually existing neoliberalism'." *Antipode* 34(3):349–79.

Brett, E. A. 1973. *Colonialism and underdevelopment in East Africa: The politics of economic change.* New York: NOK Publishers.

Brett, Edward, A 1996. "Structural adjustment, efficiency and equity in Uganda." In *Limits of adjustment in Africa: The effect of economic liberalisation, 1986–1994,* ed. Poul Engberg-Pedersen, Peter Gibbon, Philip Raikes, and Lars Udsholt, 324–25. Copenhagen: Centre for Development Research.

Breznitz, Dan. 2007. *Innovation and the state: Political choice and strategies for growth in Israel, Taiwan, and Ireland.* New Haven: Yale Univ. Press.

Breznitz, Dan, and Michael Murphree. 2011. *Run of the red queen: Government, innovation, globalization, and economic growth in China.* New Haven: Yale Univ. Press.

Brhlikova, Petra, Ian Harper, and Allyson Pollock. 2007. Good manufacturing practice in the pharmaceutical industry. Unpublished manuscript.

Briggs, Ryan C. 2017. "Does foreign aid target the poorest?" *International Organization* 71(1):187–206.

Bristol, Nellie. 2008. "NGO code of conduct hopes to stem internal brain drain." *Lancet* 371(9631):2162.

Broadman, Harry G. 2007. *Africa's silk road: China and India's new economic frontier.* Washington, DC: World Bank.

BroadReach Healthcare. 2011. Market analysis of public and private sector capacities to expand access to aubsidized ACTs in Kenya. Arlington: BroadReach Healthcare.

Bumpas, Janet, and Ekkehard Betsch. 2009. Exploratory study on active pharmaceutical ingredient manufacturing for essential medicines (Health, Nutrition and Population Discussion Paper). Washington, DC: World Bank.

Burnside, Craig, and David Dollar. 2000. "Aid, policies, and growth." *American Economic Review* 90(4):847–68.

Burt, Ronald S. 1992. *Structural holes: The social structure of competition.* Cambridge, MA: Harvard Univ. Press.

Byaruhanga, Frederick K. 2013. *Student power in Africa's higher education: A case of Makerere University.* New York and London: Routledge.

Cable, Vincent. 1969. "The Asians of Kenya." *African Affairs* 68(272):218–31.

Çakmaklı, Anıl Divarcı, Christophe Boone, and Arjen van Witteloostuijn. 2017. "When does globalization lead to local adaptation? The emergence of hybrid Islamic schools in Turkey, 1985–2007." *American Journal of Sociology* 122(6):1822–68.

Campbell, Horace, and Howard Stein. 1992. "Introduction: the dynamics of liberalization in Tanzania." In *Tanzania and the IMF: The dynamics of liberalization,* ed. Horace Campbell and Howard Stein, 1–20. Boulder: Westview Press.

Cardno. 2011. Implementation of the WTO decisions on TRIPS public health COMESA member states—Seminar series paper. Survey of pharmaceutical industry. London: Cardno Emerging Markets.

Cardoso, Fernando H. 1967. "The industrial elite." In *Elites in Latin America,* ed. Seymour Martin Lipset and Aldo Solari, 94–114. New York: Oxford Univ. Press.

Carpenter, Daniel. 2010. *Reputation and power: Organizational image and pharmaceutical regulation at the FDA.* Princeton: Princeton Univ. Press.

CCMCentral. 2013. Zinc/ORS scale-up in Kenya. Washington, DC: Integrated Community Case Management of Childhood Illness.

CEHURD. 2013. Promoting local pharmaceutical production in Uganda. Kampala: Center for Health, Human Rights and Development.

Center for Pharmaceutical Management. 2003. Access to essential medicines: Tanzania, 2001 (Report prepared for the Strategies for Enhancing Access to Medicines Program). Arlington: Management Sciences for Health.

Chachage, Chambi S. L. 1987. "The Arusha Declaration and developmentalism." *African Review* 14(1&2):103–115.

Chandler, Alfred D. 2005. *Shaping the industrial century: The remarkable story of the evolution of the modern chemical and pharmaceutical industries.* Cambridge, MA: Harvard Univ. Press.

Chang, Ha-Joon. 2002. *Kicking away the ladder: Development strategy in historical perspective.* London: Anthem Press.

Chaudhuri, Sudip. 2005. *The WTO and India's pharmaceuticals industry: Patent protection, TRIPS, and developing countries.* New Delhi: Oxford Univ. Press

Chaudhuri, Sudip. 2008. "Ranbaxy sell-out: reversal of fortunes." *Economic and Political Weekly,* , July 19, 11–13.

Chaudhuri, Sudip. 2013. "The pharmaceutical industry in India after TRIPS." In *The new political economy of pharmaceuticals,* ed. Hans Löfgren and Owain David Williams, 111–133. London: Springer.

Chaudhuri, Sudip, Maureen Mackintosh, and Phares G. M. Mujinja. 2010. "Indian generics producers, access to essential medicines and local production in Africa: An argument with reference to Tanzania." *European Journal of Development Research* 22(4):451–68.

Chaudhuri, Sudip, Chan Park, and K. M. Gopakumar. 2010. Five years into the product patent regime: India's response. New York: United Nations Development Programme.

Chemical & Engineering News. 2005. "The pharmaceutical golden era: 19301960." 83(25).

Chibber, Vivek. 2003. *Locked in place: State-building and late industrialization in India.* Princeton: Princeton Univ. Press.

Chibber, Vivek. 2005. "Reviving the developmental state? The myth of the 'national bourgeoisie.'" *Socialist Register* 226–46.

Chorev, Nitsan. 2012a. "Changing global norms through reactive diffusion: the case of intellectual property protection of AIDS drugs." *American Sociological Review* 77(5):831–53.

Chorev, Nitsan. 2012b. *The World Health Organization between north and south.* Ithaca: Cornell Univ. Press.

Chorev, Nitsan. 2015. "Narrowing the gaps in global disputes: The case of counterfeits in Kenya." *Studies in Comparative International Development* 50(2):157–86.

Chorev, Nitsan, Tatiana Andia, and David Ciplet. 2011. "The state of states in international organizations: From the WHO to the Global Fund." *Review* XXXIV (3):285–310.

Ciuri, Simon. 2015. "Siblings grow drugs firm into Sh1.5bn turnover enterprise." *Business Daily,* May 25.

Claessens, Stijn, Danny Cassimon, and Bjorn Van Campenhout. 2009. "Evidence on changes in aid allocation criteria." *World Bank Economic Review* 23(2):185–208.

Collier, Paul. 2007. *The bottom billion: Why the poorest countries are failing and what can be done about it.* New York: Oxford Univ. Press.

Comaroff, Jean. 1993. "The diseased heart of Africa." In *Knowledge, power and practice: The anthropology of medicine and everyday life,* ed. Shirley Lindenbaum and Margaret Lock, 305–29. Berkeley: Univ. of California Press.

Coulson, Andrew. 2013. *Tanzania: A political economy.* Oxford: Oxford Univ. Press.

Croke, Kevin. 2011. "Foreign aid, child health, and health system development in Tanzania and Uganda, 1995–2009." PhD diss, Johns Hopkins Univ., School of Advanced International Studies.

Cygnus. 2008. Top 200 pharma companies profile. Hyderabad: Cygnus Business Consulting & Research.

*Daily Nation.* 2015. "Pharmaceutical firm in Sh2bn expansion bid," Aug. 4.

*Daily Star.* 2018. "Square Pharmaceuticals begins constructing Kenya plant," Jan. 10.

Das, Sohini 2011. "Africa hot favourite among Gujarat pharma firms." *Business Standard*, Apr. 18.

Ddumba-Ssentamu, J, and Adam Mugume. 2001. The privatisation process and its impact on society: A report submitted to Uganda National NGO Forum (Secretariat, Kampala), Structural Adjustment Participatory Review Initiative (SAPRI). Kampala: Makerere University Institute of Economics.

Deaton, Angus. 2010. "Instruments, randomization, and learning about development." *Journal of Economic Literature* 48(2):424–55.

de Freytas-Tamura, Kimiko. 2017. "For dignity and development, East Africa curbs used clothes imports." *New York Times*, Oct. 12.

Delf, George. 1963. *Asians in East Africa.* Oxford: Oxford Univ. Press.

de Mesquita, Bruce Bueno, and Alastair Smith. 2009. "A political economy of aid." *International Organization* 63(2):309–40.

Deng, Rongling, and Kenneth I. Kaitin. 2004. "The regulation and approval of new drugs in China." *Drug Information Journal* 38(1):29–39.

Devarajan, Shantayanan, David Dollar, and Torgny Holmgren. 2001. *Aid and reform in Africa: Lessons from ten case studies*: Washington, DC: World Bank.

Dietrich, Simone. 2013. "Bypass or engage? Explaining donor delivery tactics in foreign aid allocation." *International Studies Quarterly* 57(4):698–712.

Dietrich, Simone. 2016. "Donor political economies and the pursuit of aid effectiveness." *International Organization* 70(1):65–102.

DND*i*. 2013. Annual Report. Geneva: Drugs for Neglected Diseases *initiative*.

Dodge, Cole P. 1986. "Uganda—rehabilitation, or redefinition of health services?" *Social Science & Medicine* 22(7):755–61.

Dorbian, Iris. 2016. Catalyst buys Tanzanian generic drugs maker Zenufa. Pe Hub Network, Oct. 10.

Dore, Ronald. 1986. *Flexible rigidities: Industrial policy and structural adjustment in the Japanese economy, 1970–1980.* London: Bloomsbury Academic.

Doucouliagos, Hristos, and Martin Paldam. 2011. "The ineffectiveness of development aid on growth: An update." *European Journal of Political Economy* 27(2):399–404.

Due, Jean M., Andrew E. Temu, and Anna A. Temu. 1999. Privatization in Tanzania: A case study. Unpublished manuscript.

Duflo, Esther, and Michael Kremer. 2008. "Use of randomization in the evaluation of development effectiveness." In *Reinventing foreign aid*, ed. William Easterly, 93–120. Cambridge, MA: MIT Press.

Dunning, Thad. 2004. "Conditioning the effects of aid: Cold War politics, donor credibility, and democracy in Africa." *International Organization* 58(2):409–23.

East African. 1999. "Kenya: Hard times hit pharmaceuticals manufacturers," July 19.

East African. 2008. "Mengi's ARV firm placed under receivership," Dec. 27.

East African. 2010. "Kenya misses out on AIDS funds," Feb. 12.

East African Court of Justice. 2015. Magezi vs. the Attorney General of the Republic of Uganda. In the East African Court of Justice First Instance Division at Arusha.

Easterly, William. 2006. *The white man's burden: Why the west's efforts to aid the rest have done so much ill and so little good.* Oxford: Oxford Univ. Press.

Easterly, William, ed. 2008. *Reinventing foreign aid.* Cambridge, MA: MIT Press.

Easterly, William. 2014. *Tyranny of experts.* New York: Basic Books

Easterly, William, Ross Levine, and David Roodman. 2004. "Aid, policies, and growth: Comment." *American Economic Review* 94(3):774–80.

Easterly, William, and Claudia R Williamson. 2011. "Rhetoric versus reality: The best and worst of aid agency practices." *World Development* 39(11):1930–49.

Economic Times. 2016. "Drug firm Strides acquires controlling stakes in Kenyan, Australian cos," Feb. 8.

Edwards, Sebastian. 2014. *Toxic aid: Economic collapse and recovery in Tanzania*. Oxford: Oxford Univ. Press.

Eglin, Richard. 1979. "The oligopolistic structure and competitive characteristics of direct foreign investment in Kenya's manufacturing sector." In *Readings on the multinational corporation in Kenya*, ed. Raphael Kaplinsky, 96–133. Nairobi: Oxford Univ. Press.

Elinaza, Abduel. 2013. "Tanzania: Indian firm to invest in Keko Pharmacy." *Tanzania Daily News*, Apr. 25.

Eberstadt, Nicholas. 1988. *Foreign aid and American purpose*. Washington, DC: American Enterprise Institute.

Epstein, Helen. 2015. "The strange politics of saving the children." *New York Review of Books*, Nov. 5.

Escobar, Arturo. 1995. *Encountering development: The making and unmaking of the Third World*. Princeton: Princeton Univ. Press.

Evans, Peter B. 1976. "Foreign investment and industrial transformation: A Brazilian case study." *Journal of Development Economics* 3(2):119–39.

Evans, Peter B. 1979. *Dependent development: The alliance of multinational, state, and local capital in Brazil*. Princeton: Princeton Univ. Press.

Evans, Peter B. 1995. *Embedded autonomy: States and industrial transformation*. Princeton: Princeton Univ. Press.

Evans, Peter, and William H Sewell. 2013. "The neoliberal era: Ideology, policy, and social effects." In *Social resilience in the neoliberal era*, ed. Peter A Hall and Michèle Lamont, 35–68, New York: Cambridge Univ. Press.

Evans-Pritchard, Ambrose 2004. "Tories face more scandal over MEP's travel expenses." *Telegraph*, May 11.

Ewen, M., W. Kaplan, T. Gedif, M. Justin-Temu, C. Vialle-Valentin, Z. Mirza, B. Regeer, M. Zweekhorst, and R. Laing. 2017. "Prices and availability of locally produced and imported medicines in Ethiopia and Tanzania." *Journal of Pharmaceutical Policy and Practice* 10(1):7.

Fafchamps, Marcel. 2000. "Ethnicity and credit in African manufacturing." *Journal of Development Economics* 61(1):205–35.

Fafchamps, Marcel, Tyler Biggs, Jonathan Conning, and Pradeep Srivastava. 1994. Enterprise finance in Kenya. Washington, DC: World Bank, Regional Program on Enterprise Development, Africa Region.

Fahnbulleh, Miatta. 2006. "In search of economic development in Kenya: Colonial legacies & postindependence realities." *Review of African Political Economy* 33(107):33–47.

FEAPM. 2012. Yearbook. Arusha: Federation of East African Pharmaceutical Manufacturers.

Ferguson, Douglas E. 1980. "The political economy of health and medicine in colonial Tanganyika." In *Tanzania under colonial rule*, ed. Martin H. Y. Kaniki, 307–43. London: Longman.

Ferguson, James. 1990. *The anti-politics machine: 'Development,' depoliticization and bureaucratic power in Lesotho*. Minneapolis: Univ. of Minnesota Press.

Ferrand, David Vaughan. 1999. "Discontinuity in development: Kenya's middle-scale manufacturing industry." PhD thesis, Univ. of Durham.

Festel, Gunter, Andreas Kreimeyer, Udo Oels, and Maximilian von Zedtwitz, eds. 2005. *The chemical and pharmaceutical industry in China: Opportunities and threats for foreign companies*. Berlin: Springer.

Finkel, Steven E, Aníbal Pérez-Liñán, and Mitchell A Seligson. 2007. "The effects of US foreign assistance on democracy building, 1990–2003." *World Politics* 59(3):404–39.

FinnFund. 2009. Additional financing granted to Kenyan-Finnish drug maker. Helsinki: FinnFund.

FinnFund. 2012. WHO approves AIDS drug made by Finnish-Kenyan company. Helsinki: FinnFund.

FinnFund. 2016. Drug producer sets an example for others in Africa. Helsinki: FinnFund.

Fischer, Christiane, Claudia Jenkes, and Denis Kibira. 2014. "Poor and forgotten: Examination of the business behavior of Boehringer Ingelheim, Bayer and Baxter in Uganda." In *Pharma-Brief Special*. Bielefeld: BUKO Pharma-Kampagne.

Foster, Susan D. 1986. Some issues relating to domestic production of pharmaceuticals in developing countries. Geneva: World Health Organization, Action Programme on Essential Drugs.

Foster, Susan D. 1999. Drug production in low- and middle-income countries: An issues paper. Boston: Boston Univ., School of Public Health, Dept. of International Health.

Fourcade, Marion, and Sarah L Babb. 2002. "The rebirth of the liberal creed: Paths to neoliberalism in four countries." *American Journal of Sociology* 108(3):533–79.

Frank, Charles R, and Mary Baird. 1975. "Foreign aid: Its speckled past and future prospects." *International Organization* 29(1):133–67.

Freeman, Charles, and Xiaoqing Boynton. 2011. *China's emerging global health and foreign aid engagement in Africa*. Washington, DC: Center for Strategic & International Studies.

Frieden, Jeffry. 2006. *Global capitalism: Its fall and rise in the twentieth century*. New York: W.W. Norton.

Friedmann, Harriet. 1982. "The political economy of food: The rise and fall of the postwar international food order." *American Journal of Sociology* 88:S248–86.

Frontani, Heidi 2015. "Success story from Tanzania: Reginald Mengi supports corproate responsibility." *WorldPress.com*.

Gachino, Geoffrey. 2009. "Industrial policy, institutions and foreign direct investment: The Kenyan context." *African Journal of Marketing Management* 1(6):140–60.

Gereffi, Gary. 1983. *The pharmaceutical industry and dependency in the third world*. Princeton: Princeton Univ. Press.

Gereffi, Gary, and Olga Memedovic. 2003. *The global apparel value chain: What prospects for upgrading by developing countries*. Vienna: United Nations Industrial Development Organization.

Gettleman, Jeffrey. 2015. "Meant to keep malaria out, mosquito nets are used to haul fish in." *New York Times*, Jan. 24.

Ghai, Yash P., and Dharam P. Ghai. 1971. *The Asian minorities of East and Central Africa (up to 1971), vol. 4*. London: Minority Rights Group.

Global Fund. 2012a. Guide to Global Fund policies on procurement and supply management of health products. Geneva: Global Fund.

Global Fund. 2012b. Audit of Global Fund grants to the Republic of Kenya. Geneva: Global Fund.

Global Fund. 2012c. Review of audit of Global Fund grants to the Republic of Kenya. The Office of the Inspector General. Geneva: Global Fund.

Global Fund. 2017. Guide to Global Fund policies on procurement and supply management of health products. Geneva: Global Fund.

Goh, Nancy, and Katherine Pollak. 2016. Progress over a decade of Zinc and ORS scale-up. Diarrhea & Pneumonia Working Group.

Goldsmith, Arthur A. 2003. "Foreign aid and state administrative capability in Africa." In *Beyond structural adjustment: The institutional context of African development*, ed. Nicolas van de Walle, Nicole Ball, and Vijaya Ramachandran, 183–211. New York: Springer.

Goldthorpe, John Ernest. 1965. *An African elite: Makerere College students 1922—1960*. Nairobi: Oxford Univ. Press/East African Institute of Social Research.

Gomanee, Karuna, Oliver Morrissey, Paul Mosley, and Arjan Verschoor. 2005. "Aid, government expenditure, and aggregate welfare." *World Development* 33(3):355–70.

Gopalan, Sasidaran, and Ramkishen S. Rajan. 2016. "Has foreign aid been effective in the water supply and sanitation sector? Evidence from panel data." *World Development* 85(C):84–104.

Governance. 2011. Governance assessment of the public sector drug management system: Uganda. Basel: Basel Institute on Governance.

Grace, Cheri. 2004. The effect of changing intellectual property on pharmaceutical industry prospects in India and China. London: DFID Health Systems Resource Centre.

Granovetter, Mark. 1995. "The economic sociology of firms and entrepreneurs." In *The economic sociology of immigration: Essays on networks, ethnicity, and entrepreneurship*, ed. Alejandro Portes. New York: Russell Sage.

Greene, Jeremy A. 2015. "Vital objects: Essential drugs and their critical legacies." In *Reimagining (bio)medicalization, pharmaceuticals and genetics: Old critiques and new engagements*, ed. Susan E. Bell and Anne E. Figert, 89–111. New York: Routledge.

Greene, William. 2007. The emergence of India's pharmaceutical industry and implications for the US generic drug market (Office of Economics Working Paper). Washington, DC: US International Trade Commission.

Gregory, Robert G. 1993. *South Asians in East Africa: An economic and social history, 1890- 1980*. Boulder: Westview Press.

Grindle, Merilee S. 2004. "Good enough governance: Poverty reduction and reform in developing countries." *Governance* 17(4):525–48.

Grosh, Barbara. 1991. *Public enterprise in Kenya: What works, what doesn't, and why*. Boulder: Lynne Rienner.

Grover, Dhruv, Sebastian Bauhoff, and Jed Friedman. 2018. "Using supervised learning to select audit targets in performance-based financing in health: An example from Zambia." (Working Paper 481). Washington, DC: Center for Global Development.

GTZ. 2009. Study on the feasibility of conducting bioequivalence studies in East Africa. Eschborn: German Technical Cooperation Agency.

Guimier, Jean-Marc, Evan Lee, and Michel Grupper. 2004. Processes and issues for improving access to medicines: The evidence base for domestic production and greater access to medicines. London: DFID Health System Resource Centre.

Gyezaho, Emmanuel 2011. "Wikileaks: China gave Uganda uncertified malaria drugs." *Daily Monitor*, Sept. 13.

Haak, Hilbrand, and Hans V Hogerzeil. 1991. Drug supply by ration kits: Report of an evaluation. Geneva: World Heatlh Organization, Action Programme on Essential Drugs.

Haak, Hilbrand, and Hans V Hogerzeil. 1995. "Essential drugs for ration kits in developing countries." *Health Policy and Planning* 10(1):40–49.

Haakonsson, Stine Jessen. 2009a. "The changing governance structures of the global pharmaceutical value chain." *Competition & Change* 13(1):75–95.

Haakonsson, Stine Jessen. 2009b. "'Learning by importing' in global value chains: Upgrading and south–south strategies in the Ugandan pharmaceutical industry." *Development Southern Africa* 26(3):499–516.

Häfele-Abah, Christine. 2010. "Improving access to high-quality low-cost essential medicines in Tanzania—assessing an NGO's contribution." Master's thesis, , Heidelberg Univ., Dept. of Tropical Hygiene and Public Health.

Hanley, Eric, Lawrence King, and István Tóth János. 2002. "The state, international agencies, and property transformation in postcommunist Hungary." *American Journal of Sociology* 108(1):129–67.

Harris, Gardiner. 2014. "Medicines made in India set off safety worries." *New York Times*, Feb. 14.

Herbert, Bob. 2001. "In America; Refusing to save Africans." *New York Times*, June 11.

Hermann, Rachel M. 2013. "East African Community doubles efforts to boost local drug production." *Intellectual Property Watch*, Mar. 28.

Hillmann, Henning. 2013. "Economic institutions and the state: Insights from economic history." *Annual Review of Sociology* 39:251–73.

Himbara, David. 1994. "The failed Africanization of commerce and industry in Kenya." *World Development* 22(3):469–482.

Hirschman, Albert O. 1968. "The political economy of import-substituting industrialization in Latin America." *Quarterly Journal of Economics* 82(1):1–32.

Honey, Martha. 1974. "Asian industrial activities in Tanganyika." *Tanzania Notes and Records* 75:55–69.

Hook, Steven W. 1995. *National interest and foreign aid*. Boulder: Lynne Rienner.

Hopcraft, Peter. 1979. Industrialization, balance of payments, and trade policy in Kenya: The effects of protectionism and government intervention on prices, exports, and income distribution. Nairobi: Univ. of Nairobi, Institute for Development Studies.

Hope, Kempe Ronald. 2011. *The political economy of development in Kenya*. New York: Bloomsbury Publishing.

Hopkins, Raymond F. 1971. *Political roles in a new state: Tanzania's first decade*. New Haven: Yale Univ. Press.

Horner, Rory. 2013. "Strategic decoupling, recoupling and global production networks: India's pharmaceutical industry." *Journal of Economic Geography* 14(6):1117–40.

Hossain, Amjad 2018. "Square Pharmaceuticals to initially invest $25m in Kenya." *Dhaka Tribune*, Jan. 10.

Hout, Wil. 2002. "Good governance and aid: Selectivity criteria in development assistance." *Development and Change* 33(3):511–27.

Huang, Yanzhong. 2013. Enter the dragon and the elephant: China's and India's participation in global health governance. New York: Council on Foreign Relations.

Hutchinson, Paul. 2001. "Combatting illness." In *Uganda's recovery: The role of farms, firms, and government* ed. Ritva Reinikka and Paul Collier, 407–50. Washington, DC: World Bank.

IFC. 2007. The business of health in Africa: Partnering with the private sector to improve people's lives. Washington, DC: International Finance Corporation.

Ikiara, Gerrishon K. 1995. "Kenya." In *Exporting Africa: Technology, industrialism and trade*, ed. Samuel M. Wangwe, 296–343. London: Routledge.

Iliffe, John. 1998. *East African doctors: A history of the modern profession*. Cambridge, UK: Cambridge Univ. Press.

Ingram, Paul, and Peter W. Roberts. 2000. "Friendships among competitors in the Sydney hotel industry." *American Journal of Sociology* 106(2):387–423.

IRIN News. 2012. "Tanzania: New pharmaceutical plant to produce ARVs." *IRIN News*, Mar. 6.

IRIN News. 2013. "Uganda government under pressure to boost ARV funding." *IRIN News*, Mar.14.

Jennings, Michael. 2015. "The precariousness of the franchise state: voluntary sector health services and international NGOs in Tanzania, 1960s–mid-1980s." *Social Science & Medicine* 141:1–8.

Johnson, Michael, Oliver Hazemba, Janet Kimeu, Rosalind Kirika, and Michael Thuo. 2008. Assessment of Kenya Medical Supplies Agency (KEMSA). Nairobi: Management Sciences for Health/Strengthening Pharmaceutical Systems Program Regional Office.

Jonsson, Urban. 1986. "Ideological framework and health development in Tanzania 1961–2000." *Social Science & Medicine* 22(7):745–53.

Jørgensen, Jan Jelmert. 1981. *Uganda: A modern history*. New York: St. Martin's Press.

Joseph, Reji K. 2009. India's trade in drugs and pharmaceuticals: Emerging trends, opportunities and challenges. New Delhi: Research and Information System for Developing Countries.

Jouet, Josiane. 1984. "Advertising and transnational corporations in Kenya." *Development and Change* 15(3):435–56.

Juma, Victor. 2011. "Drug maker in Sh1bn expansion drive." *Business Daily*, July 11.

Kaaya, Sadab Kitatta 2014. "Uganda: Closed drug company sues for Shs 2.4 billion." *Observer*, 8 June.

Kafeero, Stephen. 2013. "Uganda: Who was swindling Global Fund money?" *Independent*, 5 July.

Kajubi, Senteza. 1985. "Integration and national development from the viewpoint of education in Uganda." In *Crisis in Uganda: The breakdown of health services*, ed. Cole P. Dodge and Paul D. Wiebe, 15–24. Oxford: Pergamon Press.

Kakamwa, Charles. 2010. "Uganda: Jinja drugs factory closes." *New Vision*, 6 Jan.

Kalyango, Ronald. 2006. "Uganda: KPI builds Sh182bn laboratory." *New Vision*, 30 Mar.

Kanji, Najmi, Gaspar Munishi, and Goran Sterky. 1989. An evaluation of WHO's Action Programme on Essential Drugs. Tanzania country case study submitted to AEPD management advisory committee. London and Amsterdam: London School of Hygiene and Tropical Medicine and the Royal Tropical Institute.

Kapczynski, Amy. 2009. "Harmonization and its discontents: A case study of TRIPS implementation in India's pharmaceutical sector." *California Law Review* 97(6):1571–1649.

Kaplan, Warren, and Richard Laing. 2005. "Local production of pharmaceuticals: Industrial policy and access to medicines" (World Bank Health, Nutrition, and Population Discussion Paper). Washington, DC: World Bank.

Kaplan, Warren, and Colin Mathers. 2011. Global health trends: Global burden of disease and pharmaceutical needs. Geneva: World Health Organization.

Kaplinsky, Raphael. 1979a. *Readings on the multinational corporation in Kenya*. New York: Oxford Univ. Press.

Kaplinsky, Raphael. 1979b. "Technical change and the multinational corporation: Some British multinationals in Kenya." In *Readings on the multinational corporation in Kenya*, ed. Raphael Kaplinsky, 201–260. Nairobi: Oxford Univ. Press.

Kaplinsky, Rafael. 1980. "Capitalist accumulation in the periphery—the Kenyan case re-examined." *Review of African Political Economy* 7(17):83–105.

Kasujja, Carol 2016. "NDA gets new boss." *New Vision*, Dec. 25.

Kazmin, Amy. 2015. "Indian drugs: Not what the doctor ordered." *Financial Times*, Sept. 9.

Kenyunko, Karama. 2014. "Madabida, five others in court over fake drugs." *Guardian*, 11 Feb.

Kevlihan, Rob, Karl DeRouen, Jr., and Glen Biglaiser. 2014. "Is US humanitarian aid based primarily on need or self-interest?" *International Studies Quarterly* 58(4):839–54.

Khisa, Isaac. 2015. "Uganda: Balancing trade—Uganda, Kenya sign bilateral framework on health, medicines." *East African*, 15 Aug.

Kibikyo, David Lameck. 2008. "Assessing privatization in Uganda." PhD diss, Roskilde Univ., Graduate School of International Development Studies.

Kilonzo, Eunice. 2015. "Kenya: USAID, KEMSA in Sh65bn medical supplies deal." *Nation*, 9 Nov.

Kimani, Dagi. 2003. "Nairobi firm ready to make generics." *AllAfrica*, 15 Sept.

Kimani, Dagi. 2006. "Roche gives Kenyan firms right for AIDS Drug." *East African*, Oct. 23.

Klissas, Nicholas, Charles Schwartz, Wade Channell, and Nathan Kline. 2010. Health Climate Legal and Institutional Reform (HealthCLIR) assessment: Uganda. Washington, DC: US Agency for International Development (USAID).

Kohli, Atul. 2004. *State-directed development: Political power and industrialization in the global periphery*. Cambridge, UK: Cambridge Univ. Press.

Kosack, Stephen. 2003. "Effective aid: How democracy allows development aid to improve the quality of life." *World Development* 31(1):1–22.

Kosack, Stephen, and Jennifer Tobin. 2006. "Funding self-sustaining development: The role of aid, FDI and government in economic success." *International Organization* 60(1):205–43.

Krasner, Stephen D. 1999. *Sovereignty: Organized hypocrisy*. Princeton: Princeton Univ. Press.

Krasner, Stephen D., and Jeremy M. Weinstein. 2014. "Improving governance from the outside in." *Annual Review of Political Science* 17:123–45.

Kukunda, Charlotte. 2001. "Uganda: Drugs firm seeks help." *New Vision*, 30 June.

Kwon, Seok-Woo, Colleen Heflin, and Martin Ruef. 2013. "Community social capital and entrepreneurship." *American Sociological Review* 78(6):980–1008.

Lakoff, Andrew. 2017. *Unprepared: Global health in a time of emergency*. Oakland: Univ. of California Press.

Lall, Sanjaya. 1978. *The growth of the pharmaceutical industry in developing countries: Problems and prospects*. Vienna: UN Industrial Development Organization.

Lall, Sanjaya. 1992. "Structural problems of African industry." In *Alternative development strategies in subSaharan Africa*, ed. Frances Stewart, Sanjaya Lall, and Samuel M. Wangwe, 103–44. London: Springer.

Lall, Sanjaya, and Carlo Pietrobell. 2002. *Failing to compete*. Cheltenham: Edward Elgar.

Lancaster, Carol. 2007. *Foreign aid: Diplomacy, development, domestic politics*. Chicago: Univ. of Chicago Press.

Lee, Suejin A., and Jae-Young Lim. 2014. "Does international health aid follow recipients' needs? Extensive and intensive margins of health aid allocation." *World Development* 64(C): 104–120.

Leys, Colin. 1978. "Capital accumulation, class formation and dependency—The significance of the Kenyan case." *Socialist Register* 15(15):241–66.

Leys, Colin. 1980. "Kenya: What does 'dependency' explain?" *Review of African Political Economy* 7(17):108–13.

Li, Tania M. 2007. *The will to improve: Governmentality, development, and the practice of politics*. Durham: Duke Univ. Press.

Lifesaver, The. 2011. The Kenya National Medicines Information and Pharmacovigilance Centre Newsletter. Nairobi: Pharmacy and Poisons Board.

Ligami, Christabel. 2012. "Kenyan firm to manufacture 4 million ARV tablets." *East African*, Feb. 18.

Light, Donald W., Joel Lexchin, and Jonathan J. Darrow. 2013. "Institutional corruption of pharmaceuticals and the myth of safe and effective drugs." *Journal of Law, Medicine and Ethics* 14(3):590–610.

Liu, Chenglin. 2012. "Leaving the FDA behind: Pharmaceutical outsourcing and drug safety." *Texas International Law Journal* 48:1–32.

Livingstone, Ian. 1998. "Developing industry in Uganda in the 1990s." In *Developing Uganda*, ed. Holger Bernt Hansen and Michael Twaddle, 38–58. Nairobi: East African Educational Publishers.

Lofchie, Michael F. 2014. *The political economy of Tanzania: Decline and recovery*. Philadelphia: Univ. of Pennsylvania Press.

Löfgren, Hans, and Owain David Williams, eds. 2013. *The new political economy of pharmaceuticals: Production, innovation and TRIPS in the global South*. London: Springer.

Losse, Karen, Eva Schneider, and Cristoph Spennemann. 2007. The viability of local pharmaceutical production in Tanzania. Eschborn: German Technical Cooperation Agency.

Lubwama, Siraje. 2012. "NDA tightens drug regulation." *Observer*, July 8.

Luoma, Marc, Julie Doherty, Stephen Muchiri, Tiberius Barasa, Kate Hofler, Lisa Maniscalco, Charles Ouma, Rosalind Kirika, and Josephine Maundu. 2010. Kenya health system assessment 2010. Bethesda: Health Systems 20/20 project.

Mackintosh, Maureen, Geoffrey Banda, Watu Wamae, and Paula Tibandebage. 2016. *Making medicines in Africa: The political economy of industrializing for local health*. London: Palgrave Macmillan.

Mackintosh, Maureen, and Phares G. M. Mujinja. 2008. "Pricing and competition in essential medicines markets: The supply chain to Tanzania and the role of NGOs." Innovation, Knowledge and Development Working Paper 32.

Macrae, Joanna, Anthony B. Zwi, and Lucy Gilson. 1996. "A triple burden for health sector reform: 'Post'-conflict rehabilitation in Uganda." *Social Science & Medicine* 42(7):1095–1108.

Mamdani, Mahmood. 1976. *Politics and class formation in Uganda.* New York: Monthly Review Press.

Mamdani, Mahmood. 1983. Imperialism and fascism in Uganda. Nairobi: Heinemann Educational Books.

Mamdani, Masuma. 1992. "Early initiatives in essential drugs policy." In *Drugs policy in developing countries*, ed. Najmi Kanji, Anita Hardon, Jan Willen Harnmeijer, Masuma Mamdani, and Gill Walt. London: Zed Books.

Mans, Darius 2002. "Tanzania: Resolute action." In *Adjustment in Africa: Lessons from country case studies*, ed. Ishrat Husain and Rashid Faruqee, 352–426. Washington, DC: World Bank.

Matsuzawa, Setsuko. 2016. "A donor influenced by local dynamics." *Sociology of Development* 2(1):51–69.

Mbabazi, Pamela , and Gladys Mokhawa. 2005. "The developmental state and manufacturing in Botswana and Uganda." In *The potentiality of 'developmental states' in Africa: Botswana and Uganda compared*, ed. Pamela Mbabazi and Ian Taylor, 133–46. Senegal: Council for the Development of Social Science Research in Africa.

Mbilinyi, Marjorie J. 1979. "African education during the British colonial rule 1919–1961." In *Tanzania under colonial rule*, ed. Martin H. Y. Kaniki, 86–127. Boston: Addison-Wesley Longman.

McDonnell, Erin Metz. 2017. "Patchwork Leviathan: How pockets of bureaucratic governance flourish within institutionally diverse developing states." *American Sociological Review* 82(3):476–510.

*Medical Journal of Therapeutics Africa.* 2009. "Pharmaceutical manufacturing in Kenya." 3(2):59.

Mehri, Darius Bozorg. 2015. "The role of engineering consultancies as network-centred actors to develop indigenous, technical capacity: The case of Iran's automotive industry." *Socio-Economic Review* 13(4):747–69.

Melrose, Dianna. 1983. "Double deprivation: Public and private drug distribution from the perspective of the Third World poor." *World development* 11(3):181–86.

Meyer, John W., and Brian Rowan. 1977. "Institutionalized organizations: Formal structure as myth and ceremony." *American Journal of Sociology* 83(2):340–63.

Mhamba, Robert M, and Shukrani Mbirigenda. 2010. The pharmaceutical industry and access to essential medicines in Tanzania. Equinet Discussion Paper 83. Harare: Training and Research Support Centre.

Mkony, Charles A. 2012. "Emergence of a university of health sciences: Health professions education in Tanzania." *Journal of Public Health Policy* 33 (1):S45-S63.

Mkumbwa, Sonia Henry. 2013. "Challenges of medicines registration process in Tanzania." MSc. pharmaceutical management diss., Muhimbili University of Health and Allied Sciences.

MMS. 2010. Kenya pharmaceutical country profile. Nairobi: Ministry of Medical Services.

MMS and MPHS. 2009. Access to essential medicines in Kenya: A health facility survey. Kenya: Ministry of Medical Services and Ministry of Public Health and Sanitation.

MMS and MPHS. 2010. Sessional paper on national pharmaceutical policy. Kenya: Ministry of Medical Services and Ministry of Public Health and Sanitation.

Mnookin, Robert H., and Lewis Kornhauser. 1979. "Bargaining in the shadow of the law: The case of divorce." *Yale Law Journal* 88(5):950–97.

MoH Kenya. 2003. Assessment of the pharmaceutical situation in Kenya: A baseline survey. Kenya: Ministry of Health.

MoH Tanzania. 1990. National health policy. Tanzania: Ministry of Health.

MoH Uganda. 2002. National pharmaceutical sector strategic plan 2002/3–2006/7. Uganda: Ministry of Health.

MoH Uganda. 2011a. Uganda pharmaceutical country profile. Uganda: Ministry of Health.

MoH Uganda. 2011b. Status report on the Global Fund grants in Uganda. Uganda: Ministry of Health.

Mohamed, Nazeem. 2009. "The role of local manufacturers in improving access to essential medicines." *Africa Health* 32(1):40–42.

Mohan, Giles, and Marcus Power. 2008. "New African choices? The politics of Chinese engagement." *Review of African Political Economy* 35(115):23–42.

MOHSW. 2009. Assessment of the pharmaceutical human resources in Tanzania and the Strategic Framework. Tanzania: Ministry of Health and Social Welfare.

MOHSW. 2011. Situational analysis report of the domestic production of medicines in paediatric dosage forms in Tanzania. Tanzania: Ministry of Health and Social Welfare.

MoI, MMS and UNIDO. 2011. Strengthening the production of essential generic medicines in Kenya (Draft Kenya pharmaceutical sector development strategy). Kenya: Ministry of Industrialization and Ministry of Medical Services and the UN Industrial Development Organization.

Moore, Gerald D. 1982. "Essential drugs for Kenya's rural population." *World Health Forum* 3(2):196–99.

Moran, Theodore H. 2006. *Harnessing foreign direct investment for development: Policies for developed and developing countries.* Washington, DC: Center for Global Development.

Morgan, Kimberly J., and Ann Shola Orloff. 2017. *The many hands of the state: Theorizing political authority and social control.* Cambridge, UK: Cambridge University Press.

Mosley, Paul, John Hudson, and Arjan Verschoor. 2004. "Aid, poverty reduction and the 'new conditionality'." *Economic Journal* 114(496): F217-F243.

Moss, Todd , Gunilla Pettersson, and Nicolas van de Walle. 2008. "An aid-institutions paradox? A review essay on aid dependency and state building in Sub-Saharan Africa." In *Reinventing foreign aid*, ed. William Easterly. Cambridge, MA: MIT Press.

MOTI. 2014. "Rwanda and Uganda agreed on a bilateral cooperation in pharmaceutical industry." Rwanda: Ministry of Trade and Industry.

Muchangi, John. 2011. "ARVs to cost 30% less as WHO clears manufacturer." *Nairobi Star*, Nov. 2.

Mugarula, Florence. 2013. "Government clears Arusha firm in ARVs scam." *Citizen*, May 13.

Mugunga, Jim. 2016. "Tackling questions on privatized companies." *New Vision*, Mar. 18.

Mujinja, Phares G. M., Maureen Mackintosh, Mary Justin-Temu, and Marc Wuyts. 2014. "Local production of pharmaceuticals in Africa and access to essential medicines: 'Urban bias' in access to imported medicines in Tanzania and its policy implications." *Globalization and Health* 10(1):12.

Mukisa, Lydia. 2005. "Uganda: Buteera withdraws case against National Drug Authority bosses." *The Monitor,* 8 Apr.

Mulupi, Dinfin. 2014a. "Meet the boss: Ajay Patel, MD, Dawa Limited." *Howwemadeitinafrica.com,* 31 Oct.

Mulupi, Dinfin. 2014b. "Made in Kenya: Pharmaceutical firm has pan-African ambitions." *Howwemadeitinafrica.com,* 4 Nov.

Mutegi, Mugambi. 2011a. "Local drug maker takes a shot at global market." *Business Daily,* 26 Sept.

Mutegi, Mugambi. 2011b. "Kenyan firm wins entry into global drug market." *Business Daily,* Oct. 27.

Muwanga, David. 2002. "NEC seek new joint ventures." *New Vision,* Nov. 3.

Mwase, N., and Benno J. Ndulu. 2008. "Tanzania: Explaining four decades of episodic growth." In *The political economy of economic growth in Africa, 1960–2000*, ed. Benno J. Ndulu, Stephen A. O'Connell, Jean-Paul Azam, Jan Willem Gunning, and Dominque Njinkeu, 426–70. Cambridge, UK: Cambridge Univ. Press.

Mwega, Francis M., and Njuguna S. Ndung'u. 2008. "Explaining African economic growth performance: The case of Kenya." In *The political economy of economic growth in Africa, 1960–2000*, ed. Benno J. Ndulu, Stephen A. O'Connell, Jean-Paul Azam, Robert H. Bates, Augustin K. Fosu, Jan Willem Gunning, and Dominque Njinkeu, 325–68. Cambridge, UK: Cambridge Univ. Press.

Mwilongo, Sophia Josephat. 2011. "Challenges perceived by local pharmaceutical manufacturers that hinder adequate production of essential medicines in Tanzania." Master's thesis, Muhimbili Univ. of Health and Allied Sciences, Dar es Salaam.

Mwiti, Lee. 2016. "Kenyan firm buys Tanzanian drugs manufacturer." *The Standard,* Oct. 11.

NACC and NASCOP. 2012. Kenya AIDS epidemic update 2011. Nairobi: National AIDS Control Council and National AIDS and STI Control Programme.

Nagar, Richa. 1996. "The South Asian diaspora in Tanzania: A history retold." *Comparative Studies of South Asia, Africa and the Middle East* 16(2):62–80.

Nairobi Business Monthly. 2015. "Dawa Limited acquires KEL Chemicals," 10 Nov.

Nakaweesi, Dorothy 2016. " 'Our pricing is transparent.' " *Daily Monitor,* 6 Sept.

Narlikar, Amrita. 2010. "India's rise to power: Where does East Africa fit in?" *Review of African Political Economy* 37(126):451–64.

Nassaka, Flavia. 2016. "Uganda: NMS, Cipla bickering over expensive HIV/AIDS drugs." *Independent,* 25 Oct.

Naturinda, Sheila, and Yasiin Mugerwa. 2011. "Minister sacks NDA board." *Daily Monitor,* July 20.

Ndulu, Benno J, and Joseph J Semboja. 1995. "The development of manufacturing for export in Tanzania: Experience, policy and prospects." In *Manufacturing for export in the developing world,* ed. G. K. Helleier, 167–210. London: Routledge.

Nee, Victor, and Sonja Opper. 2012. *Capitalism from below: Markets and institutional change in China.* Cambridge, MA: Harvard Univ. Press.

Nossiter, Adam. 2014. "Fear of Ebola breeds a terror of physicians." *New York Times,* July 27.

Nyanje, Peter. 2017. "Shock as CCM expels ex-minister, 11 strong cadres." *Citizen,* Mar. 12.

Nyong'o, P. Anyang'. 1988. "The possibilities and historical limitations of import-substitution industrialization in Kenya." In *Industrialization in Kenya: In search of a strategy,* ed. Peter Coughlin and Gerrishon K Ikiara, 6–50. Nairobi: Heinemann Kenya.

Observer, The. 2009. "Pharmaceutical dealers fighting over business," Dec. 10.

Obwona, Marios, Isaac Shinyekwa, Julius Kiiza, and Eria Hisali. 2014. The evolution of industry in Uganda. (*Learning to Compete. Working Paper 9*). Washington, DC: Brookings Institution.

Ody-Brasier, Amandine, and Isabel Fernandez-Mateo. 2017. "When being in the minority pays off: Relationships among sellers and price setting in the champagne industry." *American Sociological Review* 82(1):147–78.

Okuku, Juma A. 2006. "Informing industrial policy in Uganda: Interaction between institutions, technology and market reforms." PhD diss, Univ. of Witwatersrand.

Okwembe, Arthur. 2004. "Kenya now producing AIDS drugs." *Daily Nation,* Apr. 1.

Oonk, Gijsbert. 2006. "South Asians in East Africa (1880–1920) with a particular focus on Zanzibar: Toward a historical explanation of economic success of a middlemen minority." *African and Asian Studies* 5(1):57–90.

ÓRiain, Seán. 2004a. *The politics of high tech growth: Developmental network states in the global economy.* Cambridge, UK: Cambridge Univ. Press.

ÓRiain, Seán. 2004b. "The politics of mobility in technology-driven commodity chains: Developmental coalitions in the Irish software industry." *International Journal of Urban and Regional Research* 28(3):642–63.

Orubuloye, I. O., and O. Y. Oyeneye. 1982. "Primary health care in developing countries: The case of Nigeria, Sri Lanka and Tanzania." *Social Science & Medicine* 16(6):675–86.

Osewe, Patrick L., Yvonne K. Nkrumah, and Emmanuel K. Sackey. 2008. *Improving access to HIV/AIDS medicines in Africa: Trade-Related Aspects of Intellectual Property Rights (TRIPS) flexibilities utilization.* Washington, DC: World Bank.

Otieno, Jeff. 2011. "Grant to boost lucrative drug market." *East African*, Nov. 13.

Owino, Pius S. W. 1985. "The pharmaceutical industry in Kenya." Master's thesis, Univ. of Nairobi.

Owino, Pius W. 1991. "The pharmaceutical industry: Excess capacity, missed opportunities, and planning failures." In *Kenya's industrialization dilemma*, ed. Peter Coughlin and Grrishonn K Ikiara, 57–76. Nairobi: Heinemann Kenya.

Packard, Randall M. 2016. *A history of global health: Interventions into the lives of other peoples.* Baltimore: Johns Hopkins Univ. Press.

Parliament of Uganda. 2015. The report of the Committee on Defence and Internal Affairs.

Patel, Surendra J. 1983. "Editor's introduction." *World Development* 11(3):165–67.

PATH. 1992a. Marketing assistance to Medipharm: Technologies for Primary Health Care Project. Washington, DC: US Agency for International Development?

PATH. 1992b. Quarterly and final report: Follow-on technical assistance to Medipharm Industries, Ltd. Washington, DC: US Agency for International Development.

PATH. 1992c. Technical production assistance visit to Medipharm Industries. Washington, DC: US Agency for International Development.

Patwardhan, Nandini 2007. "India on African safari." *Express Pharma*, June 16–30.

Pefile, Sibongile , Zezhong Li, Wan Ke, Chen Guang, Claudia Chamas, and Hiro Bhojwani. 2005. Innovation in developing countries to meet health needs: Experiences of China, Brazil, South Africa, and India. Oxford: Centre for the Management of Intellectual Property in Health Research and Development.

PEI. 2014. "The Africa Special 2014." London: Private Equity International.

People's Daily. 2001. "Sino-Tanzanian pharmaceutical factory starts production." Mar. 20.

Peterson, Kristin. 2012. "AIDS policies for markets and warriors: Dispossession, capital, and pharmaceuticals in Nigeria." In *Medicine, mobility, and power in global Africa: Transnational health and healing*, ed. Hansjörg Dilger, Abdoulaye Kane and Stacey A. Langwick, 138–62. Bloomington: Indiana Univ. Press.

Peterson, Kristin. 2014. *Speculative markets: Drug circuits and derivative life in Nigeria.* Durham: Duke Univ. Press.

PharmaAfrica. 2011. "New production plant set up for HIV/AIDS medication in Tanzania." Apr. 12.

PharmaAfrica. 2012. "New Kenyan drug regulation guidelines." Feb. 3.

Pharma Letter. 1996. "Indian firm invests in Uganda." Oct. 21.

Pharma Letter. 2000. "Uganda's NEC in JV with German group." Feb. 17.

Pharmexcil. 2013. List of Indian companies/sites registered at USFDA as on 11 March, 2013. New Delhi: Pharmaceuticals Export Promotion Council of India.

Philemon, Lusekelo 2011. "Arusha firm to manufacture ARVs." *Guardian*, 16 Aug.

Picciotto, Robert. 2012. "Experimentalism and development evaluation: Will the bubble burst?" *Evaluation* 18(2):213–29.

Portes, Alejandro. 1997. "Neoliberalism and the sociology of development: emerging trends and unanticipated facts." *Population and Development Review* 23(2):229–59.

Portes, Alejandro, Luis Eduardo Guarnizo, and William J Haller. 2002. "Transnational entrepreneurs: An alternative form of immigrant economic adaptation." *American Sociological Review* 67(2):278–98.

Portes, Alejandro, and Julia Sensenbrenner. 1993. "Embeddedness and immigration: Notes on the social determinants of economic action." *American Journal of Sociology* 98(6):1320–50.

Portes, Alejandro, and Min Zhou. 1992. "Gaining the upper hand: Economic mobility among immigrant and domestic minorities." *Ethnic and Racial Studies* 15(4):491–522.

Powell, Robert. 1999. *In the shadow of power: States and strategies in international politics.* Princeton: Princeton Univ. Press.

Prasad, Monica. 2006. *The politics of free markets: The rise of neoliberal economic policies in Britain, France, Germany, and the United States.* Chicago: Univ. of Chicago Press.

Prasad, Monica, and Andre Nickow. 2016. "Mechanisms of the 'aid curse': Lessons from South Korea and Pakistan." *Journal of Development Studies* 52(11):1612–27.

Printz, Naomi, Johnnie Amenyah, Brian Serumaga, and Dirk van Wyk. 2013. Tanzania: Strategic review of the national supply chain for health commodities. Tanzania: Ministry of Health and Social Welfare.

Quick, Jonathan D., and Francis Ndemo. 1991. Pharmaceutical and medical supplies system assessment: Kenya Ministry of Health (Trip report and technical notes). Health Planning and Sustainability Project.

Radelet, Steven. 2006. A primer on foreign aid. Kenya: Ministry of Health.

Radelet, Steve, Michael Clemens, and Rikhil Bhavnani. 2004. Aid and growth: The current debate and some new evidence. Washington, DC: Center for Global Development.

Ravallion, Martin. 2009. "Evaluation in the practice of development." *World Bank Research Observer* 24(1):29–53.

Ravishankar, Nirmala, Paul Gubbins, Rebecca J. Cooley, Katherine Leach-Kemon, Catherine M. Michaud, Dean T. Jamison, and Christopher J. L. Murray. 2009. "Financing of global health: Tracking development assistance for health from 1990 to 2007." *Lancet* 373(9681):2113–24.

Reich, Michael R. 1987. "Essential drugs: Economics and politics in international health." *Health Policy* 8(1):39–57.

Reinikka, Ritva. 2008. "Donors and service delivery." In *Reinventing foreign aid*, ed. William Easterly, 179–200. Cambridge, MA: MIT Press.

Reinikka, Ritva, and Paul Collier. 2001. *Uganda's recovery: The role of farms, firms, and government.* Washington, DC: World Bank.

Remmer, Karen L. 2004. "Does foreign aid promote the expansion of government?" *American Journal of Political Science* 48(1):77–92.

Riddell, Roger C. 2007. *Does foreign aid really work?* Oxford: Oxford Univ. Press.

Roberts, Muriisa. 2005. "The privatisation experience in Uganda: Prospects and challenges in its implementation." In *The potentiality of 'developmental states' in Africa*, ed. Pamela Mbabazi and Ian Taylor, 122–32. Senagal: Council for the Development of Social Science Research in Africa.

Roche. 2008. "Roche engages in four additional AIDS technology transfers to strengthen local manufacturing in world's poorest countries." *The Corporate Social Responsibility Newswire*, Jan. 9.

Roche. n.d.a Corporate responsiblity: The AIDS technology transfer intiiative. Unpublished pamphlet (https://www.roche.com/dam/jcr:32d134ce-e114-4dde-8020-f81e514e3c7a/en/sus_acc _tti.pdf).

Roche. n.d.b. Organization, Country Roche AIDS TTI Visit: Visual Report. Unpublished pamphlet.

Rodrik, Dani. 2008. *Normalizing industrial policy.* Washington, DC: World Bank.

Romer, Paul. 1993. "Idea gaps and object gaps in economic development." *Journal of Monetary Economics* 32(3):543–73.

Rweyemamu, Justinian. 1973. *Underdevelopment and industrialization in Tanzania.* Nairobi: Oxford Univ. Press.

Sachs, Jeffrey. 2005. *The end of poverty: How we can make it happen in our lifetime.* London: Penguin.

Sachs, Jeffrey. 2014. "The case for aid." *Foreign Policy*, Jan. 21.

Sachs, Jeffrey 2015. *The age of sustainable development.* New York: Columbia Univ. Press.

Sachs, Jeffrey, and Pia Malaney. 2002. "The economic and social burden of malaria." *Nature* 415(6872):680–85.

Sachs, Jeffrey, John W. McArthur, Guido Schmidt-Traub, Margaret Kruk, Chandrika Bahadur, Michael Faye, and Gordon McCord. 2004. "Ending Africa's poverty trap." *Brookings Papers on Economic Activity* 2004(1):117–240.

SADC. 2009. Country data profile on the pharmaceutical situation in the Southern African Development Community. Tanzania. Southern African Development Community.

Saez, Catherine. 2014. "Interview With Nazeem Mohamed, CEO Of Kampala Pharmaceutical Industries." *Intellectual Property Watch*, Feb. 20.

Saiboko, Abdulwakil, and Anthony Tambwe. 2012. "Tanzania: Fake ARVs not ours, says TPI." *Tanzania Daily News*, 12 Oct.

Sambo, John. 2016. "East Africa: Imports rule EAC pharmaceuticals." *East African Business Week*, 7 Nov.

Samford, Steven. 2017. "Networks, brokerage, and state-led technology diffusion in small industry." *American Journal of Sociology* 122(5):1339–70.

Samila, Sampsa, and Olav Sorenson. 2017. "Community and capital in entrepreneurship and economic growth." *American Sociological Review* 82(4):770–95.

Sampat, Bhaven N., and Kenneth C. Shadlen. 2015. "TRIPS implementation and secondary pharmaceutical patenting in Brazil and India." *Studies in Comparative International Development* 50(2):228–57.

Sampat, Bhaven N., Kenneth C. Shadlen, and Tahir M. Amin. 2012. "Challenges to India's pharmaceutical patent laws." *Science* 337(6093):414–15.

Sandbrook, Richard. 1993. *The politics of Africa's economic recovery*. Cambridge, UK: Cambridge Univ. Press.

Sanjaya, Lall. 2004. Reinventing industrial strategy: The role of government policy in building industrial competitiveness. Geneva: United Nations Conference on Trade and Development.

Sanyal, Paromita. 2009. "From credit to collective action: The role of microfinance in promoting women's social capital and normative influence." *American Sociological Review* 74(4):529–50.

Savun, Burcu, and Daniel C Tirone. 2012. "Exogenous shocks, foreign aid, and civil war." *International Organization* 66(3):363–93.

Saxenian, AnnaLee. 2007. *The new Argonauts{name}: Regional advantage in a global economy*. Cambridge, MA: Harvard Univ. Press.

Saxenian, AnnaLee, and Jinn-Yuh Hsu. 2001. "The Silicon Valley–Hsinchu connection: Technical communities and industrial upgrading." *Industrial and Corporate Change* 10(4):893–920.

Schrank, Andrew. 2008. "Homeward bound? Interest, identity, and investor behavior in a Third World export platform." *American Journal of Sociology* 114(1):1–34.

SCRIP. 1991a. "Roche and Wyeth to 'Indianize.'" *SCRIP* 1584:12.

SCRIP. 1991b. "Support for Third World ORS production." *SCRIP* 1644:21.

SCRIP. 1999. "India to firm up on quality control." *SCRIP* 2433:18.

SCRIP. 2001. "More Indian AIDS drugs for Africa." *SCRIP* 2650:16.

SCRIP. 2003. "India steps up to assist Africa." *SCRIP* 2823:20.

SDC. 2016. Production of antimalarial drug successfully moved to Tanzania. Bern: Swiss Agency for Development and Cooperation.

Sell, Susan K. 2003. *Private power, public law: The globalization of intellectual property rights*. Cambridge, UK: Cambridge Univ. Press.

Sempijja, David. 2009. "Uganda: U.S.$20 million drug plant opens in Mukono." *New Vision*, Sept. 30.

Sen, Amartya. 2000. *Development as freedom*. New York: Alfred A. Knopf.

Sen, Kunal, and Dirk Willem Te Velde. 2009. "State business relations and economic growth in Sub-Saharan Africa." *Journal of Development Studies* 45(8):1267–83.

Sensenbrenner, Julia S. 1987. "Medicines for millions: The struggle to raise standards and rationalise production in the pharmaceutical industry." *China Business Review* 14(6):35–40.

Shadlen, Kenneth C. 2007. "The political economy of AIDS treatment: Intellectual property and the transformation of generic supply." *International Studies Quarterly* 51(3):559–81.

Shah, Keval. 2009. "An exploratory study of the use of organisational network analysis for a business case for change in Sumaria Group." Stellenbosch: Univ. of Stellenbosch.

Shen, James J. 2008. "China's rising importance in pharmaceuticals." *China Business Review* 35(3):20–23.

Shweiki, Omar. 2014. "Before and beyond neoliberalism: The political economy of national liberation, the PLO and *'amal ijtima'i*." In *Decolonizing Palestinian political economy: De-development and beyond*, ed. Mandy Turner and Omar Shweiki. London: Springer.

Siggel, Eckhard, and Germina Ssemogerere. 2004. "Uganda's policy reforms, industry competitiveness and regional integration: A comparison with Kenya." *Journal of International Trade & Economic Development* 13(3):325–57.

Simmons, Beth A., Frank Dobbin, and Geoffrey Garrett. 2006. "Introduction: The international diffusion of liberalism." *International Organization* 60(4):781–810.

Simonetti, Roberto, Norman Clark, and Watu Wamae. 2016. "Pharmaceuticals in Kenya: The evolution of technological capabilities." In *Making medicines in Africa*, ed. Maureen Mackintosh, Geoffrey Banda, Watu Wamae, and Paula Tibandebage, 25–44. London: Palgrave Macmillan.

Srinivasan, Priya 1999. "Euro MP of Indian origin to work for pro-Third-World tariffs." *Rediff*, June 23.

Ssekamwa, John C. 1997. *History and development of education in Uganda*. Uganda: Fountain Publishers.

Stallings, Barbara, and Eun Mee Kim. 2017. *Promoting development: The political economy of East Asian foreign aid*. Singapore: Springer.

Steinberg, Richard H. 2002. "In the shadow of law or power? Consensus-based bargaining and outcomes in the GATT/WTO." *International Organization* 56(2):339–74.

Stewart, Frances, Sanjaya Lall, and Samuel M Wangwe. 1992. "Alternative development strategies: An overview." In *Alternative development strategies in subSaharan Africa*, ed. Frances Stewart, Sanjaya Lall, and Samuel M. Wangwe. New York: Springer.

Stiglitz, Joseph E. 2002. *Globalization and its discontents*: New York: W.W. Norton.

Stoutjesdijk, E. J. 1967. *Uganda's manufacturing sector: A contribution to the analysis of industrialisation in East Africa*. Nairobi: East African Publishing House.

Strides Shasun. 2016. Strides Shasun to acquire controlling stake in Universal Corporation, Kenya. Press Release, Feb. 8. Banglore: Strides Shasun.

Summa Foundation. 2003. Assessment of financing and business training needs for partners of the MSH SEAM project in Tanzania. Washington, DC: Summa Foundation.

Sun Pharmaceutical Industries. 2016. Annual Report 2015–16. Mumbai: Sun Pharmaceutical Industries.

Sundet, Geir, and Eli Moen. 2009. Political economy analysis of Kenya (NORAD Report 19/2009 Discussion Paper). Norwegian Agency for Development Cooperation.

SURE. 2012. Annual progress report (year 3), October 2011 to September 2012. Kampala: Securing Ugandans' Right to Essential Medicines.

Sutton, John, and Donath Olomi. 2012. *An enterprise map of Tanzania*, vol. 3. London: International Growth Centre.

Swainson, Nicola. 1977. "The rise of a national bourgeoisie in Kenya." *Review of African Political Economy* 4(8):39–55.

Swainson, Nicola. 1979. "Company formation in Kenya before 1945 with particular reference to the role of foreign capital." In *Readings on the multinational corporation in Kenya*, ed. Rafael Kaplinsky, 22–95. Nairobi: Oxford Univ. Press.

Swainson, Nicola. 1980. *The development of corporate capitalism in Kenya, 1918–77*. Berkeley: Univ. of California Press.

Swainson, Nicola. 1987. "Indigenous capitalism in postcolonial Kenya." In *The African bourgeoisie: Capitalist development in Nigeria, Kenya and the Ivory Coast*, ed. Paul M. Lubeck, 137–63. Boulder: Lynne Rienner.

Swamy, Gurushri. 1994. "Kenya: Patchy, intermittent commitment." In *Adjustment in Africa: Lessons from country case studies*, ed. Ishrat Husain and Rashid Faruqee, 193–237. Washington, DC: World Bank.

Tambwe, Masembe. 2015. "Tanzania: State sets drugs registration ultimatum." *Tanzania Daily News*, Apr. 11.

Tang, Shenglan, Jing Sun, Gang Qu, and Wen Chen. 2007. "Pharmaceutical policy in China: issues and problems: Background Paper for the Study on China's Health System Reform." Beijing: World Health Organization, Beijing Office.

Tangri, Roger, and Andrew Mwenda. 2001. "Corruption and cronyism in Uganda's privatization in the 1990s." *African Affairs* 100(398):117–33.

Tangri, Roger, and Andrew M. Mwenda. 2013. *The politics of elite corruption in Africa: Uganda in comparative African perspective*. London and New York: Routledge.

Tanzania Daily News. 2015. "Tanzania: Bank pushes to sell Dar businessman's house," 2 Jan.

Tewathia, Nidhi. 2014. "Foreign direct investment in Indian pharmaceutical industry: An assessment." *International Journal of Social Science and Humanities Research* 2(3):20–26.

Thoithi, G. N., K. O. Abuga, J. M. Nguyo, O. K. King'Ondu, G. G. Mukindia, H. N. Mugo, J. K. Ngugi, and Isaac O. Kibwage. 2008. "Drug quality control in Kenya: Observation in the drug analysis and research unit during the period 2001–2005." *East and Central African Journal of Pharmaceutical Sciences* 11(3):74–81.

Tibandebage, Paula, Samuel Wangwe, Maureen Mackintosh, and Phares G. M. Mujinja. 2014. "Pharmaceutical manufacturing in decline in Tanzania: How possible is a turnaround to growth?" In *Making medicines in Africa*, ed. Maureen Mackintosh, Geoffrey Banda, Paula Tibandebage and Watu Wamae. London: Palgrave Macmillan.

Tremblay, Jean-Francois. 2007. "China strides toward global pharma role." *Chemical and Engineering News* 85(11):15–19.

Tripp, Aili Mari. 1997. *Changing the rules: The politics of liberalization and the urban informal economy in Tanzania*. Berkeley: Univ. of California Press.

Turshen, Meredeth. 1984. *The political ecology of disease in Tanzania*. Rutgers: Rutgers Univ. Press.

Ubwani, Zephania. 2016. "Tanzania: CTI pharmaceutical industry hit." *Citizen*, 1 Dec.

Uganda Business News. 2017. "Company profile: Cipla Qualty Chemicals Industries Ltd.," 25 Feb.

Uganda Invest. 2002. The pharmaceutical industry. http://s3.amazonaws.com/zanran_storage/www.ugandainvest.com/ContentPages/45342012.pdf, accessed May 9, 2018

Uganda Law Reform Commission. 2011. Study report on legislation for HIV and AIDS. ULRC publication 48. Uganda: Republic of Uganda.

UNAIDS. 2013. Issue brief on TRIPS transition period extensions for least-developed countries. Geneva: Joint United Nations Programme on HIV/AIDS.

UNCTAD. 2001. *An investment guide to Uganda*. Geneva: United Nations Conference on Trade and Development.

UNCTAD. 2011a. Local production of pharmaceuticals and related technology transfer in developing countries: A series of case studies by the UNCTAD Secretariat. Geneva: United Nations Conference on Trade and Development.

UNCTAD. 2011b. *Investment in pharmaceutical production in the least developed countries: A guide for policy makers and investment promotion agencies*. Geneva: United Nations Conference on Trade and Development.

UNCTC. 1979. *Transnational corporations and the pharmaceutical industry*. New York: United Nations Centre on Transnational Corporations.

UNCTC. 1984. *Transnational corporations in the pharmaceutical industry of developing countries.* New York: United Nations Centre on Transnational Corporations.

UNDP. 2016. How local production of pharmaceuticals can be promoted in Africa. The case of the United Republic of Tanzania. New York: United Nations Development Programme.

UNIDO. 1975. Lima declaration and plan of action on industrial development and co-operation. Second General Conference of the United Nations Industrial Development Organization. Lima, Peru, 12–26 March 1975.

UNIDO. 1980. Appropriate industrial technology for drugs and pharmaceuticals (*Monographs on Appropriate Industrial Technology* 10). Vienna: United Nations Industrial Development Organization.

UNIDO. 1997. Review of pharmaceutical industries in selected developing countries of Africa south of the Sahara. Vienna: United Nations Industrial Development Organization.

UNIDO. 2010a. Pharmaceutical sector profile: Kenya. Vienna: United Nations Industrial Development Organization.

UNIDO. 2010b. Pharmaceutical sector profie: Uganda. Vienna: United Nations Industrial Development Organization.

UNIDO. 2010c. Annual survey of industrial production and performance, 2008 (statistical report). Vienna: United Nations Industrial Development Organization.

UNIDO. 2011a. Conference of African Ministers of Industry. Roundtable on pharmaceutical industries. Summary of senior officials, Algeirs, 27–28 March 2011.

UNIDO. 2011b. Pharmaceutical sector profile: Nigeria. Vienna: United Nations Industrial Development Organization.

UNIDO. 2014. Kenya GMP roadmap: A stepwise approach for the pharmaceutical industry to attain WHO GMP standards. Vienna: United Nations Industrial Development Organization.

UNIDO. n.d.a Supporting pharmaceutical production in Africa. Vienna: United Nations Industrial Development Organization.

UNIDO. n.d.b UNIDO global project: Strengthening the local production of essential generic drugs in Developing Countries (DCs). Vienna: United Nations Industrial Development Organization.

USAID. 2008. USP DQI Good Manufacturing Practices assessment for manufacturers of zinc sulfate formulations. The United States Pharmacopeia Drug Quality and Information Program. Washington, DC: US Agency for International Development.

USAID. 2011a. External evaluation of the President's Malaria Initiative final report. Washington, DC: US Agency for International Development.

USAID. 2011b. Introducing improved treatment of childhood diarrhea with zinc and ORT in Tanzania. Washington, DC: US Agency for International Development.

Vandenberg, Paul. 2003. "Ethnic-sectoral cleavages and economic development: reflections on the second Kenya debate." *Journal of Modern African Studies* 41(3):437–55.

Van Den Bulcke, Danny, Haiyan Zhang, and Xiaorong Li. 1999. "Interaction between the business environment and the corporate strategic positioning of firms in the pharmaceutical industry: A study of the entry and expansion path of MNEs into China." *MIR: Management International Review* 39(4):353–77.

Venkatesh, Kartik K., Kenneth H. Mayer, and Charles C. J. Carpenter. 2012. "Low-cost generic drugs under the President's Emergency Plan for AIDS Relief drove down treatment cost; more are needed." *Health Affairs* 31(7):1429–38.

Verma, Anuradha. 2015. "Cipla to acquire 51% stake in Ugandan firm Quality Chemicals for $30M." *VCCircle*, May 22.

Viterna, Jocelyn, and Cassandra Robertson. 2015. "New directions for the sociology of development." *Annual Review of Sociology* 41:243–69.

von Massow, Friderich. n.d. The German funded PPP project. Nairobi: PharmaQuality Catalogue.

Wade, Robert. 1990. *Governing the Market: Economic Theory and the Role of Government in East Asian Industrialization*. Princeton: Princeton Univ. Press.

Wang, Yongfeng. 1999. "China meets the medicine market." *Chemistry and Industry*, Jun. 21, 462–66.

Wangwe, Samuel, Paula Tibandebage, Edwin Mhede, Caroline Israel, Mujinja Phares, and Maureen Mackintosh. 2014a. "Reversing pharmaceutical manufacturing decline in Tanzania: Policy options and constraints." *REPOA Brief*, July, no. 43.

Ward, Andrew. 2016. "China's biotech revolution ushered in by entrepreneurs." *Financial Times*, Mar. 7.

Watanabe, Mariko, and Luwen Shi. 2011. "Sufficient but expensive drugs: A double-track system that facilitated supply capability in China." In *Intellectual property, pharmaceuticals and public health: Access to drugs in developing countries*, ed. Kenneth C. Shadlen, Samira Guennif, Alenka Guzmán, and Narayanan Lalitha, 253–85. London: Edward Edgar.

Whittaker, D. Hugh, Tianbiao Zhu, Timothy Sturgeon, Mon Han Tsai, and Toshie Okita. 2010. "Compressed development." *Studies in Comparative International Development* 45(4):439–67.

WHO. 1975. Alternative approaches to meeting basic health needs in developing countries. Geneva: World Health Organization.

WHO. 1978. Declaration of Alma Ata: International conference on primary health care, Alma Ata, USSR, 6–12 Sept. 1978. Geneva: World Health Organization.

WHO. 1988. The world drug situation. Geneva: World Health Organization.

WHO. 1994a. Draft report of a mission to Uganda. Geneva: World Health Organization.

WHO. 1994b. East and Central African essential drugs programmes management meeting. Geneva: World Health Organization.

WHO. 1995a. Use of the WHO certification scheme on the quality of pharmaceutical products moving in international commerce. Geneva: World Health Organization.

WHO. 1995b. Action Programme on Essential Drugs. Collaboration and coordination in national drug policy development. Geneva: World Health Organization.

WHO. 1997. Local production of pharmaceuticals in the WHO African region. Geneva: World Health Organization.

WHO. 1999. The World Health report, 1999: Making a difference. Geneva: World Health Organization.

WHO. 2002. Effective drug regulation: A multicountry study. Geneva:World Health Organization.

WHO. 2003. Scaling up antiretroviral therapy: Experience in Uganda (case study). Geneva: World Health Organization.

WHO. 2004. The world medicines situation. Genva: World Health Organization.

WHO. 2006. Medicine prices surveys and proposed interventions to improve sustainable access to affordable medicines in 6 sub-Saharan African countries. Geneva: World Health Organization.

WHO. 2007a. Quality assurance of pharmaceuticals: A compendium of guidelines and related materials—Good manufacturing practices and inspection. Geneva: World Health Organization.

WHO. 2007b. Towards universal access: Scaling up priority HIV/AIDS interventions in the health sector (progress report). Geneva: World Health Organization.

WHO. 2009. Improving access to medicines in developing countries through pharmaceutical-related technology transfer: Preliminary findings on capacities, trends, challenges and opportunities. Geneva: World Health Organization.

WHO. 2010. Experience with supporting pharmaceutical policies and systems in Kenya: Progress, lessons and the role of WHO. Geneva: World Health Organization.

WHO. 2011a. Global strategy and plan of action on public health, innovation and intellectual property. Geneva: World Health Organization.

WHO. 2011b. Local production for access to medical products (policy brief). Geneva: World Health Organization.

WHO. 2011c. Pharmaceutical production and related technology transfer. Geneva: World Health Organization.

WHO. 2011d. Survey of the quality of selected antimalarial medicines circulating in six countries of sub-Saharan Africa. Geneva: World Health Organization.

WHO. 2011e. Trends in local production of medicines and related technology transfer. Geneva: World Health Organization.

WHO. 2016. "WHO rotational fellowships: An update." *WHO Drug Information* 30(1):40–45.

WHO and Global Fund. n.d. Pharmaceutical sector country profile questionnaire: United Republic of Tanzania. Geneva: World Health Organization and Global Fund.

Wilson, Kinsley Rose. 2009. "A manufactured solution? The transfer of technology to developing countries for the local production of affordable antiretrovirals: Case Studies from Tanzania and South Africa." PhD diss, Univ. of Toronto, Leslie Dan Faculty of Pharmacy.

Wood, Robert Everett. 1986. *From Marshall Plan to debt crisis: Foreign aid and development choices in the world economy*. Berkeley: Univ. of California Press.

World Bank. 1971. Industrial development in East Africa: Progress, policies, problems and prospects, vol. III: Tanzania. Washington, DC: World Bank.

World Bank. 1983. Kenya: Growth and structural change (*Country study series*). Washington, DC: World Bank.

World Bank. 1988. Staff appraisal report. China pharmaceuticals project. Washington, DC: World Bank.

World Bank. 1990. Staff appraisal report. Tanzania health and nutrition project. Washington, DC: World Bank.

World Bank. 1994. Limitations and rewards in Kenya's manufacturing sector: A study of enterprise development (*Country study series*). Washington, DC: World Bank.

World Bank. 2010. Tanzania—Privatization and private sector development project. Washington, DC: World Bank.

Wortzel, Lawrence H. 1971. *Technology transfer in the pharmaceutical industry*. Geneva: United Nations Institute for Training Research.

Wright, Joseph. 2009. "How foreign aid can foster democratization in authoritarian regimes." *American Journal of Political Science* 53(3):552–71.

Wright, Joseph, and Matthew Winters. 2010. "The politics of effective foreign aid." *Annual Review of Political Science* 13:61–80.

WTO. 2015. "News Item. WTO members agree to extend drug patent exemption for poorest members." Geneva: World Trade Organization, Nov. 6.

Yadav, Prashant. 2014. Kenya Medical Supplies Authority (KEMSA): A case study of the ongoing transition from an ungainly bureaucracy to a competitive and customer-focused medical logistics organization. Washington, DC: World Bank.

# INDEX

A.A. Pharmaceuticals, 165, 166, 169
Abacus Parenterals Drugs Ltd., Uganda, 191,
    192, 194, 196; 205–6; ownership of, 209;
    registered drugs of, 203
Abbott Laboratories, 45
action medeor, 23, 159, 177–78, 185
Action Programme on Essential Drugs
    (APED), 65. *See also* Essential Drugs List
active pharmaceutical ingredient (API):
    definition of, 231n.2; production of in
    China, 235n.78
Aerosols Ltd., 115
Affordable Medicines Facility–malaria
    (AMFm), 200, 216, 254n.5, 261n.35
African Kenyans, 55–56, 237n.4; in the phar-
    maceutical sector, 135–36, 138; preferen-
    tial hiring of, 75–76
African Ugandans, in the pharmaceutical
    sector, 123–26
Aga Khan. *See* Industrial Promotion
    Services (IPS)
Aga Khan Development Network (AKDN),
    194
Aga Khan Fund for Economic Development,
    123
Agaba, Amon Ganafa, 207, 220
Aggarwal, Aradhna, 36, 37
Aid for Poverty-Related Diseases in
    Development Countries, 178
AIDS. *See* HIV/AIDS
AIDS drugs. *See* antiretrovirals (ARVs)
AIDS Technology Transfer Initiative.
    *See* Roche
Aiyar, Sana, 73
Alesina, Alberto, 218
Alexander, Myrna, 144
Alma Ata Declaration, 86
Altincekic, Ceren, 220
Amin, Idi, 39, 109; coup, 114; educational
    resource cutbacks by, 119–20; expulsion of
    Indian Ugandans by, 4, 120–21; health care
    and access to medicines under, 110–11;

pharmaceutical sector under, 114–16; seek-
    ing foreign technical assistance, 251n.40
Amin, Tahir M., 45
Amsden, Alice, 3, 7, 8, 13–19, 36, 46, 53–54,
    214, 268n.11
Amutabi. Maurice N., 62
Anderson, Tatum, 133–34, 157
Andia, Tatiana, 58, 141, 217
Andreoni, Antonio, 9
antimalarial drugs: changed treatment
    guidelines of, 163; from China, 52; global
    programs for, 206. *See also* artemether/
    lumefantrine (AL); artemisinin-based
    combination therapies (ACTs)
antiretrovirals (ARVs): access to in Kenya,
    148–50; debate over spending on,
    256n.31; foreign funding for in Tanzania,
    174; global programs for, 206; high prices
    of, 140; Indian production of, 44–45;
    international funding of, 141; local
    production of, 1, 4–5; slow rollout of in
    Tanzania, 171; in Uganda, 197–98
artemether-lumefantrine (AL), 131, 138, 163,
    168, 196, 200, 261n.35
artemisinin-based combination therapies
    (ACTs), 52–53, 131; access to in Kenya,
    149–50; CiplaQCIL certification to
    produce, 200; foreign funding for in
    Tanzania, 174; local production of, 5
Arusha Declaration, 85–86, 88–90, 94,
    99–101, 114
Aspen Pharmacare, 138, 168; acquisition of
    local manufacturers by, 226; reducing
    number of registered drugs, 175
Aurobindo Pharma, 45

Babb, Sarah, 38, 213
Baliamoune-Lutz, Mina, 17
Baran, Charlie, 174
Barigaba, Julius, 144
Barkan, Joel D., 63
Barker, Carol, 19, 34, 88, 99–101

## A NOTE ON THE TYPE

This book has been composed in Adobe Text and Gotham.
Adobe Text, designed by Robert Slimbach for Adobe,
bridges the gap between fifteenth- and sixteenth-century
calligraphic and eighteenth-century Modern styles.
Gotham, inspired by New York street signs, was designed
by Tobias Frere-Jones for Hoefler & Co.